D1604377

FLESHING OUT AMERICA

FLESHING OUT AMERICA

Race, Gender, and the Politics of the Body in

American Literature, 1833–1879

Carolyn Sorisio

THE UNIVERSITY OF GEORGIA PRESS

ATHENS AND LONDON

© 2002 by the University of Georgia Press
Athens, Georgia 30602
All rights reserved
Designed by Mary Mendell
Set in 9 point Trump Mediaeval by Bookcomp, Inc.
Printed and bound by Maple-Vail Book Group
The paper in this book meets the guidelines for permanence
and durability of the Committee on Production Guidelines for
Book Longevity of the Council on Library Resources.
Printed in the United States of America
06 05 04 03 02 C 5 4 3 2 1

Library of Congress Cataloging-in-Publication Data
Sorisio, Carolyn, 1966–
Fleshing out America : race, gender, and the politics of the
body in American literature, 1833–1879 / Carolyn Sorisio.
p. cm.
Includes bibliographical references and index.
ISBN 0-8203-2357-8 (hardcover : alk. paper)
1. American literature—19th century—History and criticism. 2. Body, Human, in literature. 3. Politics and literature—
United States—History—19th century. 4. Sex role in
literature. 5. Race in literature. I. Title.
PS217.B63 S67 2002
810.9'35—dc21
2002001359

British Library Cataloging-in-Publication Data available

To Robert and Barbara Sorisio

CONTENTS

ACKNOWLEDGMENTS

Writing this book has been a wonderful, and in many respects a collective, experience. I would like to thank those who have made it so. To begin, I would like to thank the staff members of Library Company of Philadelphia, particularly Phillip Lapsansky, for their help in providing me with material on the science of race and gender in the antebellum era. Users of the library are well aware of how valuable are not only its resources but also its staff, who points you to the relevant aspects of the collection. I would also like to thank the editors at the University of Georgia Press, especially Margaret Nunnelley and Marlene Allen, for their support of this project.

Miles Orvell and Rachel Blau DuPlessis deserve particular note. Miles Orvell contributed not only his advice and encouragement at many phases of this project, but also his valuable insight into the study's structure and theoretical viewpoint. Rachel Blau DuPlessis contributed a combination of theoretical questioning and astute attention to writing style to this project in its early form. Nancy Bentley was kind enough to read the manuscript in its initial form, and her insights helped me reconceptualize my work in respect to the representation of torture and spectatorship in the writings of Lydia Maria Child and Frances E. W. Harper. Carla L. Peterson and Karen L. Kilcup both made vital suggestions for revision that contributed positively to the work's final form. Martha J. Cutter and Debra J. Rosenthal helped me develop further several sections of the book, including the introduction, my work on Child and Harper, and my chapter on Fuller. Lisa Brawley helped me reconceptualize my argument regarding Margaret Fuller and progressive feminism.

I would also like to thank my family. My husband, Gregory Fornia, continuously astonishes me with his unwavering support, from seemingly mundane to exceedingly generous gestures. He is simply the reason why I am able to accomplish what I do. My parents, Robert and Barbara Sorisio, to whom the book is dedicated, encouraged a lifelong love of reading and supported my education during its many stages. My earliest teachers were my sisters, Cheri O'Neill and Cathy Lang, with whom I would "play school"; they have taught me much and continue to provide their encouragement. In addition I want to acknowledge two very special people who passed away during the time I was writing this book, my grandfather Mario Sorisio and my father-in-law, John Fornia. They are missed.

As someone who spends a large portion of her career teaching, I also want to acknowledge those who did not contribute to this study per se but were instrumental in my development as a scholar and writer, those who take seriously their charge to nurture a love of literature in their students. When I was an undergraduate at Pennsylvania State University, John W. Moore Jr., Carla J. Mulford, and John Secor always encouraged me, even when I was preoccupied with other activities. Additionally, Sanford Schwartz and Deborah Clarke were some of the first to spark my interest in literary theory. As a graduate student at Temple University, I was privileged to work with many faculty members who took that most precious of all commodities in higher education today—time—and spent it generously upon their students, particularly Sharon Harris and Sally Mitchell, who taught me a great deal about historical research and writing.

Finally, I want to thank Carolyn L. Karcher, a remarkable mentor and friend. From my days as a doctoral student to the present, she has generously critiqued my work with care and patience. She has read and reread, discussed and further discussed, conceptualized and reconceptualized this project with me so many times and in so many forms that it is truly impossible for me to imagine its taking shape without her energy, enthusiasm, and expertise. She is an exceptional scholar and teacher, and those like myself who have had the privilege to work with her have benefited incalculably from the experience.

FLESHING OUT AMERICA

INTRODUCTION

Remapping the Nineteenth-Century

Literary Landscape

This is a common cause; and if there is any burden to be borne in the Anti-Slavery cause—anything to be done to weaken our hateful chains or assert our manhood and womanhood, I have a right to do my share of the work.—Frances E. W. Harper, "I Have a Right to Do My Share"

But if you ask me what offices [women] may fill; I reply—any. I do not care what case you put; let them be sea-captains, if you will.—Margaret Fuller, *Woman in the Nineteenth Century*

Here is not merely a nation but a teeming nation of nations.—Walt Whitman, *Leaves of Grass*

When the escaped slave Harriet Jacobs received a letter from her owner's family attempting to trick her into returning to the South, she recognized the snare and commented: "Verily, he relied too much on 'the stupidity of the African race.'" Published in 1861, Jacobs's remark may just as well have been directed at many Americans who—impressed with scientists' "proof" of Negro inferiority—had been lulled into a false sense of racial superiority. As this anecdote suggests, the first half of the nineteenth century ushered in an era of powerful scientific and quasi-scientific disciplines that assumed permanent and innate difference between the "types" of humankind. A new set of scientific "laws," supposedly establishing the physical inferiority of women, Negroes, and Aboriginals, were said by some proponents of slavery and opponents of women's rights to replace the Declaration of Independence's "higher law." For many American writers, who connected the individual body symbolically with the body politic, the new science was fraught with possibility and peril. This book explores the representation of the body in the work of seven authors: Lydia

Maria Child, Frances E. W. Harper, Ralph Waldo Emerson, Margaret Fuller, Walt Whitman, Harriet Jacobs, and Martin R. Delany. These writers were involved to some degree with women's rights or abolition or both, yet respond to these movements and the changing conceptions of the body in diverging, even conflicting, ways. Rarely, then, does this book posit a binary of scientific action and literary reaction. Rather, it investigates how these authors struggled in a tumultuous period to *flesh out* America, to grapple, in other words, with the discourses of abolition, women's rights, and science—all of which had the cumulative effect of debunking the myth of the disembodied "person" of Revolutionary rhetoric. This rhetoric held forth the promise of natural and higher laws of innate equality, but often masked the reality that political rights were allocated only to those who inhabited bodies marked white and male. Karen Sánchez-Eppler summarizes the corporeal paradox of Revolutionary rhetoric: "All the 'men' who, Thomas Jefferson declared, 'are created equal' shed their gender and their race; in obtaining the right to freedom and equality they discard bodily specificity." By the decades preceding the Civil War, the theory of an allegedly disembodied "person" entitled to political rights was no longer rhetorically valid. Rather, as Sánchez-Eppler argues, "the development of a political discourse and a concept of personhood that attests to the centrality of the body erupts throughout antebellum culture."[1] The authors my book studies assume their place in the mid-nineteenth-century contest to demarcate the body of the nation.

A century and a half later, antebellum theories of identity may strike us as remnants of a lamentable past. Yet even though they have been discredited, can we argue that they do not reverberate in our society today? One of the nineteenth century's legacies to this one is a vague, yet significant, sense in many Americans that race, gender, and sexuality are natural categories of difference. For this reason, my study joins late-twentieth-century efforts to explore the historical construction of the categories that define us in an effort to move beyond the polarization that is deeply rooted in our culture. Although these authors' representations of corporeality merit study in their own right, this project is in part also an attempt to forge answers to some contemporary pedagogical and theoretical problems I find troubling. As my reliance upon scholars such as Michel Foucault indicates, I am resistant to the idea that physiological essentialism can be knowably "true," and instead I explore nineteenth-century science as a discourse that connects in complex ways knowledge and power. Our embodied experiences are united inextricably to our culture's multifaceted constructions of corporeality. Nonetheless, as resistant as I am to the concept of physiological essentialism, I am just as skeptical about the idea that our corporeal experience is solely the result of ideology. In short, I fear that when we view the body's manifestations only as socially constructed, we continue a Western insistence upon a Cartesian split between corporeality and identity that is blind to the complex relationship between these components of the construction of self. Like many writers in this study, I believe our bodies influence us in both comprehensible and unknowable ways. Therefore it is important to make tentative leaps between what we can surmise about authors' embodied experiences and their representations of corporeality. When doing so, we face the challenge of framing the question of how the body influences experience and representation in such a way as to avoid inaccurate and potentially harmful conceptions of corporeal essentialism and binaries of racial, gendered, and sexual difference.

This dilemma, which also plagued the writers I investigate, confronts many who teach in contemporary American classrooms. As students at institutions of higher learning increasingly reflect the nation's diverse population, the question of how to teach about representations of the body becomes more obvious and pressing. When it is not done carefully, teaching about race, gender, and sexuality reaffirms polarization as natural. Henry Louis Gates Jr. summarizes this paradox in relation to race, reminding us that race "has become a trope of ultimate, irreducible difference between cultures, linguistic groups, or adherents of specific belief systems" despite the fact that it is "so very arbitrary in its application." Yet, Gates argues, "we carelessly use language in such a way as to *will* this sense of *natural* difference into our formulations." Like Gates, I worry about our culture's tendency to "engage in a pernicious act of language, one which exacerbates the complex problem of cultural or ethnic difference, rather than to assuage or redress it."[2] Part of the solution, Gates intimates, is to teach the invention of race, to probe the historical construction of racial categories. *Fleshing Out America* attempts to do just that by investigating America's racial history to study the roots of scientific racism. Because I also encounter the difficulties that Gates describes about race when teaching about gender and sexuality, it is neither possible nor desirable to fragment my investigation of the politics of the body and concentrate solely on one of these classifications of identity. All components, in addition to others beyond the scope of this study, may contribute to one's embodied experiences and representations of corporeality.

The authors I focus on help us investigate the complex relationships among corporeal categorizations, embodied experiences, and textual representations. I selected some authors, such as Child, Delany, and Harper, who are less written about, to situate them in relation to both canonical writers (Emerson and Whitman) and writers who are fast becoming included as part of what we might tentatively identify as a newer, more multicultural "canon" (Fuller and Jacobs). In doing so, I hope to provide a context for rethinking how we teach about writers from seemingly disparate backgrounds. The past decades of feminist and multicultural criticism have produced an explosion of archival and theoretical work that transforms our understanding of literary and cultural production. Indeed, I am awed by, and grateful for, the recovery work that has enabled this project. In particular, I recognize that my chapters on Child, Fuller, Harper, and Jacobs are indebted to the pioneering work of Carolyn L. Karcher, Bell Gale Chevigny, Jean Fagan Yellin, and Frances Smith Foster—among many others. *Fleshing Out America* is also inspired by recent scholarship on the politics of corporeal representation. The book most closely related to this project is Sánchez-Eppler's *Touching Liberty: Abolition, Feminism, and the Politics of the Body* (1993). Sánchez-Eppler's work is noted for her significant investigation of the precarious relationship between abolition and women's rights rhetorics. Another related work is Robyn Wiegman's *American Anatomies: Theorizing Race and Gender* (1995), which begins its interrogation of theories of race and gender by examining science's relationship to racial domination in the nineteenth century.

Despite the impressive work by scholars such as those mentioned above, literature by women and people of historically oppressed races is still not adequately represented in the classroom.[3] The reasons for this resistance are multifold. Certainly, they can be attributed to the generally slow pace of educational innovation as well as to political resistance stemming from the "majority's" profound attachment to its own myths of superiority. Nonetheless, can we not also ask if this lack of curricular revision results, in part, from a cycle of compartmentalization that relegates feminist and race criticism and its related texts to their own classrooms, departments, journals, and conferences? Although it is imperative to examine the works of women and people of color within their own contexts, we must also attempt—as many now do—to integrate American literary studies in order to generate a more complete understanding of the cultural and literary contributions of all Americans. Likewise, we must follow in the footsteps of scholars such as Reginald Horsman, Dana D. Nelson, and David R. Roediger, who study the construction of "whiteness" as a category in American history and literature, as well as of those who investigate the meaning of masculinity.[4] My work aids in this process by bringing together women and men, African Americans and Anglo-Americans, and canonical and noncanonical authors. Although some of the authors may be labeled "traditional" and some "nontraditional" today, during their era many of them can be understood as participating with one another in a cultural conversation. The separation between these authors that the late-twentieth-century American literary canon naturalized simply does not describe adequately their relationships. Therefore, I view my work as part of the ongoing process of reintegration and hope that my study will encourage readers to reconsider the nature of nineteenth-century literary associations.

If part of the gap between scholarly work and curricular change can be attributed to professional categorization and compartmentalization, Judith Fetterley points to another possible explanation: the disparity between recovery work and feminist criticism focusing on the writing strategies of nineteenth-century women's texts. Fetterley wonders "if we have this investment in recovery because persons interested in these writers are having difficulty finding ways to write *about* them."[5] She traces this difficulty, in part, to two factors. First, she notes the paradoxical status of many nineteenth-century American women writers who "are no longer seen as sufficiently marginal to justify literary history about them simply because they are marginal" and yet are "virtually absent from whatever literary history we have." Second, Fetterley remarks that the interest in nineteenth-century American women's writing "coincided with the dismantling of the interpretive strategies developed during the 1950s and '60s . . . the strategies of close reading and thematic study" and suggests that those interested in these writers "may need to find ways to revitalize modes of criticism no longer fashionable because these modes may represent stages in the process of literary evaluation that we cannot do without."[6] In this respect, my study is focused on the work of the authors themselves, blending close attention to often underread texts with techniques and inquiries most often associated with New Historicism. In providing both close reading and attention to theme—if we can consider such an explosive topic as representation of corporeality in the face of scientific essentialism and reform efforts a "theme"—I integrate less-read authors with writers such as Emerson and Whitman. By placing Whitman and Emerson in comparison with these women writers and Delany in what scholars have designated a "contact zone,"[7] I hope to contribute to the remapping of the nineteenth-century literary and political landscape.

In addition to these pedagogical dilemmas, my work also stems from contemporary concerns in gender and race studies. Like scholars today, the writers in this study grapple with the question of how to respond to the interrelationships among their own bodies, theories of identity, and the body politic. As a feminist, I am attentive to the politics of the body, which are closely related to questions about the effectiveness of identity politics. What does it mean to "speak essentially"—as a woman or man, an African American or white person, a homosexual or lesbian—when these categories are neither pure nor natural? Do we merely replicate perilous constructs formed more than a century ago? Yet what do we lose if we take away notions of essential knowledge or difference—the right to claim our bodies, our identities, as *our very own*? How can we form a space for ourselves in the political sphere as a particular group if we give up notions of difference?

Tania Modleski tackles this question in *Feminism without Women*. She argues that feminist scholarship drawing upon recent literary and social theory to emphasize the constructed aspects of gender generally benefits women. "Since feminism has a great stake in the belief . . . that one is not *born* a woman, one *becomes* a woman (for if this were *not* the case it would be difficult to imagine social change)," she contends, "thinkers like [Jacques] Lacan and Foucault have provided the analytical tools by which we may begin the arduous task of unbecoming women."[8] However, Modleski cautions that when an antiessentialist position is taken too far, it can dismiss the different embodied experiences of men and women, creating political paralysis. The "once exhilarating proposition that there is no 'essential' female nature," she argues, "has been elaborated to the point where it is now often used to scare 'women' away from making *any* generalizations about or political claims on behalf of a group called 'women.'"[9] Barbara Christian also questions the political timing of the so-called death of the subject, arguing that "the language it creates" is "one which mystifies rather than clarifies our condition, making it possible for a few people who know that particular language to control the critical scene." She points out "that language surfaced, interestingly enough, just when the literature of peoples of color, of black women, of Latin Americans, of Africans began to move to the 'center.'"[10] With these cautions in mind, I have tried to strike a balance between employing a language suitable to the complex connections between corporeality and identity and my desire to write a book that clarifies rather than mystifies. I hope that by examining the challenges that confronted these authors, as well as the strategies they invented in response, we can have a better vantage point from which to address our own complicated politics of the body.

By examining these authors' corporeal depictions, we begin to understand that essentialism, or knowledge claimed through the body, became both an obstacle in people's efforts to attain full access to the literary and political spheres and a tool to deploy cautiously when advantageous. Because antebellum conceptions of the body are crucial to understanding literary representations of corporeality, my first chapter analyzes scientific works, medical guides, and advice books from the Revolutionary era to the Civil War. When relevant in this chapter and throughout the book, I interpret these texts in light of theories by scholars such as Michel Foucault, Stephen Jay Gould, Thomas Laqueur, and Elaine Scarry. Rather than presenting my own theory of corporeality, then, this chapter is intended as a synthesis of contemporary and nineteenth-century theories of the body for readers less familiar with these debates. Because writers in the past few decades have produced such an impressive amount of secondary work on the history of the body and because primary sources are also extensive, I focus on concepts of race, gender, and sexuality that most influenced the authors in this study. Clearly, a fourth factor—that of class—is intertwined with race, gender, and sexuality, and I address class issues when relevant throughout this study. One senses, of course, that more has been, could, and should be said on the complex relationship between class and representations of corporeality. However, in a study of this scope, one risks becoming diffuse to the point of unhelpfulness. Therefore, my analysis of class is embedded in this study, but not in its forefront.

As my summary of individual chapters below indicates, the authors I study generated any number of responses to corporeality. One strategy was to replicate the discourse of science and claim knowledge through the body. Delany, for example, repeatedly points to his status as the "blackest of the black" men to establish his authority among the African American community and whites. Similarly, as chapter 5 demonstrates, Fuller claims a special female nature— "the genius of woman"—because it benefits her within the romantic epistemological framework. Whitman, Child, and Harper point to the body either as a source of knowledge or as evidence of societal injustice. Yet speaking knowledge from the body carried with it certain risks—always came the possibility that your presence merely reified existing structures. By replicating an idea of essential difference one opened the way for exclusion from various political rights. By using the body as a testimony of pain, one risked making certain groups into permanent victims. By pointing to oneself as evidence against a scientific theory, one hazarded becoming an "exceptional" or "unnatural" spectacle. Due to these and other factors, many writers, such as Emerson, Fuller, and Jacobs, were tempted to claim a transcendent identity. But no writer could simply ignore the changing conceptions of the body in the antebellum era. All struggled with the problems of how best to represent corporeality and how to define, even defend, the nation's body.

My study of individual authors begins with Child, whose 1833 *Appeal in Favor of That Class of Americans Called Africans* (1833) helped usher in the second wave of American abolitionism. Child's decision to confront the corporeal aspects of slavery drew criticism during her time and continues to do so today. I consider the correlation between nineteenth- and late-twentieth-century concerns about the appropriateness of Child's literary representations of slaves' corporeality by placing Child's introduction to Jacob's *Incidents in the Life of a Slave Girl* in relation to Child's *Appeal* and fictional antislavery writing of the 1840s and 1850s. I argue that Child's portrayals of corporeality do not rest, as some claim, upon the binary of a disembodied white female self and embodied slave "other." Because Child wants to avoid the charges of indelicacy that confront any woman entering the public sphere, she develops methods to reveal slavery's corporeal nature without soliciting readers' voyeuristic spectatorship. In part, she does so by interrogating the sentimental assumption of the universality and translatability of pain. The tactics Child develops to elude accusations of indelicacy in her era also answer contemporary critics who charge feminist-abolitionist writers with appealing to an "allure of bondage" and exploiting the slave's body in the literary marketplace.

My next chapter, on Harper, considers further the dilemma that is outlined in relation to Child's antislavery work: How can a woman participating in the abolition movement address corporeal issues without drawing an unbearable amount of indelicate attention to herself or to the bodies of those she wants to aid? In Harper's case this dilemma was complicated because she was an African American woman, whose body could be too easily aligned with what Carla L. Peterson has identified as the "unruly, grotesque, carnivalesque."[11] The first section of this chapter focuses on Harper's antebellum poetry, demonstrating how she diverts the public's inappropriate gaze from her own body and the bodies of the slaves she represents. However, Harper goes beyond merely deflecting her readers' gaze. Through the use of temperance rhetoric, Harper turns readers' attention toward deracialized or Caucasian characters to challenge damaging beliefs about governance, corporeality, and control. The final section of this chapter shows how Harper encourages readers to turn their gaze inward by proposing self-discipline as a liberatory strategy in the postbellum era.

Chapter 4 focuses on Emerson and is situated in relation to the following chapter on Fuller. Rather than calling for a sentimental understanding based on experiences of pain, or using pain (as Scarry suggests many do) as the paradoxical starting point for expression, Fuller and Emerson represent pain as distinct from their essential selves. If Emerson's and Fuller's transcendent impulse seems conventional when viewed through romanticism, it takes on increased interest and radicalism when considered in relation to the rise of scientific essentialism. Emerson mocks science's relegation of identity to corporeality, and some of his most fiery and committed antislavery speeches show his commitment to a philosophical premise of the unity of humankind. However, Emerson's romantic philosophy is not without contradictions. Analyzing Emerson's essays from the 1840s and 1850s, I argue that Emerson's transcendent "metaphysical selfhood" relies upon a dynamic that often traps women and "other" races in an embodied identity. Emerson's reluctance to apply his potentially radical theory of identity to women may derive from his anxiety over the position of Anglo-Saxon men in antebellum America. We can best assess this anxiety by juxtaposing his antislavery lectures with *English Traits*, the travel book he was developing and lecturing upon during the same years he delivered many of his antislavery speeches. Seeking to define unique American characteristics as he traveled to England, Emerson creates definitions of national identity that endorse stereotypical conceptions of male Anglo-Saxon superiority.

Elaborating upon the relationship between the search for national identity and travel addressed in my chapter on Emerson, chapter 5 argues that Fuller revises Emerson's conception of an aggressively masculine republic in her travel work, *Summer on the Lakes*, and in her feminist manifesto, *Woman in the Nineteenth Century*. Certainly, Fuller is more consistent than Emerson about the need to reform Euro-American women's societal roles and opportunities. However, the radical potential of *Woman* must be read in relation to Fuller's problematic representations of Native Americans in *Summer*. Unlike Child, who does not use an "other" race to deflect attention from her own body, Fuller's feminist vision depends on the symbolic transference of unwanted corporeal associations to the bodies of Native Americans. On the one hand, Fuller wants to assume an identity based on the female body, because this is a benefit within her romantic epistemological framework. On the other hand, she does not want to align herself with "physiologists" who "bind great original laws by the forms which flow from them," and entrap women in presumably permanent and limited embodied roles.[12] By assuming the role of ethnologist in *Summer*, Fuller is able to divert the scientific gaze from the Euro-American woman's body and claim (at least temporarily) the role of a disembodied observer. Once she accomplishes this, she is free to expand further on her theory of gender identity in *Woman*, particularly her simultaneous claim to a special female nature ("the genius of woman") and equality. Although she wants to claim corporeal knowledge, she also recognizes that a woman in the nineteenth century has cause to fear an association with the natural sphere (including her body), which too often justifies her oppression.

In this respect Fuller complicates the answer to a question that begins my sixth chapter. In his 1855 edition of *Leaves of Grass*, Walt Whitman brazenly demands to know: "Who need be afraid of the merge?" As my chapter on Fuller suggests, many people who were defined by their corporeality would have an understandable resistance to Whitman's methodology of defining himself through his body. As such, I juxtapose Whitman's trust in the body as an equal partner on the journey toward knowledge with Emerson's and Fuller's faith in transcendence. If, as Laqueur suggests, earlier interpretations of sexuality relied upon an "unimaginably—indeed terrifyingly—porous body,"[13] then Whitman harkens back to these conceptions to defy his day's rigid corporeal categories. By creating an epistemology of the body, Whitman fundamentally challenges the modern structures of knowledge that were coming to dominate his age. He replaces what Foucault identifies as *scientia sexualis* with an *ars erotica*. However, by envisioning a new race of North Americans that is predominantly masculine and Caucasian, Whitman, much like Emerson, weakens the liberatory potential of his early work. As the last section of my chapter details, Whitman had doubts after the Civil War about who could reside in what he called the "white neighborhood" of America.

Unlike Whitman, who proposes sexuality as a site of, and source for, knowledge, Jacobs must learn to become knowing not through sex, but, rather, through sexuality. She has to turn corporeal knowledge and the complex politics of sexuality and slavery into a source of power. Chapter 7, then, shows how neither Emerson's and Fuller's optimistic transcendence nor Whitman's glorification of identity through the body could fit the experiences of a mulatto woman who was once a slave. Instead, in a move similar to Fuller's, Jacobs creates a both/and strategy, simultaneously claiming the importance of knowledge from the body and a transcendent will. Like Harper, this dual strategy allows her to evade the essentialism and voyeurism that haunted so many African American women during her era and also enables her to carve out literary, philosophical, and political space in the debates that dominate her time. Because Jacobs is defined, in part, by a binary of black womanhood that juxtaposes her to passionless white women, it is not enough for her merely to extend the privileges of true womanhood to African American women. Rather, she has to break the racial binary on which true womanhood relies.

My epilogue addresses Martin R. Delany's *Condition, Elevation, Emigration, and Destiny of the Colored People of the United States* (1852), "The Political Destiny of the Colored Race" (1854), and *Principia of Ethnology* (1879), to reconsider some of the major issues and themes addressed in *Fleshing Out America*. Perhaps more than any other author's, Delany's rewriting of scientific discourse demonstrates not only the powerful nature of this discourse, but also the complicated responses to it. If Delany risks, as Frederick Douglass argues, having gone "about the same length in favor of black, as the whites have in favor of the doctrine of white superiority," he nonetheless dares to do "what white men have ever dared and done," namely, to build upon and reinvent theories of racial essentialism that not only served his personal politics, but also provided the theoretical background for his vision of the globalized destiny of people of color.

As my description of the chapters and epilogue indicates, I assume that race, gender, and sexuality are historically constructed and therefore flexible classifications. As such, I move away from universalized and essential definitions of identity and ask instead how corporeal experiences may have led these authors to respond to conceptions of difference. At times I use biographical information about the authors to surmise how they may have experienced their corporeality. In doing so, I am aware that the relationship between biography and textual representation is complicated, and my intent is not to find one easily identifiable (and reductive) biographical explanation of why a particular author represents corporeality in a specific way. Rather, I trust that my speculation about embodied experiences will be read in the spirit of inquiry in which it was written. It is designed to consider the relationship between corporeality and textuality in a way that moves beyond merely seeing an author as representative of a particular race, gender, or sexuality. Fuller, for example, is not only a woman in the nineteenth century. She is also an unmarried, middle-class, intellectual white woman with a specific corporeal history of bodily pain that influenced her understanding of corporeality and identity. Although we cannot surmise the full nature of this influence, I do not want to exclude the consideration of it from this work.

Despite the logic dictating my choice of authors and what I see as the conversational structure of this study, there is no linear narrative with which I can neatly define the politics of the body in these writers' texts. Their literary representations neither fall into an oppositional structure between science and literature, nor move in an orderly chronological progression from a faith in a "transcendent" or "metaphysical" body early in the century to an acceptance of identity as embodied by the Civil War. Perhaps it is the nature of this topic to resist totalizing narratives and conclusions. As Nelson says in her excellent work *The Word in Black and White: Reading "Race" in American Literature, 1638–1867*, she too did not try to "write a continuously progressing history because fictions of 'race'" seem to her "neither continuous nor progressive." Like Nelson, I try to "avoid forcing these diverse texts into a preconceived thesis."[14] Instead, I pose the questions that propel my investigation in relation to individual authors: How do discourses of scientific difference influence an author's representation of the body? Can the new politics of the body be liberating or useful? How can authors engage in a critique of nineteenth-century sciences if those very discourses define them as incapable of participating in the debate? When and why do authors decide to deploy "strategic essentialism" and speak the knowledge that comes from their body or from their embodied experiences? How do authors deploy "strategic essentialism" to enact political change without reconfirming notions of themselves as defined primarily by their corporeality? How do authors negotiate the dynamics of spectatorship in relation to either their own bodies or the bodies of those they represent?

These questions, in one way or another, relate to the overall inquiry that dominates this book: Can we combat the disturbingly divisive nature of the politics of the body through the imaginary space that literature provides? As I pursued this question, I found some of the answers disturbing. In particular, my analysis of Fuller was difficult at times, as was the realization that Emerson, Whitman, and Delany, like so many Americans, reacted to political crises with an increased interest in concepts of innate difference. Yet it seems crucial for us to continue to chart the ways in which the politics of identity and corporeality can splinter reform efforts and seep into texts, deconstructing their overt radical and liberative aims. The fact that writers such as Emerson, Fuller, Whitman, and Delany incorporate scientific essentialism into aspects of their texts is neither coincidental nor extraordinary. The discourses were so pervasive as to be unavoidable; no one is outside the influence of culture. Yet no one is totally controlled by ideology. All these authors—some more than others—are able to imagine through literature a space in which to reshape the politics of the body that shaped the politics of their times. This is an imaginative feat worthy of our attention and appreciation. And it is to those efforts that this work now turns.

1

THE BODY IN THE BODY POLITIC

Race, Gender, and Sexuality in

Nineteenth-Century America

Away, therefore, with all the scientific moonshine that would connect men with mon-
keys; that would have the world believe that humanity, instead of resting on its own
characteristic pedestal—gloriously independent—is a sort of sliding scale, making one
extreme brother to the ou-rang-ou-tang, and the other to angels, and all the rest interme-
diates!—Frederick Douglass, "The Claims of the Negro Ethnologically Considered"

In 1854, Frederick Douglass stood before the Literary Societies of Western
Reserve College. The first African American to speak at a commencement ceremony for an American institution of higher education, the former slave and current author, editor, and lecturer had been invited by the graduating class. Over
three thousand people assembled to hear him speak, a larger crowd than
attended the official graduation ceremony.[1] Contrasting the students' eagerness
to hear the renowned orator, the school's administration was primarily conservative, doubted the ability of slaves and free people of color to become viable
members of the body politic, and favored their removal to Africa. One cannot
help but reflect on the spectacle of Douglass's speech. He stood before them, a
guest revered by some, but also a sort of curiosity, a specimen of the race so
often subject to intense scrutiny and cynicism, a representative, yet exceptional, Negro. If Douglass was, as he said, "on trial" as the first African American to deliver an address before such a gathering, he understood that the
"manhood of the negro" was also, in effect, on trial in the United States during
this decade. He therefore used the occasion to challenge one of his era's most
divisive subjects, ethnology, and to argue for the common unity of all men, and
thus for his own manhood. "There was a time," he told his audience, "if you
established the point that a particular being is a man, it was considered that

such a being, of course, had a common ancestry with the rest of mankind. But it is not so now."

This time, Douglass told his audience, was "before the Notts, the Gliddons, the Agassiz[es], and Mortons made their profound discoveries in ethnological science." In other words, the time was the late-eighteenth and early-nineteenth centuries, an Enlightenment era that held forth the promise of the natural and inalienable rights of all men. When the framers of the Declaration of Independence wrote that "all men are created equal," the various races, although not considered equal, were nonetheless generally assumed to be descended from a common ancestry. This biblical conception—monogenesis—attributed racial characteristics primarily to climatic variation. It allowed for the possibility that however "inferior" members of a group might be considered, changes in conditions could alter their status and create the potential for citizenship in the newly formed Republic. However, by the mid–nineteenth century, monogenesis had yielded to polygenesis, the theory that races were produced in separate acts of creation. Samuel Morton's career aptly demonstrates this shifting conception of race. A proponent of monogenesis when he published *Crania Americana* in 1839, Morton maintained that humans were separated into races after the biblical Flood, when they were marked with "a primeval difference" that was part of the "all-pervading design" giving Caucasians "unquestionable superiority over all the nations of the earth." By 1850 Morton had altered his view, alleging that humankind was created "in many pairs; and they were adapted, from the beginning, to those varied circumstances of climate and locality."[2]

Morton's evolving concept of race signifies a general trend in the first half of the nineteenth century, during which various scientific or quasi-scientific disciplines were forming, chief among them phrenology, ethnology, and craniometry. These disciplines, led in part by the men Douglass names, assumed from their inception not only classifiable differences between the races and sexes, but also what we may understand as internal and innate (what Michel Foucault would call *invisible*) qualities of race and gender. Wittingly or not, scientists were fleshing out the implications of Revolutionary rhetoric and contributing to the invention of a biologically determined subject whose corporeality contradicted any claim to the Declaration of Independence's higher law of equality by means of creation.

The fact that the Revolutionary promise of equality was just that—a promise, unfulfilled (and generally unintended)—demonstrates how much bodies mattered in Colonial and Revolutionary literary, political, and philosophical discourses, and it cautions us not to misinterpret Douglass's description of the earlier era as naive. Certainly Douglass was aware that late-eighteenth-century racial discourse did not assume a fundamental equality but rather had an alternative understanding of the origin and implication of racial difference. Indeed, Foucault describes the natural historians' obsession with classification in the seventeenth and eighteenth centuries, highlighting their reliance on *difference* as a primary means of classification. In classical terms, he argues, "a knowledge of empirical individuals can be acquired only from the continuous, ordered, and universal tabulation of all possible differences."[3] This drive toward classification and distinction is evidenced in one of the most influential works of natural history, Carl von Linné's *System of Nature* (1735), in which Linné separates "Homo" into two main categories (sapiens and monstrosus) and then distinguishes further between the wild man, the "copper-coloured" (American), the "fair, sanguine, brawny" (European), the "sooty, melancholy, rigid," and the "black, phlegmatic, relaxed." His subsequent categories of description reveal the hierarchy implicit in his method and world view: the European's eyes are described as "acute," and he is said to be "*governed* by laws"; the "black," we learn, "anoints himself with grease" and is "[g]*overned* by caprice."[4] By 1758, Linné aligned these categories with the Wild Man, American, European, Asiatic, and African sapiens. Mary Louis Pratt says of this shift that "[o]ne could hardly ask for a more explicit attempt to 'naturalize' the myth of European superiority,"[5] and scholars such as Henry Louis Gates Jr. demonstrate that the Enlightenment era linked literacy and humanity, often defining Africans as incapable of literacy and therefore as a lesser grade of humanity.[6]

When we compare, for example, the claim of the politician Thomas Jefferson that "all men are created equal" with the assertion of the natural historian Jefferson in his *Notes on the State of Virginia* (1787) that "never yet could I find that a black had uttered a thought above the level of plain narration" and that "[i]t is not their condition then, but nature, which has produced the distinction [between the races]," we can see how literary and philosophical discourses in the late eighteenth century established a racial hierarchy that belied the political myth of disembodied equality.[7] Antebellum scientists would draw upon the Enlightenment's hierarchal understanding of race and faith in objective knowledge as they created new concepts of race.[8] Reginald Horsman notes that while Enlightenment "thinkers stressed the unity and general improvability of mankind, they also accelerated the process of secularization of thinking" and separated "science from theology."[9] The sheer volume of statistics collected, skulls and skeletons studied, tables calculated, and cadavers dissected in the antebellum era points to an intense desire to classify, to master humankind as one would any other natural object, a desire these thinkers shared with their predecessors.

If there is not an absolute division between late-eighteenth-century and mid-nineteenth-century racial discourse—if we cannot draw as clear a line as does Foucault between "classical" and "modern" understandings of race when we consider the United States—we can nonetheless delineate a shift in emphasis that was profound, the movement from visible classification based upon a climatic explanation of race in the late eighteenth century to a classification of race based on invisible factors rendered "real" by newer technologies and controlled by an increasingly elite group of specialists in the antebellum era. Prior to the 1830s race was not usually considered a phenomena located in the internal structure of the body itself.[10] It is this climatic view of race that the former slave Olaudah Equiano endorses in his *Interesting Narrative of the Life of Olaudah Equiano* (1789), where he provides examples of Spaniards and Portuguese who become in some respects *"perfect Negroes"* in the African climate, a fact that demonstrates how "complexions of the same persons vary in different climates." This argument, he hopes, will "remove the prejudice that some conceive against the natives of Africa on account of their color."[11] In effect, the climatic understanding of race depends upon what Foucault identifies as the classical age's reliance on the *"historical* knowledge of the visible,"* a knowledge that the modern age would replace with the *"philosophical* knowledge of the invisible,"* a shift marked by the substitution of "anatomy for classification" and "organism for structure."[12] Robyn Wiegman argues that the "full force" of both systems was "nonetheless contingent on the status of an observer, whose relation to the object under investigation was mediated and deepened by newly developed technologies for rendering the invisible visible" in the nineteenth century.[13] Although both systems certainly privileged the status of the observer (who, as Pratt notes, is aligned with the European colonizer),[14] the development of the new technologies that Wiegman refers to— technologies that would render the allegedly invisible qualities of race visible to the culturally knowledgeable and empowered observer—points to the critical shift in cultural authority with which many of the authors in this study struggle. Who has access to these technologies and to the discourses that deploy them? Who can speak, in other words, the science of the body in the nineteenth century? Who can answer the devastating accusations of scientists regarding the innate inferiority of particular races and of almost all women? In this context it is arguable that premodern racial concepts had more latitude for dissent, more room to argue for commonality of origin, even for equality, than did their successors of the nineteenth century. Indeed, despite the prevalence of cultural racism, George Fredrickson argues that from 1817 to the 1830s one cannot find "a single clear and unambiguous assertion of the Negro's inherent and unalterable inferiority" because, "[a]long with such assertions of the Negro's *de facto* cultural inferiority, there were many statements which strongly affirmed a basic equality of human capacities."[15]

This study, then, is concerned with two phenomena that we can understand as essential to the debates over citizenship and the representation of corporeality in antebellum America. First, as Karen Sánchez-Eppler argues, the late-eighteenth-century "higher law" of equality was predicated on an allegedly disembodied person who in fact inhabited a white and male body, and "success in masking this fact has secured and legitimized the power that accrues to that body."[16] We can detect an unmasking of this theoretically disembodied person in the antebellum era, due in part to the combined and often contradictory discourses of abolitionism, women's rights, and science, all of which called attention to the specificity of the body and forced Americans to flesh out the implications of their Revolution and Constitution. Second, as the concept of race shifted from the realm of the visible/climatic to the realm of the invisible/inherent, the urgency of a discourse to counter the political implications of this shift became increasingly intense, and much of the literature analyzed in this book results from that urgency. The antebellum concept of race was, as Wiegman argues, neither stable nor totalizing.[17] However, during the antebellum era, scientific "laws" were cited by many to argue for the exclusion of women of all races from full participation in the democratic process and public spheres, the removal of Native Americans from the eastern United States, the enslavement of some African Americans, and the relegation of all African Americans to a secondary political and social status. This shift in emphasis between the late-eighteenth century and mid-nineteenth century was intense and devastating. For example, in 1860 the proslavery writer Sidney George Fisher, who popularized scientific beliefs, argued that the theory of polygenesis and the permanent inferiority of Africans were indisputable facts. Calling for a recognition of "higher laws" that supersede those established by the United States Constitution, he argued: "They *must* rule our politics and our destiny, either by the Constitution or over it. . . . They are the higher law, to which we must submit on pain of destruction, just as we must submit to the laws of steam and electricity, of winds and waves, of earth and iron, of acid and alkali, and as Lord Bacon says, by submitting, govern, and direct them to our advantage."[18] Likewise, Josiah C. Nott and George R. Gliddon conclude that groups of races "heretofore comprehended under the generic term Caucasian" have always been rulers and are destined to conquer "every foot of the globe where climate does not interpose an impenetrable barrier. No philanthropy, no legislation, no missionary labors, can change this law: it is written in man's nature by the hand of his Creator."[19]

Douglass's audience, therefore, would have been forewarned by respected members of the scientific community such as Nott, the coauthor of the monumental 1854 ethnological work *Types of Mankind*, that any rationality on Douglass's part came "in proportion to the amount of white-blood in his veins." Readers who did not want to struggle with scientific texts could turn to widely selling proslavery writers such as the physician J. H. Van Evrie, who translated science for a general readership. Van Evrie cautioned that the "most essential feature" of the Negro was his faculty for "imitating the qualities and for acquiring the habitudes of the white man." Try as they might, men like Douglass would never be able "to speak the language of the white man with absolute correctness." Van Evrie represented the views of many when he zealously announced that for the first time in history difference could be determined far beyond the visible and amorphous categories of cultural practice or skin color, because the "minutest particle, the single globule of blood even" demonstrated Negro inferiority. Indeed, as Fredrickson contends, throughout the 1850s science became "a principal weapon against proponents of emancipation and racial equality."

Just as science was deployed against African American men and women, so too did it hinder some women's activities outside the domestic sphere. For example, J. H. Pulte, the author of the *Woman's Medical Guide*, reminds readers that the "duties and mode of life" are "clearly pointed out to the female in her bodily construction." Scientific discourses on race and gender from this time period, although not identical, nonetheless share methodologies and assumptions. Nancy Leys Stepan demonstrates that, as the century progressed, "gender was found to be remarkably analogous to race, such that the scientist could use racial difference to explain gender difference, and vice versa." Through science, rational man could study the female object to define her separate sphere. If opponents disagreed, such as the supporters of women's rights, whom Pulte criticized fiercely, scientists deduced that they were unnatural:

"Nature has drawn a line, and its existence can only be doubted by those whose inclinations have carried them already beyond its limits."

Scientific analysis of race and gender was tied to a third component of identity, sexuality. As Robert Young reminds us, in the nineteenth century "[t]heories of race" were "also covert theories of desire" because so much attention was paid to the possibility of racial hybridity and thus focused attention on "sexual unions between whites and blacks." Because these three constructs—race, gender, and sexuality—are inextricably connected with conceptions of American identity in the antebellum era, I organize my analysis in this chapter around them. In doing so, I hazard participating in the trend toward division that Douglass warns us against. Yet if this chapter divides these components of identity in theory, the rest of this work demonstrates that, in practice, they were inextricably bound.[20]

Constructing Race

May you be faithful, and enter into a consideration as to how far you are partakers in this evil, even in other men's sins. How far, by permission, by apology, or otherwise, you are found lending your sanction to a system which degrades and brutalizes three million of our fellow beings.—Lucretia Mott, "A Sermon to the Medical Students"

Stephen Jay Gould argues that one of the nineteenth century's most devastating legacies to our era is the general perception of race as a legitimate, natural, and biologically demonstrable category of difference. "Racial prejudice may be as old as recorded human history," he contends, "but its biological justification imposed the additional burden of intrinsic inferiority upon despised groups, and precluded redemption by conversion or assimilation." If, as I suggest below, the motives of American scientists came in part from a complex mixture of racism, professional territorial competition, and the desire for cultural authority, the new classifications of race were quickly seized upon by proponents of slavery and Indian Removal, who felt little need to mask their overt political agenda. Van Evrie's attack on abolitionists reveals the strategical use of science to reconcile the bodies of enslaved people with a body politic that supposedly cherished freedom and equality:

They have a theory . . . that the negro is a *black*-white man . . . a creature like ourselves except in color, and therefore placed under the same circumstances . . . he will manifest the same qualities, etc. On this foolish assumption legislatures and individuals have acted, and both in the South and in the North considerable numbers of these people have been thrust from their normal condition into what? Why, into the condition of widely different beings.

This passage demonstrates how supporters of slavery used science to argue that "widely different beings" should not be legislated into the false equality promised by Revolutionary rhetoric. The shift from mono- to polygenesis was particularly devastating because it provided a justification for excluding African and Native Americans from American identity. Once groups were considered distinct, there was no longer any need to discuss political equality, and often a natural hierarchy and animosity was alleged, as in the case of Nott, who concludes that "[n]o two distinctively-marked races can dwell together on equal terms."[21]

Theories of origin were only one way of constructing difference; scientists also delineated facial/cranial, anatomical, and sexual/reproductive determinants of racial identity. By the time Morton published *Crania Americana* in 1839, the idea that the brain's physical attributes indicated moral and intellectual qualities was already prevalent due to phrenology, which had gained popularity throughout the mid-1820s and 1830s. Until the 1840s, Horsman notes, phrenology was treated with seriousness by the scientific community, although "it later lost its intellectual support." Phrenology linked individual characteristics to the relative size of distinct areas of the brain. Each section was said to reflect a certain trait—such as sexual desire, love of children, or love of one's native land. After it was dismissed by respected scientists, phrenology was still very popular, and "practical" phrenologists continued to disseminate widely "the arguments regarding innate differences between races." Although phrenological practice was not always supported by "legitimate" scientists after the 1820s, many accepted its basic concept: the brain (or skull) of a person or race was used to ascertain innate characteristics and prescribe respective social status. For example, Morton cautions first-year medical students against too readily accepting phrenology's specifics but nonetheless credits it for teaching that the brain is "the seat of the mind," containing intellectual and moral capabilities. Robert E. Bieder indicates that we can locate the shift from an environmental understanding of racial difference to the perception of race "in deterministic terms and as the source of civilization" if we consider Morton's choice of skulls as his objects of study. By using skulls to collect data, Morton turned away from earlier categories of determining difference (such as language) in part because he was turning away from an environmental or cultural understanding of race. To prove that race is innate and permanent, Morton needed to demonstrate that the skulls he studied were "immune to environmental forces" and, to do so, he turned to "a comparison of the crania of prehistoric North and South American Indians with those of recently deceased Indians of both continents." Such a method dismissed cultural and historical explanations of difference, offering instead an onslaught of data to establish permanent racial difference. Craniometry, according to Gould, was the first discipline to support a biological theory of race by extensive quantitative data.[22]

Morton follows this quantitative method in *Crania Americana*, a work that was lauded by many, and earned Morton considerable cultural status. Hailed in the *American Journal of Science and Arts* as "the most extensive and valuable contribution to the natural history of man, which has yet appeared on the American continent," Morton's 1839 work is massive, illustrated by 78 plates and a colored map. Through the depiction of various crania and tabulation of skulls, Morton "proves" that Aboriginals are a distinct race and concludes that the Caucasian brain is the largest, with the Aboriginal's inferior to the Caucasian's, but larger than the African's. Morton accentuated the political implications of his book by asking George Combe to write its appendix. Combe, a Scottish proponent of phrenology, was very interested in the "power and reputation" of Great Britain and stressed "racial differentiation" and "genetic inheritance." It is not surprising, then, that in the appendix he concludes that "the present work . . . will be an authentic record in which the philosopher may read the native aptitudes, dispositions and mental force of these families of mankind." The "mental force" to which Combe makes reference was considered to be inferior in Indians, and this inferiority was linked to the policy of Indian Removal in the 1830s. Bieder notes that Morton "shared with other phrenologists the assumption that the Indians' rejection of civilization lay not in willfulness but in their mental inability, given the size of their brains, to absorb civilization." Assimilation, therefore, was not considered a reasonable option by some scientists, and even Indian Removal was not always considered sufficient to save the physiologically fated Indians because, as Bieder argues, for the "polygenist critic, Indian removal was the next logical step toward Indian extinction." Mid-nineteenth-century science had the effect of making the Indian, in Bieder's words, both a "tragic figure" and a "specimen for science." The Indian was visible before a Euro-American audience as a specimen, an object of scientific and literary study. Yet, paradoxically, Morton and others also participated in the symbolic vanishing of Indians. Certainly, as Bieder notes, many "had prophesied a tragic end for the Indian even before Morton began his investigations, but Morton seemed to provide the scientific proof for Indians' inevitable extinction." The prediction of extinction signifies a cultural desire to "disappear" Indians, to erase markers of their corporeal presence. Science, then, made Indians visible as objects of study and contributed both literally and figuratively to the removal of Indians' corporeality from the visibility of many inhabitants of the eastern United States. Margaret Fuller participates in this process, often drawing upon the works of men of science to authorize herself as a scientific/ethnological observer who simultaneously erases and preserves Indians in her text.[23]

It should come as no surprise that Morton followed up his work on Indians in *Crania Americana* with a more extensive study of Africans, his 1844 *Crania Aegyptica*. Although the findings and political implications of the science of race often differed for Indians and African Americans, the discourse was nonetheless unified in its creation of space for Caucasian superiority. Morton's work was accepted by many as fact, and his followers (associated with the American School of Anthropology) continued his work of racial categorization based on physical attributes. Nott and Gliddon, for example, in *Types of Mankind*, pointed to the alleged deficiency in brain size to "prove" that nature intended Negroes in Africa to stay "in that same benighted state wherein Nature has placed them, and in which they have been for at least 5,000 years." Repeatedly, proslavery writers compared the intellectual capacity of Africans to that of orangoutangs, but even so-called objective scientists concluded that "[n]o line can be drawn between men and animals on the ground of 'reason,' and more than one of the savage races of men possess no perceptible moral or religious ideas." In addition to brain size, the proportion of anterior to posterior cranial segments and facial angle were employed to distinguish racial characteristics. The anterior portion was thought to provide intelligence and rationality, and the posterior one was believed to be responsible for passion and sensation. Perhaps not coincidentally, scientists "proved" that Africans had a larger percentage of posterior brain mass, thus making them more sensual, passionate, and animal-like. These findings confirmed two of the most common nineteenth-century stereotypes of the African American: the oversexed "animal" and the romanticized natural primitive. Facial angle was said to connect Africans more closely with apes. Colfax reported that anatomists measured the facial angle of Europeans at 80 degrees; Negroes at 70 degrees; orangoutangs at 58 degrees; and all brutes below 70 degrees. Citing the shape of the Negro head as both proof of, and the cause for, their "inability" to learn, he concluded that it is *"improper and impolitic"* that they should be allowed the privileges of citizenship in an *"enlightened country."*[24]

Although facial/cranial calculations were most often cited as proof of innate capability, as the century progressed, scientists tended to view the body's overall anatomy as indicating racial difference. The writings of Charles Caldwell best demonstrate the zealous racialization of every component of the body. Caldwell emphasizes that the microscope reveals "striking" differences, and his extensive list of these distinctions is a celebration of the Caucasian through the degradation of the Negro. His catalogue of body parts reads like a racist precursor to Walt Whitman's "I Sing the Body Electric." This quote indicates the extreme level that the taxonomy of difference had reached by 1852:

> In the upper and lower extremities, then, the teeth, the maxillary bones with their muscles, and the head generally, the differences between these two races of men are numerous and great. . . .
>
> But all the differences between the two races are not yet enumerated. In the African the stomach is rounder, and the blood and brain of a darker color. . . . In their genital organs they also differ much from each other. . . . It extends, as already intimated, to the head and face, the arms, hands—especially the fingers and nails—the flatness of the sides of the chest, the bones of the pelvis and the muscles that cover them, the lateral flatness and thinness of the thigh, its depth in the opposite direction, its length compared to that of the leg, the forward bend of the knee, the general form of the foot and its connections with the leg, and the length and taper of the toes, together with the form and position of their nails.[25]

For physicians such as Caldwell, every part of the body indicated racial difference and hierarchy. Technology in the form of the microscope made the previously invisible visible and enabled a particular group of elites to interpret this newly visible phenomena for their ends. Similarly, Van Evrie assures readers that no matter how one looks at the Negro body, it shows subservience. "[W]hile the analysis of a single bone or a single feature" will suffice, "the *tout ensemble* of the anatomical formation" betrays inferiority. The closer one gets to the body, the more pronounced large-scale categories of difference become. This is a grammar of difference that delves into the microcosm to reaffirm a basic order of the macrocosm. Each part and particle of the Negro or Aboriginal reaffirms the overall racialized order of the Caucasian's universe. Once these scientific paradigms were established, it was not a difficult gesture to generalize about the proper societal position of African Americans and Native Americans and to conclude that they were only fit to be slaves or noncitizens. "Heavily emphasized," Fredrickson explains, "was the historical case against the black man based on his supposed failure to develop a civilized way of life in Africa." Van Evrie chided the Negro for not taking "one step" toward mental development: "the negro is a blank, a wilderness, a barren waste," whose "mental powers are unable to grapple with science or philosophy, or abstractions of any kind." The denigration of African culture, along with assertions that Egyptians were non-Africans, prompted Douglass to remark in reference to Morton that "[t]o be intelligent is to have one's negro blood ignored."[26]

Douglass's observation reflects the profound ambivalence of many in the dominant culture toward people of mixed races, a population who generated hatred, fear, and patronizing romanticization. Although scientists alleged permanent categories called Caucasian and Negro, the presence of numerous mixed-raced people challenged these structures. Therefore, inconsistencies abound between concepts of fixed racial features and fear over commingling. Nott, for example, professes that "[c]ertain races would be stationary and barbarous for ever, were it not for the introduction of new blood and novel influences." Maintaining that the Negro and Caucasian are permanent types, he nonetheless warns that "the infusion of even a minute proportion of blood of one race into another, produces a most decided modification of moral and physical character." The contradiction between an assumed permanent racial identity and dread of racial disintegration indicates anxiety over categories that, while fixed in theory, were, through the presence of real bodies, constantly flaunting their fiction. Strident efforts were made to reaffirm the naturalness of racial categories despite their apparent breakdown. Van Evrie's declaration that the southern American "knows that a negro is a negro . . . just as clearly, absolutely and unmistakingly as he knows that black is black, and is not white, that a man is a man and is not a woman" can be read as an almost hysterical insistence on categorization in the face of an inability to distinguish race (and perhaps gender) in some individuals. Clearly, concerns over the mulatto underscore the anxiety over racial purity, especially in the seemingly susceptible white race. Although the term "miscegenation" was not generally in use until 1864, abolitionists were said to propose "amalgamation" of the races as a design to end slavery, a charge that was deployed to categorize white abolitionists as traitors to their race. Proslavery writers, like their Reconstruction counterparts, incited popular abhorrence of racial mixing and of the abolitionists who supposedly proposed it. The merging of any two races, according to Nott and Gliddon, results in the superior race's debasement and eventual extinction. The fact that the majority of "mixing" was due to white southern males exploiting, raping, and prostituting slave women rarely enters into their rhetoric. Rather, amalgamation was represented as the degradation of the white woman and, therefore, of the white race. Van Evrie warned that if four million slaves formed couples with four million whites, all would suffer from an "ulcer on the body politic" that would end in the nation's demise.[27]

Medical and scientific beliefs about the nature of the mulatto differed greatly, in part because people of racially mixed heritage represented a challenge to racial order. A system that allowed for biological superiority had to concede that "white" blood benefited its recipients. Accordingly, scientists generally classified the mulatto as an "intermediate" being, whose intelligence was attributable to Caucasian blood. Therefore, it was possible theoretically for a person to "become" white through repeated generations of "up-breeding," a scenario that was becoming increasingly imaginable as generations of Americans commingled and Negroes existed who were visibly white. To disavow this possibility, the majority of scientists classified the mulatto as naturally fragile, diseased, and unable to produce healthy offspring. The term "mulatto" derives from Spanish and Portuguese and, more obscurely, from *mulo* (mule). It refers to a "young mule, hence one of a mixed race." As a cross between the horse and the donkey, the mule cannot produce offspring. Although animal hybrids may be barren, most scientists recognized that to apply this same rule to human racial "hybrids" directly contradicted physical evidence. Consequently, some proposed that racial "hybrids" were weak, less prolific, and prone to become sterile in about four generations when kept separate from their "parent stock." Nott classified mulatto women as "bad breeders, bad nurses," who were "liable to abortions," and whose "children generally die young." Likewise, he concluded that when a Negro man had a child with a white woman, it was more likely to be Negro.[28] White identity, then, could never be obtained through amalgamation; the only outcome racial mixing could produce was the degeneracy of the Caucasian race and, by extension, the breakdown of American prosperity.[29] In this context we can understand the dilemma facing writers such as Harriet Jacobs. By identifying herself as a mulatto, she may have appealed to the dominant culture's sense that she was more akin to them than a Negro, but she also had to contradict notions that she was inherently weak and prone to poor mothering skills.

If mulattoes challenged racial order, so too did the influx of immigrants, and the presence of both groups tended to contribute to the construction of white identity. As various ethnic groups arrived in the United States throughout the century, many people began to distinguish even more specifically between the lower and higher types of Caucasians. At the same time, many began to insist upon a white democratic order. Fisher demonstrates this tension when he resists the colonization of Mexico because it would weaken the Saxon American blood and allow "mongrel" people to participate in democracy. "Now, at least, Saxon, Celt, and German, live together harmoniously," he argues, "though, perhaps, this is only because as yet the Saxon practically predominates and governs." Indeed, Horsman argues that the "catalyst in the overt adoption of a racial Anglo-Saxonism was the meeting of Americans and Mexicans in the Southwest."[30] Although the Saxon/Caucasian identity was not always secure, proslavery writers used African Americans to solidify white identity across class.[31] Van Evrie's 1862 *Free Negroism* declares that slavery benefitted working-class northerners by allowing for affordable prices on otherwise luxury items, raising their standard of living and reducing labor competition. His conclusion that the "'slave' negro is the poor man's friend" and "the 'freed' negro is his bitter and unrelenting enemy" announces his class appeal. So too does the ending of *Negroes and Negro "Slavery,"* which outlines how racism assists in the formation of a white American identity. Van Evrie believes that the presence of Africans stimulated democracy because the juxtaposition of races revealed the natural connection between white men. He concludes: "[T]he existence of an inferior race . . . has resulted in the creation of a new political and social order, and relieved the producing classes from that abject dependence on capital which in Europe, and especially in England, renders them mere beasts of burthen to a fraction of their brethren." Van Evrie's suggestion that the existence of an "inferior race" created a "new political and social order" echoes one of two racial ideologies that dominate his age. Horsman reports that although "[p]ractically all expansionists" enthusiastically endorsed the concept of a "superior race imposing its will on a variety of inferior races," not all accepted the idea that Americans were "simply transplanted Anglo-Saxons." Instead, many thought of Americans as a "special, progressive branch of the Anglo-Saxon race" or even a "separate, superior, unique race."[32] As Van Evrie hints in his discussion of a "new political and social order," and as contemporary scholars such as David Roediger and Noel Ignatiev confirm, the formation of a new "white" identity resulted in part from the presence of African Americans in the antebellum era.[33] If the writings of Ralph Waldo Emerson,

Fuller, and Whitman all testify to the appeal of the myth of a unified white/ national identity in the antebellum era, many of Martin R. Delany's texts point to the equally powerful pull of the discourse of racial difference for African Americans seeking to establish literal and symbolic space in the nineteenth-century body politic.

As I argue above, one result of racial science was to "disappear" the Indian. It can be argued that the science of race had the opposite outcome for African Americans. More than any other body, the African American body was the one that was scrutinized, taxonomized, and chattelized. It was whipped, worked, sold, raped, and studied with a ferocity close to frenzy. Publicly accessible—through the slave auction or the medical examination table—the body of the African American was figuratively, and quite often literally, public.[34] The process was one that attempted to reduce the identity of the Negro to that of his or her body, to subordinate moral or intellectual attributes to physiological phenomena. It is in the face of these obstacles that abolitionists like Lydia Maria Child appealed for "Africans" to be considered "Americans." It is in this context that writers like Jacobs and Frances E. W. Harper bravely avowed their full humanity—physical, intellectual, and spiritual. Their task was made all the more difficult by the links between scientific racism and scientific sexism.

To the Bones: Essentializing Gender

The same ignorance of organization, which, in its blind fanaticism, would compel the Negro, or would seek to compel the Negro, with his different and inferior organization, to perform the functions of the white man, also busies itself about "woman's rights" . . . indeed, the advocates of "human rights" and "woman's rights" are, from very necessity, associated together, and the delusion in one case is certain to exist in the other.—Van Evrie, *Negroes and Negro "Slavery"*

Van Evrie's observation that the "advocates of 'human rights' and 'woman's rights' are, from very necessity, associated together" may be more astute than he intended. He not only reveals the historical ties between the two groups, inasmuch as the abolition movement aided in the birth of the American women's movement, but also demonstrates how both encountered the obstacle of scientific essentialism. Many scientists defined women and people of color as "other" and "object" and deemed any challenge to this subordinate societal status "delusional." Analogies between white women and allegedly inferior races saturate nineteenth-century science; just as brain size, the nervous system, and overall anatomy were said to demarcate the "races," so too were they used to categorize women as inferior beings. Many believed that the male Negro, for example, was more feminine than the male Caucasian. Similarly, scientists considered women of all races and African Americans childlike, in a permanent stage of adolescence that would eventually be labeled "arrested development."[35]

As in the case of race, phrenology was instrumental in birthing new scientific conceptions of the body, in this case initiating analysis of the brain to ascertain women's capabilities and societal roles.[36] Phrenologists believed brains were proportioned differently in males and females and presumed that women naturally tended to feminine behavior. One of phrenology's most ardent advocates, Lorenzo Fowler, summarized the applicability of phrenological principles to domestic relations in his 1842 pamphlet "The Principles of Phrenology and Physiology Applied to Man's Social Relations." He stressed that women had more "benevolence," "veneration," "conscientiousness," "secretiveness," and "philoprogenitiveness" (love of children). Men, on the other hand, dominated in "amativeness" (sexual longing), "combativeness," "destructiveness," "firmness," "causality," and "comparison."[37] Through assertions such as these, phrenologists supported the Doctrine of Separate Spheres by translating social behavior generally deemed "masculine" and "feminine" into innate attributes of men and women. Craniometry, the science evolving from phrenology, was, according to Cynthia Eagle Russett, "the characteristic achievement" of physical anthropology. Like ethnology, the new anthropology "preached permanence and scoffed at reform." Generally, craniologists assumed that the larger the brain, the more intellectual and developed the person and, at first, women were deemed to have 10 percent less brain mass than men, a perceived deficit that became known as the "missing five ounces of female brain." By midcentury, physicians could confidently declare that women were physically unfit for intellectual labor.[38]

Privileging cranial capacity created problems, one of which was that, based on size alone, whales and elephants outclass humans. Also, one could reason that the female brain, in relation to body weight, is proportionally larger than that of the male. Scientists negotiated these discrepancies in a variety of ways. Generally, they hypothesized that the female skull was in a stage of semidevelopment, with an analogy made to the proportionately larger brain of maturing children. After the 1860s scientists proposed that the frontal lobes of the brain were more vital and, not surprisingly, men were credited with having more of this essential mass.[39] Pulte contends that females' larger brains were a disadvantage, as their nerves were "finer, more tender and weaker, making them disproportionate to the size of the brain." If cranial disproportion rendered a woman unable to execute long-term thinking, Pulte reassured readers that she was nonetheless perfectly constituted to become the "constant companion of man, who is well fitted by nature to carry out her designs."[40]

Pulte's classification of women as more "nervous" than men was common. According to Ludmilla Jordanova, men's supposedly greater muscular structure was often compared to women's more susceptible nervous system. Pulte repeats the widely held assumption that the female nervous system is more vulnerable than the male but less likely to be seriously sick, as "[i]ts impressions are not so deep and lasting."[41] Therefore, even before hysteria became a category of disease for middle-class women in the last half of the nineteenth century, scientists had established the perception of middle-class women as highly nervous and sensitive, yet not seriously ill.[42] As Pulte's discussion of the female nervous system suggests, physicians presumed that women had different anatomical structures than men. Londa Schiebinger traces the construction of the first specifically female skeletons to the mid-eighteenth century. By the nineteenth century, scientists presumed that the skeleton revealed not only a person's sex, but also his or her natural duties. In this manner, difference was taken, quite literally, to the bones.[43]

Even though gender difference was taken "to the bones" in antebellum scientific discourse, all women were not understood as essentially the same. Rather, concepts of women's capabilities and physiology differed according to their race and class. Much of the scientific discourse from this era naturalizes the Doctrine of Separate Spheres, the concept that a true woman was pious, pure, submissive, and domestic. Clearly, this doctrine (always more rhetoric than reality) was race- and class-based, as it established and legitimized the white, middle-class home.[44] We can best understand the race- and class-based definitions of true womanhood by focusing on two related areas: childbearing and illness. During this time period, the middle-class Caucasian woman was understood by many as the producer of the dominant race, a role at odds with the drop in reproduction rates from slightly over seven children at the turn of the nineteenth century to an average of 4.24 by 1880. Nonetheless, according to Horsman, proponents of racial Anglo-Saxonism had a "boundless faith in the reproductive capacity of the white American people" and connected "commercial penetration and population growth" to America's future global domination.[45]

Caught in these changes was the Caucasian middle-class woman, who symbolized the future of the state as well as the family. Often, rhetoric focused on pregnant white women's health, encouraging them "to regard the sacrifice of good health and personal comfort as the price of motherhood" and suggesting that "failure to do whatever was necessary to assure their own health and that of their unborn child was to be negligent." Dixon warned firmly in 1859 that from the moment of quickening "thou has no right to trifle with thy life: from this moment it is sacred to nature, and to God."[46] The pregnant woman, and by extension any women who could and should become pregnant, had a responsibility to conserve energy and maintain health for her most important duty, giving birth to Caucasian citizens. Any activity—social, political, or intellectual—that detracted from this duty was regarded as not only unnatural, but also as endangering future generations. Given the simultaneous call for the progress of the race and the drop in white birth rates, it should come as no surprise that this era produced the first large-scale antiabortion movement. Prior to the 1830s abortion was considered immoral, but not illegal. By the 1830s and 1840s members of the middle class in several states began to agitate for criminalizing abortion. Smith-Rosenberg emphasizes that antiabortion rhetoric targeted middle-class married women as the worst offenders, accusing them of seeking to "avoid marital responsibilities so as to live a life of endless pleasure without responsibility or pain," to escape, in effect, a life defined solely by biology.[47]

Paradoxically, then, the allegedly passionless and pure Caucasian woman was demarcated by a biology of sex. Also ironic, but not coincidental, was that, as birthrates dropped and technological advances spiraled, middle-class women had more time to pursue activities outside the domestic sphere, yet motherhood was increasingly viewed as their sole role.[48] Smith-Rosenberg points to the two primary means by which reproductive functions determined women's identities. First, femininity was perceived as incarnated in the female body, specifically in the organs of reproduction. Second, women's lives were presumably structured around their biological capabilities for motherhood. Thomas Laqueur defines the 1843 discovery of spontaneous ovulation in some mammals as a critical turning point in the conception of female identity. Previously, most believed that ovulation was dependent on coition. Now, because of their "discovery" of spontaneous ovulation, scientists compared women to animals in estrus. Laqueur states that "[t]he ovary, whose distinction from the male testes had only been recognized a century earlier, became the driving force of the whole female economy, with menstruation the outward sign of its awesome power."[49] Scientists defined women by their ovaries or uterus, and some, such as Dixon, claimed that any woman without these organs was not womanly at all: "The saying of a distinguished writer 'On account of the uterus, woman is what she is,' becomes most forcibly apposite in the extraordinary moral and physical peculiarities of those females in whom there exists a complete absence of the ovaria. . . . The passion of love is unknown to them, and they present an aspect altogether at variance with the harmony of nature."[50]

If new information about the ovary often reduced women's identity to their reproductive capabilities, as Smith-Rosenberg suggests, this did not mean that during other periods of her life a woman could hope to define herself in different ways. Rather, women's identities were linked to their maternal potential throughout their lives. Medical advice books often divided the female life cycle into three phases: menstruation, marriage/childbirth, and cessation of menstruation. Because scientists envisioned the body as a closed system with limited energy, they warned young females that too much intellectual or physical exertion would squander stamina needed for motherhood.[51] As Pulte explained to his readers in his best-selling medical guide, marriage and childbirth were a woman's greatest accomplishment and "the natural destiny of her existence." "Menstruation," the physician Edward H. Dixon told readers in 1859, "is the first great era in the life of a female. . . . Should it not be established, all the charms of her person vanish." With menstruation, Pulte announces, the "girl, talkative, roguish and romping, becomes at once reserved, retiring, sometimes even sad, and easily moved to tears. She begins to dress with more care, and is more observing anxiously and silently; her whole soul is filled with gentle emotions."[52] As this passage reveals, physicians prescribed social behavior by defining feminine characteristics as natural. Menstruation transformed a previously energetic girl into an anxious, silent, and still woman—the domesticated true woman.

Coinciding, then, with the rise of the category of the biologically true woman was the simultaneous categorization of the deviant women as unnatural, a powerful charge against women who threatened the social order. After elaborating on the physiological foundations for woman's identity, Pulte reaches a rhetorical rapture cushioning an implicit threat: "No triumph of the victorious soldier, the subtle statesman, the eloquent advocate, successful physician, or faithful minister, can equal in reality and sublimity a mother's happiness, when fondling her infant. . . . There is no reason, then, why the woman, with true motherly feelings, should engage in any other but the business assigned to her by nature."[53] This passage indicates that a "true" woman "should" (and presumably would) not "engage in any other" activity beyond her sphere. Additionally, considered passionless, Caucasian women indicated their gentility by feeling no sexual longing. Therefore, women who exhibited sexual passion or "deviancy," such as prostitutes or proponents of free love, were categorized as unnatural.[54] Many of the writers in this study question the notion of the "unnatural" or "monstrous" woman, but it is in Whitman's poetry that we see the most direct challenge to the alleged passionlessness of the middle-class white female; relatedly, it is in Whitman's poetry that we also see the most glorification of motherhood, a rhetoric that echoes many of the medical writers of the day.

Certainly, scientific discourse could be employed to limit women's political and social roles. However, many middle-class women—consciously or not—exploited the concept of being biologically different, even inferior, to solidify or emphasize their middle-class standing. As stated above, puberty, pregnancy, and menopause were all considered critical periods in a woman's life, leaving her especially susceptible to disease.[55] By its title alone, Dixon's *Woman and Her Diseases, from the Cradle to the Grave* popularizes the idea of the hopelessly infirm woman. In this advice book, first published in 1847 and going through ten editions by 1859, Dixon maintains that it is an "act of humanity" to instruct women about their bodies as they are "subjected to so many causes of physical degeneration from the evident design of nature."[56] According to Sylvia Hoffert, by midcentury pregnancy was generally viewed as pathological. Although not all doctors went as far as Benjamin Rush, who early in the century encouraged physicians to bleed birthing women, many agreed with Pulte's overall presumption that "a pregnant woman can never be free from one or the other disease."[57] In part, the conception of pregnancy as a malady resulted from physicians' efforts to wrestle control of the birthing process away from midwives and bring it into the realm of professional medical men. Yet in this process, the medical men were helped by many middle-class women, who, as Hoffert illustrates, subscribed to the concept of pregnancy as an ailment to demonstrate their class status conspicuously through both the employment of a respected physician and the display of expendable time for medically required rest.[58] Their "weaker" status, then, became a way to mark their middle-class genteel societal standing. By contrast, many African American women and working-class women of all races were considered naturally capable of performing strenuous labor and quickly recovering from childbirth, with the exception of mulatto women, whose alleged weakness was asserted to reaffirm racial division. Jacobs's narrative exposes and critiques the racial and class-determined category of the "frail" woman.

Women of color, then, were caught in the changing conceptions of gender and sexuality. Whereas non-Caucasian races were categorized as inferior and animalistic, Caucasian women were generally categorized as "different." Although "difference" was associated with subordination and rationalized political exclusion, it also suggested that Caucasian women were specially equipped for their duties as mothers of the superior, dominant, "American" race. A precarious balance was maintained between the ideology of superior white womanhood and political oppression; this equilibrium was achieved by emphasizing difference. John and Robin Haller aptly summarize how by "the end of the century, medical science had depicted women as creatures inferior to men yet somehow kin to the angels."[59] In order to elevate Caucasian women to their questionable status of private, passionless mothers, many disparaged African American women as public, passionate breeders. Deborah Gray White explores the connections between reproduction and privacy in the slave community. "Just as with reproduction," she argues, "that which was private and personal became public and familiar" for slave women, whose bodies were often exposed or semiexposed while they were working in the fields, being tortured, or sold on the auction block.[60] This was, after all, a century that witnessed uncensored sexual abuse of slave women. During this era, the nation also relied on the strenuous labor of slave and working-class women. Whereas the cult of motherhood thrived on the belief that Caucasian women were designed to be the tender nurturers of future citizens, southern law marked slave children as the property of slave owners. To maintain this radical discrepancy between the practice and theory of womanhood, scientists invented means of differentiating Negro from Caucasian middle-class women. As Hazel V. Carby argues, any investigation of the cult of true womanhood that does not recognize the "dialectical relationship with the alternative sexual code associated with the black woman" is sterile.[61] In the nineteenth century, scientists helped establish an "alternative sexual code" by arguing that maternal and sexual qualities were racially determined characteristics. Scientists deemed sexuality, like many qualities, innate. Van Evrie echoes common beliefs when he contends that the white female's "blush of maiden modesty" exhibits natural purity. He then asks: "Can any one suppose such a thing possible to a black face? . . . And if the latter cannot reflect these things in her face—if her features are utterly incapable of expressing emotions so elevated and beautiful, is it not certain that she is without them—that they have no existence in her inner being, are no portion of her moral nature?"[62]

Van Evrie reiterates what was by then a given: the Negro woman was sexually accessible and desirous. Likewise, Nott comments upon "the want of chastity among mulatto women which is so notorious as to be proverbial."[63] These scientific and popular representations of the passionate Negro woman coincided with textual depictions. White summarizes this phenomenon in relation to the figure of the African American "Jezebel character," a black woman "governed almost entirely by her libido," who "was the counterimage of the mid-nineteenth-century ideal of the Victorian lady." Differences between fertility rates of slave and Caucasian women may have contributed to perceptions of the Negro woman's promiscuity. As White indicates, "once slaveholders realized that the reproductive function of the female slave could yield a profit, the manipulation of procreative sexual relations became an integral part of the sexual exploitation of female slaves." This was particularly the case once the importation of slaves from Africa was outlawed in 1808, after which many slave owners exploited their slave women to increase their capital. In part due to these practices, African American women's birth rates did not decrease until the postbellum era.[64]

Even if the theory of mulatto and Negro women's innate immorality helped to justify wide-scale sexual exploitation, slavery was still susceptible to criticism for separating children from their mothers. Proslavery writers rebutted these charges by citing physiological distinctions between Negro and Caucasian mothers and children. To the Caucasian women, Van Evrie argued, motherhood is "a profound instinct" and "a lofty sentiment," one that reflects the race's intellectual abilities and defines a Caucasian woman's life. Negro women's maternal instincts, however, are "more closely approximate to the animal" and consequently fade quickly after the birth of a child. While the Negro mother has a "boundless affection" for her infant, at twelve to fifteen she "is relatively indifferent to it" and "at forty she does not recognize it." Additionally, scientists postulated that Negro children, like certain animals, developed more rapidly than Caucasians. Therefore, it was appropriate to separate them from their mothers at an earlier age.[65] Science, once again, defended legal and social practice. Children could be separated from their mothers because the two had no "natural" affection after a certain age. The mulatto woman, as noted previously, was considered to be a particularly inadequate mother, and her "mixed" children were labeled fragile and likely to die.

Certainly, nineteenth-century scientists constructed woman as a category linked to biological foundations of femininity or sexuality or both. It is against these convictions that Fuller would formulate her provocative theory of gender in *Woman in the Nineteenth Century*. Scientists also justified the exploitation of African American women by defining their gender racially, a move that Child, Harper, and Jacobs would refute with might. However, the relationship between science and gender cannot be viewed solely as a white "masculine" discourse dominating the female body. White men were also defined and confined by scientific theories, particularly, as suggested below, in relation to sexuality. The nineteenth-century Caucasian male hardly enjoyed a natural or uncomplicated identity, for he was caught between conflicting notions of masculinity and civility. Physiologically the Saxon male was considered superior, but also prone to conquest, violence, and lust. Despite the young eastern male's purported weakness, he was bombarded with an enticing frontier-based myth of sexuality, violence, and fierce independence.[66] In contrast to such images— but equally strident—were calls reminding white men to govern their "natural" aggression and perform their social duties as Christians, fathers, and husbands. "Every man," one of the most popular young men's guides emphasized, "lives for his wife, his children, his neighbors, his friends, his country; yea, for the world." Haller and Haller maintain: "The white man's burden became the young man's burden, and on his slender shoulders the young male Caucasian had to carry the weight of the century's ideas, hopes and goals." Often this anxiety manifested itself in attempts to control the young white male's body. Haller and Haller note that "[a]nything which weakened his vital energy in youth detracted from his potential greatness in maturity. The evils of smoking, chewing, drinking, and swearing stood ominously in the doorway to progress."[67] The "progress" that a young male hindered by abusing his body was not only his own, but also that of his race and nation. The health of the Republic relied on his ability to control corporeal impulses, especially sexual ones. Writers such as Emerson and Whitman were both attracted and repulsed by the rhetoric of corporeal control and racial responsibility. These men were not alone. Sexuality became a critical site of struggle in an age desperate to control the constitution of the body politic.

Controlling Sex

Often envisioned as an age of sexual repression, the nineteenth century in fact exhibited a complex combination of expression and repression. Although public outcry against prostitution, seduction, and nonprocreative sex gained force throughout the century, private choices repeatedly clashed with public discourse. Foucault points to the century's fundamental ambiguity:

> In terms of repression, things are unclear. There was permissiveness, if one bears in mind that the severity of the codes relating to sexual offenses diminished considerably in the nineteenth century and that law itself often deferred to medicine. But an additional ruse of severity, if one thinks of all the agencies of control and all the mechanisms of surveillance that were put into operation by pedagogy or therapeutics.[68]

I point to the contradictions that Foucault notes because this section focuses on a rhetoric of sexuality that is often restrictive and regulatory. However, as my subsequent chapters demonstrate, sexual theory and practice were far more multifaceted than an analysis of medical discourse indicates, and efforts to control the body politic were not totalizing. Nonetheless, science in general, and medicine in particular, became a powerful player in societal struggles over sexuality. "As if it was essential that sex be inscribed," Foucault suggests, "not only in an economy of pleasure but in an ordered system of knowledge."[69]

The tension between pleasure and knowledge to which Foucault refers is evidenced in one of the century's most pervasive beliefs, that of the body as a closed system of energy. As Russett details, from the 1820s to the turn of the century, one branch of biology envisioned the body as a machine, with all functions competing for energy.[70] Brainwork was considered most exhausting, and the brain was understood to have a direct impact on the nervous system.[71] One popular lecturer, Sylvester Graham, explained the body's interrelatedness to his 1837 audience: "Hence the influences of the brain may act directly on the genital organs; and of these latter on the brain. Lascivious thoughts and imaginations will excite and stimulate the genital organs, cause an increased quantity of blood to flow into them, and augment their secretions and peculiar sensibilities; and, on the other hand, an excited state of the genital organs, either from the stimulations of semen, or from diseased action in the system, will throw its influence upon the brain, and force lascivious thoughts and imaginations upon the mind."[72] According to Graham, sexual arousal could disease the mind, and the implication is clear: sexual activity, even within marriage, was potentially dangerous. One very popular guide reminded young couples in 1856 that intercourse would lead to its "ultimate purpose" of procreation only if performed sparingly. Overindulgence could sabotage health, sicken offspring, and produce barrenness.[73] Couples were advised to limit sexual activity to an average of once a month and to abstain entirely during pregnancy and nursing. Seduction, physicians warned, could take place even within marriage, as wives could be led by selfish husbands to licentiousness that corrupts themselves and their children.[74]

More dangerous than sex within the heterosexual procreative context was any activity threatening this norm. In relation to men, societal anxiety was evidenced in the fervor over anti-onanism, a term that referred to masturbation and dispersion of "seed" outside the female body. In part, fear of masturbation and other nonprocreative acts stemmed from an ancient belief in semen as an almost sacred fluid. Prior to the nineteenth century, semen was thought to be a combination of brain and spinal marrow and was regarded as the vital component of conception.[75] As "Aristotle," the pseudonymous author of a popular series of sexual-advice guides, tells his readers: "The purest blood we find if well we heed, / Is in the testicles turned into seed." Although nineteenth-century physicians generally dismissed the idea that too frequent loss of semen resulted in debilitation, they nonetheless replicated the concept that male sexual excitement resulted in a dangerous depletion of energy. Alcott warned that "it is the great agitation of the nervous system . . . and the waste of the vital energies, which accompany or rather precede the discharge, and not the mere discharge of the fluid itself—which do the mischief."[76] Throughout the century, physicians, clergymen and advice books cajoled and tormented young American males into avoiding masturbation.[77] At times the rhetoric reached quite a pitch, as in the case of Graham, who in 1837 described the decline of a masturbator, who "finally becomes a confirmed and degraded idiot, whose sunken and vacant, glossy eye, and livid, shriveled countenance, and ulcerous, toothless gums, and foetid breath, and feeble, broken voice, and emaciated and dwarfish and crooked body, and almost hairless head . . . denote a premature old age—a blighted body—and a ruined soul!" Resulting in impotence, idiocy, and premature death, masturbation exhausted the body in addition to revealing an individual's lack of will. The young white male's body correlated to the body politic because the ruling class needed to be able to command itself to govern others. "[T]he aggregate of individual character and individual will," Graham emphasizes, "constitutes the foundation and efficiency of all our civil and political institutions."[78] To keep the body politic Caucasian, orderly, and clean, the young white, middle-class male needed to purge himself of filth. In this sense, sexual control, D'Emilio and Freedman remark, "helped differentiate the middle class from the working class, and whites from other races."[79]

Underlying the apprehension over masturbation was the understanding of the male as being naturally lustful and bordering on being depraved. The sexual male and passionless female were concepts generally new to the nineteenth century. At least from the Renaissance to the late eighteenth century, sex in Western culture was viewed as an activity that, if not indulged in too frequently and if confined within the heterosexual marital context, benefited men and women.[80] Conception was considered to be dependent on the "heat" generated by friction during intercourse and, more specifically, on female orgasm.[81] However, by the late eighteenth century, biologists began to theorize about conception without female orgasm, and by midcentury many believed that too much enthusiasm or "violence" during intercourse actually hindered procreation. The conviction that procreation was linked to a lack of female passion evidences critical changes in the construction of sexuality.

Laqueur's *Making Sex* traces a related shift in the understanding of sexuality throughout the eighteenth and nineteenth centuries. Challenging the assumption that biological "facts" of sexual difference are universally fixed attributes to which gender roles are appended for political reasons, he argues convincingly that the perception of two distinct and incommensurable sexes is a relatively recent phenomenon. Prior to the eighteenth century, Laqueur shows, the one-sex model was the dominant mode for understanding sex. Sex was viewed on a continuum of maleness, with the male as the perfect body and the female as an inverted, imperfect male. In other words, female genitalia were perceived as internalized male genitalia. A commonly quoted poem from the pseudonymous "Aristotle" is generally interpreted to show the inferior status granted to women in this model:

> And that though they of different sexes be,
> Yet on the whole they are the same as we.
> For those that have the strictest searches been,
> Find women are but men turned outside in.[82]

Yet Laqueur interprets this passage as emphasizing the general sameness of the sexes. In pre-Enlightenment texts, and some later ones, "*sex*, or the body, must be understood as the epiphenomenon, while *gender*, what we would take to be a cultural category, was primary or 'real.'" The poem continues in an 1821 American edition:

> And men if they but cast their eyes about,
> May find they're women with their inside out.

"Aristotle" reveals a system in which the male and female body mirror one another. When "Aristotle" describes the female body, he emphasizes these parallels: "The action and use of the neck of the womb, is the same with that of the Penis, that is, erection." The clitoris also is described as "like the yard of a man . . . the bigness of it only differs."[83] Although the one-sex model privileges the male by identifying the semen as the most essential element in conception, it nonetheless presents women and men as more similar than different. There are no clear borders between male and female; from a modern perspective the one-sex body seems "unimaginably—indeed terrifyingly—porous."[84] For writers such as Whitman, the conception of a "porous" body provided a site from which to challenge the increasingly prescriptive sexual codes of his day. Nonetheless, as in the case of his representation of middle-class white female sexuality, Whitman's poetry once again poses the most substantial paradox in relation to sexual reform writing, because he echoes the purity movements of the day while challenging the concept of sexuality as depletion.

The two-sex model greatly affected men's and women's perceptions of themselves and each other. It also provided a biological justification for the Doctrine of Separate Spheres and allowed for women's identity to be linked primarily to their sexuality. In a one-sex model, women—as mirrors of men—could not have been defined by their sexuality without reflecting on men. However, the "discoveries" Laqueur traces radically altered constructions of male and female sexuality. Men, who already through phrenology were thought to possess more "amativeness," were generally considered the active agents of corruption and vice. Two of the most popular midcentury advice books show these new distinctions: "[W]herever impurity can be found, man is, directly or indirectly, the cause," Alcott argues; "He is ever, at least since the days of the first pair, the grand seducer."[85] Woman, by comparison, "as is well known, in a natural state—unperverted, unseduced, and healthy—seldom, if ever, makes any of those advances which clearly indicate sexual desire; and for the very plain reason that she does not feel them."[86] Although both sides of the sexual binary were constricting, men had one advantage. With effort, they could control their impulses; the mind could triumph over the body. Women, however, were naturally passionless and, therefore, any deviance could be defined as abnormal and diseased. In this context, the "fallen woman" could be considered irredeemable.[87]

Struggles over seduction in general and prostitution in particular reflect the overall tendency toward the criminalization of deviant sexuality that gained force throughout the century. The fallen woman, the prostitute, the masturbating male, the aborting woman, the Jezebel slave were all accessible figures on which anxiety over social, economic, and political changes could be transcribed. "Homosexual" and "lesbian" identities were also solidified and criminalized beginning in the late nineteenth century. During the century, D'Emilio and Freedman contend, the meaning of same-sex relationships changed. In the Colonial era, the concept of homosexuality as a personal identity did not exist. Rather, individual acts of sodomy, defined as anal sex between men, were thought of as distinct sins for which men could repent. Until 1880 most same-sex relationships, even when extremely close or sensual, were assumed to be "devoid of sexual content."[88] However, by midcentury, and with greater intensity toward the end, sodomy laws increased in severity. Whereas previously only nonconsensual acts of sodomy were punished, laws began to be applied to consenting adult males. No longer an individual act, sodomy represented the homosexual personality, which was associated with disease.[89] As Foucault argues, the "nineteenth-century homosexual became a personage, a past, a case history, and a childhood, in addition to being a type of life, a life form, and a morphology, with an indiscrete anatomy and possibly a mysterious physiology. Nothing that went into his total composition was unaffected by his sexuality."[90] Indeed, the homosexual and lesbian identity can be read as yet another step in the nineteenth century's journey to embody identity through race, through gender, and through sex.

Why, we might ask, did this century produce such obsessive tellings and retellings of the body? Wiegman asks a similar question in *American Anatomies*, acknowledging the difficulty of explaining the "social violence of race and gender" that haunt United States history. Echoing Toni Morrison's narrator in *The Bluest Eye*, Wiegman turns her energy toward investigating *"how"* as a "response to the difficulties of handling *why.*"[91] Like Wiegman, I am suspicious of too readily assuming *why* the complex and devastating politics of the body in nineteenth-century America came to be. Nonetheless, we may gesture toward a few possible and partial considerations of *how*, which in turn imply a *why*. Certainly, several historical events contributed. In many parts of the nation, economic competition intensified during the 1830s and 1840s, and racial difference could be used "to call attention to the guaranteed social status of a white skin."[92] This enthusiasm for the "Anglo-Saxon stock was heightened" in the mid-1840s, according to Horsman, by "a growing concern about the rapid increase in Irish Catholic and in German immigration." In an era of

"constant change, many were to find security in the certainty of a racial heritage that stretched back into the distant past." While factors in the North as
well as the South made new concepts about race appealing to many, the institution of slavery elevated the science of race to a prominent position as proslavery advocates defended their peculiar institution. The invention of the cotton
gin, and subsequent expansion of slavery to new territories, increased slavery's
profitability to the extent that by the 1830s lingering hopes for gradual emancipation had all but vanished. Once Britain emancipated its slaves in the West
Indies in 1834, the institution needed additional social justification. Perhaps
more than any other factor, the increased agitation from abolitionists spurred a
scientific backlash. In the 1830s abolitionists gained new energy, broke with
colonization efforts, and, conceiving of slavery as a social and individual sin,
called for immediate emancipation. Fredrickson argues that it "took the
assault of the abolitionists to unmask the cant about a theoretical human
equality that coexisted with Negro slavery and racial discrimination and to
force the practitioners of racial oppression to develop a theory that accorded
with their behavior."[93] Additionally, as I have already suggested, the politics of
corporeal essentialism can be regarded as a reaction to the promise offered by
Enlightenment and Revolutionary rhetoric; the theoretically disembodied citizen was forced figuratively into flesh in part by the combination of abolitionism, the women's rights movement, and scientific investigations of the body.
As reform activity intensified, distinctions had to be made between the bodies
of American citizens and the bodies of those subjugated within a society pur-
porting individual liberty.

Clearly, the body in nineteenth-century America took on a new and perhaps
intensified political significance, and control of individual bodies came to symbolize control over the body politic. What, after all, would this body look like?
How could it keep itself orderly, clean, and productive? In this context, Foucault's contention that the middle-class's obsession over its body was a means of
maintaining its newfound power is helpful. He argues that the primary concern
of much discourse on the body was "not repression of the sex of the classes to be
exploited, but rather the body, vigor, longevity, progeniture, and descent of the
classes that 'ruled.'"[94] Here Foucault points to one major concern of this
study—how discourses of science were deployed by the ruling class to naturalize their status. Yet Foucault's analysis only tells part of the story. The paradigm
he describes rests on an alternative code of corporeal disorder, which was transferred onto "lower" classes and "other" races. D'Emilio and Freedman argue

that minority races became a foil against which "whites redefined themselves": "Throughout much of the nineteenth century, the meaning of sexuality for white, middle-class Americans balanced uncomfortably between the
reproductive moorings of the past and the romantic and erotic leanings of the
present, between female control and male license, between private passion and
public reticence. No wonder that the sexuality of minority races became a foil
against which whites redefined themselves. Alternative sexual systems threatened the precarious balance of white sexuality."[95] Foucault, D'Emilio and
Freedman, and others help us understand that to the three categories that mark
the divisions of this chapter—race, gender, and sexuality—we must add
another, class. All factors were put into competition and contradiction with
one another, as Americans struggled to flesh out the promise of equality written into the "higher law" of their Declaration of Independence in a nation that
allowed for slavery, Indian Removal, anti-immigration movements and legislation, and the political and legal subordination of women of all races and classes.

The question of *why* individual scientists were led to assert theories of racial
difference despite evidence that we now see as largely to the contrary continues to be debated. Gould, for example, acknowledges that white leaders "did
not question the propriety of racial ranking" in the eighteenth and nineteenth
centuries and suggests that "the pervasive assent given by scientists to conventional rankings arose from shared social belief, not from objective data gathered
to test an open question." However, he argues that in "a curious case of reversed causality, these pronouncements were read as independent support for
the political context." Gould, whose work investigates the methodology of
some of the most prominent nineteenth-century men of science, finds Morton's methods and conclusions particularly troubling because Gould can
"detect no sign of fraud or conscious manipulation" in Morton's work. Rather,
all he can "discern is an a priori conviction about racial ranking so powerful
that it directed his tabulations along preestablished lines." Nonetheless, as
Dana D. Nelson points out, prejudice "did not necessarily have to be against
'black' people for it to work on behalf of racist practices and structures. Rather,
Morton's prejudice seems to have been located in supporting whiteness." Nelson investigates the means by which Morton's scientific inquiries and methods
served to consolidate the "discursive, subjective, and professional spaces of
white, scientific manhood."[96] Nelson's analysis of how Morton bolsters polygenesis in order to "discredit theology's right to interpret 'natural order,' and
claim that authority as the spoils of the 'battle' for 'science'" is astute. Indeed,

if Morton and his colleagues were invested with authorizing the sciences within the United States, they also had their sights on an international audience. Polygeny, Gould argues, was "one of the first theories of largely American origin that won the attention and respect of European scientists—so much so that Europeans referred to polygeny as the 'American School' of anthropology."[97] Also critical in Nelson's assessment is the link between the science of race and the status of women in the antebellum era. Nelson suggests that we consider "how the contemporary emergence of scientific professionalism works in part as a cultural countermove against women's growing claims to a civic agency formulated through the moral logic of domesticity." In other words, as women began to increase their public action under the rubric of domesticity, some white men responded by bolstering their cultural authority through scientific professionalism.[98]

In the midst of these cultural debates stood the literary men and women that this study investigates, writers struggling to add their voices to the national debate and determine what the body of America should look like, how it should act, and who should control it. During the antebellum era, both occupations—that of the writer and that of the scientist—became increasingly professionalized.[99] Yet, as Nelson's work indicates, scientists repeatedly claimed a privileged status for their methodology and discourse. Indeed, when one reviews the discourse of scientific difference, one comes to recognize how much it reasserts its authority, establishing the subject of the Caucasian male scientist who, by definition, studies "others" as objects. Repeatedly, scientists stress the selectivity of their specialized knowledge and point to the overwhelming "evidence" of others' inferiority. In the preface to his *Evidence Against the Views of the Abolitionists* (1833) Richard Colfax reminds readers "whose religious sentiments may be startled" by his argument that "the details of this subject (as a philosophical question) are perfectly known only to Anatomists and Physiologists" and come from knowledge that "can be acquired only in the medical profession." Similarly, Combe objects that the "causes of the difference of national characters . . . has been investigated by philosophers in general, without any knowledge of, or reference to, the functions of different parts of the brain." Nott and Gliddon contend in their introduction that the "great fundamental laws of humanity to which all human passions and human thoughts must ultimately be subject" are "questions upon which science alone has the right to pronounce."[100]

Even more significant than scientists' assertion of authority was the tautology they presented in relation to those studied. Although many of the disciplines could support various ideological positions, some by their very structure endorsed racist and sexist hierarchies. For example, Nott quotes from the *London Ethnological Journal* and defines ethnology as a "science which investigates the mental and physical difference of mankind, and the organic laws upon which they depend; and which seeks to deduce from these investigations, principles of human guidance, in all the important relations of social existence." By definition, then, ethnology presumed that social relations were based on a priori differences, and that ethnologists should study these differences to deduce "principles of human guidance."[101] Similarly, when defining the male Caucasian, Caldwell asserts that "[a]s relates to intellect, a vast pre-eminence belongs to the Caucasian. . . . It is as truly the gift of nature as his complexion and figure." He proceeds to explain that the Caucasian's ability to study nature demonstrates his superiority, as he "is so endowed, by reason of a higher and better organization, that he can instruct himself, by attending to the objects of nature around him, observing their phenomena, and studying their laws."[102] Thus the circle is complete. By studying the object of nature (the African American, the Native American, the woman), the Caucasian scientist reaffirms his status as subject. To return to Fisher's paraphrase of Bacon, scientists can "govern and direct" their findings to their advantage. Science, to which only an elite few had access, defined people as intellectually and physically unable to understand the evidence that categorized them as inferior. How could one dispute such a tautology?[103]

Many did. However much science gained in importance in the nineteenth century, it is not appropriate to think of it as totalizing. Although the quantity of publications attests to the increasing significance of science, it also hints that this was a time not of *constructed* race, gender, and sex difference, but of *construction*; the process was neither complete nor final. Even among scientists, the categories of difference were slippery at best.[104] Douglass responds to these scientific authorities by questioning their motives and methods, by pointing—finally—to the underlying problem of classification based on difference. "This," he told the crowd, "is an age of science, and science is favorable to division." He continues: "It is somewhat remarkable, that, at a time when knowledge is so generally diffused, when the geography of the world is so well understood—when time and space, in the intercourse of nations, are almost annihilated—when oceans have become bridges—the earth a magnificent ball—the hollow sky a dome—under which a common humanity can meet in a friendly conclave . . . I say it is remarkable—nay, it is strange that there should arise a phalanx of learned men—speaking in the name of *science*—to forbid the magnificent reunion of mankind in one brotherhood.[105]

By mid-nineteenth century, there was still room to critique the "phalanx of learned men—speaking in the name of *science*," and the authors in this study would provide that critique, even while, at times, replicating the structures and suppositions of corporeality that the scientists proposed. Classification, hierarchy, division, an invisible basis for difference—these were the methodologies and ideologies deeply embedded in American culture, influencing in conscious and unconscious ways the authors in this study. They respond to the challenges posed by these methods and ideologies and to the changing conceptions of corporeality and identity in vastly different ways. Only one factor remains consistent: the body in fiction and nonfiction in mid-nineteenth-century America came to the text signifying any number of weighty possibilities.

2

THE SPECTACLE OF THE BODY

Corporeality in Lydia Maria Child's

Antislavery Writing

❧❧

A few years hence, the opinion of the world will be a matter in which I have not even the most transient interest; but this book will be abroad on its mission of humanity, long after the hand that wrote it is mingling with the dust.—Lydia Maria Child, *An Appeal in Favor of That Class of Americans Called Africans*

I am well aware that many will accuse me of indecorum for presenting these pages to the public; for the experiences of this intelligent and much-injured woman belong to a class which some call delicate subjects, and others indelicate. This peculiar phase of Slavery has generally been kept veiled; but the public ought to be made acquainted with its monstrous features, and I willingly take the responsibility of presenting them with the veil withdrawn.—Lydia Maria Child, introduction to Harriet Jacobs's *Incidents in the Life of a Slave Girl, Written by Herself*

To those familiar with Lydia Maria Child's commitment to social progress, her claim in *An Appeal in Favor of That Class of Americans Called Africans* that "the opinion of the world" will not be of interest to her as long as her writing can be "abroad on its mission of humanity" sounds sincere.[1] Child was a woman who sensed early in her professional life, as Carolyn L. Karcher argues, that she was called to "reconsecrate her art to the service of her sisters and brothers in bonds," to create literature that would perform the cultural work she believed was necessary to help end slavery and promote racial justice.[2] Yet even if she privileged the collective good over her individual literary reputation, Child might have thought it an odd twist of history that she "is most often reintroduced to the public these days not as an author in her own right," not as the prolific and talented woman whom William Lloyd Garrison once called "the first woman in the republic," but as the editor of Harriet Jacobs's *Incidents in the Life of a Slave Girl, Written by Herself*.[3]

Speculating further, we could imagine that Child would be pleased with the current interest in Jacobs's text. Besides offering advice on the manuscript and expediting its publication by attesting to its veracity, Child continued to promote *Incidents* throughout the Civil War, printing selections from it in several publications.[4] However, Child might be surprised at the subtle, yet consistent, suspicion expressed by contemporary scholars, who often frame her relationship with Jacobs as representative of "vexed alliances" between white and African American women. Despite the authentication of Jacobs's text by Jean Fagan Yellin and the examination of Child's role as an editor by Karcher, Child is accused of everything from "editorial colonization" to bypassing "Jacobs's authorship."[5] For example, the editors of *Harriet Jacobs and Incidents in the Life of a Slave Girl: New Critical Essays* believe that *Incidents* "will *forever* both unite and *alienate* the black and white academics who promote, interpret, and teach it" (emphasis mine).[6]

As the coeditors' comments indicate, reasons for suspicion are many, and their comments reveal as much about our racial environment as they do about tensions in Child's era. At the root of nineteenth- and twentieth-century concerns is the relationship between spectatorship and corporeality. What causes the most misgiving is the appropriateness of a Caucasian woman taking "the responsibility of presenting . . . the veil withdrawn" to expose slavery's "monstrous features."[7] Child's wording, which literally indicates an uncovering of slavery rather than the slave woman's body, nonetheless could be said to evoke figuratively a show, a public exhibition of the female slave's embodied wrongs. This, in turn, could be interpreted as drawing upon what Hazel V. Carby has identified as the "dialectical relationship" of true womanhood, a dynamic that (as chapter 1 outlines) relied upon an "alternative sexual code associated with the black woman" to bolster white women's alleged passionless gentility.[8] In this scenario, the delicate/nonsexual white woman, by disclosing the indelicate/ sexual African American woman's story, manages to sustain her polite status—even when undertaking a socially transgressive act—by the implied juxtaposition of herself to the black woman's embodied, sexual nature. If this were the case, Child's unveiling of Jacobs's "face" would deflect attention from her own "face," Child's own body, in the public sphere.

The wording of Child's introduction to *Incidents* can be interpreted in a variety of ways, and it is not the intent of this chapter to engage in a prolonged defense of Child's editorship of Jacobs's text. Rather, I place Child's introduction to *Incidents* in relation to her 1833 nonfictional and 1840s and 1850s fictional antislavery writing; suggest that her portrayals of corporeality do not rest upon a binary of a disembodied white female self and embodied slave "other"; and consider the correlation between nineteenth- and late-twentieth-century concerns about the appropriateness of Child's literary representations of slaves' corporeality. As early as in her 1833 *Appeal*, Child had to invent strategies for holding the tortured slave's body (both male and female) before the public's eye. In part because Child wanted to avoid charges of indelicacy that confronted any woman entering the public sphere, and in part because she herself was particularly aware of the conflicts one faced when revealing oneself—either literally or figuratively—to the public's gaze, she developed methods to reveal slavery's corporeal nature without soliciting readers' voyeuristic spectatorship of either her body or the bodies of slaves. She did so by interrogating the sentimental assumption of the universality and translatability of pain. The tactics Child developed to elude accusations of indelicacy in her era also answer contemporary critics who charge feminist-abolitionist writers with appealing to an "allure of bondage" and exploiting the slave's body in the literary marketplace.

Going Public with the Body

Although Child was not predominantly a sentimental writer, she was influenced by the antebellum culture's sentimental constructions of female identity in a conflicting and at times atypical manner, especially when she sought to include antislavery themes in genteel fiction in the 1840s. As Karen Halttunen explains, sentimental culture and fiction had as its central premise the belief that "private experience was morally superior to public life." White women from the middle class were not only supposed to maintain the private sphere by their homemaking activities, but also were thought to *embody* sentimentality and its related virtue, sensibility.[9] If we recall, for example, the physician J. H. Pulte's insistence that when one compared the "female system" with that of the male, one could only conclude "that the former was destined to move in a different sphere of action from the latter" because the "duties and mode of life" were "clearly pointed out to the female in her bodily construction,"[10] we begin to recognize how scientific discourse increasingly defined what constituted a normal woman in antebellum America and how any deviation from normality could be viewed as unnatural. Because women were said to embody private virtues, any activity outside the domestic sphere was often responded to by metaphoric attacks upon their bodies, attacks that suggested they were transgressing natural laws and crossing into the realm of the monstrous. For example, lurking behind many of the rhetorical attacks against women abolitionists in antebellum America was the implication that they were taking physical pleasure in their "indelicate" activities. One need only turn to what Phillip Lapsansky calls the "lacerating graphics" created by antiabolitionists in the popular media to discern the corporeally based nature of these anxieties. Repeatedly white women were shown as gazing "lasciviously" on men of color or walking arm in arm with African American escorts. In these representations the implied sexuality indicates the most extreme form of a multitude of possible "immoral" pleasures that abolitionist women might be pursuing under the guise of an allegedly moral cause.[11] The fact that opponents inscribed their condemnation on women abolitionists' bodies is not coincidental; it results from their perception of the abolitionist woman as acting in opposition to natural laws dictating their role in society and their "proper" sexual partner.

Despite these prohibitions, as I indicate in my introduction, and as Karen Sánchez-Eppler also demonstrates, "the development of a political discourse and a concept of personhood that attests to the centrality of the body erupts throughout antebellum culture." The decision of the 1837 Anti-Slavery Convention of American Women to endorse visual images to promote their cause demonstrates the "centrality of the body" to which Sánchez-Eppler refers. As Yellin indicates, such tactics were common in the antislavery movement as "hundreds of images dramatizing the violence related to the institution of slavery—the separation of families, the seizing, branding, selling and torturing of men, women, and children—appeared in broadsides, newspapers and books" in the 1830s and 1840s.[12] By endorsing the use of these images, abolitionist women were joining with antislavery men in making representations of slaves' bodies available to the northern public. A gathering of about two hundred women paying such close attention to corporeal tactics was certain to draw censure and, according to Karcher, the antiabolitionist press "viciously lampooned the convention as an 'Amazonian farce' staged by 'a monstrous *regiment* of women.'" Child's prominent role at the conference made her, along with Angelina and Sarah Grimké, a particular target for criticism.[13]

The participants also issued "An Appeal to the Women of the Nominally Free States," written under the primary authorship of Angelina Grimké, to rouse northern women to action.[14] Characteristically, the pamphlet faced readers', and perhaps the authors', fear of association with anything deemed "monstrous."

Once again, the image of the "veil" is employed to help negotiate the complex relationship between the public and private spheres. After referring elusively to slaveholders' relations with slave women, the authors continue: "But we forbear to lift the veil of private life any higher; let these few hints suffice to give you some idea of what is daily passing *behind* that curtain which has been so carefully drawn before the scenes of domestic life in Christian America." Here the women are aware of the indelicacy of peeping "behind the curtain" of "private life." Halttunen demonstrates that at the height of sentimental culture all domestic "behind the scenes" activity was to be kept out of view by polite society, as it was not considered genteel.[15] Much has already been written about how antislavery women defined slavery as invading the private sphere, thus justifying their public political activities.[16] However, to fight slavery a woman had not only to enter the public sphere, but also to invade the private space of the southern white woman's home. The authors grasp the difficult nature of this undertaking and reveal only "hints" of what the women need to know, allowing readers to remain more genteel than the authors. They also transfer accusations of indelicacy onto slaveholding women, suggesting that they are particularly culpable when they order a slave woman whipped because they expose the slave woman "to the gaze of the executioner of a *woman's* command." By locating inappropriate behavior in slaveholding women, northern women separate the act of representing or reading about torture from participation in it. Once they create this distinction, they are free to urge northern women to educate themselves about all facets of slavery, including torture. A passage that follows this discussion of southern "ladies," for example, details a whip's size and specifications. Clearly, one way to investigate slavery was to study torture, in effect, to probe figuratively the slave's body. However, a woman needed to do so while avoiding any indication that the author, speaker, or reader could take pleasure in such an illicit and public activity.

Child was cognizant of these and other risks associated with writing about the body in general and slavery in particular. Her first novel, *Hobomok, A Tale of Early Times* (1824), depicts a marriage between a Native American man and a Colonial woman. Karcher notes that the "subversive possibilities" of this plot did not escape contemporary reviewers, who "united in pronouncing [it] 'in very bad taste, to say the least.'"[17] However, Child was not one to fear reproach. Having guided the children's magazine *The Juvenile Miscellany* to financial and popular success and having gained respect and financial security through the publication of *The Frugal Housewife* and *The Mother's Book*,

Child jeopardized her livelihood to write *Appeal*.[18] In fact, the book "outraged a public that had just canonized Child as a paragon of feminine virtue," creating rifts between herself and friends and family members. Besides having incited public condemnation, Child was professionally blacklisted and lost the support of many influential Boston patrons, as well as her free access to the Boston Athenaeum.[19] Whereas these attacks against Child were not physical, female abolitionists also braved bodily harm, as did all abolitionists, who incurred the very real possibility of mob violence. In 1835 the English abolitionist George Thompson visited the United States and was a threatened target. Child traveled with Thompson and tried, along with others, to secure his safety, sometimes using her own body as a shield. The tone of her letter to Louisa Loring while Child was in Brooklyn shows the potential danger she faced:

> I have not ventured into the city, nor does one of us dare to go to church to day, so great is the excitement here. You can form no conception of it—'Tis like the times of the French Revolution, when no man dared trust his neighbor. Private assassins from N. Orleans are lurking at the corners of the streets, to stab Arthur Tappan; and very large sums are offered for any one who will convey Mr. Thompson into the slave states. I tremble for him. . . . We have managed with some adroitness to get along in safety so far; but I have faith that God will protect him, even to the end.—Yet why do I make this boast?[20]

One can certainly wonder if in this environment of agitation and hostility even a woman as courageous as Child would not want to devise some method for defending her private body, her private self, from public harm. Yet Child's relationship to her body and to genteel expectations of womanhood was complicated and often contradictory. As Karcher points out, Child's class status (she took "pride in her identity as a baker's daughter") freed Child somewhat from the inhibitions faced by her older brother, who married into a genteel family and shied away from the political commitments that Child embraced. Early in her career, Child—according to Karcher—"seems never to have suffered from either the fear of unsexing herself or the paralyzing sense of inadequacy that inhibited so many other nineteenth-century women writers."[21] At times, Child's corporeality may have justified her ability to participate in ungenteel and rather masculine activities, as was demonstrated by the 1841 phrenological reading of her head by L. N. Fowler, which Child reacted to with pleasure. Examining the bumps in Child's head, Fowler remarked upon several characteristics that we would certainly understand as masculine, including Child's preference for intelligent and cultivated male society, her pleasure with a *"book and pen more than in household arrangements,"* her *"more than . . . ordinary degree of moral courage"* and her ambition to *"excel in some department"* from child-hood.[22] Like Walt Whitman, who also had an interest in phrenology and was proud of the phrenological examination of his head, Child's corporeality con-firmed characteristic traits that she took pride in as innate and, therefore, as sanctioned by nature if not society.

Likewise, Child may have sought in her physical appearance a reprieve from gendered expectations. As addressed in chapter 5, Margaret Fuller is said to have adopted a strategy of being "bright and ugly" at one point in her life, in part to cope with the pressures and desires that she faced as an intellectually driven woman. Although Child's decision may not have been as conscious, she also may have labeled herself "ugly" to cope with the conflicts she faced as a highly intelligent and ambitious woman. Karcher notes that "[p]hysically, this petite, dark-haired, dark-eyed young woman did not cut an arresting figure," even if many commented on her ability to transform her appearance once ani-mated with interest or expression. Child frequently called herself "very ugly," going so far as to object to a 1826 portrait of herself by the French painter Fran-cis Alexander because he wanted to "pour over my very ugly face the full tide of inspiration."[23] Although this self-definition may have expressed some long-ing to be conventionally beautiful, at times it helped Child defy societal con-ventions. Such was the case in Child's relationship in the early 1840s with John Hopper, a man thirteen years her junior, to whom Child was extremely attached and with whom she roamed through much of New York City while she was separated from her husband. Responding to a friend who expressed concern about the intensity of Child's relationship with Hopper, Child wrote: "My charms were *never* very formidable, and at this period I think can hardly endanger a young man of 26, passionately fond of the beautiful." Here, Child shields herself by means of her apparent lack of "charms," thus allowing for a most unconventional relationship with a younger man (whom she also charac-terized as her son).[24]

Likewise, Child literally shielded herself from the public's gaze in her sub-mission to societal rules and restraints prohibiting women's speaking in front of "promiscuous audiences" of men and women. The reasons why Child did not lecture are unclear.[25] She certainly admired excellent orators such as Thompson and Angelina Grimké, and, at least in private, longed to join them.

In 1837 Child describes in a letter her argument over abolition petitions with an unidentified opponent, a debate she evidently won with force. "Oh, if I was a man, how I *would* lecture!" she declares. "But I am a woman, and so I sit in the corner and knit socks."[26] Whatever her motivation, Child often followed a strategy of laying the groundwork for women's rights while never fully taking a leadership role in the women's movement. Although she published the comprehensive two-volume *History of the Condition of Women* in 1835, she declined to draw direct political implications from her cross-cultural and historical investigation.[27] When Angelina and Sarah Grimké began to lecture, Child supported them, although she told them it was best for women "not to *talk* about our right, but simply [to] go forward and *do* whatsoever we deem a duty."[28] As this hesitation suggests, Child may have been at least partially inhibited by a sentimental culture that defined her role as private. Although she was willing to manipulate and break sentimental rules of fiction and dared to participate actively and consistently in public political causes, she nonetheless maintained some sense of privacy by not revealing her body as a lecturer. Given her reluctance to display herself before a crowd, one could ask if she transfers the obligation of corporeal revelation onto slaves in her literary representations. Does she, as some suggest of abolitionist-feminists, unveil slaves' bodies in order to deflect attention from her own? If so, does this process play into a desire on the part of the audience for illicit corporeal knowledge?

Representing the Body in Pain

Some contemporary scholars echo nineteenth-century concerns about the alleged pleasure that could be received from reform texts in general and anti-slavery texts in particular, either by authors or readers.[29] For example, in her analysis of pornography and pain in the eighteenth and nineteenth centuries, Karen Halttunen argues that because a "cult of sensibility" beginning in the eighteenth century "redefined pain as unacceptable and indeed eradicable," the "growing violence of pornography" during this era "is attributable to the new shock value of pain within a culture redefining it as forbidden and therefore obscene." Reformers "were caught in a contradiction largely of their own making. To arouse popular opposition to the evil practices they sought to eradicate, they deemed it necessary to display those practices in all their horror. . . . But, by their own line of argument, viewing the spectacle of suffering could inflict terrible moral damage on the spectator, turning him or her into a 'savage' with an 'atrocious passion' for cruelty." Halttunen suggests that reformers developed rhetorical strategies to negotiate the contradictions among pain, pornography, and spectacle, but some scholars contend that women abolitionists (consciously or not) manipulated readers' desires, erotic or otherwise, to spectate on the slave's body, thus replicating through text the domination of slavery. Sánchez-Eppler, for example, expresses her concern, which is also shared by Yellin, regarding the "metaphoric linking of women and slaves" in abolitionist-feminist rhetoric.[30] She argues that the "difficulty of preventing moments of identification from becoming acts of appropriation constitutes the essential dilemma of feminist-abolitionist rhetoric," and she investigates the seemingly paradoxical activity of selling antislavery material to raise money for abolitionism, pointing out that one "important feature" of the antislavery gift book, *The Liberty Bell*, to which Child contributed, was that it was considered "saleable." She continues: "[t]he horrific events narrated in these tales attract precisely to the extent that the buyers of these representations of slavery are fascinated by the abuses they ostensibly oppose. For, despite their clear abolitionist stance, such stories are fueled by the allure of bondage, an appeal that suggests the valuation of depictions of slavery may rest upon the same psychic ground as slaveholding itself."[31]

In the above passage, Sánchez-Eppler conflates antislavery rhetoric with slaveholding, suggesting that both rest upon the "allure of bondage," terminology that points to what she views as the exploitative potential of some antislavery literature. Addressing a similar concern, Marianne Noble describes the erotic possibilities of the technique of the "sentimental wound" in Harriet Beecher Stowe's *Uncle Tom's Cabin*. Noble argues that Stowe "thrusts into readers' preexisting wounds, forcing them to 'feel for' slaves by reexperiencing their own painful separations and other forms of suffering" and that this wounding "forces a new mode of cognition upon readers, who are to understand slavery through their memories of sorrow rather than through reason." Yet the fact that it is "fundamentally impossible to bridge the gap separating one person's experience from another's" creates "an unanticipated result: representations of physical and emotional wounding constitute powerful tropes for the *desire* to achieve a perfect form of knowing," and this desire evokes an erotic response from readers. Additionally, "fantasies of wounding appear to be most fully eroticized . . . when projected onto suffering *black* bodies." Thus, slaves are positioned "as erotic objects rather than fully human subjects."[32]

Just as scholars are correct in pointing out that we cannot assume that readers' (and authors') intentions were purely philanthropical, I would also like to suggest that we cannot presume that they were only, or even primarily, self-centered. As Noble concedes, even if the texts had the potential to elicit plea-sure, "many nonetheless responded to those pleasures by taking arms against enslavement in a public arena."[33] We need to assess, then, what makes some texts particularly effective in the antislavery cause. One way to do so is to dif-ferentiate between texts that function within a sentimental framework and those that avoid sentimentality. The dilemmas presented by these scholars all point to problems associated with sentimental empathy, with the idea that the reader should be guided into a physical reaction to scenes of cruelty to be spurred to social action. Because authors who wrote in a sentimental fashion regarded pain as a universal sensation, they assumed that readers could be encouraged to imagine another person's pain and, after this act of imagining, to be stimulated to help end the cause of the pain. Underlying this method was the presumption that the body itself could function as a universal symbol, that pain was a knowable, translatable sensation, one which readers could easily access because they, too, inhabited a body susceptible to pain. As Franny Nudelman describes it, the "communication of suffering is not only sentimen-tality's object, but also its method: sentimentality relies on bodily suffering, or bodily manifestations of emotional suffering, to signify and convey feeling. The body can communicate universal sentiment most effectively because its responses, particularly to pain, are predictable and legible."[34]

Nudelman also points out that the nineteenth-century premise of sentimen-tality differs from contemporary theories of pain that scholars such as Elaine Scarry now propose. Because Scarry's theories contradict sentimental defini-tions of pain, they help to elucidate the unsentimental methods Child employs to avoid pleasurable spectatorship in *Appeal*. Scarry believes the difficulty of expressing pain comes from pain's intensely personal and almost unspeakable nature, and this premise differs greatly from sentimentalism which, as Nudel-man argues, does not "signify an effort to articulate an essentially private expe-rience," because it assumes that "community, in the form of shared sentiment, already exists and must simply be revealed." Rather, Scarry contends that physical pain destroys one's world by annihilating the ability to articulate or even imagine the world beyond the limits of the body. As a person undergoes the process of torture, for example, she begins to lose cognitive connection with the objects through which she usually defines herself, and this loss culmi-nates in the erasure of the language with which she names them. Scarry argues that "[p]hysical pain does not simply resist language but actively destroys it, bringing about an immediate reversion to a state anterior to language, to the sounds and cries a human being makes before language is learned."[35] Scarry's assertion that pain can destroy an individual's connection to the world is supported by former slaves. For example, Frederick Douglass and Harriet Jacobs understood that torture, whether it be through deprivation of bodily necessities or the application of pain, can eradicate one's ability not only to resist, but also to conceptualize the idea of resistance.[36]

Although pain destroys one's world by destroying one's language, it must, paradoxically, be represented, because "the act of verbally expressing pain is a necessary prelude to the collective task of diminishing pain." One must verbalize pain, Scarry suggests, because "the relative ease or difficulty with which any given phenomenon can be *verbally represented* also influences the ease or difficulty with which that phenomenon comes to be *politically represented*" (12). Like today's Amnesty International, which Scarry uses as an example, abolitionists wanted to help end pain, in this case by encouraging readers to become active in the political struggle against slavery. Doing so, they faced at least two major obstacles. First, readers generally question the validity of the suffering person's experience. "To have pain is to have *certainty*," Scarry proposes; "to hear about pain is to have *doubt*" (13). Certainly, Child had to dismiss proslavery claims that reports of torture were contrived, exceptional, or exaggerated. For example, Bruce Mills demonstrates that through the influence of periodicals such as the *North American Review*, many northern readers during the 1830s were urged to perceive patience and restraint as marks of their own good taste when considering the question of slavery. Accounts of corporeal cruelties inflicted upon slaves within the United States were usually denied and their authors often charged with fabrication.[37]

Second, as noted above, when one represents pain, one faces the problem of articulating an intensely personal and inexpressible experience. A tactic often employed, according to Scarry, is the objectification of pain by projecting it onto the weapon that inflicts it. As a "perceptual fact" the weapon can "lift pain and its attributes out of the body and make them visible. The mental habit of *recognizing* pain *in* the weapon . . . is both an ancient and an enduring one" (16). To return to the pamphlet written after the 1837 convention, for example, the authors include a detailed description of the whip to represent the pain it produces. However, this strategy "permits a break in the identification of the referent and thus a misidentification of the thing to which the attributes belong" (17). As Scarry suggests, the text of pain can slip into a narrative about the power used to induce pain by means of the weapon. Scarry notes that the iconography of weaponry does not ordinarily assist those in pain, but rather those who wish to assert power. How, then, can someone express the pain of others without reinforcing the power of the torturer? How can one authenticate pain in order to end it?

This dilemma must be placed within the social transformation of pain and punishment in the nineteenth century in both Europe and the United States, changes that Michel Foucault illuminates in *Discipline and Punish*. By the end of the eighteenth and beginning of the nineteenth century, "the gloomy festival of punishment was dying out," the desire to create a spectacle of punishment fading away.[38] Rather than attempting to torture the truth out of the body, the penal system began to withhold individual rights in a show of supposed rationality. The goal of punishment, therefore, shifted from the desire to inflict corporeal pain to an effort to save the disembodied soul (16). In the United States, these changes were part of a public debate. Richard Brodhead contends that in the 1830s, and more prominently in the 1840s and 1850s, "the picturing of scenes of physical correction emerges as a major form of imaginative activity in America, and arguing the merits of such discipline becomes a major item on the American public agenda." Through debates over corporal punishment in the home, school, and military, readers were already concerned about the relationship between pain and effective discipline.[39] Debates over slavery, then, must be viewed as taking place within a general conversation about the relationships among corporeality, punishment, and power. Foucault examines substantive changes in the penal system, but his analysis of the United States focuses primarily on penal experiments in the northern states. The tendency he describes directly contradicted southern slave law as represented by Child, which not only sanctioned but also regulated the infliction of pain on the slaves' bodies throughout the antebellum era. In fact, as Child articulates, the corporeal nature of slave law intensified as slavery became increasingly entrenched in the southern economy (62–68). Whereas northern states curtailed public spectacles of torture, southern states such as Maryland still permitted the following punishment for slaves found guilty of "petit treason, or murder, or wilfully burning of dwelling-houses": "to have the right hand cut off, to be hanged in the usual manner, the head severed from the body, the body divided into four quarters, and the head and quarters set up in the most public places of the country" (58). When analyzing Child, we can assume that many of her readers would have been aware, at least on some level, of the movement from "punishment" to "discipline," a shift that was not reflected in the treatment of slaves. This discrepancy provided a fracture in the conception of punishment that Child manipulated to her advantage.

Child was aware of debate over the use of corporal and capital punishment, and she abhorred public spectacles of pain. In her first collection of newspaper columns, *Letters from New York*, Child exhibits concern over the savage spectatorship of the New York City mob gathered at the 1842 execution of John C. Colt. She faults the participants for their desire to witness another person's pain, deploring that "[t]he hearts of men were . . . rabid to witness a fellow-creature's agony." Repeatedly, she defines the act of spectating as morally degrading, as likely to produce "murderers *outside* the prison, each as dangerous as would be the one inside."[40] Child's decision to represent torture despite her misgivings about the dangers of viewing it indicates that she believed people could distinguish reading about torture from either watching or enacting it if the scene was carefully constructed and contextualized. In *Appeal*, Child's representations of torture enable readers to move beyond spectacle and into the analytical framework she believed was necessary to produce political action. Once again, Scarry's work helps delineate Child's strategy. As Scarry notes, moments of intense pain defy language. Yet if pain is invisible in part because of its resistance to language, "it is also invisible because its own powerfulness ensures its isolation, ensures that it will not be seen in the context of other events, that it will fall back from its new arrival in language and remain devastating" (61). By its very nature, pain is divorced from the political context that enables it. Child provides that context. She does not ask readers to grapple directly with a slave's pain, for that cannot be adequately articulated. Rather, she invents strategies to represent and politicize pain without soliciting readers to participate imaginatively in it. She directs them to understand the pain in a larger framework, to consider it as it relates to northern efforts at penal reform and southern abuse of corporeal punishment, shifting readers from the sentimental idea of the universality of pain to an investigation of the mechanisms of power in slave society.

The Tortured Body in Child's Appeal

Immediately addressing accusations of indelicacy, Child tells readers in her preface to *Appeal* that she "*expect*[s] ridicule and censure" but does not fear

them. After pleading with readers not to "throw down this volume," she provides several reasons why they might continue. Finally, she implores: "Read it,
from sheer curiosity to see what a woman (who had much better attend to her
household concerns) will say upon such a subject." Her plea attempts to capi-
talize on the rarity of an American woman's leaving her "household" to write
on slavery and focuses curiosity—the attention of spectacle—on Child herself
rather than on the slave bodies she represents. Indeed, it is no coincidence that
Child confronts scenes of torture in the first chapter of her first major antislavery work published at the beginning of her career as a public abolitionist. It is
also significant that only the first chapter of *Appeal* contains sustained narratives
of torture that focus on slaves who are at least partially identified as individuals.[41]

Although some might contend that Child places the graphic scenes of torture
in the first chapter to appeal to an "allure of bondage," I believe she evokes
spectatorship to control and regulate it.[42] To convince her audience of the reality of slaves' suffering, she must reveal the tortured slave; however, to politicize pain in order to help end it, she has to move from narratives of pain to the
context of power that allows—even necessitates—torture. Child completes
this necessary shift in her first two chapters, with her first chapter highlighting
specific narratives of torture and her second chapter moving from these corporeal depictions to an analysis of slave law. This analysis still relies on corporeal
examples of the punishments deemed proper under slave law, but it does not
contain any sustained personal narratives of torture. Having moved from the
corporeal to the less corporeal in the first two chapters, the remainder of
Appeal becomes increasingly noncorporeal, refraining from descriptions of victimization and torture. Instead, Child gives examples of the benefits of free
labor and possibilities of safe emancipation, analyzes the history and politics of
the United States in relation to slavery, offers evidence of the ineffectiveness of
the Colonization Society, provides positive images of Africans throughout the
diaspora, and argues boldly for an end to discrimination in northern states.

Chapter 1 begins with a brief history of the slave trade and description of the
middle passage and then moves into a discussion of slavery's effects on slave
owners. It is in this section that we find the most sustained and graphic
descriptions of torture. The two longest accounts include the story of Kate, a
slave in the Bahamas who dies after severe and prolonged torture, and the
story of a seventeen-year-old Kentucky slave who was ostensibly punished
because he had accidentally dropped a pitcher. Typical of much of *Appeal*,
the latter account blends Child's narrative voice with material abstracted

from various sources. In this case, she draws upon an 1826 volume of letters by the Reverend John Rankin, which in turn refers to a story from the Reverend William Dickey. She begins:

> (Reader, what follows is very shocking; but I have already said we must not allow our nerves to be more sensitive than our consciences. If such things are done in our country, it is important that we should know of them, and seriously reflect upon them.) "The door was fastened, that none of the negroes, either through fear or sympathy, should attempt to escape; he then told them that the design of this meeting was to teach them to remain at home and obey his orders. All things being now in train, George was called up, and by the assistance of his younger brother, laid on a broad bench or block. The master then cut off his ancles with a broad axe. In vain the unhappy victim screamed. Not a hand among so many dared to inter- fere. Having cast the feet into the fire he lectured the negroes at some length. He then proceeded to cut off his limbs below his knees. The suf- ferer besought him to begin with his head. It was in vain—the master went on thus, until trunk, arms, and head, were all in the fire. Still protracting the intervals with lectures, and threatenings of like punishment, in case any of them were disobedient, or ran away, or disclosed the tragedy they were compelled to witness." (25–26)

In this account, the levels of narration reveal the struggle to control the mean- ing, the context, of the torture. The master attempts to use the slave's body to create a text, a type of diabolical didactic sermon, to teach slaves the cost of transgression. Repeatedly, he arrests the torture to lecture his audience on the lesson they should learn through observation. Although the victim is first able to articulate his desire to die and asks to have his head cut off, he is eventually reduced to inarticulate screams and then rendered speechless through the sheer intensity of pain. The victim, then, cannot communicate his pain or control how it is interpreted, and the torturer attempts to mold the victim's pain into his own narrative of reality. As Foucault suggests, it is through the act of tor- ture that the sovereign creates truth (41).

The lesson of the torture necessarily relies on the spectacle of the victim's body, the slaves being literally imprisoned and forced to watch as the victim is slowly dismembered. In order for the master to have a text of power, he must have an audience. Yet the master is also aware that the potency of his text rests not only on control of its interpretation—and hence the constant interruption of the torture to reimpose his meaning—but also on domination of the audience witnessing the event. The slaves are repeatedly warned that this spectacle must remain a secret, with similar torture the cost of telling. The power of the master's text depends on his being able to control its circulation and reception. As it turns out, the master cannot manipulate his text or keep his secret, because "some of the negroes whispered the horrid deed," and his neighbors discover the corporeal remains of the slave and testify against the owner. Rather than face trial by the white community and reconfigure the meaning of his torture for a different audience, the master kills himself.

The master can neither keep his secret among the slaves, nor confine it to the southern states. It is brought north in several versions, in this case through the aid of Child, and is revealed to a much wider audience than originally intended. At this point the meaning of the torture is already separated from the victim, whose anguish has left him incapable of framing the moral of his death. Likewise, the slaves who witness the event, although obviously able to articulate enough details to make it semipublic, cannot comment freely on their interpretation. The struggle is not, then, over who will articulate the slave's pain, because its intensity has left the experience severed from language. Rather, the various "spectators" (whether present or not) will vie with each other to furnish the context and lesson of the spectacle. Like the master, Child, as the editor of the text, exposes the act of torture to create meaning for an audience. Before presenting the repulsive details of the story, Child warns her readers that what follows is "very shocking" and through the use of "is" versus "may be" suggests that there is only one context within which to read the material. Readers will naturally be startled, even disgusted, by it. At the same time, by comparing "nerves," which represent corporeality, to "consciences," which suggests disembodied morality, Child indicates that readers can transcend the corporeal nature of the events depicted through the exercise of morality. Likewise, by asking readers to "seriously reflect" upon the deeds done in "our country," she appeals to another disembodied action, reflection, as the correct means of assessing the corporeal material of the passage. This reliance on and call to unemotional, noncorporeal reason and reflection increases throughout *Appeal*, during which Child rarely manipulates her readers' emotions through sentimental strategies. Torture, then, is gradually transferred to a disembodied site from which it can be investigated.

Although Child's readers were generally more apt to doubt corporeal cruelty than to identify with it voyeuristically, Child addresses the issue of taking pleasure in pain through the inclusion of the master's comments to his wife. When his wife inquires as to the cause of the screams she heard, her husband replies that "he had never enjoyed himself so well at a ball as he enjoyed himself that evening." For him, torture is a pleasurable enactment of his fantasies of unlimited power. That Child and Rankin both disapprove of his gluttony for power is evident in the comparison of the master to the devil. The scene itself evokes a satanic ceremony, as the master oversees the fires that are reminiscent of hell, and just at midnight "heaven and earth" send "a sudden shock" to eradicate his ability to conceal his sinful deeds. By characterizing the master as diabolic, Child distances herself and her readers from him. Not even the wife is capable of enjoying or entirely ignoring the cries of the victim, which she deems "dreadful." Child's depiction of the master as diabolic hazards shifting the narrative focus from a critique of slavery to a commentary on an individual master's obsession with power. Yet she strives to illuminate the general mechanisms of slave power rather than reiterate individual narratives of pain or power. She accomplishes this goal by situating this story, and others like it, within a larger framework. As the title of her first chapter, "Brief History of Negro Slavery—Its Inevitable Effect upon All Concerned in It," suggests, Child does not ask readers to imagine the slave's pain in isolation but rather wants them to consider the overall institution of slavery. Before she repeats the stories of Kate and the Kentucky slave, for example, she tells readers that she includes the stories of torture to demonstrate "the effects of slavery on the temper" of slave owners (23). Child displays the master as an extreme case of what slavery permits and asks readers to investigate the system that produces such spectacles, guiding them to conclude that slavery necessitates unregulated tyranny.

If, as Foucault argues, the penal system generally masked itself as rational in the first half of the nineteenth century, Child represents slave law as random, and the slave owner as an unchecked sovereign, noting that "[w]hat is a trifling fault in the white man, is considered highly criminal in the slave" (40), and that "the negro's fate depends entirely on the character of his master," his very life depending on "chance" (28). Because masters controlled slaves as property, and because no slave or free person of color was allowed to testify against a white person, slave law established the master as monarch, with the ability to punish or pardon subjects at will. Rather than asking readers to imagine the slave's pain, Child focuses their attention on the arbitrary nature of the state's ability to inflict corporeal punishment, a topic under serious scrutiny in the North. This analysis of unregulated power continues throughout *Appeal*. For example, in her description of the slave trade, she argues that sea captains become "as hard hearted and fierce as tigers" because they view slaves as "cattle, or blocks of wood" (16). If readers think that the "despotic powers" of the captains will only be enacted upon African bodies, Child demonstrates how violence extends to white workers, arguing that many sailors on slave ships "have died under the lash or in consequence of it" (16). What is at stake, she suggests, is tyranny's dependency on corporeality and spectacle. Similarly, Child extends her critique beyond investigating specific scenes of torture between master/slave to the more general sphere of torturer/tortured, telling readers that although it may seem "incredible to some that human nature is capable of so much depravity, history abundantly proves that despotic power produces a fearful species of moral insanity. The wanton cruelties of Nero, Caligula, Domitian, and many of the officers of the Inquisition, seem like the frantic acts of madmen. . . . The public has, however, a sense of justice, which can never be entirely perverted" (18).

By linking the torture of slaves to the relationship between victims and tyrants throughout history, Child contextualizes the discussion and encourages readers to consider why such acts can exist. In part, her answer rests on her analysis of torturers, whom she categorizes as insane, thus differentiating them from the overall social body, which has a less corruptible "sense of justice." Unlike the early essays of Ralph Waldo Emerson, which express his faith in the individual rather than the social body, Child believes the social body has to regulate the actions of insane individuals who may want to torture, be they emperors, priests, or slaveholders. The method of regulation, Child implies, is the law.

Consequently, Child bases her second chapter on an analysis of slave law. Because slaves cannot testify on their own behalf—and perhaps because the testimony of fugitive slaves was relatively scarce in the 1830s—Child turns to southern slave law to trace the corporeal marks of oppression.[43] Child's analysis is notable for replacing explicit descriptions of an individual slave's pain (as recorded in her first chapter) with a general investigation of the language of law. She organizes her discussion into fourteen "propositions" designed to show "the true aspect of slavery" and "supported by the evidence of actually existing laws." One of the chapter's most striking passages can be found under the rubric of proposition thirteen: *There is in this country a monstrous inequality of law and right*" (39–40). In it, Child catalogs the infractions slaves may be punished for, and it is worth quoting at some length to compare with the personal narratives that appear in chapter 1. Although what follows is only a part of the catalog, it captures the overall style of the passage:

For hunting with dogs, even in the woods of his master, thirty lashes.

For running away and lurking in swamps, a negro may be lawfully *killed* by any person. If a slave *happen* to die of *moderate* correction, it is likewise justifiable homicide.

For endeavoring to entice another slave to run away, if provisions are prepared, the slave is punished with DEATH; and any negro aiding or abetting suffers DEATH.

Thirtynine stripes for harboring a runaway slave one hour.

For disobeying orders, imprisonment, as long as the master chooses.

For riding on horseback, without written permission, or for keeping a dog, twentyfive lashes.

For rambling, riding, or going abroad in the night, or riding horses in the day without leave, a slave may be whipped, cropped, or branded on the cheek with the letter R, or otherwise be punished, not extending to life, or *so as to unfit him for labor.*

For beating the Patuxent river, to catch fish, ten lashes. (57–58)

In the above passage the repetition of "for," followed by a crime and subsequent punishment, is almost numbing. By the time readers get to the end of this section, they may not remember specific crimes and punishments, because there does not seem to be any logical relationship between punishment and crime, or any connection to individual slaves. What readers receive, instead, is the sense of a constant lashing, a continuous maiming of the collective slave body. Rather than looking at the marks on any one slave's body or trying to represent his or her individual pain, Child focuses on the scars made on the overall body of the slave population. One advantage Child gains through this technique is that readers cannot dismiss any particular story as false. They have to consider the level of pain that is consistently applied to slaves' bodies. Indeed, if this level of violence is permissible by law, she insinuates, how much must exist in reality? Just as laws permitting torture indicate the level of violence in the South, so too do laws that allegedly protect the slave from cruel punishment. After analyzing the abuses prohibited under southern law, Child asks: "If negroes have never been scalded, burned, mutilated, &c. why are such crimes forbidden by an express law, with the marvellous proviso, except said slave *die* of '*moderate* punishment'?" (69).

As this question reveals, Child wields the testimony of southerners themselves to bear witness to the slave's pain.[44] If individual slaves are rendered silent through the application of torture, Child invents a way to speak the slave's pain so that the social body listens. But given the elaborate framework from which Child analyzes slavery, it is fair to ask if she has fallen into the representational quandary that Scarry describes. Does she elude representation of the body in pain by transforming the sensation of pain into an abstract argument—into the "object" of analysis—and therefore erase the body itself? To some extent, the dilemma Scarry describes is unavoidable, and Child does objectify pain to represent it politically. For example, answering advocates of the slave trade who claim that slave ships offer an "exceedingly comfortable portion of existence" that makes slaves "dance and sing" in merriment, Child introduces engravings of the torture devices commonly employed on slaves during their journey to "give a vivid idea of the Elysium enjoyed by negroes, during the Middle Passage" (19). She then enters into a technical summary that includes the following: "E is a thumb-screw. The thumbs are put into two round holes at the top; by turning a key a bar rises from C to D by means of a screw; and the pressure becomes very painful. By turning it further, the blood is made to start; and by taking away the key as at E, the tortured person is left in agony, without the means of helping himself, or being helped by others" (19–21).

In this description, the experience of pain is subordinated to a technical explanation of its application, or—to return to Scarry's argument—Child demonstrates the common "mental habit" of "*recognizing* pain *in* the weapon," a move that benefits those wishing to maintain power. In Child's description of the thumbscrew we cannot feel any one victim's individual pain. Rather, we understand the mechanisms of torture and the tyranny of the captain, who can apply such a device at his "discretion." However, while Child locates pain in the weapon, she does not pretend to represent adequately the slave's experience. Rather than calling for sentimental communication through the body, which might invite either pleasurable spectatorship or a moment of "identification" that could turn into an "act of appropriation," Child moves her readers to a disembodied site from which to place pain in its political context. This strategy worked. Although we obviously cannot trace all readers' responses to *Appeal* in general or to Child's representations of the body in particular, we do know that her text influenced men and women who would become leaders in the abolition movement. She politicized and contextualized pain to help end it.[45]

If her strategies for representing corporeality display ingenuity and sensitivity, there are points when Child acquiesces to the limits of polite discourse for a woman author. For example, although Child includes the story of the torture of Kate, she does not incorporate narratives of sexual exploitation of slave women into *Appeal*. Instead, Child presents the topic in a general and cryptic way:

There is another view of the system, which I cannot unveil so completely as it ought to be. I shall be called bold for saying so much; but the facts are so important, that it is a matter of conscience not to be fastidious.

The negro woman is unprotected either by law or public opinion. She is the property of her master, and her daughters are his property. They are allowed to have no conscientious scruples, no sense of shame, no regard for the feelings of husband or parent; they must be entirely subservient to the will of their owner, on pain of being whipped as near unto death as will comport with his interest, or quite to death, if it suit his pleasure.

Those who know human nature would be able to conjecture the unavoidable result, even if it were not betrayed by the amount of mixed population. (22)

Karcher comments that Child's remarks on slave women are "muffled in circumlocutions," indicating that she "cannot speak as plainly as she ought to because to do so would be to compromise her womanhood." Likewise, Child's critique of interracial marriage laws may be influenced by her need to retain at least a semblance of gentility. Her final chapter argues against an "unjust" law in Massachusetts that pronounces "marriages between persons of different color" illegal (187). Yet even as Child defends interracial marriage theoretically, as Sánchez-Eppler points out, she distances herself from women who choose to engage in sexual relations with men of another race by saying that they "are merely guilty of differing from us in a matter of taste" (188), thereby categorizing herself as someone who has more refinement than women who marry men of another race.[46] As I argue below, Child's hesitancy must be placed in the context of her career; her antislavery fiction (some of which I analyze below) and editorship of Jacobs's text indicate that her willingness to tackle sexual issues increased throughout the antebellum era.

Although I have focused on Child's representation of torture in *Appeal*, Child did not concentrate solely or even primarily on pain in her examination of the corporeal implications of slavery. As my first chapter details, the scientific enterprise of categorizing Negroes as an inferior and separate species began in the 1830s but reached its full force in the 1840s, and especially the 1850s. However, even if scientific essentialism was not manifested fully by the publication of *Appeal*, Child had to dismiss suspicions that the inferiority of the Negro might be permanent. Karcher argues that Child's title reveals the means by which she fought these perceptions, because Child represents Africans as "an assimilable 'class,' not a biologically separate race." Also, Karcher suggests,

Child devotes chapters 6 and 7 to demolishing "the rationale for prejudice—the myth of the Negro's biological inferiority and savage past."[47] Besides refuting charges of Negro inferiority, several of Child's chapters balance her earlier depictions of torture. For example, if the story of Kate's torture and Child's comments about slave women could leave readers visualizing slave women solely on a corporeal level, Child balances these representations with the powerful and detailed description of the African princess Zhinga in chapter 6, "Intellect of Negroes." This chapter catalogs Africans in Africa and throughout the diaspora who have exhibited talents in a multiplicity of fields, including business, education, politics, philosophy, religion, law, medicine, science, and the military. Almost no one receives as much attention as Zhinga, the seventeenth-century queen of Angola, whom Child includes as an example of "bravery, intelligence, and perseverance" (145). If slavery and the racism that justified it have the effect of corporealizing African Americans in general and African American women in particular, Child's inclusion of Zhinga once again exemplifies her desire to work against this injurious construct. As early as 1833, when she published her *Appeal*, then, Child was concerned with creating strategies to represent adequately the corporeal cruelties inflicted on slaves while not leaving readers with an inaccurate sense of slaves' permanent victimization or solely corporeal identity. Her nonfiction work of the 1840s and 1850s advances this project in a new form and also highlights the challenges of representing corporeality in the genre of genteel fiction.

Writing the Body into Antislavery Fiction

Choosing nonfiction as the mode of her first antislavery work was a radical act for Child, as it decidedly placed her in the unsentimental public sphere. By appealing primarily to her readers' reason rather than to sentiment, she challenged audience expectations of a woman author.[48] Yet if her nonfiction contained these subversive possibilities, it also shielded her from what would become one of her most difficult literary quandaries. When writing nonfiction, Child could address an audience not specified by gender and not limited by the rules of polite fiction. However, Child recognized the power of fiction to reach readers who would not approach a work such as *Appeal*, and as she advanced in her antislavery commitment, she wanted to attract as wide an audience as possible. Included among her antislavery texts are four fictional pieces first published in *The Liberty Bell* (the antislavery gift book that

Sánchez-Eppler critiques as appealing to readers' voyeuristic desires): "The Black Saxons" (1840), "The Quadroons" (1841), "Slavery's Pleasant Homes: A Faithful Sketch" (1842), and "The Stars and Stripes: A Melo-Drama" (1857). Of these, the last three are particularly relevant to my analysis of representations of corporeality, especially in relation to sexuality and gender.[49] Reading these three texts in relation to one another shows that Child continued to struggle with how to best represent the corporeal aspects of slavery. Also, by interpreting "The Stars and Stripes: A Melo-Drama" as a revision of Child's earlier work, we understand how Child became increasingly able to challenge sentimental assumptions in her genteel fiction, as she did in her earlier nonfictional *Appeal*.

As Karcher demonstrates, Child confronted important personal and professional hurdles as she set about writing fictional works in the 1840s. Separated from her husband and frustrated by a marriage that had failed to satisfy her passionate and domestic desires, Child was—as Karcher notes—"astonishingly candid" in her August 1846 letter to Frances Shaw, commenting, "*I do not wonder that so many men are libertines; I had* almost *said, I do not* blame *them. Nature is so outrageously damned up, her strongest instincts are so repressed, her plainest laws are so violated, in the present structure of society, that nature* will *revenge herself, in spite of all we can do.*"[50] Clearly, by the 1840s, Child was frustrated by societal restrictions on women's (and men's) sexuality; Karcher argues that "[f]ailed marriages, thwarted or forbidden sexuality, and erotic fantasies haunt" Child's 1846 collection of short stories, *Fact and Fiction*. She suggests that fiction "allowed Child the distance and imaginative freedom to examine aspects of her life too painful to confront directly" (such as her failed marriage and desire for at least two men while in New York City). Indeed, we see in the themes that Child chooses to write about a constant concern with restrictions on women's lives and sexuality. It seems all the more remarkable, then, that Child's fiction does not transfer her corporeal anxieties solely or even primarily onto the bodies of women of color. Again, I would argue that her personal experience, if anything, stimulated a sympathy for the need to tenuously balance the public and private in women's lives, a sympathy that results more often than not in fiction that challenges conventional gender and racial stereotypes.

In addition to struggling with personal conflicts in her own life, Child was also concerned about what was proper for a woman to write, and for anyone in the feminized parlor to read. While Child "recognized that fiction had the potential to arouse the 'benumbed' sympathies of hostile or indifferent readers by impelling them to imagine themselves in the place of slaves" (a sentimental tactic), she also "recognized that fiction would lose its attraction for such readers if it strayed too close to the disturbing contents of the antislavery tract."[51] Perhaps due to these obstacles, one of Child's best-known and earliest short fictional works, "The Quadroons," is noticeable for its overall acquiescence to sentimental tropes and racial platitudes, characteristics that are particularly evident in her decision to weave the story around the tragic mulatto plot.[52] Child creates the beautiful quadroon Rosalie, who falls in love with a wealthy white Georgian, Edward, with whom she has a child, Xarifa. When Edward deserts Rosalie to marry the daughter of "a very popular and wealthy man" (90), Rosalie dies within a year due to emotional stress. After Edward dies, it is discovered that Rosalie was never officially emancipated by her master, and Xarifa is sold at auction, raped by her master, and kills herself by hitting her head against the wall in the "frenzy of despair"(98).

By employing the figure of the tragic mulatto, Child gestures toward several genteel expectations that contradict her antislavery and antiracism goals. First, as is common in tragic mulatto fiction, she appeals to white readers by making the characters racially close enough to them to merit their sympathy, thus reinforcing their racial notions of personal worth. Therefore, unlike *Appeal* and "Slavery's Pleasant Homes," "The Quadroons" relies upon a sentimental premise of universally communicable suffering, even if Child does not locate this suffering in the tortured body. Second, Rosalie's and Xarifa's deaths imply that their "problem" bodies cannot find an earthly home; as women of an "other" race they are written out of the text. Third, despite the narrator's repeated praise of Rosalie for her "purity and bright intelligence" (89), Child reinforces racial stereotypes by making Rosalie more passionate than Edward's new wife, Charlotte, who is prouder by nature and responds to her husband's sexual history with the "polite propriety" (94) that readers could expect from a genteel white woman. One could therefore argue that in this story Child projects sexuality onto the African American woman's body. The passionate African American woman, "gushing" (94) with love and emotion, contrasts with the white lady who "could not miss the impassioned tenderness she had never experienced" (93). Indeed, at first reading, it appears as if the quadroons' race dooms them to tragedy and death, a suggestion that Child adds to by telling readers at the end of the story that "[t]he world does not afford such materials for tragic romance, as the history of the Quadroons" (98).

However, even in this sentimental and seemingly conservative story, Child

complicates the "dialectical relationship" between white and black womanhood, a move that would become more pronounced in "Slavery's Pleasant
Homes: A Faithful Sketch" and "The Stars and Stripes: A Melo-Drama." She
does so by making Charlotte a commodity in the public marketplace of marriage while situating Rosalie and Edward's relationship, at least temporarily,
beyond commodification. Rosalie tells Edward early in the story that if his affec-
tions for her changed, "I would not, if I could, hold you by a legal fetter" (89).
Although she lives in a society structured around slavery, Rosalie will not (and,
in reality, cannot) participate in its legal dynamics as a subject; she rejects the
(imagined) possibility of using a "fetter" (a chain) to hold Edward captive.
Repeatedly, Child portrays the marriage as a domestic retreat sanctioned by natural law, which she represents as higher than state law. In contrast, Edward and
Charlotte's marriage originates and remains entirely in the public sphere. The
narrator describes Edward's new interest in politics as "the arena where so
much American strength is wasted," as a "contagion" that lures him from his
idealized home (90). Unlike Rosalie, whom he loves passionately and purely,
Charlotte awakens in Edward only "vanity" and thoughts of the "great worldly
advantages connected with a union" (91). Even their marriage enacts a trade, as
Edward gives careful kindness in lieu of love. Despite the "polite propriety" that
marks Charlotte's conduct, the story reveals her status as relying, ultimately, on
the public and political exchange of her body. By making such a comparison,
Child risks conflating the distinctions between the slave woman's and the
white woman's experiences; she implies that Xarifa, who on the auction block
suffers from "the rude hands that examined the graceful proportions of her
beautiful frame" (97) and dies by the story's end, is akin to Charlotte, who maintains her wealth, polite societal status, and life. Returning to Sánchez-Eppler's
analysis, this is a moment of "identification" that could become an "appropriation." Yet if Child hazards a sentimental blurring of difference, she also shows
that the lives of all women in this story are ultimately reduced to their corporeality in a corrupt society and thus avoids shifting the entire corporeal burden
onto African American women's bodies. She underscores this point early in the
story, when Edward, just entering into an engagement with Charlotte, begins to
associate Rosalie, whose race would usually mark her as containing an
unchecked sexuality, with "the idea of restraint" (91).

Interestingly, Xarifa is not the only "desecrated" body in the story. Edward is
also, in effect, "desecrated" by his own weakness in succumbing to corporeal
temptations. The first sign of Edward's deficiency comes not in his love of Ros-

alie, but in the fact that although he does not truly love Charlotte, "the ardent young man," "unfettered by laws of the land," decides to act on the allure of "variety in love" (91). The choice of the word "unfettered" is significant. For the quadroon woman would not hold Edward with the "fetter" of legal marriage, and her love is portrayed as incorruptible and transcendent, as having "a far deeper sentiment than belongs merely to excited passion" (89). Yet Edward, when left "unfettered" by "law," acts on his instinct, which directs him to seek "variety in love." Unchained, the white man surrenders to corporeal cravings. Likewise, although the story does not linger on it in much detail, Child draws upon temperance rhetoric to elaborate further upon Edward's weakness. Unlike Xarifa, who steadfastly tries to keep the "pure temple" of her body free from her master's corruption, Edward seeks "relief for his wretched feelings in the free use of wine," a habit that the story implies leads to his fatal fall from his horse (95). Like Frances E. W. Harper's antebellum poetry and postbellum fiction (see chapter 3), Child implicitly contrasts "desecrated" white men, who can't control their bodily impulses, with African Americans who risk everything to maintain their corporeal dignity. Such a process necessarily complicates the "dialectical relationship" between African American and white bodies, both male and female.

Published just one year after "The Quadroons," "Slavery's Pleasant Homes: A Faithful Sketch" also complicates corporeal depictions of slave and free women while continuing the work of *Appeal* by providing a context for the spectacle of the slave's body.[53] The story opens as Frederic Dalcho, a wealthy slave owner, returns home with his new wife, Marion, who brings with her a "foster-sister" (240) and a slave, Rosa. Although Rosa has fallen in love with George, Frederic's "handsome quadroon brother" and "favorite slave," Frederic begins to lust for Rosa and eventually forces her into a sexual liaison. After George discovers the rapes and urges Rosa to stay out of Frederic's way, Rosa's defiance outrages Frederic and "one severe flogging succeeded another," until Rosa miscarries and dies. That night, Frederic is murdered. George's rival is judged guilty and condemned to die, but just before he is about to be hung, George confesses. As packed as the plot of "Slavery's Pleasant Homes" is with sensationalist events (including adultery, rape, torture, and murder), it was not, as Sánchez-Eppler suggests about the stories in *The Liberty Bell*, marketable. In fact, Child decided to include "The Quadroons" in her 1846 collection of writings, *Fact and Fiction*, but excluded "Slavery's Pleasant Homes," most likely because she believed it would not appeal to her readers. As Karcher argues, "No amount of rhetorical tact could have made a story that portrayed the slave-holding elite so starkly—much less one that justified a slave's murder of his master—acceptable to readers of the class antislavery fiction sought to reach. Its penetrating insights into the interlocking systems of racial and sexual oppression . . . condemned Child's masterpiece to burial in a coterie publication."[54] Karcher's comments indicate that one major distinction between "The Quadroons" and "Slavery's Pleasant Homes" is the newly included presence of the male slave who is eager to retaliate for the sexual wrongs done to slave women. This story also examines in much greater detail the effects of sexual abuse on an entire household.

Despite the differences between the two pieces, "Slavery's Pleasant Homes" builds on and makes more explicit themes Child begins to explore in "The Quadroons," especially those involving women. Just as she revealed Charlotte's commodified status in society, Child once again places white women in the marketplace, this time making the sexual nature of the marketplace more explicit. Marion arrives from New Orleans, the home of the "fancy" slave trade where white men often went to purchase slave women for sexual use. We are told that she has been "nurtured in seclusion, almost as deep as that of the oriental harem," and that she is a "pretty little waxen plaything" (238). Clearly, Child is comparing Marion to a "fancy" slave woman, who is bought as an object for the master's pleasure.[55] At first Frederic is "too much absorbed" in his own "honey-moon" to notice any other woman, but eventually is drawn to Rosa as she has "the charm of novelty," a phrase calling to mind Charlotte's appeal to Edward as representing "variety in love" (239). In these representations, the white woman is not the asexual antithesis of the African American woman; she has the capability to "absorb" her husband in the presumably sexual honeymoon stage of their marriage and is shown to be one of his many sexual playthings. However, even while blurring the distinctions between slaves and slaveholding women, Child shows that a recognition of mutual oppression based on corporeally defined roles does not necessarily result in the sentimental understanding that "The Quadroons" implies may be possible. Rosa wants "to tell her mistress" about her problems and "claim her protection; but she dared not" (239). When Marion discovers Rosa's sexual role in the household, she strikes her, which leads to a brief period of shared emotion as they embrace and weep. Yet these tears—helpful as they are in sentimental scenes in Harriet Beecher Stowe's *Uncle Tom's Cabin*—cannot bridge the gap between the women's experiences: "neither sought any further to learn the other's secrets"

(240). After their violent confrontation, Rosa and Marion are never placed together in the narrative, and Marion does not act to save Rosa from Frederic's abuse, not even to save Rosa's life.[56]

Once Child has dismissed the possibility of sentimental identification with another person's pain based on shared gender identity, she continues the task she began in *Appeal*, that of placing the spectacle of the abuse of slaves in a proper context. Here again, Child demonstrates that slave law is random in its application, leaving the lives of slaves to chance. As Child describes it, the punishment of George's rival, Mars, is planned as an exercise of power, not justice: "The fatal hour came. Planters rode miles to witness the execution, and stood glaring at their trembling victim, with the fierceness of tigers. The slaves from miles around were assembled, to take warning by his awful punishment" (242). The verbs Child uses in the above passage highlight the spectacle's nature. The "planters," who are presumably white, but not all slaveholders, "*rode* miles to witness the execution" and "*stood* glaring at their trembling victim" (emphasis mine). Active verbs such as "rode" and "stood" suggest that they are willing participants in the spectacle, probably because the execution reconfirms the power of their whiteness. By contrast, the slaves are passively grouped together and forced to view the spectacle of the white man's "awful punishment." Child suggests that it does not really matter to the crowd who dies; their fury is directed equally at both the relatively innocent Mars and the guilty George. The point is not to condemn a guilty man to death, but rather to present the spectacle of *a* death to the crowd.

George is not unaffected by the power of this ceremony, as he stands by "very pale and haggard, and his breast was heaving with tumultuous thoughts" (242). It is one thing, Child suggests, to die. It is another to die in front of a crowd of "tigers" hungry for your blood. Yet George reasons that the only power the slaveholders have is corporeal, which is both absolute and limited. "[T]hey can do no more than hang me," he concludes. He confesses his deed, and the crowd "kicked and cursed him; and hung up, like a dog or a wolf, a man of nobler soul than any of them all" (242). By including George's confession, Child reconfigures the spectacle. The crowd (and reader) understand that George has heroically succumbed to the spectacle of power and his own death rather than wrongly accusing an innocent man. No longer a lesson about the power of the slaveholders, George's death becomes his symbolic gesture toward retaining a sense of justice within the slave community. By making this choice, George turns a moment of disempowerment—the instant when the slave body is about to be hanged before the crowd—into a paradoxical statement of power. He chooses to die, and his last words are those of a hero. By revealing this spectacle to her readers in a different context, Child encourages them to reread George's death as signifying the power of slave men, rather than the power of slaveholders. Like Harper in "The Tennessee Hero," Child turns a public hanging into a subversive statement against unchecked tyranny.

To direct readers to reconsider further spectacles of slave punishment, Child ends her story with the authoritative voice of the narrator, who comments on the representation of the events by the media.[57] Both northern and southern press accounts describe the murder of Frederic as *"fiend-like"* and allege that "one of our most wealthy and respected citizens, was robbed and murdered last week, by one of his slaves. The black demon was caught and hung; and hanging was too good for him" (242). Responding to the media, the narrator comments that "not one was found to tell how the slave's young wife had been torn from him by his own brother, and murdered with slow tortures" (242). What the press has omitted, she indicates, is the corporeal cruelties perpetrated against slaves, particularly the rape and torture of Rosa and the near hanging of Mars. By reframing the events, Child turns the spectacle of hanging into a commentary not only on the arbitrary nature of southern "justice," but also on the factors that lead to violence in the slaveholding community. After all, Frederic dies with his own dagger in his heart. The slaveholder has created and perpetuated a system of violence that he cannot contain.

Child returns to the themes she explores in "Slavery's Pleasant Homes" in the final antislavery piece she contributes to *The Liberty Bell*, her 1857 story "The Stars and Stripes: A Melo-Drama," a work that traces the escape of a slave couple from their abusive masters.[58] If "The Quadroons" and "Slavery's Pleasant Homes" contain moments of possible identification between slaveholding and slave women, this work denies any sentimental identification. The central protagonist, Ellen, a very light-skinned slave, is hounded by her master. When she reports his actions to her husband, William, she informs him that she is "afraid" to tell her mistress as "they will sell *me* to Georgia traders, and keep you." Despite Ellen's reluctance to talk, "misses begins to mistrust something; for she has been terribly cross . . . lately," burning Ellen's "arm with hot sealing-wax" because she broke a comb (144). Here Ellen does not even attempt to garner empathy from her mistress, despite their supposedly close relationship. Likewise, the blow that Marion gives Rosa in "Slavery's Pleasant Homes," described as more symbolic than painful, has turned into an act that could be labeled as torturous, the pouring of "hot sealing wax" on Ellen's arm. Child has come a long way from "The Quadroons," where both Charlotte and Rosalie want to protect the "other" woman. By 1857 Child is not inclined to portray any possibility of a sentimental relationship between a slaveholding woman and her slave. Nor is Child inclined to portray the slave woman as merely a victim. Whereas both Rosa and Xarifa are raped in the previous stories, Ellen manages to escape north with William and elude rape. The plot of "Stars and Stripes: A Melo-Drama" returns again to "Slavery's Pleasant Homes" to rewrite it, this time reaching a conclusion of freedom, not death.

Child also evokes "Slavery's Pleasant Homes" through the inclusion of the subplot of William's sister Peggy. Although Ellen has feared her master for some time, she tells William that she has "been afraid to tell you all my troubles, for fear you would do something rash, and then they would burn you alive," as they did "Peggy's husband" (142). Earlier the reader has learned that William's "handsome sister" (presumably Peggy) was sold to a New Orleans trader to pay for an expensive piano (139). Although the story is not given in detail, it is revealed that after Peggy was sold, her husband did "something rash." The fact that he was burned alive indicates that his "rash" act might have included violence or the threat of violence to a white man, perhaps the trader, overseer, or master. Like George in "Slavery's Pleasant Homes," Peggy's husband seems to have been tortured to death in a public spectacle of white power. Ellen wants to avoid Peggy's fate; in effect, she—and perhaps Child—wants to get beyond the plot of "Slavery's Pleasant Homes" and allow herself and William to live. Having learned from Peggy's experience, Ellen waits until her owners are away and then tells William about her potential abuse: "Massa has gone away, and you will have time to get cool before he comes back" (142). In this state of excitement and reflection, they resolve to flee, and the rest of the text shows their successful trip north. Because they escape before Ellen is raped, William does not have to enter into a dynamic that forces him to become either an emasculated spectator to his wife's abuse or a "rash" defender of her virtue. As this story suggests, Child consistently rethought and rewrote anti-slavery plots, even her own. Her struggle to reveal the corporeal implications of slavery in the most effective manner was ongoing, and by the late 1850s she had mastered her ability to represent corporeality and challenge political and racially precarious tropes of sentimentality in genteel fiction, as she had done earlier in her nonfictional appeal.

The concern over how to represent the slave's body, then, was nothing new to Child as she undertook the project of editing Jacobs's autobiography. Even as she worked with Jacobs's text, one of the major changes she made was to "put the savage cruelties into one chapter, entitled 'Neighboring Planters,' in order that those who shrink from 'supping on horrors,' might omit them, without interrupting the thread of the story."[59] Once again, this decision shows Child's effort to negotiate between what a reader *had to know*, and what he or she *was able to read*. Clearly, for Child there was no easy way to manage the relationships among readers, the slave's body, and authors or editors. Throughout her career, she develops and redevelops strategies for striking what she hopes will be the correct balance between spectacle and context. From what we know of the relationship between Jacobs and Child, there is every reason to believe that Jacobs trusted Child to carry out her editorship with tact and skill.[60]

Child wrote during an era when scientists were rigidly establishing identity as corporeally determined. As these and other authorities painstakingly tabulated embodied difference to justify oppression and exclusion, it must have been tempting to avoid representations of the body. When the scientific "evidence" against all women was added to the vicious rhetorical attacks on women abolitionists and the real danger many of them braved, we might not be surprised if Child's body weighed heavily on her, and we would certainly understand if she sidestepped depictions of corporeality that could, in her audience's mind, highlight her "inferior" and vulnerable body. Likewise, it is reasonable to suggest that some white women emphasized African American women's corporeal identity to deflect the public's gaze from their own bodies. As chapter 5 demonstrates, Margaret Fuller deploys such a strategy in relation to Native Americans in *Summer on the Lakes*. Yet it is just as reasonable to suggest that some white women—subjected as they were to charges of indelicacy, and exposed, as they were, to ridicule for their public antislavery work—would have been made more sensitive by their own experiences to the vulnerability (and paradoxical power) that comes from making a private body public. As I have suggested, for Child this was the case. Nonetheless, we should not conflate Child's sensitivity to corporeal concerns with an uncomplicated sentimental bond; she never claims to know completely or to represent adequately the slave's pain. Rather, she develops a variety of methods to represent the corporeal nature of slavery without evoking a sentimental understanding of pain or appealing to an "allure" of "bondage." Her antislavery writing commands readers to look with intelligence on the physical evidence of slavery's obscene injustices.

As chapter 3 argues, Harper, like Child, negotiates the dilemma of how to best represent the corporeal oppression of slavery while avoiding the trap of pleasurable spectatorship. Her task is made all the more difficult because, unlike Child, Harper ascends the lecture platform and brings her message before "promiscuous" audiences. Moreover, as an African American woman, Harper could be all too easily aligned with what Carla L. Peterson has defined as the "unruly, grotesque," and "carnivalesque."[61] Harper met these challenges with personal courage and literary finesse.

3

DEFLECTING THE PUBLIC'S GAZE

AND DISCIPLINING DESIRE

Harper's Antebellum Poetry and Reconstruction Fiction

I don't know but that you would laugh if you were to hear some of the remarks which my lectures call forth: "She is a man," again "She is not colored, she is painted."—Frances E. W. Harper, "Almost Constantly Either Traveling or Speaking"

In 1853, when Frances Ellen Watkins Harper was twenty-eight years old, her home state of Maryland passed a law preventing free people of color from entering it, with imprisonment and sale into slavery the punishment for transgression. When one man broke the law, he was forced into slavery and, after a failed attempt to escape, died of exposure. "Upon that grave," Harper is quoted as saying, "I pledged myself to the Anti-Slavery cause."[1] Why, one might ask, does Harper select this incident to represent her baptism into abolitionism? As chapter 7 details, slave women such as Harriet Jacobs endured almost unimaginable physical restraint (forced, as she was, to retreat into a garret space for seven years). Yet "free" people of color such as Harper also confronted physical restriction and potential bodily harm. Their bodies, although technically not confined within the chattel system of slavery, were nonetheless considered by many to be part of the public domain because they were identified as Negro. Harper's letters indicate the oppression she faced due to her corporeality. Writing from Pennsylvania in 1858, she comments: "I have been travelling nearly four years, and have been in every New England State, in New York, Canada and Ohio: but of all these places, this is about the meanest of all, as far as the treatment of colored people is concerned. I have been insulted in several railroad cars."[2]

As these remarks indicate, even if Harper had never ascended the lecture platform, her body would have been understood by the public in a very different manner than those of white abolitionist women such as Lydia Maria Child; she was more vulnerable to public scrutiny and abuse. Chapter 1 demonstrates how scientific discourse often defined women of color as innately lustful, a definition that enabled their rhetorical and actual abuse. We can recall, for example, John H. Van Evrie's echoing of common beliefs when he contends that the white female's "blush of maiden modesty" exhibits natural purity and then asks: "Can any one suppose such a thing possible to a black face? . . . And if the latter cannot reflect these things in her face—if her features are utterly incapable of expressing emotions so elevated and beautiful, is it not certain that she is without them—that they have no existence in her inner being, are no portion of her moral nature?"[3] In effect, scientific discourse contributed to the stereotype of the Jezebel character, a black woman "governed almost entirely by her libido," who "was the counterimage of the mid-nineteenth-century ideal of the Victorian lady."[4] Despite the serious implications of such theories, Harper, as Frances Smith Foster notes, "decided that her personal survival and well-being were inextricably linked with the survival and well-being of the larger society and that confrontation, not silence, was the way to mental, if not physical, health."

In 1854 Harper gave her first antislavery lecture. Although antislavery women of both races had prepared Harper's way, she still faced significant challenges on the lecture circuit. As Carla L. Peterson details, despite the ability of African American women to participate effectively in the domestic, ethnic community, ethnic public, and national public spheres, they were "officially excluded" from black national institutions because that arena was "dominated by men of the elite," who worked, in what they believed were the best interests of the community, "to contain heterogeneity, silence difference, and gender blackness as male."[5] Because blackness was gendered male (and, I would add, because African American women were defined scientifically as naturally lustful), women speaking on behalf of their race were often considered oddities and were perceived as reconfirming notions of their bodies as "unruly, grotesque, carnivalesque."[6] In addition, as Peterson demonstrates, when women like Harper lectured, they did so without the cushion of race, class affiliation, or family ties that many white women had the privilege to call upon.[7] The audiences that Harper might have faced in the antebellum years can be partially surmised by reaction to her postbellum lectures. In 1870, for example, the editor of the southern *Mobile Register* recorded his trip to hear Harper speak. He went primarily out of "curiosity," both to ascertain how the "colored citizens" were managing and because the lecturer was a woman. As a type of curio, Harper was particularly scrutinized for any "grammatical inaccuracy of speech, or the slightest violation of good taste in manner or matter." Finding no error, the reviewer confesses that he then asked: "What is her color? Is she dark or light?"[8] This question does not appear to be atypical. Harper comments in a letter written in 1870: "I don't know but that you would laugh if you were to hear some of the remarks which my lectures call forth: 'She is a man,' again 'She is not colored, she is painted.'"[9] These accounts reveal that Harper not only risked being viewed as a spectacle, but also confronted questions about the authenticity of her gender and race when her demeanor and abilities contradicted her audiences' stereotypical expectations.

Because Harper was "identified" with a race whose bodies were all too often considered part of the public sphere, and because she chose a career that risked associating herself with preconceived notions of the African American woman's body as "unruly, grotesque" and "carnivalesque," she developed strategies to represent corporeality while figuratively avoiding the public's inappropriate gaze. The first section of this chapter examines the strategies evidenced in Harper's antebellum ballads, tactics that enabled her to counter the popular conception of the Negro body as a spectacle available for public use and abuse. When Harper shifts her audience's gaze away from the bodies of slaves to the bodies of deracialized and Caucasian characters in her antebellum poetry and postbellum fiction, she participates in a reversal of power. Chapter 2 notes the fracture between what, in Michel Foucault's terms, we can identify as the application of punishment in the antebellum South and the shift toward discipline in the antebellum North. However, I do not want to overemphasize the dominance of punishment in the South. As my discussion of Harriet Jacobs in chapter 7 indicates, discipline, especially the use of surveillance, was also a major mechanism for maintaining power over slaves. As Foucault reminds us, in "discipline, it is the subjects who have to be seen. Their visibility assures the hold of the power that is exercised over them."[10] Like Child, Harper developed strategies in her antislavery poetry to deflect the reader's gaze from her "body" and the bodies of the male and female slaves she represents. Yet unlike Child—who, in *Appeal*, may muffle the slave's voice to avoid the possibility of pleasurable spectatorship and appropriation—Harper's subjects are able to speak or act or both and can therefore participate, at least figuratively, in their own liberation.

Not only does Harper deflect the gaze from her body and the bodies of the slaves she represents, but she also turns the gaze toward the bodies of Caucasians or deracialized characters through her deployment of temperance rhetoric. As the second section of this chapter argues, Harper's relationship to the temperance movement (a common affiliation in the antebellum African American community) can be understood as intimately connected to her anti-slavery message in general and her representation of corporeality in particular. Although Harper, as Debra J. Rosenthal notes, crafts most of her temperance literature as a "deracialized discourse," eliding specific racial identification of her characters and representing intemperance as a "racially transcendent" affliction, her temperance texts do not signal a *release* from racial issues but rather an *extension* of her corporeal strategy.[11] The structure of her antebellum poetry volumes and the chronological order of her three recently rediscovered postbellum novels juxtapose intemperate deracialized or Caucasian bodies with the temperate, even heroic, bodies of slaves and free African Americans. I end this chapter by suggesting that we consider Harper's corporeal strategy in relation to Foucault's conception of the coercive nature of discipline. Harper demonstrates the vast difference between being punished, surveyed, or disciplined by an exterior force and disciplining oneself. For Harper, self-discipline was not the coercive mechanism of power that Foucault intimates. Rather, it was a means of asserting power for African Americans, who were not only denied control of their bodies, but also labeled as disorderly, unruly, and in need of restraint by the dominant culture. In her postbellum novels *Sowing and Reaping* and *Trial and Triumph*, the concept of self-restraint, of self-discipline, enables Harper to shift the location of corporeal power and challenge rhetorically the concepts of governance, body, and control that were fundamental in her era.[12] In this sense, it is possible to read Harper's move toward discipline as a paradoxically liberating act, much in the same way that Claudia Tate and Ann duCille have suggested that marriage is represented as a liberating institution by African American women writers in the late nineteenth century.[13]

As the rest of this chapter argues, Harper worked throughout the antebellum and Reconstruction eras to invent a multifaceted strategy of corporeal representation: she averted the public's inappropriate gaze from her own body and the bodies of those she represented textually; she redirected public scrutiny toward the intemperate body, often either deracializing that body or hinting that it may be Caucasian; and she proposed self-regulation and self-discipline as a liberational strategy for African Americans in the ante- and postbellum periods. All of these strategies resulted, at least partially, from the complex negotiation of corporeality that Harper faced as a woman of color who dared travel throughout the antebellum North, calling for abolition, and throughout the Reconstruction South, calling for racial equality and uplift.

The Public Body and the Antebellum Ballad

As the previous section indicates, Harper braved not only censure, but also physical harm when she lectured and read her poetry. Peterson analyzes reactions to Harper's public performances and concludes that in order to reconcile Harper's intelligence and morality with conceptions of the "grotesque, carnivalesque" female African American body, Harper's audience tended figuratively to decorporealize her. "What results is a complex compromise between presence and absence," Peterson argues; "the body is rendered 'quiet' and 'modest,' the language represented as 'pure' and 'chaste,' and the voice promoted as intangible music." Although audiences may have decorporealized Harper by transforming her metaphorically into pure voice, Peterson argues that Harper crafts her speeches and literature to negotiate the extremes of corporeality and transcendence. In her textual work she mediates between "the plentitude of passion and the hollowness of pure sound . . . between, finally, the audience's image of the black woman as body and the poet's construction of self."[14] To negotiate these extremes, Harper replaces the image of the African American woman lifted onto the auction block with the picture of the African American woman on the lecture "block," uplifting men and women from both races. The challenge of this transformation is revealed in the comments of one of Harper's reviewers who saw her in Philadelphia: "As I listened to her, there swept over me, in a chill wave of horror, the realization that this noble woman had she not been rescued from her mother's condition, might have been sold on the auction-block, to the highest bidder—her intellect, fancy, eloquence, the flashing wit, that might make the delight of a Parisian saloon, and her pure, Christian character all thrown in."[15]

The scene the reviewer asks readers to imagine (the slave auction) and the scene reviewed (Harper's lecture) feature the prominent display of an African American woman's body. However, in both cases, the reviewer focuses on disembodied elements of personality, such as "intellect, fancy, eloquence" and "Christian character." Here Harper is perceived, as Peterson argues about Harper's lectures in general, as disembodied despite the corporeally charged atmosphere she appears in. As this review suggests, Harper often succeeded in figuratively *concealing* her physical presence from her audience even as she *revealed* herself to them. Just as Harper "covered" herself while lecturing in a public forum, so too her manipulation of the ballad form enables her to veil her body while revealing her antislavery message.

For Harper, the use of the ballad accomplished several related feats. In part, she evokes the folk tradition she wants to represent. Maryemma Graham notes that although poets writing in the sentimental tradition often employed the rhymed quatrain, "Harper's addition of dramatic details, vivid imagery, and her effective understanding of Afro-American life, together with her political sensibility, transformed the common ballad into a distinctly Afro-American discourse."[16] By choosing an accessible form, Harper also appealed to the wide array of people who attended her lectures.[17] Politically and poetically, Harper wanted to seize her audience's attention, to fill them with a sense of the urgency of emancipation. Again, the ballad lends itself to this goal. Susan Stewart notes that even "when a traditional ballad works by means of third-person narration, the speaker 'voices' quotes and makes statements with the authority of an observer in context or witness. The ballad is thereby a form continually marked by immediacy—immediacy of voice, immediacy of action, immediacy of allusion." What better form, then, to stress the exigency of antislavery activity? In addition to fulfilling these goals, the ballad also provides a literary shield for the poem's presenter, a cover that Harper might have found appealing given her precarious position as an African American woman lecturer and poet. Stewart argues that the Anglo-Scottish tradition of holding "the body rigidly still and letting the ballad speak *through* oneself" creates "the appearance of tradition speaking through someone." In a similar way, Peterson—drawing upon the work of Lawrence Buell—argues that the ballad serves as an appropriate form in which to deploy an "aesthetics of restraint" through narrative and meter, a restraint which contains emotions within formal limits.[18] Returning again to Peterson's observation that Harper's audience decorporealized her in order to reconcile her intelligence and morality with her corporeality, we can begin to understand how the ballad aided, perhaps even initiated, this process. Harper is able to speak the stories of slaves without calling attention to herself; her voice eclipses her body.

We can argue, then, that Harper's awareness of the dynamics of spectatorship, to an even greater degree than Child's, enabled her to create a method of representation that emphasized the importance of corporeal oppression without positioning the African American woman as a passive object available to anyone's vulgar gaze. Like Jacobs, who becomes quite the "peeper" in *Incidents in the Life of a Slave Girl*, Harper perceives the power that accrues from reversing the gaze of surveillance in slave society. Two of Harper's 1854 poems, "The Slave Mother" and "The Slave Auction," challenge readers to reconsider the overall meaning and context of the public female slave body and can be understood as addressing the dilemma of the allegedly licentious reader/spectator that I analyze in chapter 2. Both poems draw upon what Philip Fisher has identified as the sentimental dynamic of family separation.[19] Doing so, they emphasize the psychological infliction of mental anguish that results from the slave auction rather than a physical scene of torture (which I analyze below in relation to "The Tennessee Hero"). "The Slave Mother" describes a mother and child about to be separated from one another:

> Heard you that shriek? It rose
> So wildly on the air,
> It seemed as if a burden'd heart
> Was breaking in despair.
>
> Saw you those hands so sadly clasped—
> The bowed and feeble head—
> The shuddering of that fragile form—
> That look of grief and dread?
>
> Saw you the sad, imploring eye?
> Its every glance was pain,
> As if a storm of agony
> Were sweeping through the brain.[20]

Ignoring concerns about the delicacy of witnessing slavery, these stanzas call upon readers not merely to observe the auction, but to scrutinize it meticulously for details. Each stanza begins with the speaker questioning the reader's perception: "Heard you that shriek?"; "Saw you those hands?"; "Saw you the sad, imploring eye?" If the slave mother can have such suffering, the reader must be able to witness it. However, Harper refuses to leave interpretation of the spectacle to the reader's discretion. Rather, she follows an "aesthetics of restraint," which Peterson defines further as a poetics in which "sentimentality became a mode whose purpose was not to unleash an excess of emotion in the reader but rather to channel feelings toward benevolent and moral ends."[21] "The Slave Mother" reveals this strategy. By following each question with a description of what readers should actually see or hear, Harper guides their responses to the scene. For example, she begins by telling readers to note the mother's "shriek," an animalistic sound. However, she follows this image with the simile: "It seemed as if a burden'd heart / Was breaking in despair." The reader should not concentrate on the inhuman sound—the shriek of pain that defies language—but the human characteristics that lead the slave mother to make this noise, the intense psychological pain caused by the potential loss of her child. Harper's movement from specific corporeal features to abstract conceptualizations of the victim's pain (a tactic she repeats in the third stanza) urges readers to view the slave mother not as a curiosity or spectacle, but as a suffering human being.[22]

Once she has dismissed concerns about the propriety of spectating a slave auction, Harper reverses the gaze of the reader and the slave woman. Although the poem's readers have been repeatedly told to scrutinize the woman, what Harper suggests we see, if we look hard enough, is that the slave mother actually peers at the audience. The second stanza begins, "Saw you those hands so sadly clasped" and carries the question of what the reader/spectator sees to its end, finishing by asking if the reader comprehends "[t]hat look of grief and dread." By focusing attention on the look of the slave mother, the poem forces the reader to consider her face. Harper continues in the next stanza: "Saw you the sad, imploring eye?" At this moment, the gaze of the reader is met by the gaze of the slave mother. What does the reader see? Presuming it is a woman reader, does she see a reflection of herself, a reminder that she too is property in a patriarchal system, that she too would suffer unbearable pain if she was separated from her child? Or is the slave's experience so different that this moment defies sentimental communication? In this instance, Harper leaves the lesson ambiguous. However, by reversing the spectator/spectacle dynamic, she not only alleviates concerns about the propriety of looking at a slave auction (as the reader is being examined by the slave woman and vice versa) but also challenges conventional depictions of the slave woman as a passive object. Even on the auction block, the slave woman commands attention not with her body, but with her gaze.

Like "The Slave Mother," "The Slave Auction" also reconfigures the dynamic of spectacle. Once again, we see slaves viewing an auction, but this time they look at one another: mothers "stood with streaming eyes, / And saw their dearest children sold"; and a woman "[g]az'd on the husband of her youth, / With anguish none may paint or tell." Unlike "The Slave Mother," which leaves open the possibility of sentimental understanding, this poem complicates identification between the reader and the slave, challenging the assumption that suffering is universally communicable. This challenge appears in the beginning of the fifth stanza of this six-stanza poem:

> Ye who have laid your love to rest,
> And wept above their lifeless clay,

Know not the anguish of that breast,
Whose lov'd are rudely torn away.

Ye may not know how desolate
Are bosoms rudely forced to part,
And how a dull and heavy weight
Will press the life-drops from the heart.

Here Harper confronts readers who try to understand the condition of slavery within their own framework, as in the painful separation experienced at the death of a loved one. These stanzas evoke one of the passages in Harriet Beecher Stowe's *Uncle Tom's Cabin* that is often used to define sentimentalism, the scene in chapter 9 in which the fugitive slave Eliza Harris, in an effort to justify having fled her allegedly benevolent masters, asks Senator Bird's wife if she has "ever lost a child." The Birds, who are mourning their son's death, are able to empathize with Eliza because of their own suffering. As addressed in chapter 2, Marianne Noble interprets this scene as forcing "a new mode of cognition upon readers" through the technique of the sentimental wound, as readers are "to understand slavery through their memories of sorrow rather than through reason, and thereby apprehend the 'plain right thing' that logic conceals." Yet unlike Stowe, Harper (like Jacobs) implies that the experience of separation is not universally communicable. To understand it, you cannot turn to your own life; instead, readers must accept slave testimony and slave experience as authority. They must, paradoxically, attempt to traverse a divide that, in reality, cannot be crossed. According to John Ernest, Jacobs demonstrates a similar dynamic between the reader and slave woman, because the paradoxical "lesson" of *Incidents* is that "white mothers and daughters cannot identify with Brent, but that they must learn to do so if they are to achieve their own moral ideals."[23] In effect, Harper transforms the moment of the slave mother's corporeal vulnerability into a site that confirms the significance of her knowledge. This knowledge, she hopes, will lead her audience to participate in the struggle to end slavery.

Although Harper was particularly concerned about slave women, she—like Child in "Slavery's Pleasant Homes"—also reconfigures the spectacle of slave men's torture. "The Tennessee Hero" converts a moment of intense victimization and corporeal passivity (the beating and murder of a slave) into a triumphant statement of subversive agency, particularly through its comparison of the tortured hero to the tortured, but triumphant, Christ. The poem, which

was added to the 1857 edition of *Poems on Miscellaneous Subjects*, purports to
be based on truth and begins by informing readers that the hero "had heard his
comrades plotting to obtain their liberty, and rather than betray them he
received 750 lashes and died." Recalling Child's description of crowds who
gather to watch the hanging of John C. Colt that I address in chapter 2, Harper's
ballad begins by showing the nature of the crowd as "savage":

> He stood before the savage throng,
> The base and coward crew;
> A tameless light flashed from his eye,
> His heart beat firm and true.
>
> He was the hero of his band,
> The noblest of them all;
> Though fetters galled his weary limbs,
> His spirit spurned their thrall.
>
> And towered, in its manly might,
> Above the murderous crew.
> Oh! liberty had nerved his heart,
> And every pulse beat true.
>
> "Now tell us," said the savage troop,
> "And life thy gain shall be!
> Who are the men that plotting, say—
> 'They must and will be free!'"

The first four stanzas contrast the hero and the crowd. Unlike the hero, who
stands in his "manly might" as the exemplary individual, this "throng" finds
strength through anonymity. The epithets thrown at the crowd—"savage,"
"base," "coward," and "murderous"—reverse stereotypes commonly used to
discredit African Americans in general, and slave men in particular. By focusing readers' attention on this contrast, Harper reshapes the slave as an ideal
American male, a strong revolutionary hero who defies a mob for his honor and
his comrades.

Despite this active depiction, the hero is about to be tortured, and we know
in advance that he will die. The spectacle of torture has the potential to render
him a silent, passive victim and to reinforce the power of the mob. Yet Harper
highlights and arrests this possibility when the crowd, hoping to beat a confession out of the hero, asks him to reveal the names of his comrades. As Elaine

Scarry indicates, the motive generally given for torture is interrogation that leads to confession, yet "what masquerades as the motive for torture is a fiction." The torturer really yearns for his victim's abdication of self. She continues: "In compelling confession, the torturers compel the prisoner to record and objectify the fact that intense pain is world-destroying. It is for this reason that while the content of the prisoner's answer is only sometimes important to the regime, the form of the answer, the fact of his answering, is always crucial."[24] When the hero is asked to reveal his comrades' plans, then, the torturer really wants him not only to renounce his solidarity with his fellow slaves, but also to announce his annihilation.

Yet by relying on a public attempt to torture truth out of the slave, the slave owners invite the subversive potential of the spectacle, a possibility that Harper manipulates. As Foucault indicates, public execution allowed for "momentary saturnalia, when nothing remained to prohibit or punish. Under the protection of imminent death, the criminal could say everything and the crowd cheered." The identification between the spectators and the "criminal" led to the popularity of what Foucault names the genre of the "last words of a condemned man," which transformed a criminal into a hero. Harper seeks this transformation through her poem, as her readers—witnessing the spectacle solely via her text—are asked to consider the "criminal" slave a hero by admiring his manipulation of the spectacle of his torture. After the crowd asks the hero to reveal the "truth," he responds with his only dialogue in the poem:

> I know the men who would be free;
> They are the heroes of your land;
> But death and torture I defy,
> Ere I betray that band.
>
> "And what! oh, what is life to me,
> Beneath your base control?
> Nay! do your worst. Ye have no chains
> To bind my free-born soul.

The hero's "last words" defy the crowd and the law, and the challenge is one that readers may find appealing, especially, as Foucault notes, "if the conviction was regarded as unjust,"[25] if they too sense a schism between purported reform in the justice system and slave law. In his short speech, the hero, through Harper, accomplishes several things. First, he lets the torturers know that he has the "truth" they desire, but will not reveal it; he intends to control the discourse of torture. Second, he rewrites the meaning of those who are conspiring, calling them the "heroes of your land." In an argument resembling Child's, Harper exposes slave law as linked inextricably to Old-World tyranny and juxtaposes it to an American admiration for personal liberty, a sensibility that she suggests her readers and the tortured slave share. Third, the hero exposes the power of the torturer as paradoxically both absolute and limited. All they can take, he tells them, is his life. Like Linda Brent in Jacobs's *Incidents*, the hero in Harper's poems insists on a disembodied identity that cannot be enslaved or killed.

Significantly, these are the only words the hero speaks in the poem; we do not hear him once the torture begins. In the final two stanzas of the poem Harper moves quickly from a state of embodiment to the disembodied soul, to the reunification of the body and soul in the afterlife:

> Like storms of wrath, of hate and pain,
> The blows rained thick and fast;
> But the monarch soul kept true
> Till the gates of life were past.

> And the martyr spirit fled
> To the throne of God on high,
> And showed his gaping wounds
> Before the unslumbering eye.

By moving readily from "blows" raining "thick and fast" on the body to the monarch soul, Harper avoids the part of torture that Scarry describes, the moment when the body is so broken that the person has no heroic (or even linguistic) capability. One of the reasons Scarry cautions against mistaking interrogation for the goal of torture is that it inverts moral responsibility, shifting the burden to the victim, who is given the almost impossible charge not to "betray" himself despite the application of intense world-destroying pain.[26] Harper's refusal to depict the torture in detail allows the reader to envision the slave dying before such a moment of so-called betrayal; he remains heroic. It also enables her to circumvent the "allure of bondage" that chapter 2 indicates could be associated with a prolonged torture scene.

The poem's final two stanzas perform several important feats. As noted previously, the spectacle of torture is supposed to display the absolute power of the sovereign. However, here the victim is shown to have a "monarch soul" and therefore to be his own ruler. Moreover, as the hero/monarch is followed by the poet to "the throne of God on high," we are made to understand that he will now be heard in a superior court of justice. Significantly, Harper depicts death as, ultimately, an embodied state. In this court, Harper implies, the "gaping wounds" of torture will be read correctly. They will evidence not only the hero's suffering and the crowd's sins, but also the hero's physical and moral courage. His wounds link him with Christ, who was also tortured in a public spectacle to reveal the power of the earthly sovereign. As he hung dead on the cross, a soldier pierced his side. Once Christ was resurrected, the apostle Thomas refused to believe in the miracle "[u]nless I see the mark of the nails in his hands, and put my finger in the mark of the nails, and my hand in his side."[27] Like Christ, Harper implies, the Tennessee hero will reveal his wounds to show the severity of his suffering, the strength of his character, the immortality of his soul, and the eventual reunification of the body with the soul in a more just court.

Through this allusion to Christ, Harper evokes one of the most spectated fictional bodies in her day, that of the martyred Tom in *Uncle Tom's Cabin*. Stowe's best-selling antislavery work was serialized in 1851, just six years before Harper published "The Tennessee Hero." Like Harper's hero, Stowe's Tom dies because he refuses to betray information about fellow slaves' plot to be free, and like the hero's, Tom's death is compared to the torture of Christ. To question whether an author can transform the tortured victim into an active agent by alluding to Christ is to repeat the same unresolved debate about the radical potential of Uncle Tom. For some, this association evokes victimization and colonization.[28] For writers like Harper (who was clearly influenced by Stowe),[29] Christianity is a powerful political force, and a comparison to Christ was the most radical analogy possible. The tortured body, in both Harper's and Stowe's text, testifies to the sovereignty of the "victim," not to the power of earthly punishment.

A Slave to Desire: Discipline and Race

In the poems highlighted above, Harper turns the potentially passive bodies of slaves into sites of symbolic triumph, in part by reversing the dynamics of spectatorship and victimization. However, if one considers these poems in the context of the book they appear in, it becomes evident that Harper is not only deflecting the reader's gaze away from slaves' bodies, but also directing her audience to look at the bodies she considers degraded. When we compare Harper's antislavery poems with her temperance writing, Harper's poetic strategy can also be understood as a political strategy through which she regulates figuratively the body politic and reverses common stereotypes about African Americans. Peterson argues that Harper's "aesthetics of restraint" derives in part from her Unitarian background. Instead of encouraging "the free flow of emotions," Unitarians believed that "individual 'character' must be attended to in order to create moral beings whose duty it would be to work for social cohesion in a disordered world."[30] Just as Harper's poetics channels her audience's emotions into a site from which they can reason political and social solutions to their era's problems, so too does her prose fiction attempt to convince her audience that the regulation of their emotions, and particularly their desires, is the best path toward freedom. As the narrator at the end of Harper's short story "The Two Offers" (1859) states, "true happiness consists not so much in the fruition of our wishes as in the *regulation of desires*" (emphasis mine).[31] For this reason, the bodies of those who cannot control their appetites tend to garner Harper's most negative representations in her poetry and prose.

Several of Harper's antebellum poems reveal the strategy she develops more extensively in her serialized temperance novel *Sowing and Reaping* (1876–1877). In these poems Harper not only deflects her readers' gaze from slaves' bodies, but also directs readers to consider either their own intemperate body or the bodies of deracialized and/or Caucasian characters as corporeally weak and possibly ungovernable. In effect, she uses the same strategy that Walt Whitman employs in "I Sing the Body Electric," asking readers to reconsider the true location of corporeal corruption in nineteenth-century America (see chapter 6). For example, "The Drunkard's Child" (1854) focuses on the death of a boy whose last wish is the redemption of his "drunkard" father. As in the case of "The Two Offers" and *Sowing and Reaping*, the race of the family is not specified. However, she intimates that they are either white or very light-skinned by describing the child's "pale and fair" appearance, his "marble brow," and "golden curls." Although we do not learn much about the boy's corporeality, we are told a great deal about his father, who returns home to watch his son die. He has a "dim and bloodshot eye," a "slow and staggering tread," a "vague, unmeaning stare," and a "bloated face," scathed by "guilt, remorse, and shame." Indeed, the father's body is one of the few bodies in *Poems on Miscellaneous Subjects* to be described with so much negative specificity. Likewise, in "Lessons of the Street" (1858), the speaker of the poem surveys the various faces she meets in the street. She first encounters a beggar and immediately warns readers not to judge him by his body: "Neath that wrecked and shattered body / Doth a human soul reside." If we are not to judge the beggar corporeally, the speaker does let us know whom we can assess based on physical appearance. Her only negative comments are about those who have sacrificed their morality for material possessions. By juxtaposing the seemingly ugly face of the beggar with the depraved faces of those who have succumbed to their appetites, Harper once again indicates that the most degraded are those who have the comfort and ability to strive for moral behavior, but trade it for fulfilling material or sensual needs.

"Lessons of the Street" was not published in Harper's antebellum volumes of poetry. However, "The Revel," a temperance poem that specifies no race, and "The Drunkard's Child" appear in both antebellum editions of *Poems on Miscellaneous Subjects*. The inclusion of temperance poems in a work containing antislavery material is not exceptional. The two movements, as I suggest below, were often related in the African American community in particular, and in antebellum American culture in general. Yet we can read these poems as connected not only through Harper's involvement with these related groups, but also as exhibiting an overall structure that follows her strategy of corporeal representation. Foster, drawing on the work of Dickson D. Bruce Jr., suggests that we read Harper's Reconstruction poetry in light of the fact that African American poets often organized their volumes with a specific structure to appeal to a wide readership. If we apply Foster's argument that "one must consider the effect of the entire volume, the order of its poems and its dominant tone, as well as the themes and subjects of the individual poems"[32] to the antebellum work *Poems on Miscellaneous Subjects*, we surmise that Harper may have desired to alter radically the politics of the body that dominated her age. It is also possible to read the chronological "structure" of Harper's three previously "lost" postbellum novels (*Minnie's Sacrifice* [1869], *Sowing and Reaping* [1876–77], and *Trial and Triumph* [1888–1889]) as replicating and extending the structure of Harper's antebellum volumes of poetry. The first and third novels Harper wrote designate race as an important determinant in characters' lives and chronologically envelop a "deracialized" novel concentrating primarily on temperance. Instead of reading Harper's use of a deracialized discourse as releasing her "from the burden of race" and freeing her to focus on marriage and temperance,[33] we could interpret *Sowing and Reaping* (and the earlier antebellum temperance poems) as implicitly addressing the issues of race, corporeality, and governance that her other work explicitly confronts. The structure of her poems and the chronological order of her novels urge us to read these works in relation to one another.

As Foster notes in her introduction to the rediscovered novels, Harper serialized her work in the *Christian Recorder*, the journal of the African Methodist
Episcopal Church. Foster emphasizes that consideration of the place of publication "requires us to revise our notions that early African American publications were directed to white readers and that the black readership was too
small and too dependent to count for much." Therefore, she argues, "we can no
longer subscribe to the common conclusion" that African American writers'
"implied or actual audiences were white or that their works should be read as
attempts . . . to imitate the literary productions of Euro-Americans."[34] Indeed,
when we consider that what is thought to be the first African American journal
of its type, the *Anglo-African*, declared that all articles "not otherwise designated" were "the products of the pens of colored men and women,"[35] then we
might assume that Harper's characters are also African American unless otherwise specified. Yet one must question why Harper chose to publish three novels, *only one of which elides racial designations*, in the same press. Writing to
the same audience, Harper left out race in her temperance novel while making
it of central importance in the other two works. The racially ambivalent characters in *Sowing and Reaping* create several reading scenarios: the characters
could be considered deracialized; some or all of the characters could be understood as white; and some or all of the characters could be assumed to be African
American. By leaving all of these possibilities open and encouraging readers to
tease out the various political/racial implications of the text, Harper is able to
present several related arguments about corporeality and self-governance
through her strategy of racial indeterminacy.

Tate argues that when confronted with racially ambivalent characters in
works written by African American authors, scholars have "generally presumed that such characters are white," thereby erasing the "political statement of racelessness." What, we might then ask, would Harper gain politically
by erasing race? One thing she might achieve is the ability to shift doubt about
self-governance away from race and onto individual character. By creating
racially ambivalent characters in *Sowing and Reaping*, Harper opens up the
debate as to which bodies are ungovernable and who is capable of self-rule in
the Reconstruction era. As Tate argues about other African American women
writers, Harper may want to "eliminate race as the absolute determinant for
qualifying personal esteem, access to virtuosity, and social and financial success."[36] In this sense, creating racially ambivalent characters allows her to
destabilize beliefs that race is the determining factor in defining an individual's
identity.

This strategy continues in Harper's *Minnie's Sacrifice* (1869). In this novel, two characters who look white, but are in fact the children of light-skinned slaves and white slaveholders, believe themselves to be white in their formative years. When they discover their heritage, they struggle with the fact that they will be associated with a race that is "hated and despised for what" it cannot help,[37] but decide they have to identify themselves with their "mother's race" (MST, 60). Eventually they marry and dedicate their lives to the service of what the female protagonist, Minnie, now calls "our" race (MST, 67). The plot of *Minnie's Sacrifice* immerses the reader in questions about what constitutes true identity: is race something that is in the blood, in one's heritage, or is it something that one can decide to identify with? By concentrating on light-skinned characters who are categorized as African Americans only because they reside in a nation obsessed with making distinctions even when physical evidence does not support them, Harper implies that race is hardly a natural category of difference, but rather a constructed category that one has to chose to identify with given the politics of the time.

At the end of the novel, Harper provides an author's conclusion to the work. Referring, perhaps, to Lydia Maria Child's *Romance of the Republic* (1867), she laments that "some of the authors of the present day have been weaving their stories about white men marrying beautiful quadroon girls who, in so doing were lost to us socially." Harper, however, has "conceived of one of that same class" to whom she gave "a higher, holier, destiny; a life of lofty self-sacrifice and beautiful self-consecration, finished at the post of duty, and rounded off with the fiery crown of martyrdom, a circlet which ever changes into a diadem of glory" (MST, 91). Harper suggests that she has created Minnie to show how, given the historical moment her readers reside in, one is forced into a racial identity. As such, if one has any amount of African heritage in one's background, one should identify with that race. However, by using a character who looks white, Harper also suggests that the very "race" she asks people to identify with is a classification that does not hold up to scrutiny. The lesson for her African American readers seems to be the nobility of identifying with a race that needs assistance because of its oppression. The lesson for white readers, however, might be less clear and, perhaps, disturbing. Like Whitman—who asks in his 1855 "I Sing the Body Electric": "Who might you find you have come from yourself if you could trace back through the centuries?"—Harper prods readers to question the racial foundation on which they stand. Will their allegedly white bodies betray racial indeterminacy? Will the benefits that they accrue because of their whiteness suddenly be stripped away?

These same questions can be asked about *Sowing and Reaping*. The fact that Harper published in an African American journal, as Foster indicates, certainly suggests that we cannot assume her intended audience was white. Nonetheless, *Sowing and Reaping* hints that Harper might be playing with the possibility that some of the characters could be white. At times, the indications are minor and inconclusive. For example, in the beginning of the novel, two cousins, Jeanette Roland and Belle Gordon, discuss their future prospects. Belle, an advocate of temperance and a serious thinker, suggests to Jeanette that she needs to have a higher "idea of life." Jeanette responds that she prefers to "drift along the tide of circumstances." She continues by singing a song, the last two lines of which declare: "I'd never languish for wealth or for power / I'd never sigh to have slaves at my feet" (MST, 103). Although it is not outside the realm of possibility that an African American character would make this statement, it is more likely that a character who considered herself white would do so. Minor references like these are suggestive, but Harper's introduction of a couple that Belle helps lift out of the devastation caused by the husband's intemperance is even more provocative. This couple is not related to any of the other characters in the novel, and therefore their racial identity is not dependent on anyone else in the book. By calling these characters Mary and Joe Gough, Harper alludes to a famous ante- and postbellum white temperance speaker and author, John Bartholomew Gough. Gough's *Autobiography*, published in 1845, was one of the best-selling temperance narratives, going through thirty-one reprints between 1845 and 1853.[38] It seems likely that, given Gough's popularity and Harper's connection with the temperance movement, she would have known of his work. Why, then, does she name a character Joe Gough in her novel? Perhaps she wants to suggest to her readers that at least some of the characters are white. If we heed these hints, then we must ask what Harper gains by such a move.

One answer is that creating white intemperate characters allows her to reverse the concept of the uncontrollable African American body and propose—at least temporarily—that some white bodies are desperately in need of restraint and reform. Certainly Harper's familiarity with the black temperance movement would have provided her with the background for this type of rhetorical argument. As John W. Crowley argues, white temperance writers and speakers often drew analogies between the tyranny of the bottle and Britain's tyranny prior to the American Revolution. This trope served to "*elide* all reference to chattel slavery."[39] By contrast, Donald Yacovone demonstrates that by "the 1840s, temperance and abolitionism had become virtually synonymous" within African American reform movements.[40] Certainly, *Sowing and Reaping* is quite explicit about the connections between intemperance and enslavement, as Jeanette's song indicates. Belle, for example, alludes to the historical connection between the slave and rum trades, explaining why she refuses to attend the party of a man who made his fortunes by selling alcohol: "[T]here are two classes of people with whom I never wish to associate . . . and they are rum sellers and slave holders" (MST, 110). A character whom we meet just once says he feels like a slave to alcohol, and although it is too late to break his chains, he can nonetheless warn young men not to "make slaves and fools" of themselves (MST, 134). What distresses the narrator of *Sowing and Reaping* is that the characters who are intemperate are totally enslaved by their corporeal appetites. Repeatedly characters are said to be "misguided slaves of appetite" (MST, 165) who struggle "with the monster that had enslaved" them (MST, 172).

Among the many reasons for the strong association between black temperance groups and abolitionists was that temperance rhetoric provided African American authors with the necessary tools to reverse rhetorically the idea of a vulnerable, susceptible Negro body that needed to be controlled by excessive governmental and/or slaveholder restraint. When we consider Van Evrie's 1861 statement that "legislatures and individuals" in both the North and South were acting on the "foolish assumption" that "the negro is a *black*-white man . . . a creature like ourselves except in color" and therefore erroneously thrusting African Americans "from their normal condition" into "the condition of widely different beings," we understand how pervasive and powerful scientific definitions of innate difference were in defining the African American body as incapable of the rights or responsibilities of self-governance, characteristics linked inextricably to citizenship. To combat such harmful assumptions, leaders in the antislavery and temperance movements emphasized that people from all races should call upon an internal restraint, or what we could understand in Foucauldian terms as the eventual manifestation of a disciplinary society in the surveillance and regulation of self. Robert Levine argues that the idea of intemperance as a form of slavery "remained central both to antislavery and temperance discourse during the antebellum period, helping white and black abolitionists to develop a trenchant critique of slave owners as 'intoxicated' by, or 'enslaved' to, the unlimited power vouchsafed them by their culture." Levine notes that for "black temperance writers and abolitionists in particular, the image of the slave owner as a beast enslaved to appetite was an attractive one, as it allowed black writers to turn upside down the proslavery stereotype of blacks as brutes in need of restraint."[41] Yet why would Harper return to this antebellum trope in the postbellum period? Hazel V. Carby notes that whites' fear of uncontrollable African American bodies continued in the Reconstruction era. White southerners often defended their reluctance to extend voting rights to newly emancipated slaves by asserting that African Americans were naturally impulsive and easily duped.[42] As we know too well, the stereotype of the unruly African American body, especially the male body, was ultimately used to justify large-scale violence, particularly lynching.

Therefore a figure like Gough allows Harper to enact a corporeal reversal, destabilizing notions of race that were harmful to African Americans, while arguing that ultimately everyone could be redeemed through self-governance and self-control. If, for example, a reader considered the possibility that Belle and her relatives might be African American, then Gough's character becomes representative of the figure of an intemperate white man—a slave to his appetite—who is redeemed through the intervention of a temperate African American woman. It is not that the white man is incapable of redemption; both Harper's novel and Gough's *Autobiography* show that one can master oneself through self-restraint. However, Harper suggests that given his tendency toward disorder, Gough can hardly be called upon to rule others. Comparisons between representations of gender in *Sowing and Reaping* and Gough's *Auto-biography* suggest a similar strategy of reversal. Whereas Gough mentions his first wife's marriage and death only briefly (and is just as reticent about his second marriage),[43] Harper frames her account of Joe Gough by examining the influence of his intemperance on his wife, Mary. How, a reader wonders, can we expect Joe to govern his home, let alone the nation? By crafting Mary and Belle into figures of redemption, Harper once again suggests that the body often classified as incapable of participation in governance—in this case the female body of both races—is hardly less qualified than that of the male.

These examples demonstrate that one issue at stake in the rhetoric of slavery and temperance is the question of whose bodies are capable of the self-control and self-regulation necessary in a democracy. After the character I quoted above speaks at the bar, for example, another man responds that if he can't "govern" himself, then "more's the pity for you" (MST, 134). In a nation that was supposedly shifting from the antebellum realm of punishment to the internalization of societal values and control, the question of who could demonstrate self-control was, in part, the question of who would be entitled to full rights of citizenship. Therefore it is no accident that Belle defines self-control as a type of freedom: "Believing that the inner life developed the outer, she considered the poor, and strove to awaken within them a self-reliance, and self-control, feeling that one of the surest ways to render people helpless or dangerous is to crush out their self-respect and self-reliance" (MST, 124). To Belle, happiness and power comes through the regulation of one's desire. I will return to this idea below, but for now I point to it to indicate that by opening up the possibility that some characters were white males, Harper creates a space where the reader can question the white male's supposed natural right to govern others. She could, as Levine argues about black temperance rhetoric in the section I quote above, "turn upside down the proslavery stereotype of blacks as brutes in need of restraint."

As I have argued, Harper countered accusations of African American incapability of self-governance by suggesting that some white bodies were often in need of restraint. In this context, the first two possible readings of her racially indeterminate characters—that they are purposely deracialized or potentially white—make sense in terms of the corporeal politics of her era. Yet the third suggestion, that because Harper is writing for an African American press the characters can be presumed to be African American, is also plausible and reveals the multifaceted aspect of Harper's corporeal strategy of racial indeterminacy.[44] Belle's comments about the "poor" people she works with and the narrator's lesson at the end of "The Two Offers" demonstrate how Harper often delivers to her readers a message of self-control, or the idea that "true happiness" comes from the "regulation of our desires." If we assume that Harper's characters are African American, this may make us reconsider the meaning of physical restraint and discipline in the postbellum context. By drawing upon Foucault's terminology of a *disciplinary* society, we can understand how in Harper's fictional worlds self-discipline was not an extension of external coercive power, but a paradoxical path to freedom. Chapter 2 illustrates how Foucault's argument that the late-eighteenth and early-nineteenth centuries saw "the disappearance of the tortured, dismembered, amputated body" from the public's view does not apply to the antebellum South. Southern society depended upon what Child, Jacobs, and others saw as an increase in the spectacle of torture and surveillance to maintain power over the enslaved. It should be no surprise, then, that given the preponderance of punishment in antebellum slave society, the postbellum period marked an era of increasing calls to discipline. As Foucault notes about discipline in general:

These methods, which made possible the meticulous control of the operations of the body, which assured the constant subjection of its forces and imposed upon them a relation of docility-utility, might be called "disciplines." Many disciplinary methods had long been in existence—in monasteries, armies, workshops. But in the course of the seventeenth and eighteenth centuries the disciplines became general formulas of domination. They were different from slavery because they were not based on a relation of appropriation of bodies; indeed, the elegance of the discipline lay in the fact that it could dispense with this costly and violent relation by obtaining effects of utility at least as great.[45]

To Foucault, the shift from punishment to discipline represents another form of coercion, as the "elegant" disciplines obtain an effect of utility and force production from docile bodies. A possible implication of Foucault's argument is that as "general formulas of domination" become more sophisticated and pervasive, they could shift from external methods of surveillance and regulation to internal. We could, for example, extend Foucault's notion of discipline to include temperance movements and efforts at uplift through self-regulation of seemingly unproductive desires. However, doing so, we come to understand the vast difference between being disciplined or surveyed by an exterior force and surveying oneself. Having survived a period in which *punishment* and *surveillance* by an exterior power (the slaveholder, the slave state, the Fugitive Slave Law, the kidnapper) was a reality for many people embodied as African American, the ability to claim control of oneself (to repress one's desires and channel one's emotions for a greater cause) can be viewed as liberational, however odd that liberation might seem to a reader today.[46] Peterson also makes this point in relation to Harper's postbellum work, arguing succinctly that "[t]his disciplinary ideology reinforced African American antebellum concepts of self-control as a strategy of resistance and survival for both slave and free black populations."[47]

Sowing and Reaping and *Trial and Triumph* represent self-discipline as a positive alternative to punishment and external surveillance. For example, when Jeanette and her fiancé, Charles, discuss why Charles was previously rejected by Belle (because of his intemperance), Jeanette comments that Charles might be better off under Belle's "discipline" (MST, 114). Charles later disparagingly relates Belle's insistence upon self-regulation to his father's methods of correction, which he did not "enjoy" (MST, 116). Yet Harper's novel implies that the shift from patriarchal "correction" to maternal/feminine "discipline" is positive and substantially different. Often the "sainted mother" (MST, 119) appears as a figure capable of urging characters to self-control and temperate behavior even after her death. *Sowing and Reaping* is a novel centered around an education in self-discipline, sometimes through the help of a woman or temperance group, and sometimes on one's own. The successful character is one who subordinates desire (whether it be the desire to drink or, in Belle's case, her desire for an intemperate man) in order to be a more productive person in his or her community.

Likewise, *Trial and Triumph* addresses the relationship between discipline and punishment. Among other interests, the novel is concerned with educating African American mothers "for the home" (MST, 183), and one of its implicit goals is to shift mothers from using corporeal punishment toward discipline. It opens with the character of Annette, a young girl who, reminiscent of Stowe's Topsy, "specs" she does bad things "for the devil" (MST, 183). Indeed, the novel suggests that she may have inherited her impulsiveness from her mother, a woman whose lack of self-control manifests itself in her decision to enter into a sexual liaison with a man to whom she is not yet married. A typical fallen woman, she dies shortly after childbirth, leaving Annette's grandmother to struggle with Annette's mischievous nature. The grandmother, as a result, has "scolded and scolded" until her "tongue is tired," and "whipping don't seem to do her a bit of good" (MST, 180). Although the novel represents the grandmother in a somewhat positive light, she is juxtaposed to the kind neighbor, Mrs. Lasette, whose method of instruction through teaching and example helps Annette internalize the proper ways to behave in society, without interfering with her creative need for expression. The lesson, then, seems clear: Mrs. Lasette's method of discipline is preferable to the grandmother's use of "whipping," or punishment.

The capstone of Annette's education in self-regulation comes with the conflict presented by her love for Clarence, a man who pursues her not for her physical beauty (which, the novel says, she does not have much of) but for her intelligence and companionship. Shortly before they are to be married, Clarence's first wife (whose impulsive nature made her disgrace and desert him) suddenly reappears, absolving Clarence of responsibility and telling him that he is free to "apply for a divorce" on "the plea of willful desertion" (MST, 279). When Clarence asks Annette if she would blame him if he sought a divorce, she says she would and that she must give him up. "This, Clarence," she tells him, "is the saddest trial of my life. . . . But, Clarence, the great end of life is not the attainment of happiness but the performance of duty and the development of character. The great question is not what is pleasant but what is right" (MST, 280). Desire must be subordinated to duty. When Annette and Clarence are reunited after Clarence's first wife dies, they join in an effort to uplift and help others. Thus, they are "strengthened by duty, purified by that faith which works by love, and fitted for life's highest and holiest truths" (MST, 285). As Tate notes, African American women writers in the late-nineteenth century often represented love "not characterized as impassioned pronouncements of dedication to their mutual happiness; to the contrary, their love is buttressed against 'the threshold of a new era and labor' for the advancement of black people."[48] Their subordination of personal love to community uplift points again to Harper's overall pattern of representing passion as a force that needs to be subjected to an individual's control in order to alter radically the politics of the time. In Harper's works, through the disciplining figures of temperance groups, mothers, and concerned neighbors, free people of color assert their freedom by learning to regulate desire.

I conclude this chapter with a discussion of Harper in relation to self-discipline to suggest the historical and geographical specificity of corporeal strategies. Although my use of Foucault throughout this study indicates the helpfulness of his work when one investigates the dynamics of power, corporeality, and knowledge, his theory does not always apply to specific situations, especially in relation to race and slavery in the United States. As Lora Romero notes, "Foucault's assertion that the West's commitment to managing the life of its own population also entails a commitment to massive destruction of populations designated as 'other' is parenthetical" to *The History of Sexuality*. Foucault does not devote much space to analyzing the racial implications of corporeal dynamics. Because Foucault accentuates the obsession of the "ruling classes" with its own progeniture, he tends to emphasize the internalization of surveillance as a coercive power that the ruling classes "first tried" on themselves.[49] However, in ante- and postbellum America, the power of surveillance was rigorously deployed on African Americans, as was corporeal punishment. This complicates Foucault's narrative of modernization and also asks us to rethink New Historical Criticism that draws upon Foucault and conflates punishment and discipline without differentiating enough between the two forms of power. All too often, this type of critical work, as Romero argues, replicates nineteenth-century narratives that presuppose "normalization" as "women's work."[50]

In effect, such New Historical work positions women as conservative adherents and advocates of a coercive regime of discipline and surveillance. If Harper's call for uplift is common in the African American community, it also typifies much of women's rhetoric in the nineteenth century. Many women appropriated the conception of themselves as innately passionless and less corrupt than men to assert some power over the "unruly" bodies of those who would presume to govern them.[51] Although it is tempting to interpret their rhetoric as the internalization of a coercive regime of discipline, this type of reading tends to elide the liberational aspects of these women's corporeal strategies, their appropriation of the discourse of discipline for political power. It also tends to overlook the subtle shifts that some women may have made when deploying a rhetoric of discipline. For example, Peterson rightly argues that Harper adapted "middle-brow notions of writing as a tutelary activity concerned with the welfare of the domestic household." Although Harper "remained committed to the values of discipline, her model was no longer that in which authority figures (often female) exercise discipline—whether through coercion or through love—over their charges. Instead, these latter must learn to discipline themselves."[52] It is fitting, then, to consider Ralph Waldo Emerson's fear of becoming a "parlor soldier" in relation to Harper's insistence that the self be regulated for the communal/national good, as well as to Child's insistence that the law must regulate insane or exploitative individuals. Likewise, it is fitting to consider Emerson's move toward an increasingly racialized rhetoric in the 1850s in relation to Harper's politically motivated deployment of racial indeterminancy in the same period. This comparison demonstrates the vastly different strategies of these writers, strategies that came, in part, from their embodied experiences. One person's liberation may be another's path to subjugation; likewise, one person's constraining discipline may be someone else's paradoxical freedom.

4

SAXONS AND SLAVERY

Corporeal Challenges to Ralph Waldo Emerson's

Republic of the Spirit

That is morning, to cease for a bright hour to be a prisoner of this sickly body, and to become as large as nature.—Ralph Waldo Emerson, "Literary Ethics"

In the spring of 1832, the twenty-eight-year-old Ralph Waldo Emerson took his daily walk to visit the grave of his first wife, Ellen. Known for her beauty and intelligence, she had died more than a year earlier after a prolonged case of tuberculosis. Her death devastated Emerson. That day he went beyond communing "with the spirit of the departed Ellen: he opened the coffin." The gesture, one of Emerson's recent biographers believes, "was essential Emerson. He had to see for himself." Later, in 1857, after he had remarried, fathered a family, and established a considerable professional reputation, Emerson would repeat this act for his first son, Waldo, whose death at the age of five had left him, once again, deeply distraught. Fifteen years after Waldo's death, when the coffin of his son was moved, Emerson had it opened to gaze upon the remains of his boy. As Robert D. Richardson notes, "[v]irtually all of Emerson's creative life was lived in the first twenty-five years between those glimpses not simply of death but of *his* dead."[1]

Although dramatic, these episodes are not atypical for Emerson, whose life was interrupted by moments of suffering, periods when his body or the bodies of those he loved seemed to frustrate the soul's potential.[2] When he was a student and early in his career, Emerson was often plagued by physical ailments that blocked his ability to work. As David Leverenz notes, "Emerson's body continually betrayed him, with eye diseases, diarrhea, pain, and simple awkwardness" and, as a result, "Emerson lumped his body together with everything else that wasn't his mind. It was his 'NOT ME.' His body took him sprawling into the world, and the world continuously made him feel inadequate, foolish, vulnerable, and open to attack."[3] No wonder, then, that when Emerson's brother Charles died in 1836, Emerson and Charles's fiancé, Elizabeth Hoar, struggled to separate "the best of Charles—what he stood for, the meaning of his life—from the actual physical person."[4] The body's mortality and susceptibility were problematic to Emerson on a personal level, a fact that probably influenced his tendency to divorce corporeality from identity, especially in *Nature* and his early essays.[5] Although Emerson certainly experienced corporeal pleasure as well as pain, he often distrusted corporeality as a site of identity or knowledge and at times tried to transcend theoretically the embodied state. It seems understandable, for example, that after having peered at the rotting remains of the wife he had loved sensually and passionately, Emerson could more quickly endorse a philosophy in *Nature* that labeled the body "Not Me."[6]

The first section of this chapter argues that Emerson's philosophical insistence on transcendence in his early essays necessitated a subordination of corporeality to spirituality and therefore was often aligned with an implicit or explicit assumption of the basic unity of humankind, what we could call a republic of the spirit. When this assumption is juxtaposed to the divisive science of race that came to fruition in the 1830s and 1840s, it has radical political implications. However, Emerson's romantic philosophy is not without contradictions. The "metaphysical selfhood" that Emerson proposes in his essays written during the 1840s and 1850s relies upon a dynamic that often traps women and "other" races in an embodied identity. As the second section of this chapter argues, Emerson was reluctant to apply his radical theory of identity to women, often portraying them as incapable of surmounting their embodied status. In the chapter's final section, I argue that this reluctance may stem from Emerson's anxiety over the position of Anglo-Saxon men in antebellum America. When we juxtapose Emerson's travel book *English Traits* (1856) with his antislavery lectures, we see how Emerson's definition of national identity endorses stereotypical conceptions of Anglo-Saxon masculinity and derives, in part, from his fear of becoming a "parlor soldier." In effect, his call for a new manhood was a racialized call for a Saxon brotherhood, a move that aligns him with the dominant culture's construction of a white national identity in the 1850s.

The past several years of Emersonian scholarship evidence an increased interest in Emerson's views on race and reform, demonstrated by the republication of Emerson's antislavery lectures by Len Gougeon and Joel Myerson. Gougeon, in particular, has forcefully reevaluated Emerson's relationship to the antislavery movement and his views on race in *Virtue's Hero*, effectively demonstrating that Emerson's antislavery efforts were more consistent and pronounced than is usually assumed. Gougeon reinitiates debates over the nature of Emerson's relationship to reform movements, asking us to reconsider the image of Emerson as a man who remained aloof from reform for most of his career, an image David S. Reynolds reinforces in *Beneath the American Renaissance*. In that work, Reynolds argues that Emerson and other "major" writers of the mid-nineteenth-century "carefully took note of their age's variegated reforms, experimented regularly with reform rhetoric and imagery, but above all learned to give literary expression to the vibrant reform impulse while they escaped *the trap of prolonged dedication to individual reforms*" (emphasis mine). Differing from the view proposed by Reynolds, Gougeon and others argue that a shift occurs in Emerson's theory and practice in the 1840s. Gougeon suggests that between 1839 and 1844, Emerson believed in the "basic inferiority of the Negro," a belief that was especially problematical to Emerson because of his commitment to self-reliance.[7] However, Gougeon interprets 1844 as a turning point for Emerson, marking his increased commitment to abolition and (thereafter) consistent public denial of African American inferiority. Gougeon notes that in his 1844 address celebrating Emancipation in the British West Indies, Emerson "attacked those who insisted upon Negro inferiority as an excuse for slavery," a belief Gougeon claims Emerson maintained publicly thereafter even if his journals "reveal on occasion, especially in the early and mid-1850s, some doubt about the Negro's equality and ability to compete successfully in the struggle for survival."[8] Likewise, David M. Robinson argues that in the late 1840s and 1850s, Emerson—motivated in part by the "fading of visionary ecstasy as a reliable religious foundation"—responded to his philosophical crisis "with an emphasis on ethical action and social criticism."[9]

The arguments suggesting an intensification of Emerson's reform activities, especially in relation to antislavery endeavors, are convincing. However, the question of whether Emerson's philosophical writings take on an increased ethical or political purpose in his later years is open to further consideration, and this chapter argues that both his early and later writings should be read as political when placed in a dialectical relationship with the science of race. In part we understand all of Emerson's work as potentially political, because his philosophy was shaped in response to the material conditions of his time. For example, Mary Kupeic Cayton demonstrates how Emerson's early work, based on a search for a natural law governing human behavior, was a means by which the young Emerson could understand, explain, and potentially transform "the raucous social order in which he lived." I do not want to elide the differences between theory and practice, but we can, as Eduardo Cadava argues, understand Emerson's work as demonstrating his belief that social change "can only happen with the transformation of the language within which and with which we encounter the world and everything in it. It can only occur, that is, through a task of thinking that is also a labor of reading and writing."[10] Indeed, when we consider the public nature of Emerson's essays and the large audiences he addressed on the lyceum circuit, we recognize the communal and ethical implications of his philosophy. This is to suggest, then, that rather than viewing the early Emerson as somehow removed from ethical concerns, we can understand that all of Emerson's essays engage the politics of his time, even if his commitment to reform activity came later in his life. Moreover, I am not convinced that the early Emerson was less radical in relation to questions of racial equality than the later Emerson. Unlike John Carlos Rowe, who views Emerson's early transcendental writings as fundamentally at "odds with the social reforms regarding slavery and women's rights," resulting in an "intellectual schizophrenia" and revealing the limitations of Emerson's transcendent philosophy, I argue that the implications of Emerson's early representations of corporeality can be viewed as more radical politically, due to their premise of humankind's spiritual equality, than his later antislavery writings, which often juxtapose calls for emancipation with language that constructs a racialized national identity privileging whiteness.

To understand fully Emerson's ability to embrace abolition in the 1840s and to remain committed to it throughout the remainder of the antebellum era, one must, as I state above, read his antislavery lectures in relation to *English Traits*, which he contemplated after his 1847–48 trip to England. As Philip L. Nicoloff argues, there is "good cause" to view Emerson's second trip to England as a "significant milestone in his intellectual career," especially as it provided a "stimulus to his interest in modern science" and concerns over race.[11] By formulating a theory of history that categorized the English as a "race" and Americans as an extension of that "race," Emerson eased many people's fear that emancipation would alter radically the composite of the American people. Therefore, despite Gougeon's extensive exploration of Emerson's antislavery activities, I argue that Emerson's *public* support of African Americans was erratic after 1844, especially if one reads his antislavery lectures in relation to the lectures he was writing and delivering in preparation for *English Traits* and those he delivered during the Civil War. Perhaps due to the fear initiated by the reality of emancipation, perhaps due to Emerson's attraction toward fatalism and conservatism later in his life,[12] or perhaps due to the increased prevalence of racial science in the antebellum era, Emerson's representations of race become increasingly dominated by the idea of difference.

Before examining Emerson's representation of gender, race, and reform, I want to address the question of his rhetoric in relation to his representation of corporeality. Emerson's work must be read in the spirit of the dialectical and metaphorical method he usually employed. Cadava argues that there "can be no reading of [Emerson's] language that does not trace the movement of his figures and tropes as they become something else" and notes that Emerson warns readers "against a literalism that refuses to recognize the figural and metaphoric elements of all language." Lawrence Buell likewise reminds us that Emerson's work "will not reveal its depths to those who ask no more of it than 'What does it say?' and 'What are the rhetorical strategies?' One must further inquire, 'What is the exact degree of commitment? How much does the style work for and against it? How much is the rhetoric an end in itself?'"[13] Emerson often debates a concept within his essays, taking several contradictory possibilities into consideration simultaneously and refusing to commit himself to any one position. This method, which is both a reaction against and a continuation of the Unitarian sermons that influenced Emerson early in his life,[14] creates the effect of an ever shifting Emersonian persona, of someone who is turning ideas over in his mind and inviting readers into his serious play. For every assertion that one makes about Emerson's beliefs, a counterassertion can be made, usually from the same text or from another text in the same volume or series of lectures. In effect, Emerson's essays construct a dialectic that to the modern reader may invite deconstruction. Therefore, when it comes to outlining a general shift from what I am identifying as Emerson's early belief in transcendence (a belief coupled with the possibility of unity and similarity of the races) to an acceptance, even promotion, of racial difference, I am aware that parts of Emerson's later essays could be interpreted as evidencing a faith in transcendence and that sections of his early essays likewise suggest his willingness to construct racial difference, which began at an earlier stage in his career. Nonetheless, when his essays are considered collectively, one can argue that a shift occurs in Emerson's emphasis in relation to corporeality in the late 1840s and early 1850s. Also, it is important to keep in mind that although

Emerson's method may invite deconstruction, included in the dialectic is a movement to synthesis that Emerson took very seriously. Stephen E. Whicher correctly suggests that when we work with Emerson, "we are dealing with a mind that makes any assertion of belief against the felt pull of its lurking opposite, the two forming together a total *truth of experience* larger than the opposing *truths of statement* of which it is composed. Such a mind of course has 'double vision,' but it has unity, too."[15] Therefore, if we end our analysis by pointing to the contradictions inherent in his work, we miss the struggle for synthesis in which his writing prompts readers to engage.

Yet, in what may at first seem a contradictory assertion, even as we understand Emerson's essays as creating a dialectic that *can* result in the favoring of one position and is, in fact, designed to lead Emerson and his readers to synthesis, it is also fair to suggest that his method destabilizes any given conclusion, especially in relation to race. This contradictory nature of Emerson's essays is one of the points I am trying to emphasize rather than elide. In part, I argue that the instability present in Emerson's 1840s writings on race, particularly his "Address on Emancipation" (1844), is attributable not only to his dialectical method of writing but also to the ambivalence Emerson felt as he struggled with the subject. The fact that we can read Emerson neither as unambivalently committed to racial equality nor as totally accepting of scientific essentialism keeps the question of racial difference in constant flux in his essays and therefore undermines calls to equality. Even if his assertions of racial difference are not as certain as the scientists', even if they don't reveal what he calls the "impudent knowingness" of physicians and phrenologists, they undercut the vision of a postemancipation multiracial democracy. Additionally, much like Thomas Jefferson's admission of "a suspicion only, that the blacks, whether originally a distinct race, or made distinct by time and circumstances, are inferior to the whites in the endowments both of body and mind,"[16] Emerson's later deployment of rhetorical stasis (especially in *English Traits*) can be understood less as a reflection of his ambivalence and more in terms of a genteel mask, one that displays a racial humility more pronounced than he may feel.

When discussing Emerson's exploration of skepticism later in his life, particularly in "Experience," Whicher argues, we should not read statements that appear at odds with Emerson's philosophy as merely speculative writing that does not "touch him personally." Often Emerson would "put his doubts of the scholar's faith into the mouth of the skeptic. By thus creating a fictitious *alter ego* to whom to attribute his more dangerous thoughts, Emerson could relieve himself of responsibility for them and yet at the same time give them expression."[17] Likewise, I would suggest, when reading Emerson's essays on race and slavery from the late 1850s and early 1860s, we cannot assume that he asserts doubts about the equality of African Americans and faith in the English American race solely to present an antithesis to his thesis. By asserting that Negroes *might* be inferior or *might* be equal, while at the same time declaring that the English American embodies civilization's future, Emerson leaves very little room for his audience to deduce a fundamental equality between the races. Indeed, as Emerson contemplates the applicability of his earlier philosophic assertions to the political question of abolition, race becomes increasingly associated with the possible limitations of his earlier faith in individualism. Cornell West notes that "Emerson's slow acknowledgment that there are immutable constraints on the human powers of individuals resulted primarily from his conclusions regarding the relation of persons to their racial origins and endowments." Therefore, race is a substantial trope in Emerson's discourse, one that "signifies the circumstantial, the conditioned, the fateful—that which limits the will of individuals, even exceptional ones."[18] Understanding Emerson's increasingly fatalistic views about race, then, is essential to exploring his call for emancipation and his move toward skepticism later in life.

The Republic of the Spirit

As West indicates, Emerson's concept of identity and individuality shifts throughout his lifetime, and he becomes increasingly willing to envision race as circumscribing a person's potential, as an indication of the limitations placed on individualism and free will. I have already suggested that Emerson's early essays tend to de-emphasize the importance of corporeality in order to emphasize Emerson's optimist faith in individualism and his philosophical premise of transcendence. Although his corporeal experiences may have influenced his philosophy, his emphasis on transcendence over corporeal fate early in his career also results from his vast, if not entirely systematic, contemplation of contemporary and classical philosophy. Two of the concepts that Emerson draws upon should be briefly reviewed. The first, that of correspondence, reflects the influence of Emanuel Swedenborg on Emerson's early thought and is fundamental to Emerson's epistemology. Buell defines this as the "idea of a metaphysical correspondence between nature and spirit," an idea that assumes humans "and the physical universe . . . are parallel creations of the same divine spirit" and, therefore, the "universe is a vast network of symbols" that the poet should "study, master, and articulate." Swedenborg's description of the concept indicates the secondary status of corporeality: "If we choose to express any natural truth in physical and definite vocal terms, and to convert these terms only into the corresponding and spiritual terms, we shall by this means elicit a spiritual truth, or theological dogma, *in place of* the physical truth or precept" (emphasis mine).[19] By suggesting that spiritual truths will take the *place of* physical truths, Swedenborg indicates a hierarchy of one over the other, as does Emerson in his early works. For example, in the second section of *Nature*, "Language," Emerson notes the correlation between the material and spiritual spheres, arguing that there is a "radical correspondence between visible things and human thoughts." Although the wording "radical correspondence" could imply an equality between the spheres, he gives precedence to the spiritual world over natural facts by arguing, like Swedenborg, that natural facts *symbolize* spiritual ones. Therefore, "[t]he world is emblematic" and "[p]arts of speech are metaphors because the whole of nature is a metaphor of the human mind."[20] Typical of Emerson, this passage assumes that the material world (including corporeality) is not an end in itself, but rather a symbol of spiritual truths. As Packer notes, the eagerness with which Emerson greeted the doctrine of correspondence must be placed in relation to the Lockean-Unitarian tradition in which he was raised and to the "hunger for raw significance" that such a tradition created. "Not that the world presented by Lockean empiricism and Unitarian theology was, strictly speaking, meaningless," Packer argues. "It simply did not mean *enough*."[21]

The second concept—the Kantian basis of Emerson's idealism—similarly represents Emerson's rejection of Lockean empiricism. Emerson, like many Romantics, emphasizes the differences between Immanuel Kant and John Locke. In "The Transcendentalist," Emerson stresses what he perceives as these key differences and tries to define the idea of transcendentalism for his audience. Reacting to Locke's conviction that the mind is a tabula rasa, Emerson endorsed the Kantian premise that the mind has an existence prior to, and independent from, materiality. As Emerson explains, the idealism of his day acquired the attribute "transcendental" from Kant, "who replied to the skeptical philosophy of Locke, which insisted that there was nothing in the intellect which was not previously in the experience of the senses, by showing that there was a very important class of ideas, or imperative forms, which did not come by experience, but through which experience was acquired; that these were intuitions of the mind itself; and he denominated them *Transcendental* forms."[22]

What attracts Emerson to Kant is the assertion that there are "intuitions of the mind itself," or a knowledge that comes prior to, and is separated from, the experience of the body. These beliefs contribute to Emerson's concept of nature that categorized materiality as secondary to spirituality, as symbolic of (but not exactly reaching) the status of the creator. Emerson aligns the material sphere with corporeality, naming it "Nature" or "Not Me," and argues that it exists, in part, as a revelation of the primary power, that of the intellect. He describes this relationship in terms of a chronology that implies a hierarchy of the "intellect" over "nature." In "The Method of Nature" (1841) he proposes that in "the divine order, intellect is primary: nature, secondary. . . . That which once existed in intellect as pure law, has now taken body as Nature."[23] This philosophical privileging of the "pure law" led Emerson to endorse a hierarchy of "Reason" (which can also signify the soul) over corporeality.[24]

Throughout his early essays Emerson separates the body from the mind and describes a struggle between the two, as in "Compensation" (1841), where he argues that the "soul says Eat; the body would feast. The soul says, the man and the woman shall be one flesh and one soul; the body would join the flesh only. The soul says, Have dominion over all things to the end of virtue; the body would have the power over things to its own ends." In this description, the body is not only secondary to the original law of intellect, but also in opposition to it. In part, Emerson is answering Locke's insistence on the primacy of the senses by describing the body's appetites as suspect. "The influence of the senses," he tell us in "The Over-Soul" (1841), has overpowered the mind, making the "walls of time and space" look real and leaving us immersed in materialism. At times Emerson's distrust of the senses becomes so spirited that he sounds like the reformers he occasionally chides. He preaches sexual chastity, not for the sake of the state but rather to serve the soul. "The sublime vision," he tells us in "The Poet" (1844), "comes to the pure and simple soul in a clean and chaste body." In "The Transcendentalist" he uses chastity as a metaphor, arguing from the perspective of a transcendentalist against participating in reform movements because the universe wants "the attestation of faith by this my abstinence."[25]

If these transcendent impulses seem conventional when viewed through romanticism and evident when considered in relation to the philosophical concepts that influenced Emerson, they take on increased interest and vigor when juxtaposed with the rise of scientific essentialism in the first half of the nineteenth century in America and help account for the contradictory tendencies in Emerson's writings on race. At times Emerson makes the implicit discrepancy between his transcendent optimism and the fatalistic implications of racial science quite explicit. In his "Experience" (1844) he links proponents of racial science to the slavery their theories support by calling them "theoretic kidnappers and slave-drivers": "I know the mental proclivity of physicians. I hear the chuckle of phrenologists. Theoretic kidnappers and slave-drivers, they esteem each man the victim of another, who winds him round his finger by knowing the law of his being, and by such cheap signboards as the color of his beard, or the slope of his occiput, reads the inventory of his fortunes and character. The grossest ignorance does not disgust like this impudent knowingness. The physicians say, they are not materialists; but they are:—Spirit is matter reduced to an extreme thinness; O *so* thin!"[26]

Here we should read Emerson's accusation against physicians and phrenologists in relation to Dana D. Nelson's argument regarding the struggle for professional control among white men in nineteenth-century America, a struggle that often pitted religious or philosophical men against scientists. If we consider, for example, the English phrenologist George Combe's dismay in *Crania Americana* that "the difference of national characters has been investigated by philosophers in general, without any knowledge of, or reference to, the functions of the different parts of the brain,"[27] in relation to Emerson's deliberations upon such topics in many of his lectures, then we might question whether it is the racial theories that Emerson objects to or the audacity of the men who practice these theories by reading others' bodies.

Nonetheless, such a reading does not dismiss the disgust with corporeal fatalism that is evident in the passage quoted nor Emerson's objection to the extreme materialism of the scientists' position. He recoils from the idea that "Spirit" could be reduced to such a cheap materiality. Not surprisingly, this is the same year he gave his address to honor the anniversary of emancipation in the British West Indies, an event, he believed, demonstrating the "annihilation of the old indecent nonsense about the nature of the negro."[28] As both essays reveal, Emerson bases his philosophy, in part, on belief in the unity of soul and the primacy of reason, conceptions that ultimately understood all human beings as creations and representations of the same source. Throughout the late 1830s and 1840s Emerson details his faith that *all* human beings are part of divinity, albeit removed and made less perfect by embodiment. In "The Poet" he describes the relationship between corporeality and the "spirit": "We were put into our bodies, as fire is put into a pan, to be carried about; but there is no accurate adjustment between the spirit and the organ, much less in the latter the germination of the former. . . . For we are not pans and barrows, nor even porters of the fire and torch-bearers, but children of the fire, made of it, and only the same divinity transmuted, and at two or three removes, when we know least about it."[29] Emerson suggests that the "adjustment" between the "spirit" and the "organ" is not perfect, as corporeality represents a flawed state, one that is at several removes from the original source. However, humans are united in this transmutation; even if they are flawed, they are still "children of the fire," members of one family, and the reflections of their creator. Emerson continues to idealize the unity of humankind in "The Over-Soul" (1841), asserting that "the heart in thee is the heart of all" because "one blood rolls uninterruptedly, an endless circulation through all men."[30] By referring to the "endless circulation," Emerson evokes a corporeal image to elicit faith in the unity of the soul. Humans symbolically share one body, he suggests, as well as one soul. To Emerson, the higher laws, which could only be hinted at through their manifestation in material form, contradict false classifications and hierarchies in American society. As Buell argues, before Emerson—and he adds Walt Whitman—"grew old and cautious" he perceived transcendentalism as the "natural religion of democracy" and expressed "a mystic awareness from which the idea of democracy is but one specific deduction: the vision of cosmic unity-in-diversity."[31]

As Buell's comment indicates, and as is true for all the writers in this study, Emerson's corporeal depictions ultimately evoke debates about the body politic that raged during his time, a connection he sometimes made explicit but often left implicit. In "The American Scholar" (1837) Emerson argues that "there is One Man . . . and that you must take the whole society to find the whole man" because "[t]he state of society is one in which the members have suffered amputation from the trunk, and strut about so many walking monsters,—a good finger, a neck, a stomach, an elbow, but never a man."[32] If each man represents a dismembered part of the overall societal body, then it follows that all members share a common destiny. As Emerson became increasingly outspoken against slavery, his use of corporeal metaphors intensified, and America became a body set against itself. "[M]an is one," he affirmed in 1844; "you cannot injure any member, without a sympathetic injury to all the members." He reminded a crowd in 1855 that "[a] high state of general health cannot coexist with a mortal disease in any part." Members of a common body, Americans were all enslaved by the peculiar institution because the "hands that put the chain on the slave are in that moment manacled."[33] If many of Emerson's early essays point to a privileging of disembodied reason over corporeality as well as the belief that all humans are unified, albeit transmuted, children of the fire, then these statements from his 1850s antislavery lectures demonstrate that Emerson never entirely abandoned the rhetoric of unity that his early essays expounded.

Gendered Complications of Disembodied Identity

Although Emerson defines all humans as children of the same source, his premise of unity was destabilized by his inability to extend this radical philosophy to women. The question as to the extent to which Emerson allowed his potentially unifying philosophy to be applied to people other than Euro-American (or "Saxon") males was raised during Emerson's lifetime and is still debated. For example, Lydia Maria Child commented upon Emerson's lecture "Being and Seeming" in her 1843 *Letters from New York*. In a piece outlining her opinions about women's rights, Child maintains that women will be "more useful and happy" when understood in relation to their true culture, which she defines as consisting "in the full and free development of individual character, regulated by their *own* perceptions of what is true, and their *own* love of what is good." Yet even as she defines women's happiness in Emersonian terms of self-reliance, Child laments that this "responsibility is rarely acknowledged, even by the most refined." Recalling Emerson's lecture, she chides Emerson because men "were exhorted to *be*, rather than to *seem*, that they might fulfill the sacred mission for which their souls were embodied; that they might, in God's freedom, grow up into the full stature of spiritual manhood; but *women* were urged to simplicity and truthfulness, that they might become more *pleasing*." After commenting on this discrepancy, Child confronts the gap between Emerson's purported philosophical premise and his refusal to acknowledge its practical and political implications: "Are we not immortal beings?" she asks; is "not each one responsible for himself and herself?"[34] Child takes Emerson to task for limiting women to the societal role of pleasing others, rather than focusing on their status as "immortal beings" or, in Emerson's terms, children of the fire. She recognizes that Emerson fails to extend his philosophy, the idea that humans are unified in their search to fulfill the "sacred mission for which their souls were embodied," to those who happen to be embodied as women. As Child's comments indicate, advocates for women's rights often questioned the extent of Emerson's commitment to their cause. The one time he spoke publicly about women's rights, at the 1855 Boston Women's Rights Convention (from which we have his brief address "Woman"),[35] audience members were uncertain about how to assess his views. As Helen R. Deese notes, a controversy broke out "with some auditors questioning whether Emerson had really endorsed the women's movement." Caroline Healey Dall, who had invited Emerson to speak, responded by supporting Emerson in a letter to him, "noting but minimizing the differences between his view of women and her own."[36]

In his reassessment of Emerson and the "woman question," Gougeon concedes that Emerson's remarks calling for women's rights are tempered by his hesitation about women's proper roles, but argues that Emerson's involvement with the women's movement "approximates the trajectory of his experience with the antislavery movement," because both began "with a troubled concern, moved to a reserved commitment, and culminated in unambiguous support."[37] Yet, just as I argue that, in relation to race and abolition, Emerson's calls for emancipation and equality are undermined by his eagerness to construct a theory of whiteness, so too are the radical implications of his philosophy undercut when considered in relation to women by his consistent use of gendered language that highlights difference. If the positive political implications of Emerson's idealized disembodied state manifest themselves in his insistence on innate unity, the negative ramifications may be that he refuses to recognize the full extent to which embodiment matters in society. This tension is best demonstrated by considering again Emerson's claim to an identity separate from his own body, a "NOT ME" that defines his true self. Early in *Nature*, he describes this binary relationship in an often cited passage: "Philosophically considered, the universe is composed of Nature and the Soul. Strictly speaking, therefore, all that is separate from us, all which Philosophy distinguishes as the NOT ME, that is, both nature and art, all other men and my own body, must be ranked under this name, NATURE."[38] By labeling the body "NOT ME," Emerson asks readers to envision themselves as separate from their corporeality. Race, gender, and any other corporeal markers are less significant than the soul. Although I have already suggested the liberatory potential of denying corporeal significance, such a move also reveals the privilege that Emerson experienced to some degree as a white male in American society. Although he was plagued with physical illness and the death of loved ones,

Emerson could assume a "me" that was not inextricably related to the embodied self. By comparison, women, such as Lydia Maria Child, Frances E. W. Harper, Margaret Fuller, and Harriet Jacobs, were all well aware of the way the "NOT ME" of the body could relegate one to a subordinate role in society.

The romantic conception of the body as a medium for the soul further complicates Emerson's hierarchy of spirituality over corporeality. In part, this belief coincides with the American spiritualist movement, which maintained that the dead could communicate with the living through a person functioning as a medium. In particular, the bodies of children, women, and Negroes were believed to be especially susceptible to spirits.[39] Although Emerson mocked spiritualism, he nonetheless evokes the romantic idea of the body as a medium. The "Supreme Being," Emerson contends, "does not build up nature around us, but puts it forth through us."[40] Therefore, the body both symbolizes spiritual facts and acts as a medium for higher truths. In one of the most discussed passages in *Nature*, Emerson evokes the body as medium: "Standing on the bare ground,—my head bathed by the blithe air, and uplifted into infinite space,—all mean egotism vanishes. I become a transparent eye-ball. I am nothing. I see all. The currents of the Universal Being circulate through me; I am part or particle of God."[41] Here, as Emerson becomes a medium for universal currents, the body appears passive in its receptivity. Julie Ellison argues that divination and intuition are marked as feminine qualities in the romantic context, and, as I argue in chapter 5, Fuller both exploits and fears this association. Although the feminine and passive sensibility displayed in this passage may seem at odds with the Emerson who fills lectures with jeremiad-like calls to manhood, Eric Cheyfitz argues that the "loss of 'individual distinctness,' or the 'personal,' is a sign for Emerson of manliness; it is women generally who exhibit the mean egotism of a soul unable to free itself from the body." According to Leverenz, Emerson links his admiration of self-abandonment with a new definition of manhood that was a response to threatening societal masculine roles. "In a society that defined manhood competitively by possessiveness and possessions," Leverenz suggests, "Emerson would define manhood paradoxically by abandonment and self-dispossession."[42]

Both Cheyfitz and Leverenz argue that Emerson linked abandonment of self with his version of masculinity and that he bound women to their corporeality, a gesture coinciding with the conception of the metaphysical self prevalent during Emerson's time. Sidonie Smith traces the rise of the metaphysical self in the eighteenth and nineteenth centuries, a self that was both disembodied and dissociated with social or communal roles.[43] It was based heavily upon Enlightenment faith in reason and rested on both the "I" and the "eye" of the subject, a self that "turns toward the world and elaborates through reason that 'transcends all situation, context and perspective,' a universalizing, unifying vision characterized as 'impartial.'"[44] Emerson exemplifies this "I/eye" in his depiction of himself as a "transparent eyeball." He abdicates self but, at the same time, becomes omnipresent. It is this I/eye that many romantic writers could take for granted, a privilege that was ironically obtained through their embodied status in society because, as Smith explains, this "self of essences" usually relied on the construction of both women and non-Caucasian races not only as embodied, but also as encumbered and defined by biology. It legitimized its transcendent existence, in part, through the examination of the "natural" world and considered women and "other" races phenomena to be studied. In this sense, although the romantic conception of self offered transcendence in an age that increasingly tended toward scientific essentialism, it nonetheless rested on a paradigm similar to that employed by scientists. Both scrutinized others as objects to authorize the status of the subject. Emerson reflects this concept when he asks the implied male audience of *Nature* to find the miraculous in the common, encouraging them to ponder: "What is summer? What is Woman? What is a child?"[45] "Woman," it appears, is an object of nature, to be examined by the "eye/I" of the poet/philosopher. The seer, presumably Emerson, can shed corporeality, a luxury that others cannot achieve. This passage indicates that even as Emerson strives toward unity, he expresses some ambivalence about the position of women, a hesitancy that is connected with his concerns about masculinity.

At times Emerson grounds women with the weight of their embodied gender and endorses implicitly the Doctrine of Separate Spheres through his call to young men for masculine, individual action. Particularly, Emerson's rhetoric often follows a typical nineteenth-century pattern of associating women with entrapment.[46] Such is the case in his 1838 "Divinity School Address," wherein Emerson uses a gendered analogy to call for masculine scholarship:

> The orators, the poets, the commanders encroach on us only as fair women
> do, by our allowance and homage. Slight them by preoccupation of mind,
> slight them, as you can well afford to do, by high and universal aims, and
> they instantly feel that you have right, and that it is in lower places that
> they must shine. They also feel your right; for they with you are open to
> the influx of the all-knowing Spirit, which annihilates before its broad

noon the little shades and gradations of intelligence in the compositions we call wiser and wisest.[47]

Here the "lower" orators and poets are associated with "fair women" and, therefore, with the feminine realm. The serious scholar, Emerson tells his audience, must slight feminized, inferior poets. When he does so, inferior writers, like any woman, will "instantly feel . . . that it is in lower places that they must shine." They know the "right" of the young man, presumably because they are also "open to the influx of the all-knowing Spirit" that teaches them not unlimited greatness, but "shades and gradations of intelligence." Emerson's statement implies that although the spirit has the power to annihilate these gradations at will, they nonetheless survive. Therefore, he represents women as open to the reception of universal truth, but this truth usually relegates them to a lower status than men.

In a similar rhetorical move, Emerson evokes women symbolically in his 1841 essay "Love." Arguing (not surprisingly) that the body only hints at the celestial sphere, Emerson describes how a man can glean universal truths through heterosexual love. He states that when a man beholds a beautiful body in "the female sex," he "runs to her, and finds the highest joy in contemplating the form, movement, and intelligence of this person, because it suggests to him the presence of that which indeed is within the beauty, and the cause of the beauty."[48] Emerson depicts the female body as an object of beauty that a young man can study to ascertain greater truth or the "cause of the beauty"; thus the woman functions as a medium. Although this representation is not at odds with Emerson's overall conception of the body as a symbol of spiritual facts, it is revealing that he provides no similar analogy for a young woman contemplating a man in this manner. It seems natural, to Emerson, that women should function as passive objects and that men should assume the role of active observers. Emerson's depiction of women in these passages suggests that he saw them differently than men, despite his overall theory of unity.

This discrepancy becomes more apparent when considering "Manners" and "Character," two 1844 essays that explicitly comment on gender and women's nature. In "Character," Emerson presents the concept of men and women as polar opposites, a theory that was not uncommon for his age, when many were interested in what they believed was the potent influence of the earth's magnetic fields on individual bodies, nor uncommon to his method of basing arguments on binary juxtapositions. Emerson aligns males with the North Pole, which symbolizes such characteristics as action and fact, and associates

women with the South Pole, which represents "spirit." Unlike Fuller's description of "radical dualism," which proposes a similar theory of complementary
behaviors of the "masculine" and "feminine" realm (see chapter 5), Emerson
uses the words "male" and "female" rather than "masculine" and "feminine,"
suggesting that for him the bipolar qualities of the universe are embodied
respectively in men and women. While these may be complementary and even
harmonious, the male remains superior. Perhaps this is why he continues his
essay by presenting an idealization of the male-male bond that foreshadows
Whitman's faith in "adhesiveness." Although "love in the sexes is the first
symbol" of this bond, Emerson believes that nothing surpasses "the profound
good understanding . . . between two virtuous men. . . . It is a happiness which
postpones all other gratifications, and makes politics, and commerce, and
churches, cheap."[49]

"Manners," which follows "Character" in *Essays: Second Series*, continues
Emerson's discussion of femininity. Much as his later essays call for emancipation while making disconcerting assertions about the natural characteristics of
the races, "Character" conflates calls for women's rights with notions of an
essential female nature. "Certainly," he asserts, "let her be as much better
placed in the laws and in social forms, as the most zealous reformer can ask."
On the one hand, Emerson endorses "reforms," showing his willingness to concede that women deserve to have certain rights extended to them. On the other
hand, he does not name any specific improvements. His lack of precision—
which can be compared with Fuller's detailed analysis of women's rights, corporeality, and sexuality in *Woman in the Nineteenth Century*—suggests that
he is not overly concerned about, or sensitive to, the particulars of women's
embodied oppression. Emerson proceeds in the same passage to echo Fuller's
language, saying it is up to women to show the way toward reform. "I confide
so entirely in her inspiring and musical nature," he comments, "that I believe
only herself can show us how she shall be served." Emerson's reference to
women's "inspiring and musical" nature draws upon essential concepts of femininity that, as my discussion of Fuller indicates, often flirt with or endorse corporeal essentialism. He proceeds to expand on women's nature, picturing them
as traditional muses. Saying that "we shall be sunny poets" if steeped in the
influence of women, he describes the Persian Lilla: "She did not study the Persian grammar, nor the books of the seven poets, but all the poems of the seven
seemed to be written upon her. For, though the bias of her nature was not to
thought, but to sympathy, yet was she so perfect in her own nature, as to meet

intellectual persons by the fulness of her heart, warming them by her senti-ments; believing, as she did, that by dealing nobly with all, all would show themselves noble."[50]

Emerson's Lilla has a great deal in common with the idealized nineteenth-century American woman. She, like the ideal woman of his day, was noted for her sympathetic, warming, sentimental, and heart-filled qualities, rather than for intellectual endeavors. She was far more likely to be "written upon" than to write. These essays were published shortly after Fuller finished "The Great Lawsuit," the work that became *Woman in the Nineteenth Century*, and they reflect Fuller's influence. Fuller, too, maintains that women (at least as ideal-ized in "Woman") are more apt to inspire than write poetry, and she espouses the complementary nature of the sexes. However, whereas Fuller complicates and expands upon these categories, Emerson never really challenges them. Instead, he reflects ideas common to his day and uses women as foils against whom a man can define his identity.

The need to delineate manhood was particularly important to Emerson, who worried about the effects of the marketplace on the "civilized" nineteenth-century Anglo-Saxon male. Like Whitman, Emerson feared that his era's in-creased urbanization and industrialization negatively affected young men. Many of his essays exhibit this anxiety, but it is especially overt in "Self-Reliance" and "Man the Reformer." In "Man the Reformer" Emerson discusses the impetus for reform. From the start, he genders the discussion, saying that reform move-ments—or "general inquests into abuses"—result from "the practical impedi-ments that stand in the way of virtuous young men," particularly in relation to trade, which he depicts as corrupt and exhausting.[51] Emerson's connection of reform to young (and presumably white) men reveals his bias, particularly because so much of the agitation during his age was directed at women's rights and abolition. Emerson disapproves of the marketplace economy because it fragments a young man's identity. "That is the vice," he comments, "that no one feels himself called to act for man, but only as a fraction of man." As a par-tial solution to this dilemma, Emerson proposes manual labor for men who have been tainted by wealth and feminized by a separation from physical work. He states, "I doubt not, the faults and vices of our literature and philosophy, their too great fineness, effeminacy, and melancholy, are attributable to the enervated and sickly habits of the literary class." Emerson's choice of words— "melancholy," "enervated," and "sickly"—all carry feminine associations, calling to mind the nineteenth-century concept of a female nervous system that dominates the muscles and mind. Because men of the ruling classes are no longer in immediate contact with their bodies and nature through manual labor, they have lost their masculine vigor. As if to emphasize the danger men face when becoming immersed in the feminine realm, Emerson urges men who have a "strong bias to poetry, to art, to the contemplative life," to opt for solitude, denounce material possessions, and even remain celibate.[52] Women and the feminine, melancholic, and potentially sexual world they represent obstruct the man who would be a seer.

"Self-Reliance" also exhibits Emerson's suspicion of the feminine/domestic realm's potential for tyranny. Throughout the essay, Emerson sets up a binary between the individual who tries to live by his beliefs and the world, which "whips you with its displeasure" for nonconformity.[53] Emerson's choice of the word "whips" is significant, because the young man is shown to be a slave to both the marketplace and feminine society. By accusing society of enslaving manhood, Emerson identifies his audience as primarily male and draws on the idea of separate spheres, representing the societal sphere (marked feminine) as a trap. Indeed, to maintain autonomy and reclaim masculinity, a man has to throw off the domestic/familial associations that advice books insisted were the Saxon man's responsibility to nation and race. If we recall, for example, William A. Alcott's 1839 claim that every man "lives for his wife, his children, his neighbors, his friends, his country; yea, for the world," then we understand why Emerson asks his audience why "we assume the faults of our friend, or wife, or father, or child, because they sit around our hearth, or are said to have the same blood? All men have my blood, and I have all men's. Not for that will I adopt their petulance or folly, even to the extent of being ashamed of it."[54] In listing whom we should not "assume the faults of," Emerson conspicuously excludes "husband."[55] In part, this implies a male audience. However, his omission also indicates that Emerson envisions the dynamic as one of a feminine/domestic realm that entraps the young male in stifling societal roles. True, the father is male, and the friends may be as well, but these men may have already been coopted by the conspiracy called society; they may be the "parlor soldiers" he later laments.[56] In any case, Emerson's radical declaration that "all men have my blood" is undercut by his reluctance to form an alliance with any member of either his direct or extended family. His primary task is to separate himself to protect his spiritual solitude.

After addressing the conspiracy of society against its members, Emerson continues with a metaphor drawn from trade, arguing in an often quoted passage that "[s]ociety is a joint-stock company in which the members agree, for the better securing of his bread to each shareholder, to surrender the liberty and culture of the eater." By comparing society to a "joint-stock" company, Emerson suggests that the communal nature of trade threatens individuality in general and manhood in particular. As Leverenz argues, "[b]ecoming a man, Emerson came to feel, meant escaping conformity either to the rivalries of the marketplace, where men became things, or to the suffocation of domestic gentility, where men become women."[57] To dodge such traps, Emerson binds women to their embodied status and allows men to escape an aggressive and increasingly troubling world by taking a traditionally feminine, but nonetheless presumably liberating, stance of abandonment and self-dispossession—the universal eyeball.

English Traits *and the Antislavery Lectures*

In addition to proposing a philosophical and spiritual abandonment of self as one answer to the problems posed by the competitive masculine sphere of trade, Emerson also offers advice to men for when they must participate in these activities, and it is in this advice that we can begin to trace the connection between Emerson's anxiety over gender and his conflicting representations of race and national identity in his antislavery lectures and *English Traits*. In "Self-Reliance," Emerson advises his beleaguered male audience to "enter into the state of war, and wake Thor and Woden, courage and constancy, in our Saxon breasts."[58] The connection between the allegedly emasculated male audience and Emerson's call for the Saxon characteristics of "courage and constancy" merits further examination. When he evokes particularly Saxon qualities and draws on Norse and Anglo-Saxon mythology, Emerson hits upon a theme common in his day. Many considered Americans to be descendants of the Saxons, a "race" that was thought to have existed before the Norman conquest, and to have a fierce love of liberty and independence.[59] Having identified his audience as civilized Saxons, Emerson mourns what the modern male has lost through his superior civilization, lamenting that the "civilized man has built a coach, but has lost the use of his feet. He is supported on crutches, but lacks so much support of muscle. He has a fine Geneva watch, but he fails of the skill to tell the hour by the sun."[60] Yet if civilization brought with it the threat of a feminized culture, this was a confinement that Emerson believed the Saxon male was programmed to resist. His desire to reclaim the American males' manhood, to emancipate them from the captivity of the feminized parlor, coincides with some of the most pronounced language of racial difference in his writings from this time period. Although the references to racial identity in "Self-Reliance" and "Man the Reformer" are not the central issues in those essays, they indicate not only Emerson's implied audience, but also his willingness to consider or appeal to racial concepts that were coming to fruition during the 1840s. His anxiety about masculinity manifests itself, in part, in a racialized language that enables him to reclaim and redefine manhood. Such a shift becomes increasingly pronounced, and is quite evident by the time Emerson publishes *English Traits* in 1856. In this book, Emerson takes comfort in envisioning the English as his ancestors, because of their masculine roots. Describing the birth of the English race, Emerson muses: "Nature held counsel with herself, and said, 'My Romans are gone. To build my new empire, I will choose a rude race, all masculine, with brutish strength. I will not grudge a competition of the roughest males. Let buffalo gore buffalo, and the pasture to the strongest!'"[61] Clearly, part of the impetus for the fantasy that Emerson constructs by locating the roots of American identity in a mythologized English past is his need to romanticize a primitive site where men once experienced uninhibited manhood, a time when the parlor could claim no soldiers.

If Emerson's shift to an increasingly racialized language was influenced in part by his anxiety over masculinity, it also reflects a more general cultural movement, one associated with American authors' search for a definitive national identity. Reginald Horsman argues that racial nationalism is an intricate part of romanticism, noting that American authors calling for a "distinctive American literature" were influenced by German writers "who saw literature and language as embodying the soul of a nation." The American romantics "were less interested in the features uniting mankind and nations than in the features separating them. Like the scientists . . . they looked for what was special and different, not what was general and alike."[62] What Horsman suggests about American romantic writers in general is applicable to Emerson, who, in his quest for an American literature based on a unique national identity, began to deliberate definitions of national identity that endorsed stereotypical conceptions of Saxon superiority. If, as Buell suggests, Emerson's earlier gestures toward a unique American identity camouflaged his commitment to European intellectual influences,[63] *English Traits* can be understood as attempting to answer seriously the younger Emerson's call for a distinctively American culture. Sacvan Bercovitch, in accordance with other

scholars who note a shift toward conservatism in Emerson's later works, argues
that *English Traits* can be read as "a sustained apologia for modern liberal culture. Indeed, its particular focus on the superiority of the Anglo-Saxon race and
the Westering progress of civilization may be said to begin the last phase of
Emerson's journey into ideology: his more or less outright identification of
individuality with industrial-capitalist 'Wealth' (1851) and 'Power' (1860), with
'American Civilization' (1862), and summarily with 'The Fortune of the
Republic' (1864)."[64] Although purportedly about the English, the theory of race
and history that Emerson proposes demonstrates that he is most interested in
what a study of the English reveals about the American "race" and national
destiny. By considering *English Traits* in relation to Emerson's recently repub-
lished antislavery lectures in general, and to his "Address . . . on . . . the Emancipation of the Negroes in the British West Indies" (1844), "The President's
Proclamation" (1862), and "Fortune of the Republic" (1863) in particular, we
understand Emerson's movement toward conservatism as interwoven with his
racial representations, representations that increasingly emphasize difference
as the United States moved toward the Civil War.

Certainly, Emerson's 1847–48 trip to England stimulated his interest in race,
particularly his interrogation of the connections between English and American identity. Perhaps because Emerson's fascination with an English American
racial identity was still a few years in the future in 1844, he was able to write
what is arguably his most radical declaration of the possible equality and future
success of the "negro" race, his "Address on Emancipation." Indeed, none of
his later writings matches the zeal with which Emerson sets about demonstrating how the British emancipation in the West Indies signifies the "annihilation of the old indecent nonsense about the nature of the negro."[65] The
address itself is filled with optimism not only about the future of the abolition
movement, but also about the positive influence of reform efforts. Gougeon
demonstrates that Emerson interpreted the British emancipation of the West
Indies, among other things, as a sign of the affirmative power of government
when it acted upon correct moral principles.[66] Toward the end of his address,
after he establishes an economic argument against the continuation of slavery,
traces a brief history of antislavery activity in England, reports on the peaceful
transformation from slavery to freedom in the West Indies, identifies those
who enslave as acting on corporeal motives, and argues for the rights of Massachusetts's free people of color when traveling south, Emerson considers the
future of the emancipated slaves, a question that he notes is not "the least

affecting part of this history of abolition." Already, in this essay, Emerson moves toward a theory of race that includes questions of melioration (a term I address below in relation to *English Traits*), a concept closely associated with what we would now identify as evolution. Nature, Emerson argues, "will only save what is worth saving; and it saves not by compassion, but by power." If men are "rude and foolish, down they must go," he declares. At this point he introduces a dialectic that is familiar to readers of Emerson, presenting the possibility of both the future success and potential failure of emancipated slaves: "If the black man is feeble, and not important to the existing races not on a parity with the best race," Emerson argues, then "the black man must serve, and be exterminated. But if the black man carries in his bosom an indispensable element of a new and coming civilization, for the sake of that element, no wrong, nor strength, nor circumstance, can hurt him: he will survive and play his part."[67]

Although Emerson introduces the question of the future of emancipated slaves with a typical thesis/antithesis structure, the remainder of the paragraph following this statement weighs heavily on the side of the possible equality and success of emancipated slaves. In particular, Emerson points to the "Haytian heroes," or "the leaders of their race in Barbadoes and Jamaica." Reaching a rhetorical climax that coincides with the approaching end of his address, Emerson proclaims: "The anti-slavery of the whole world, is dust in the balance before this,—is a poor squeamishness and nervousness: the might and the right are here: here is the anti-slave: here is man: and if you have man, black or white is an insignificance. The intellect,—that is miraculous! Who has it, has the talisman: his skin and bones, though they were of the color of night, are transparent, and the everlasting stars shine through, with attractive beams." Some may object to the erasing of race that this passage performs; the skin and bones are lightened until they become transparent. Yet by evoking the notion that intellect supersedes race, that intellect (which elsewhere he might call reason) in effect transcends corporeality, Emerson aligns this antislavery lecture with the promise of transcendent unity that appears in his less overtly political essays from the first and second series, published in 1841 and 1844 respectively. Not content in this address to leave the question of racial equality and capability up to the audience, Emerson introduces a powerful use of ethos: "I esteem the occasion of this jubilee to be the proud discovery, that the black race can contend with the white."[68] If the beginning of the paragraph is skeptical about the question of racial equality, the voice that concludes the paragraph powerfully dismisses those doubts.

However, even within his formidable 1844 address, a speech that theoretically creates space for freed slaves within the Republic by providing the positive example of emancipation in the British West Indies, Emerson cannot escape language that undercuts his calls for equality and tentatively works toward the racialized national identity that *English Traits*, "The President's Proclamation," and "Fortune of the Republic" explicitly formulate. For example, although at the end of his address Emerson foresees a brighter future for emancipated slaves, the beginning of the piece reinforces a motif of permanent racial victimization. So important to Emerson is the idea that Africans have always been weak victims that he echoes the theorists of racial science, defining the ancient Egyptians as non-African and using them as evidence for Africans' permanent victim status, assertions that Child had challenged as early as her *Appeal in Favor of That Class of Americans Called Africans* (1833). Noting that the "earliest monuments" demonstrate "that one race was victim, and served the other races," Emerson describes how the oldest temples of Egypt have "negro captives" painted on the tombs of kings. Granted, the idea that Africans are victimized does not necessarily lead to the conclusion that they always will be so or should be so, but the remainder of Emerson's essay—with the exception of the passage on the heroes of emancipation quoted above—emphasizes the "moderation" and susceptibility of Africans, and de-emphasizes any impulse of slaves to revolt. For example, when Emerson describes the torture slaves endure, he notes with sympathy the fact that pregnant female slaves were whipped for refusing to work. However, he adds that it was "not they, but the eternal law of animal nature" that refused to work.[69] Such a claim seems odd, especially given the first sentence of his address, which declares that the anniversary of emancipation represents "a day of reason"—*reason* being a word that was deeply significant to Emerson.

For Emerson, the decision of the English government to emancipate represents the progression of the English race; it is this practical application of reason that the philosopher Emerson finds appealing. Yet the pregnant slave woman who refuses to work, apparently, does so not out of any commitment to higher laws, but out of her "animal nature." Indeed, when Emerson describes why West Indian emancipation is so important, he notes that it was a "moral revolution." Whereas other revolutions "have been the insurrection of the oppressed; this was the repentance of the tyrant." Emerson later qualifies this statement, noting that the emancipation is "in part" the "earning of the blacks." However, in contrast to the emphasis on the action and deliberation of the reasonable Englishman who wins a moral victory in emancipation, Emerson notes that the blacks "won the pity and respect which they have received, by their powers and native endowments."[70] Although Emerson points to "respect" as well as "pity" (a pity evoked, presumably, by victim status), he also refers vaguely to "native endowments," a phrase rich with racial potential, especially when considered in relation to the statements about race embedded in other parts of the essay.

These examples suggest that as much as Emerson proclaims the future success and possible equality of emancipated slaves, he fills his essay with language establishing racial difference and white superiority. Working toward his theory linking English and American identity in *English Traits*, Emerson defines the nation's "civility" as deriving from the English, because "England is the strongest of the family of existing nations" and America is "the expansion of that people." Foremost of the racial attributes he ascribes to the English is that of the trader: "And we are shopkeepers, and have acquired the vices and virtues that belong to trade," Emerson proclaims. He continues by adding that England and America enslaved Africans because "we" had "found a race who were less warlike, and less energetic shopkeepers than we," a statement that not only defines racial difference, but also reinforces myths of African docility. The myth of docility hinted at in this passage is reinforced much more explicitly when Emerson discusses the "civilization of the negro." Pointing to evidence of skilled African "productions and manufactures," Emerson expresses his optimism that the emancipated African can be civilized, noting that it "now appears, that the negro race is, more than any other, susceptible of rapid civilization."[71] By suggesting that Africans are "susceptible" of civilization, Emerson not only articulates the cultural superiority of his age that assumed Africa was less civilized than Europe and America, but he also represents Africans and, by implication, African Americans, as passive and docile, as childlike and feminine, in their receptivity, a common trope of romantic racialism.[72] The idea that Negroes were more "susceptible" than other races to "civilization" also connects to debates about Native Americans. In the appendix to Samuel Morton's *Crania Americana* (1839), Combe applies Morton's data to conclude that "[t]he aspect of America is still more deplorable than that of Africa," because even with European influence Native Americans remain "the same miserable, wandering, houseless and lawless savages as their ancestors were."[73] This juxtaposition probably appealed to Emerson, who thought that the conquest of the continent was inevitable despite his opposition to Indian Removal.[74]

Language linking Africans and African Americans to docility appears throughout the essay, even in passages generally positive about the prospects of emancipation. Clearly, Emerson, like Child in her *Appeal*, has a political need to show emancipation as a peaceful possibility, and this can account in part for his tendency to downplay revolutionary characteristics of African Americans and any violence that may coincide with emancipation. Nonetheless, when Emerson describes the emancipation of slaves in Antigua, his passage repeats language (certainly influenced by the sources he used) that reflects his era's romantic racialism: "On the night of the 31st July," Emerson reports, the soon to be freed slaves "met everywhere at their churches and chapels, and at midnight, when the clock struck twelve, on their knees, the *silent, weeping* assembly became men; they rose and embraced each other; they *cried*, they *sung*, they *prayed*, they were *wild with joy*, but there was no riot, no feasting" (emphasis mine). Even as Emerson describes the transformation of slaves into "men," the language he uses ("silent," "weeping," "wild with joy") and the actions they perform (singing, crying, praying, embracing) all evoke emotional, feminine characteristics. By contrast, Emerson ends his essay—in a passage immediately following his most pronounced arguments for racial equality— with a highly racial description of his audience, whom he identifies as Saxon. "The genius of the Saxon race, friendly to liberty; the enterprise, the very muscular vigor of this nation, are inconsistent with slavery," he declares.[75] When juxtaposed with the feminine, passive description of the slaves, the Saxon race, which is defined by its "genius," by its love for "liberty," by its "very muscular vigor," is profoundly masculine and profoundly intellectual. The fact that Emerson ends his essay, which includes such a powerful argument for the successful future and the equality of African Americans in the preceding paragraphs, with language calling readers back to racial difference is not merely a rhetorical gesture to stimulate his audience to action. Rather, it suggests that Emerson had very serious doubts, conscious or not, regarding the "old indecent nonsense about the nature of the negro." Indeed, as the nation's crisis intensified after the passage of the Fugitive Slave Law, Emerson fortified his understanding of Americans as primarily English, as a single "stock" of people. He defines the Union in 1851 as "a real thing, an alliance of men of one stock, one language, one religion, one system of manners and ideas."[76] Likewise, in 1856, Emerson appeals to his audience's allegedly Saxon love of liberty and racial pride when he urges them to free the slaves because "the Saxon man, when he is well awake, is not a pirate, but a citizen, all made of hooks and eyes, and links himself naturally to his brothers, as bees hook themselves to one another, and to their queen, in a loyal swarm."[77] As these comments suggest, Emerson's call for abolition and hope for the future success and equality of African Americans were interwoven in his prewar lectures on antislavery with a language marking racial difference, even racial hierarchy.

To examine further Emerson's conflicting descriptions of race, it is helpful to analyze his *English Traits*, the book Emerson began contemplating on his 1847–48 trip to England but did not publish until 1856. Here Emerson does not concern himself explicitly with Africans or African Americans. Rather, he attempts to define what makes the English *English* and, in so doing, suggests what makes Americans both a continuation of the English and a new race. He declares that the "American is only the continuation of the English genius into new conditions" and proclaims, "The culture of the day, the thoughts and aims of men, are English thoughts and aims."[78] He identifies his implied reader when he describes his arrival in England as replicating the experiences of every American who "has arrived at the old mansion-house, and finds himself among uncles, aunts, and grandsires. The pictures on the chimney-tiles of his nursery were pictures of these people. Here they are in the identical costumes and air, which so took him."[79] By assuming that his reader would associate England with the familial and familiar, Emerson blurs the differences in Americans' backgrounds through a willfully optimistic assertion of common roots. To Emerson, Americans had to be defined as primarily English, despite the reality of a multiracial and multiethnic population.

This insistence upon a seamless connection between Englishmen and Americans becomes problematic in view of Emerson's belief that the period in which he writes represents a break between the members of this purportedly uniform race. Throughout this work he establishes his theory of history and England's place in it. The English, he notes, although for so long the rightful rulers of civilization, are now in a state of "arrested development," immersed in "corporeal civilization," with their days of greatness in the past. If "we will visit London, the present time is the best time," he tells readers, "as some signs portend that it has reached its highest point. . . . the British power has culminated, is in solstice, or already declining."[80] Here Emerson draws upon his cyclical view of history. As Buell notes, Emerson was relatively quick to adopt an "evolutionary conception of history" after the publication of *Essays: First Series* (1841), in which the latest system is the best, as it encapsulates all others.[81] Yet also implicit in his understanding of history was the necessity of the "fall," of the natural ascent and descent of civilizations. To Emerson, England was a civilization in decline, just as America was a civilization in ascent.[82] Is it any wonder, then, that Emerson took his passage to England on the *Washington Irving*? Like the author after whom the ship is named, Emerson declares England a place of the past and America the site of the future. He powerfully drives this point home in one of the final chapters, "Stonehenge," in which he relates his visit to that historical site. Standing at the ruins with Thomas Carlyle, he tells Carlyle that when he returns to Massachusetts he will "lapse at once into the feeling, which the geography of America inevitably inspires, that we play the game with immense advantage; that there and not here is the seat and centre of the British race; and that no skill or activity can long compete with the prodigious natural advantages of that country, in the hands of the same race; and that England, an old and exhausted island, must one day be contented, like other parents, to be strong only in her children."[83] This scene and conversation fittingly gesture toward the end of *English Traits*. Stonehenge symbolizes the rise and fall of cultures that Emerson believes are part of the necessary progress of humankind and, in effect, the very form of history. Standing with Carlyle in the face of the past, Emerson looks to the future and concludes that it will be found in America.

Emerson's conception of Americans as a continuation of the English race reveals the fluidity and hybridity that mark his racial categories and must be examined more specifically in relation to his theory of amelioration. In *English Traits*, as Philip Nicoloff argues, Emerson does not merely replicate scientific theories of race, but rather proposes one of his own. Nicoloff demonstrates that Emerson accepted what we would now consider evolutionary paradigms relatively early in his life and was particularly intrigued by arrested and progressive development, concepts that came to him by way of Robert Chamber's *Vestiges of Creation* (1845). "One of the discoveries of modern science which most delighted Emerson," Nicoloff suggests, "was that man carried both in his embryological and in his matured form rudiments of the lower animals." This concept attracted him because it established a sympathy between "man and all other living creatures" and because "it offered evidence of the ameliorative program which he had come to believe had been going on throughout vast biological time."[84] In part, Emerson's conception of race forms from these beliefs, particularly his faith in *amelioration in nature*, which he describes in 1844 in "The Young American" as a force "which alone permits and authorizes amelioration in mankind. The population of the world is a conditional population; these are not the best, but the best that could live in the existing state of soils,

of gases, animals, and morals: the best that could *yet* live; there shall be a better, please God."[85] Humankind, according to Emerson in this essay, has the
ability to ameliorate, to change form (in terms of races) and improve as it works
toward the fulfillment of preordained universal laws.

When considered in contrast to the declaration of the respected scientist
Samuel Morton in 1842 that "there has been a primeval difference among men;
not an accident of occurrence, but a part of that all-pervading design," the radical potential of Emerson's assumption that all races can improve becomes
clear.[86] In fact, Emerson's faith in amelioration leads him to steer away from his
friend Louise Agassiz's theory of polygenesis, a theory that denied the possibility of racial fluidity and improvement.[87] Nonetheless, Nicoloff notes, Emerson
was not that concerned with the specifics of the monogenesis/polygenesis
debate, because his "two chief final perceptions—that the races of man varied in
their abilities but were capable of painfully slow modification—could be enter-
tained without reference to historical origins." This helps explain why Emerson
begins his third chapter, "Race," with a partial critique of Robert Knox's *Races
of Men* (first published in 1850).[88] Although there is much that interests Emerson in *Races of Men*, he criticizes Knox and other scientists for imprecision, for
representing races as knowable categories while being incapable of pinpointing
the number of races or establishing definitive racial boundaries. Robinson
argues that Emerson "attacked Robert Knox's theory of the fixity of racial types,
the leading racial theory of the day, as limited and misleading," an attack that
signified Emerson's rejection of racial determinism as an adequate framework
with which to interpret history and culture.[89] However, we cannot assume that
Emerson's criticism of Knox and other scientists indicates his dismissal of the
relevance of investigating race as an organizing principle of humankind. Indeed,
Emerson's claim in *English Traits*—that the "individuals at the extremes of
divergence in one race of men are as unlike as the wolf to the lapdog," but that
"each variety shades down imperceptibly into the next, and you cannot draw
the line where a race begins or ends"—sounds very similar to the assertion of
the ethnologist Josiah C. Nott in 1854 that although interracial sexual mixing
may benefit some, "the lowest types are hopelessly beyond the reach even of
these salutary stimulants to melioration."[90] Both emphasize the fluidity of
racial categories while also marking significant (and politically devastating) differences in gradations. As Nicoloff argues, "we must note that in opening his
chapter with a repudiation of a race count, Emerson was by no means endorsing
or rejecting any particular theory, but rather pointing to the present inadequacy

of them all. Indeed, he was willing to concede to the racialists any claim which seemed consistent with the evidence."[91]

This is why Emerson, even while acknowledging the "impossibility of arriving at a satisfaction on the historical question of race," simultaneously brings up "the indisputable Englishman," who is "himself very well marked, and nowhere else to be found."[92] In any given era, according to the theory Emerson proposes throughout *English Traits*, race could have a sense of permanence and carry with it a significance that bordered on fatal. A journal entry from the 1850s indicates that Emerson was aware of the contradictory nature of his theory of race and amelioration: "I affirm melioration,—which Nature teaches in pears, in the domesticated animals, and in her secular geology and the development of complex races. I affirm also the self-equality of Nature; or that only that is true which is always true; and that, in California, or in Greece, or in Jewry, or in Arcadia, existed the same amounts of private power, as now, and the same deductions, however differently distributed. But I cannot reconcile these two statements."[93] Perhaps Emerson could not "reconcile" his belief in amelioration with his sense that "that is true which is always true" because such a contradictory theory allowed him to understand race as something fluid enough to allow for change—say, to enable the English race to form and then to transform itself into the American race—but also rigid enough to remain stable through several historical epochs. Indeed, Emerson notes, race "in the negro is of appalling importance" and is a "controlling influence in the Jew."[94]

If race appears to be fixed and fatal for the Jew and the Negro (at least in this era), it is not so for the Englishman and the American. In fact, Emerson proposes a positive scenario of racial melioration not only by asserting that Americans are an ameliorated form of the English, but also by arguing that the English themselves are hybrid. Noting that the "best nations are those most widely related," he proposes that the English race is a "composite character," betraying "a mixed origin," specifically one that fuses "distant and antagonistic elements" in such a way as to form "collectively a better race than any from which they are derived." Emerson's description of the English as a positive hybrid race and his vision of Americans as a new form of this hybrid arguably stem from his need to reconcile the diverse nature of the nineteenth-century American population by claiming that Americans are primarily English. When Emerson describes the British Empire at the beginning of his chapter "Race," he mentions that it includes the United States but immediately interjects two qualifications about the American population. First, he counts the population of the United States "exclusive of slaves," a gesture that he assumes needs no elaboration. Second, he mentions that although America's "foreign element" is "considerable," it is "rapidly assimilated."[95] In this brief passage Emerson reveals his anxiety about America's "body," which is at the center of his investigation of the British. According to Horsman, most Americans "had faith that the multiplying Anglo-Saxons could easily absorb other European stocks," in part because they assumed the dominant nature of the Anglo-Saxon race.[96] If Emerson sang the praises of racial mixing, he did so believing that the superior race would control the outcome of mixture. In an 1851 journal passage, Emerson tries to reconcile the fact of America's racial and ethnic diversity with his need to consider Americans a monolithic race. Defining the "genius of the American race," he notes that "it is to be considered that it is not indiscriminate masses of Europe that are shipped hitherward, but the Atlantic is a sieve through which only or chiefly the liberal, adventurous, sensitive, *America-loving* part of each city, clan, family are brought." Clearly, Emerson expresses anxiety about the quality of the "foreign element" that he mentions in *English Traits*, a concern he explicitly racializes in the remainder of the journal passage: "It is the light complexion, the blue eyes of Europe that come: the black eyes, the black drop, the Europe of Europe, is left."[97] By shifting from a moral definition (i.e., the "adventurous" attitude needed for immigration) to a definition that attributes physical characteristics to these traits, Emerson demonstrates his association of positive national traits with lightness, or, we could argue, with whiteness. The language in his journal is echoed in *English Traits*, where Emerson reads the face of the English to reveal their positive attributes: "On the English face are combined decision and nerve, with the fair complexion, blue eyes, and open and florid aspect. Hence the love of truth, hence the sensibility, the fine perception, and poetic construction."[98] Emerson's movement from characteristics to physiognomy, a movement charted only by a simple "hence," is not a startling practice in an age of racial science. However, it demonstrates the way he regularly identified positive national qualities with physical and racial traits.

Emerson's tendency to assert his faith in meliorative powers and his insistence that race is a critical factor when defining national identity are part of the overall strategy of rhetorical stasis he employs throughout *English Traits*. As discussed in the first section of this chapter, the dialectical method structures most of Emerson's work, and *English Traits* is no exception. He constantly poses questions, only to undermine them and then reassert them later. In one of the most poignant of these moments, Emerson asks: "It is race, is it not? that puts the hundred millions of India under the dominion of a remote island in the north of Europe." Yet typical of Emerson's method, he provides the antithesis, arguing that "whilst race works immortally to keep its own, it is resisted by other forces," including civilization, circumstance, beliefs, and the fluidity of racial categories themselves. Repeatedly Emerson asserts the power of race and then undermines his assertion by posing a question that purportedly leaves the debate open to the reader. "Is this power due to their race, or to some other cause?" he asks of the English. "Is it their luck, or is it in the chambers of their brain,—it is their commercial advantage," he ponders, "that whatever light appears in better method or happy invention, breaks out *in their race*." "Is it the smallness of the country, or is it the pride and affection of race," Emerson asks again, that gives the English such "solidarity . . . and trust in each other."[99] Repeatedly, the reader is left to ponder how to interpret Emerson's apparently balanced argument.

Scholars often evoke Emerson's dialectical method to explain the persistence of racist theories and statements in his later work on race and slavery. To Robinson, Emerson's interjection of racial determinism in *English Traits* is pivotal because it represents "a significant attempt to measure, and ultimately to limit, a determinist explanation for human achievement."[100] Gougeon notes that if some of Emerson's statements on race seem harsh, "Emerson was always a dialectical thinker, and he attempted to see not only both sides but all sides of an issue before reaching conclusions." Cadava also addresses the question of how to account for what he calls the "discursive elements in Emerson that lend themselves to racist reappropriations." He argues that although West is correct in discerning in "Emerson's language an association between Emerson and the racism of his time," nonetheless "many other elements of Emerson's thought, even sometimes the very same elements, cannot be reduced to the project of racism—that is, there are *other* possibilities in Emerson which cannot be said to be determined by the history of racism. Emerson's texts are open, multiple, and fragmented. Parts of these texts connect with racism, and parts resist racism, are stronger than racism."[101] Certainly, Emerson's style is dialectical, multiple, and fragmented. However, it is fair to argue that such a method does not dismiss the significance and effect of what Gougeon considers "harsh" racial statements. Race, to Emerson, was a factor influencing the dialectic he understood history to be—it was the "fate" that impaired freedom, the limitation that checked individualism, the force that could be of "appalling" importance to some.

Therefore one wonders if, in this text, Emerson protests a little too much about the truth of racial determinism. Although Emerson appears to create a text that juxtaposes two possibilities equally, allowing readers to determine the truth, in fact it is hard for a reader to finish *English Traits* without determining that the author believes race to be a critical factor in national identity. As Nicoloff argues, Emerson's "earnest and persistent inquiry into the role which race played in the dialectic of history made him very much responsible for the doctrines which he finally endorsed."[102] Under the guise of balance, under the mask of stasis, Emerson enacts his dialectic, one that is working toward an implied synthesis—the conclusion that race matters.

Certainly, we cannot resolve the social and political debates generated by Emerson's rhetorical style. However, one additional factor that might help us investigate this question is Emerson's discussion of methods of argumentation in *English Traits*. Although Emerson criticizes as well as praises the English legal system in his effort to provide a balanced representation, he expresses his admiration that into the English logic "an infusion of justice enters, not so apparent in other races,—a belief in the existence of two sides, and the resolution to see fair play. There is on every question, an appeal from the assertion of the parties, to the proof of what is asserted."[103] Emerson does not explicitly link the English sense of logic and justice to his own methodology, but it is safe to suggest that the process of fair deliberation that he describes as characteristic of the English also applies to the effect he strives for in the majority of his essays and lectures. This passage is suggestive because it complicates the supposedly fair play that Emerson gives to the question of racial determinism in *English Traits*. How seriously are we to take his statements dismissing the importance of race, one might wonder, when these very statements reconfirm his "Saxon" method of argumentation? How can one assert the equality of races through a methodology of logic that one has circumscribed racially?

To move from Emerson's specific comments about English law to an overall argument about the racial/political implications of Emerson's use of claims and counterclaims in relation to race is necessarily speculative. I do not mean to suggest that Emerson did not have ambivalence about race; this chapter is predicated on the assumption that his ambivalence is critical to his writing, especially to his "Address on Emancipation" (1844). However, when we read *English Traits* and his public antislavery lectures, we should keep in mind that Emerson may have been demonstrating rhetorically the "fair play" he attributed to his racial identity, and this, in turn, might lead us to question what

Gougeon calls Emerson's consistent public denial of African American inferiority. It is fair to suggest that the less overtly rhetorical ambivalence that
marks the "Address on Emancipation" gives way in *English Traits* to a rhetoric
of ambivalence that masks Emerson's conclusion regarding race as a signifier of
fate, a conclusion that Emerson had either reached or was working toward
accepting. Although *English Traits* does not explicitly comment on the question of the Negro race and slavery, it is hardly coincidental or irrelevant that
Emerson was working on this book, and delivering lectures in relation to it,
during the very years of his most intense antislavery activity. Can we understand *English Traits* as exhibiting Emerson's anxiety over what the American
race would look like after emancipation?

Two lectures that Emerson delivers late in his career, his "President's Proclamation" (1862) and "Fortune of the Republic" (1863), help explore this possibility. "The President's Proclamation," an address not particularly noteworthy
for its rhetoric, is nonetheless of interest because of Emerson's representation
of the emancipation of slaves in the United States, a representation made all
the more significant when juxtaposed with his earlier "Address on Emancipation" (1844).[104] Here Emerson focuses almost exclusively on the meaning of
emancipation to his white northern audience. Referring to the pain caused not
by slavery but by the Civil War, Emerson describes emancipation as clarifying
the meaning of the war for northerners: "It makes a victory of our defeats. Our
hurts are healed; the health of the nation is repaired. With a victory like this,
we can stand many disasters." The bodies needing healing are those that fought
in the war. This population, of course, includes former slaves and free people of
color but, as the rest of the essay's attention to his white northern audience
indicates, they are not necessarily included in this discussion. He continues
with a rather troubling passage: "It does not promise the redemption of the
black race: that lies not with us: but it relieves it of our opposition. . . . and it
relieves our race once for all of its crime and false position."[105] With his constant use of "our" and "us," Emerson reinforces the racial polarization that
marks this essay. More importantly, he repeats the gesture he makes in his
1844 lecture, leaving the question of the "redemption" of the black race open
to consideration. However, unlike his "Address on Emancipation," Emerson
follows his open-ended statement about the fate of African Americans with no
further comment or optimistic suggestion about that future. In his earlier essay
he included the dialectic to synthesize it, in part, with his powerful statement
"I esteem the occasion of this jubilee to be the proud discovery, that the black

race can contend with the white," but no similar statement appears in this address. Rather, in an essay dedicated to the prospect of emancipation, Emerson says no more about African Americans—a significant silence. One could also wonder why the "redemption" of the black race is not, by 1862, a foregone conclusion. Does he begin to doubt, even subconsciously fear, the possibilities of a multiracial democracy the more it becomes a potential reality? Does he, we might ask, entertain concerns about a postemancipation multiracial democracy similar to those that Whitman exhibits?

Just as "The President's Proclamation" can be read as revisiting Emerson's "Address on Emancipation," so too is "Fortune of the Republic" revealing when juxtaposed with Emerson's earlier speech and *English Traits*. If "An Address on Emancipation" established the possibility of an English American identity and *English Traits* transformed this possibility into a full-fledged theory of racial identity, then "Fortune of the Republic" makes the break between the English and American race that Emerson describes as inevitable in *English Traits*. By 1863, tensions between the British and northern Americans were high, as northerners believed Britain would intervene in the Civil War and help negotiate a peace that was not favorable to the interests of the United States.[106] As such, Emerson's representation of England is reversed from his 1844 address. In the earlier work, Emerson turns England into a symbol of the future, because its act of emancipation served as a possible model for America. Now the negative traits that Emerson identifies in *English Traits* (but moderates with positive descriptions of the nation and race) become the foundation for his attack on England. To Emerson, England represents solely trade and fate. "The English," Emerson explains, "have a certain childishness,—it is at once their virtue and their fault. . . . They are insular, and narrow. They have no higher worship than Fate. . . . Never a lofty sentiment, never a duty to civilization, never a generosity, a moral self-restraint is suffered to stand in the way of a commercial advantage." To Emerson, England embodies the "spirit" of fate and trade that the young American man must reject in order to bring meaning to the carnage of the Civil War. Indeed, Emerson returns to the rhetoric of "Self-Reliance," this time arguing for a practical idealism: "A man for success must not be *pure* idealist;—then he will practically fail: but he must have ideas, must obey ideas, or he might as well be the horse he rides on." For Emerson, the Civil War represented a dual opportunity: American men could reclaim manhood, and America as a nation could finally come of age. When he declares, "We are coming,—thanks to the war,—to a nationality,"[107] he reveals just how essential the conflict was to him in terms of solidifying the national identity he introduces in his essays in the 1840s and investigates more extensively in *English Traits*. We cannot dismiss, then, the importance of how often he associates this identity with race. The Civil War certainly had the potential not only to emancipate slaves but also to change radically the "body" of America. Emerson responded, in part, by defining that body in a racialized manner.

To establish the Civil War on moral principles, Emerson charges young men of the Union to make a final break from England and cement the American aspect of their English American identity. Sounding a note that would be quite familiar to readers of *English Traits*, he argues, "At every moment some one country more than any other represents the sentiment and the future of mankind. At present time, none will doubt that America occupies this place in the opinion of the nations."[108] Continuing, Emerson represents the Civil War as part of America's Manifest Destiny, a doctrine that he believes includes America's holding and administering "the continent for mankind." Having purified itself by striking "off the chains" that had been placed on the "weaker race," the stronger race of Americans was poised to set a worldwide example. Eventually, Emerson reaches rhapsodic heights that echo Whitman's glorification of the new American male:

Here let there be what the earth waits for,—exalted manhood, the new man, whom plainly this country must furnish. Freer swing his arms, further pierce his eyes, more forward and forthright his whole build and carriage, goeth, than the Englishman's, who, we see, is much imprisoned in his backbone. What a change! We are all of English race. But climate and country have told on us so that John Bull does not know us. It is the Jonathanizing of John. They have grown cosmopolitan. Once the most English of English men, hating foreigners, they have grown familiar with the foreigner, and learned to use him according to his gift.[109]

For the reader familiar with *English Traits* and with the science of race during Emerson's era, this passage is significant. The ambiguity of the line "imprisoned in his backbone" is particularly noteworthy. On the one hand, it suggests that the English man is "imprisoned in his backbone," a victim of his (fated) race, a race of excellence, but of the past. On the other hand, it suggests that the Englishman is "imprisoned" in the backbone of the American "Jonathan," thereby evoking the theories of arrested and progressive development that so fascinated Emerson. For Emerson, according to Nicoloff, these concepts were pivotal because they indicated that "while the ends of the universe had long awaited, and awaited still, their completion in time, these ends had from the beginning been complete in law."[110] Although he applied this concept to insist on a natural and organic relationship between man and the lower species, it can also apply to the relationship between the races of men. By saying that the English man is "imprisoned" in the American's backbone, Emerson portrays him as an "arrested" form of the "exalted" man, the new man whom the American, if not exactly embodying at this point in time, is moving toward as the stages of history advance. Typically, while the language evokes racial difference that is physical and innate (the backbone), Emerson also attributes change to "climate" and "country," or environmental factors. Also, to return briefly to the question of "foreigners" raised in relation to *English Traits*, it is significant that in this passage Emerson attempts to resolve the dilemma by transferring hatred of foreigners to the English and insisting that Americans have learned to "use" foreigners' gifts rather than despise them. But whatever the specifics of his definition, it is clear that to Emerson the "exalted" man is Jonathan, a man chastened by the experiences of the Civil War and therefore an American rather than an English American. The war, then, has the possibility not only of freeing the slaves, but also of freeing the new "race" of Americans from the backbone of the English. In effect, it births a new white American race. The place of the emancipated slave in what Emerson earlier called his Saxon brotherhood is, at best, uncertain.

As my analysis of these three antislavery lectures and *English Traits* suggests, not only was Emerson's public commitment to the equality of African Americans hardly unequivocal after 1844, but we can argue that he became increasingly willing to employ a language of racial difference as the nation moved toward and fought the Civil War. If earlier essays introduced the trope of race as "fate" to test the idea, in part because Emerson was ambivalent about the issue, later works may have introduced it with far less ambivalence and more as a style of argumentation that expressed his (racialized) fairness. Still, one has to ask why Emerson—who formulated a transcendent theory of identity that was based on the premise of humankind's spiritual unity, dedicated significant personal effort to antislavery reform in the late 1840s and 1850s, and publicly supported the right of emancipated slaves to obtain the vote and education[111]—would vacillate over ideas of race, ultimately endorsing a racialized national identity that, by definition, was either willfully oblivious to the heterogenous nature of the American population or, more cynically, intentionally exclusionary. I have already suggested several possibilities. To start, Emerson's anxiety over the nature of masculinity coincides with a rhetoric that both limited women to their embodied status and flirted with concepts of innate racial difference. Additionally, Emerson's move toward conservatism and fatalism later in his life coincides with his conception of race, as West points out, as a trope signifying man's limitations. Of course, as the final part of this chapter argues, we cannot dismiss the effect of the Civil War on Emerson and other writers. As the carnage continued and the formulation of a postwar America seemed distant, yet possible, many began a conservative move toward the identification of a nation reunified, in part, by whiteness. Moreover, Emerson's struggle with science and identity and his acquiescence to many scientific concepts (never swallowed whole, and always translated and challenged) underscore the increasing tendency of many Americans to understand identity as essentialized. This testifies, once again, to the pervasive influence of the powerful discourses of science in the antebellum era.

To these factors I would like to add one more exploratory suggestion. Perhaps the aging Emerson felt personally "fated" as he experienced a loss of power and his philosophies were tested in the political arena. As he fell into a cynicism regarding his early transcendentalism, Emerson may have relocated his search for power not in his singular "self-reliant" identity, but in a collective racial/national one. Whicher argues that the later Emerson shifted his sense of identity from a belief that his "real self" was primarily the "divine Self within him" to an understanding that his real self "was his whole contradictory nature, divine potentiality and mortal limits together." In part, Whicher suggests that Emerson responded to his intensified sense of self limits by transferring the search for power onto society as a whole. Rather than viewing society as a ruin "that must be rebuilt by some impossible Reformer," Emerson began to see it as "a single growing entity, in which each pulse of energy, and each following phase, are the successive stages in one evolving process."[112] I am not interested in defending or exploring the specifics of Whicher's argument, but I am intrigued by the suggestion that Emerson reacts to the realization of the limitations of human potential by transferring his quest onto the social whole, or, one could argue, onto the social body. Such a move reverses the earlier Emerson, to whom the social body represented the corruption that an individual had to resist through an examination of natural law.[113] Although Whicher is not concerned about this idea in relation to race, it is fair to argue that Emerson's sense of limitation—of fate—causes him to investigate more eagerly and consistently the idea of race in his later career, an investigation certainly helped by the preponderance of writings on race that dominated his age. Yet if he found limitation in theories of race, he also found power—the power of identifying himself (and his implied reader) with a larger social body, with an English American who was destined to dominate this historical epoch. In effect, he turns to the rhetoric of racial essentialism to associate himself with the power of whiteness, the power to embody via one's race the future of a nation and of humankind. He is certainly not the first, or last, author to respond to a personal sense of powerlessness by transferring the concept of limitation onto the bodies of others—onto the bodies of women in his 1840s essays, and onto the bodies of African Americans in his later writings. As chapter 5 demonstrates, Fuller's response to the dilemma proposed by her corporeal status and her need to claim power resulted in a similar method of transference. In her work, though, the bodies to which she most ascribes limitation and fatalism are those of Native Americans.

5

THE NEW FACE OF EMPIRE

The Price of Margaret Fuller's

Progressive Feminist Project

Yet, no doubt, a new manifestation is at hand, a new hour in the day of man. We cannot expect to see him a completed being, when the mass of men lie entangled in the sod, or use the freedom of their limbs only with wolfish energy.—Margaret Fuller, "The Great Lawsuit"

> Cast the bantling on the rocks,
> Suckle him with the she-wolf's teat:
> Wintered with the hawk and fox,
> Power and speed be hands and feet.
> —Ralph Waldo Emerson, "Self-Reliance"

We can wonder if, when commenting disparagingly on Americans' "wolfish" energy, Fuller intended to challenge Emerson, who prefaced "Self-Reliance" with the above poem. Published just two years prior to "The Great Lawsuit," Emerson's essay functions as the quintessential call for revitalized American manhood. The "bantlings" allude to the mythological story of Romulus and Remus, the two brothers who are flung into the Tiber shortly after they are born because their mother broke her vows as a vestal virgin. Washed ashore, they are suckled by a she-wolf, and eventually raised by a herdsman and his wife. When they set out to establish a new city, they quarrel, and Romulus kills Remus. Romulus then founds Rome, which prospers but has no women. Subsequently, Romulus invites the Sabines for a festival, drives the men away, and rapes the women.[1] Despite the myth's violence, Emerson employs the allusion in his enthusiastic call for young men to claim individualism and verve. His "bantlings," torn symbolically from the feminine/domestic sphere and suckled by a beast rather than a human mother, are called upon to become masculine builders of a new civilization. As his allusion to the creation of Rome suggests, his "empire" stands on a foundation of self-reliant masculinity. By contrast, Jeffrey Steele indicates that Fuller negatively associated "wolfish energy" with "Roman aggression." She aspired, instead, to an empire based on both masculine and feminine characteristics, or what she termed a "ravishing harmony of the spheres."[2]

As she makes clear elsewhere in "The Great Lawsuit: Man *versus* Men, Woman *versus* Women" (1843) and the revised version of that essay, *Woman in the Nineteenth Century* (1845), Fuller calls not only for the advancement of women in the United States, but also for the creation of space for feminine attributes within an increasingly masculine Republic. In *Woman*, Susan J. Rosowski argues, Fuller writes "her own version of America as the New World: the Old World was worn out in terms of gender roles, and a New Eden would be one in which Eve would have her chance."[3] Typical of many writers of her era, Fuller responded to the realities of American life in the East by shifting the location of her "New Eden" westward. The western territories come to represent a potential site for gender reform in her travel narrative *Summer on the Lakes, in 1843* (1844). Fuller's need to validate women as potential "creators of a nation"[4] and to envision the West as a place for the actualization of gender harmony leads her to conclude *Woman* with a rousing appeal to American women to oppose the annexation of Texas, an act she associates with masculine aggression incompatible with her New Eden.

Even though Fuller challenges the annexation of Texas explicitly and Emerson's masculine vision implicitly, she does not dispute the importance of building an American empire through westward expansion. Rather, she debates the nature of the presumed western empire, structuring *Summer* to clear the path for the expansion of Euro-American women's roles in the West, a reform that she believed would eventually rejuvenate the East. As the chronological proximity of "The Great Lawsuit," *Summer on the Lakes,* and *Woman in the Nineteenth Century* suggests, and as several scholars have also indicated, Fuller was simultaneously contemplating women's reform and the nation's destiny; her trip west was intertwined with the invention and reinvention of her feminist philosophy. However, although scholars generally agree that Fuller's trip and the book-length travel narrative that came out of it were critical to the process of revising "The Great Lawsuit" into *Woman in the Nineteenth Century,* there is no consensus over how much, and in what ways, her experiences in general and her contact with Native Americans in particular may have influenced her feminist philosophy.[5] One of the most compelling arguments about the interrelationship of *Summer*, *Woman*, and Fuller's contact with Native Americans is proposed by Christina Zwarg, who suggests that Fuller "pursues two intertwined narrative ambitions in *Summer on the Lakes*: a change in the attitude toward Native Americans and a change in the attitude toward women in general."[6] Although Zwarg recognizes that Fuller's empathy for Native Americans was troubled by several factors, including her "treacherous alignment of feminism with the discourse of progress" (105), a rhetoric that "nurtured the discourse of the vanishing American" (124), and the fact that "a concern for gender remains primary" throughout *Summer* whereas race does not (123–124), she nonetheless contends that Fuller's argument against a "fatal reading of gender" contains an "implicit critique of the fatal interpretation of Native Americans" (113). In the terms of my study, Zwarg's argument can be understood as implying that the dominant culture's fascination with Native Americans' supposedly fated bodies struck Fuller as uncomfortably resembling similar assertions about Euro-American women's allegedly inferior/fated bodies, claims that, as I demonstrate in chapter 1, were touted against women's reform efforts. According to Zwarg, because Fuller's resistance to the fated bodies of women in *Summer* implies a resistance to the similar discourse of the fated and vanishing Native American, whenever possible in *Summer* Fuller looks upon the Indians with an "anthropologist's sensitivity to the dynamic of cultural contact" (98).

Interpretations framing Fuller as a sympathetic recorder of the plight of Native Americans can be generated by looking at individual moments in the text, a fact that should not be surprising, given Fuller's dialectical method of writing. Much like Emerson, Fuller designs a style that authorizes herself as a seemingly impartial observer. Although I agree with Zwarg's contention that Fuller (consciously or not) recognized similarities between representations of Native American bodies and bodies of Euro-American women, I question Zwarg's assertion that Fuller gazed upon Native Americans with an "anthropologist's sensitivity," especially given the colonial implications of the ethnological discourse that Fuller deployed in *Summer*, and I argue that her recognition of corporeal parallels (of a "fatal" discourse) caused her to distance herself and Euro-American women from Native Americans. In effect, when Fuller goes west, she racializes herself as "white" (as corporeally and intellectually adaptable, as progressive and a part of the nation's future, as an ethnological observer, as a literate translator) while she repeats and expands upon common racialized stereotypes of Native Americans as "other" (as corporeally fated and not adaptable to progress, as ethnological and ethnographical subjects, as nonliterate and translated). The fact that Fuller solidifies an American/white identity by repeating common tropes of the vanishing and fated Indian is hardly surprising; such beliefs were common in the antebellum period. Nonetheless, the correlation between her representation of the fated/vanishing Indian and her call for a progressive feminist project merits further investigation.

In part, Fuller's position as a nineteenth-century romantic woman contributed to her conflict regarding gender and identity. On the one hand, as I elaborate upon below, Fuller wanted to assume an identity based on the female body, because this was a benefit within her romantic epistemological framework. On the other hand, she did not want to align herself with the "physiologists" who "bind great original laws by the forms which flow from them" and entrap women in limited embodied roles (*Woman*, 310). Fuller's assumption of the role of ethnologist during her trip enabled her to transfer symbolically the politically detrimental aspects of corporeality onto the bodies of Native Americans in *Summer on the Lakes* and thus to explore further the conflicting and politically precarious claims she makes in her feminist essays—assertions of both a special knowledge and identity that comes through the Euro-American women's body (which we may term essentialist) and of the fundamental equality of American women and men, which Julie Ellison aptly labels Fuller's "both/and" theory of gender.[7] Because Fuller's "both/and" theory of women's identity is so central to her feminist theory, a brief investigation of it as it appears in "The Great Lawsuit" and *Woman* precedes my analysis of Fuller's representations of Native Americans in *Summer*.

Both/And: The "Genius of Woman" and Equality

As for Lydia Maria Child, there were many reasons why Fuller, a white woman in the public sphere, might have been tempted to avoid representations or a detailed analysis of corporeality. When she wrote *Summer* and *Woman*, Fuller was unmarried and therefore even more vulnerable to rhetorical attacks challenging her purity. Indeed, Child comments on Fuller's nerve in publishing *Woman*: "It is a *bold* book," she writes in a letter to Louisa Loring; "I should not have dared to have written some things in it, though it would have been safer for me, being married."[8] In addition to the sheer courage needed to face potential insults, Fuller, who married comparably late for her era, also had to negotiate her status as someone who seemed to privilege her intellectual and professional ambitions over domestic relations. If we recall, for example, J. H. Pulte's claim in his *Woman's Medical Guide* that "[n]o triumph of the victorious soldier, the subtle statesman, the eloquent advocate, successful physician, or faithful minister can equal in reality and sublimity a mother's happiness, when fondling her infant. . . . There is no reason, then, why the woman, with true motherly feelings, should engage in any other but the business assigned to her by nature,"[9] we can begin to understand just how *unnatural* Fuller appeared to many of her contemporaries.

In addition to these dilemmas, Fuller, like Emerson, was influenced by the deaths of loved ones and by her corporeal awkwardness and pain, experiences that may have led her at times to envision identity as primarily noncorporeal. "My earliest recollection is of a death," she reflects in *Autobiographical Romance*, "the death of a sister, two years younger than myself." Although she sees "yet that beauty of death," she has "no remembrance of what I have since been told I did,—insisting, with loud cries, that they should not put the body in the ground." Later, when she was living with her family at Groton, her baby brother, Edward, died in her arms.[10] Also in Groton, her father suddenly passed away. Fuller was twenty-five, and his death, "echoing, as it did, anguished complaints about her father's emotional abandonment of her that she had expressed since her childhood—would haunt her for many years." In addition to being haunted by these deaths, Fuller also had to negotiate her body's peculiarities, both the pain she suffered and others' perception of her awkwardness. Having concentrated on her extraordinary education rather than on developing her physical agility and social skills throughout her childhood, Fuller's parents became worried about their adolescent daughter's ability to function properly as a lady in society. Their concern contributed to their decision to send Fuller (against her wishes) to Susan Prescott's Young Ladies' Seminary at Groton. Fuller also suffered from "several adolescent blemishes—some permanent, like squinting at people to compensate for her nearsightedness, and others temporary, like the rash or possible acne that her father called the 'eruption on her face.'"[11] According to Thomas W. Higginson, it was at about this time in her life that Fuller made up her mind to be "bright and ugly," wording that suggests the extent to which Fuller may have separated her intellectual self from her corporeal self.[12] In addition to awkwardness, Fuller experienced physical suffering throughout her adult years, and her letters testify to the consistent companion that pain became in her life. For example, when she was twenty-nine, she sent verses to Emerson, commenting: "[M]y sufferings last winter were almost constant and I see the journal is very sickly in its tone."[13] A letter she wrote to Elizabeth Hoar at age thirty-two provides a typical description of her misery: "I am tired out now so that there is constant irritation in my head which I can only soothe by keeping it wet with cold water, and pain, such as formerly, in the spine and side. . . . I am quite exhausted, feel as if I could not go a step further, and the day, as a whole, has no joyous energy."[14] For much of Fuller's life, each day was a struggle against pain. Despite this struggle, her relationship to corporeality was never one of mere dismissal or transcendence. In addition to being an unmarried woman plagued by corporeal complaints in antebellum America, Fuller was also a dedicated romantic, and in the romantic context pain authenticates genius.[15] Fuller capitalizes upon this association in *Woman in the Nineteenth Century*, implying that her suffering marks her as particularly gifted: "[W]omen of genius," she maintains, "even more than men, are likely to be enslaved by an impassioned sensibility . . . and they are of weaker bodily frame."[16] Typical of Fuller, she wants it both ways—dismiss her body *and* claim its special nature.

One factor that could have contributed to Fuller's seemingly contradictory approach to the politics of the body, to her tendency to represent identity as both transcendent and corporeal, is her recognition that scientific assertions of inherent gender difference were often harmful to women's reform efforts. Both "The Great Lawsuit" and *Woman* protest against the relegation of women to the domestic sphere based on claims of an essential female nature. "History jeers at the attempts of physiologists to bind great original laws by the forms which flow from them," Fuller asserts in *Woman*. "They make a rule; they say from observation, what can and cannot be. In vain! Nature provides exceptions to every rule. . . . Presently she will make a female Newton, and a male Syren" (*Woman*, 310).[17] Here Fuller explicitly distances herself from the scientists who try to relegate women to distinctive roles based on theories of physiology. However, if Fuller disavows scientific theories, she does not dismiss science outright. Indeed, her "exception" to the rule—the "female Newton"—points to Fuller's desire to inhabit, perhaps appropriate, the discourse of science. Unlike numerous women in mid-nineteenth-century America who endorsed gender distinctions and argued that women should reform society from within the domestic sphere, Fuller wanted women to be public and private, to take on any societal role, to be "sea-captains, if you will" (*Woman*, 345). Yet she also claims a "genius of woman," a quality that can be read as essentially feminine, not only in the ideal Woman, but also in the real, embodied women of the nineteenth century. By arguing that women were somehow different and yet should be allowed to fulfill any societal role, Fuller was faced with obstacles that did not confront women who acquiesced to the Doctrine of Separate Spheres.[18] How could she assert that women were distinct (thus securing a place for the feminine in what she perceived as an aggressively masculine or "wolfish" society and allowing for women's particular romantic sensibility), but not *so distinct* that they could not fulfill the full range of societal roles?

To address this dilemma, Fuller developed what Ellison aptly calls a "both/and" philosophy of gender. "The Great Lawsuit" and *Woman in the Nineteenth Century* are predicated on the romantic assumption of historical progress, as well as on Fuller's assertion that neither men nor women have as yet developed their fullest potential, their ideal. Therefore, the struggle of the nineteenth century, as indicated by the subtitle of "The Great Lawsuit" ("Man *versus* Men, Woman *versus* Women"), is the struggle between the disembodied "idea" (what we might call the ideal) of Man and Woman versus their embodied reality as men and women. Although both genders are mere "pygmies" in relation to their potential greatness, Fuller maintains that "the idea of man, however imperfectly brought out, has been far more so than that of woman" ("Lawsuit," 4–7). Arguing that it is now time for "Euridice" to "call for an Orpheus, rather than Orpheus for Euridice," in other words, for women to lead the way in the human pilgrimage to the ideal, Fuller cleverly carves a space for an expansion of women's societal roles. Only if women can be allowed to move toward their ideal (toward Woman), can men also progress on their journey, and Fuller makes clear here and elsewhere that this development depends upon women's ability to assume characteristics and roles usually deemed masculine, if they will help them obtain their destiny. Because she wants to carve space for women to fulfill masculine roles and demonstrate masculine characteristics, Fuller warns readers not to assume that masculine and feminine traits are always embodied in male and female bodies respectively, suggesting instead that "[m]ale and female represent the two sides of the great radical dualism" but are "perpetually passing into one another. Fluid hardens to solid, solid rushes to fluid. There is no wholly masculine man, no purely feminine woman" ("Lawsuit," 43). Nonetheless, if Fuller disavows any simplistic correlation between the feminine idea and the bodies of real women (of Woman extending naturally into women), she hints throughout both essays that most women, at least in the nineteenth century, embody feminine traits far more often than masculine ones, and she suggests that this tendency should be honored and cultivated. Consider, for example, Fuller's assertion of a fundamental equality of souls, an assertion that seems to argue against corporeal essentialism:

> In so far as soul is in her completely developed, all soul is the same; but as far *as it is modified in her as woman*, it flows, it breathes, it sings, rather than deposits soil, or finishes work, and that which is especially feminine flushes in blossom the face of earth, and pervades like air and water all this seeming solid globe, daily renewing and purifying its life. Such may be the especially feminine element, spoken of as Femality. But it is no more the order of nature that it should be incarnated pure in any form, than that the masculine energy should exist unmingled with it in any form [emphasis mine]. ("Lawsuit," 43)

Here Fuller begins with the concept of a fundamental equality of the soul "so far" as the soul is "completely developed," but we should read this statement in the context of Fuller's progressive romantic philosophy, which assumes that the soul is not fully developed in any "body" in the nineteenth century. Rather, women and men struggle for the fulfillment of soul in a material society and through their corporeality, which Fuller describes as the soul "modified" in the body. Therefore, in the nineteenth century, the soul is "modified" in women, a modification that aligns women more often than men with feminine (and romantic) characteristics, although Fuller is certain to end this passage and paragraph with the assertion that neither men nor women contain exclusively masculine and feminine traits. If Fuller seems to dance around the relationship between the idea/ideal Woman and real women—if the passage begins and ends with a dismissal of gender difference but includes in its middle a contradictory claim of "an especially feminine element" modified in the bodies of women—this should not be surprising. Her slippage indicates Fuller's desire to claim both difference and equality. Ellison contends that Fuller wants "women both to discover their special powers as women and . . . claim equal opportunities with men. She oscillates, therefore, between honoring divination, which proceeds out of the natural law of sexual difference, and celebrating the manifold exceptions to gender topologies."[19]

Additional passages in the "The Great Lawsuit" demonstrate further Fuller's slippage between her claim of a disembodied idea of Woman and her desire to locate "divination" in women's corporeality. For example, Fuller notes that "[t]he electrical, the magnetic element in woman has not been fairly developed at any period. Everything might be expected from it; she has far more of it than man. This is commonly expressed by saying, that her intuitions are more rapid and more correct" ("Lawsuit," 38). When Fuller claims that woman "has far more" of the electrical/magnetic element and laments that this has not been fully developed in women during any period, she slips from language of the ideal to language of the real by indicating that the seemingly disembodied characteristic ("the magnetic element") needs to be "developed" in real, embodied women. She elaborates upon her description of the special "genius of woman" by defining it as "electrical in movement, intuitive in function, spiritual in tendency" and as an ability that does not easily tend toward "classification, or re-creation, as an instinctive seizure of causes" ("Lawsuit," 43). Clearly, these assertions flirt precariously with the innate conception of gender that justified the Doctrine of Separate Spheres. Yet Fuller does so because romanticism privileges intuition, and if women are believed to be corporeally more susceptible to intuitive knowledge, then they are placed in a position of authority in relation to male romantics. When we consider Eric Cheyfitz's argument regarding Emerson, for example—that for Emerson "it is women" who generally "exhibit the mean egotism of a soul unable to free itself from the body"—we can understand why Fuller wants to locate in women's bodies the power of intuition and divination. Indeed, we can discern why Fuller defines the intellect as "cold" and "ever more masculine than feminine" (Woman, 302). Likewise, Fuller's disavowal of women's desire for "classification" is particularly telling, because "classification," according to Michel Foucault, is inextricably connected to the Enlightenment era's desire for the "tabulation of all possible differences" through the sciences, a methodology that Fuller indicates women by nature tend to shy away from. Thus Fuller again marks women as virtually embodying the romantic dependence on intuition and search for unity in opposition to Enlightenment taxonomy.[20]

Fuller expands upon her interest in women's electrical/magnetic capabilities in Summer, in which she includes a detailed description of the Seherin von Prevorst, a German woman whose body was particularly sensitive to "magnetic and ghostly influences" (Summer, 150). Although it is not clear in Summer why Fuller includes this long digression in a travel narrative ostensibly about her trip west, if one understands that the question of how to reconcile the idea of the special "genius of woman" with her belief that "all soul is the same" was very much on Fuller's mind as she traveled, its inclusion becomes more comprehensible. In fact, Fuller first mentions the seeress briefly in "Lawsuit" and returns again to the story in *Woman*, further elaborating upon its significance.[21] In *Woman*, Fuller indicates that the Seherin serves as an example of someone who might have had "a gradual and gentle disclosure of remarkable powers" but, instead, was ruined by an unsuitable marriage. Regrettably, no one was able to interpret her special revelations because to appreciate "such disclosures one must be a child, and here the phrase, 'women and children' may, perhaps be interpreted aright" (*Woman*, 304–305). In other words, Fuller argues that women and children are especially capable of both receiving and interpreting revelation that comes through the body; they are, in effect, better mediums. It is significant that further explanation of the implication of the Seherin's story comes in *Woman*, after Fuller has concluded her trip west and finished *Summer*. After all, as Zwarg points out, the Seherin's story exhibits the risk that certain feminist strategies contain. Zwarg argues that Fuller's inclusion of this story in *Summer* demonstrates how a "certain type of feminist critique," especially one that concentrates on a liminal (and, I would add, corporeal) identity, "is also subject to containment," as it can "easily become the site of political deformation or annihilation" (119–121). While Zwarg argues that the story shows the Seherin's "feminism to be complicit with the larger limits of Western civilization," an additional lesson can be garnered. It is just as possible that Fuller, after returning east, was better able to clarify and endorse the idea of the Seherin's potentially remarkable female body because she had transferred the unwanted political ramifications of such claims onto Native Americans in *Summer*.

In addition to carving a privileged space for women within romantic epistemology, Fuller's "both/and" philosophy also enables her to argue for women's reform without giving up the positive benefits of difference. If we erase bodily differences, she implies, we jeopardize the fundamental balance between masculinity and femininity, the "ravishing harmony of the spheres" she prophesies (*Woman*, 260). If we erase difference, she further argues, we might ultimately be left with a society that privileges only masculine characteristics, or "wolfish" energy. Rather than having women simply assume manly roles, Fuller envisions a society that not only liberates men and women from societal roles based on gender, but also frees the roles themselves from traditionally gendered connotations. Perhaps the most powerful example of this is exhibited in the story of Miranda, which Fuller includes in "Lawsuit" to suggest that a self-reliant woman does not want to be thought of as above her sex or as "a manly

woman" ("Lawsuit," 16–17). However, as in the case of her additional comments about the seeress, *Woman* once again elaborates upon the theory of identity and societal roles that Fuller introduces in "The Great Lawsuit" and
contemplates in the West. This time, she does so through a story that follows
the Miranda narrative in *Woman*—a story about Emily Plater, a countess in
Poland who assumed male attire, joined the army, and became a hero. Plater's
life demonstrates that women should be free to usurp roles traditionally
assigned to men, but Fuller also prods her readers into drawing an additional
conclusion. "Some of the officers were disappointed at her quiet manners; that
she had not the air and tone of a stage-heroine," Fuller notes, adding that
"[t]hey thought she could not have acted heroically unless in buskins; had no
idea that such deeds only showed the habit of her mind" (*Woman*, 265). Fuller
asks readers to consider that a woman might not only redefine herself by
becoming a warrior, but also reconstruct the warrior's role. Later in *Woman*,
Fuller elaborates upon a theory that helps to explain Plater's story, calling for a
celebration of difference that would enable some women to act in traditionally
feminine ways and suggesting that "divisions are only important when they
are never to be transcended." "We are pleased that women should write and
speak," she continues, "if they feel the need of it, from having something to
tell; but silence for ages would be no misfortune, if that silence be from divine
command, and not from man's tradition" (*Woman*, 288). By carving space for
woman's "silence" as well as voice, Fuller struggles to maintain a place for traditionally feminine characteristics in the face of gender reform that might
threaten to erase difference.

Fuller's fear of the erasure of difference and her "both/and" philosophy of
gender may be tied to her political goals as well. Although she contends women
and men are equal as souls, she recognizes that their gender matters in the
material sphere. In both "The Great Lawsuit" and *Woman*, Fuller expresses her
outrage at what she calls the "contemptuous phrase, 'Women and children.'"
("Lawsuit," 13). Adding a third term to the discussion, that of the slave, she
argues that there "exists, in the world of men, a tone of feeling towards women
as towards slaves" that manifests itself in comparisons between women and
children, comparisons that argue "the infinite soul can only work through
them in already ascertained limits; that the prerogative of reason, man's highest portion, is allotted to them in a much lower degree; that it is better for them
to be engaged in active labor, which is to be furnished and directed by those better able to think, &c. &c." ("Lawsuit," 11–12). Here Fuller makes a connection

between the oppression of women and slaves, one that is certainly not uncommon for the time period, especially given Fuller's association with antislavery activists. Both are defined outside the realm of Enlightenment reason; both are said to be limited by their bodies; both are thought of as children rather than adult participants in society.

Clearly Fuller is bothered by the manner in which concepts of innate gender difference can be used to limit women in the same way that essential concepts of race relegate many African Americans to the status of slaves. It is also significant that, despite her trip west, Fuller continues to turn to the more commonly accepted metaphoric link between women and African Americans, a move that suggests she wants to distance herself from association with Native Americans.[22] Her response to the fact that women's bodies are being used against them is telling. Rather than retreating from the topic of corporeality, she argues that the body matters in relation to the governing body of the nation. Knowing that men associate (white) women with children and slaves, she asks, "[C]an we wonder that many reformers think that measures are not likely to be taken in behalf of women, unless their wishes could be publicly represented by women?" (Woman, 258–259). Just as Fuller asserts the importance of gender difference philosophically, so too does she argue that difference matters in the body politic. Indeed, in the previous passage, it is on the basis of difference that she calls for women's participation in the political sphere. Because men are using rhetorically women's bodies against them, women's bodies must be present in the public sphere to refute essentialism. Fuller returns to this idea later in Woman, when she argues that there should be more women serving as teachers in women's schools, as they have "experienced the same wants" as their female students (Woman, 297). In effect, Fuller cannot erase the body either philosophically or politically; she needs to argue that there are embodied differences, and that they matter, at least in the nineteenth century, the time awaiting the gender harmony she prophesies.

Fuller's simultaneous assertion of a special "genius of woman" and gender equality creates tension in "The Great Lawsuit," and these contradictions are not resolved. When Fuller returns to the essay to revise it into Woman in the Nineteenth Century, many of the additions she includes, some of which I indicate above, help to clarify her complicated theory of gender identity. The fact that Fuller revisited the issue suggests that it was very much on her mind as she traveled west. As Zwarg points out, if Fuller "thought the journey would help her escape the engrossing theoretical issues she had left behind, she was quite mistaken"; the problems of "pedagogy, translation, and difference were central to her experience" (97). To these dilemmas I would add the possibility of a special "genius of woman" and the political ramifications of claiming this characteristic. As Fuller left for the West, then, her body presumably weighed heavily upon her. What did it mean to be embodied as a woman in the nineteenth century? How could one claim a special feminine self while asking to be treated as an equal in male intellectual and political circles? Although not answering these question explicitly, *Summer on the Lakes* addresses them implicitly.

Holding the "Native" Captive: Summer on the Lakes

If the problem of corporeal knowledge weighed heavily on Fuller before she departed for the West, her trip may have heightened her awareness of the relationships among corporeality, national identity, and Euro-American women's progress in at least two identifiable ways. First, as Rosowski demonstrates, the physical restraints placed upon a woman traveler often disappointed Fuller. While she departed for her trip a "traveler, creator, and adventurer," she returned a woman with a greater "awareness of the role gender was playing" in her journey.[23] Second, as I outline above, Zwarg argues that Fuller's contact with Native Americans might have intensified her concern over the political implications of a fatalistic discourse, a discourse linked to theories of corporeality in the nineteenth century. Zwarg contends that *Summer* "develops a troubling conflict between [Fuller's] faith in the limitless opportunities that might open for women and her sense of the deadly limit that had already been imposed upon Native Americans" (108).

Before examining Fuller's response to the "deadly limit" that had been imposed on Native Americans, a better understanding of the importance of the West in relation to Fuller's feminist goals is helpful. As suggested previously, Fuller's insistence on the necessity of an individual's freedom to contain and exhibit both masculine and feminine characteristics can be extended to the concept of the body politic. Certainly Fuller's imagined "empire" was quite different from that of many of her male contemporaries in that she called for the inclusion of feminine qualities in the public, as well as the private, sphere. In "The Great Lawsuit" Fuller seems to respond directly to Emerson's summons to cast the "bantling on the rocks," asking readers to imagine a community where all types of people can thrive. After discussing the progress made by extraordinary women who have entered the public sphere, Fuller remarks that the real challenge is "how to get to this platform, or how to make it of reasonably easy access." In effect, she answers Emerson's allusion with an analogy, commenting that not everyone can grow up among rocks. "Plants of great vigor will almost always struggle into blossom, despite impediments," Fuller contends, but "there should be encouragement, and a free, genial atmosphere for those of more timid sort, fair play for each in its own kind," because some plants "are like the little, delicate flowers, which love to hide in the dripping mosses by the sides of mountain torrents, or in the shade of tall trees. But others require an open field, a rich and loosened soil, or they never show their proper hues" ("Lawsuit," 19). Fuller's analogy suggests that although "plants of great vigor" (or "self-reliant" ones) will grow "despite impediments," America's task is to provide a healthy environment to encourage the flowering of all its members.

For Fuller, the moment when America would provide this nurturing environment and allow space not only for individual women but also for feminine characteristics to flourish was approaching. When she revises the Miranda story in *Woman*, she includes a passage affirming her faith that being embodied as a woman in the nineteenth century is a benefit. When Miranda's male friend compliments her by saying that she "deserved in some star to be a man," Miranda responds by declaring her "faith that the feminine side, the side of love, of beauty, of holiness, was now to have its full chance and that . . . it was better now to be a woman, for even the slightest achievement of good was furthering an especial work of our time" (*Woman*, 263). Miranda's optimism reflects the author's; Fuller often prophesies the triumphant return of feminine power. However, she needed a site to construct her new American garden, and as she gazed westward, she drew upon common cultural motifs of the frontier as a place of edenic potential, eagerly surveying the Great Lakes and Wisconsin territory as a possible site for a reformed America. Such idealization of the West is typical. As Richard Slotkin demonstrates, the West as a place of rebirth was a powerful image before colonization began, and it dominated nineteenth-century American thought.[24]

The West was also critical to Fuller's imagination. As Rosowski points out, the West represented an "extension of two major influences upon [Fuller]—the Jeffersonian thought she learned from her father, and Transcendentalism." It held symbolically the "broad promise of individualism" and freedom from "restrictions imposed by society." If Fuller believed the West was good for individuals in general, she also thought it held special promise for women and families in particular. For example, Fuller declares enthusiastically in *Summer* that in the West "whole families might live together, if they would. . . . Those painful separations, which already desecrate and desolate the Atlantic coast, are not enforced here by the stern need of seeking bread" (*Summer*, 105). Yet even if Fuller had faith in the West's potential, she "came to understand," as Annette Kolodny argues, "how that Eden might at once exist and yet be unavailable to women."[25] Nonetheless, Fuller contends that women's liberation could originate in the very obstacles they confronted in the West. Concentrating on the "unfitness of the women for their new lot," Fuller urges settlers to throw off "the fatal spirit of imitation" and devise a more appropriate education for women. Not only are women's daily household tasks made more difficult by frontier life, but "[w]hen they can leave the housework, they have not learnt to ride, to drive, to row, alone." In fact, all that eastern education has prepared them for is to become fashionable ornaments. Fuller laments: "They can dance, but not draw; talk French, but know nothing of the language of flowers; neither in childhood were allowed to cultivate them, lest they should tan their complexions. Accustomed to the pavement of Broadway, they dare not tread the wildwood paths for fear of rattlesnakes!" (*Summer*, 106–107).

In this passage, Fuller not only laments the prohibitions placed on women, but also articulates how these restrictions are based on race. In the East, to remain a white woman, one must refrain from any unladylike activities that would result in the darkening (symbolically or otherwise) of one's identity. On the frontier, Fuller implies, white women will be less restrained by prohibitions of genteel behavior and thus can "tan." Because women on the frontier will suffer fewer restrictions on their behavior, Fuller insists that the land could provide a "lot which would be full of blessings" for women who are properly prepared (*Summer*, 106). A more practical education will enable women to adjust to their new lifestyle, and therefore the West will lead the East to reform women's education out of necessity. Additionally, the ability to wander down "wildwood paths" by oneself is more than just a physical need, because observing nature on solitary walks is one way of inviting romantic inspiration. In the West, Fuller imagines, women will have the room to grow out of their decorative roles and into healthy beings, fully participating in the local economy, as well as in their own physical, spiritual, and philosophical development. The West, therefore, will be a site for the testing of America's democratic principles in relation to gender and for the renewal of American society.

By envisioning the West as a place of trial and renewal, Fuller draws upon long-standing ideas of American national identity. Before leaving for her trip, Fuller had already invested in the traditional idea that America was destined to serve as a testing site for the world's moral advancement. In a passage that she includes in both "The Great Lawsuit" and *Woman*, Fuller draws upon Puritan motifs of the "New World" as a "city on the hill," a place that would attract the world's scrutiny as it enacted a decisive struggle for progress.[26] Replacing the Puritans' religious agenda with a moral and political one, Fuller argues that "this country is as surely destined to elucidate a great moral law, as Europe was to promote the mental culture of man." She continues:

> Though the national independence be blurred by the servility of individuals; though freedom and equality have been proclaimed only to leave room for a monstrous display of slave dealing and slave keeping; though the free American so often feels himself free, like the Roman, only to pamper his appetites and his indolence through the misery of his fellow beings, still it is not in vain, that the verbal statement has been made, "All men are born free and equal." There it stands, a golden certainty, wherewith to encourage the good, to shame the bad. ("Lawsuit," 8)

Here Fuller repeats her wilful optimism, her faith that the universe ultimately advances toward justice. However, she recognizes that this destiny relies on individuals taking action. Drawing again on Puritan rhetoric—this time issuing a jeremiad-like warning—she tells readers that "[t]he new world may be called clearly to perceive that it incurs the utmost penalty, if it reject the sorrowful brother" ("Lawsuit," 8). By appropriating the language of Puritan New England, Fuller is able to link her feminist goals with the nation's past and future. Recognizing that many Americans prized the myth of national progress, she argues cleverly that for America to obtain its preordained destiny, women will have to be greeted as equal members in the body politic. However, as this analysis should make clear, Fuller's endorsement of a "progressive" national rhetoric implies her acceptance of the conquest of Native American lands. She needs the West as a site of feminist renewal, and this, in turn, implies Indian Removal.

It is during her trip west, then, that Fuller's material goals (Euro-American women's expanded roles) and philosophical/political goals (the need to claim a "special genius of woman" without relegating oneself to an inferior position in American society) strikingly converge. Nowhere is this convergence more dramatic than in the first chapter of *Summer* as Fuller begins her trip at Niagara

Falls, a scene that establishes the process of corporeal transference that the rest of the travel narrative completes. The setting is particularly significant in relation to both romanticism and the increased interest in national literature that marked the first half of the nineteenth century. Like many romantics, Fuller wants to experience a moment of sublimity as she travels through the landscape. What better place for her to search for this than at Niagara Falls, a site that Elizabeth McKinsey argues emerged as "*the* American icon of the sublime in the early nineteenth century"?[27] At first, Fuller's efforts to experience the sublime are frustrated, in part because she is blocked by her intellect, by all that she has previously read or seen about the much discussed falls. However, she finally manages to appreciate their magnitude and experience the sublime. She recreates this moment: "Before coming away, I think I really saw the full wonder of the scene. After awhile it so drew me into itself as to inspire an undefined dread, such as I never knew before, such as may be felt when death is about to usher us into a new existence. The perpetual trampling of the waters seized my senses. I felt that no other sound, however near, could be heard, and would start and look behind me for a foe." In this description, Fuller's perception of the Falls inspires her with an "undefined dread." The falls "seize" her "senses" and isolate her, leaving her unable to hear any other sound. To some extent, this scene evokes Emerson's "transparent eyeball," in that Fuller appears to reach a state where she can forget what she later calls "one's little self and one's little mind" and merge with the sublime (*Summer*, 72–75).[28] However, unlike Emerson, Fuller experiences trepidation as well as awe. What, we might ask, is the source of Fuller's dread? Isn't she, as both a romantic and a woman, particularly suited and eager for this revelation? Yet she hesitates. In part, we can read her pause in conventional terms and recognize that the sublime is supposed to inspire dread as well as revelation. However, we can also surmise that Fuller pulls back from the knowledge she claims to desire because she does not want to immerse herself so fully as to lose her unique identity. She fears self-obliteration, something akin to death, which, although ushering one to a "new existence," nonetheless obliterates a unified sense of self, the identity that comes in part through the temporary state of embodiment. Therefore, her gender is important to the scene and helps explain why her reaction to a potentially sublime moment differs so much from Emerson's transformation into a "transparent eyeball." At the falls, the philosopher Fuller seeks the sublime, but the woman Fuller resists the loss of self this implies. She distrusts merging with what too often defines her, the natural sphere. Zwarg summarizes the dilemma confronting Fuller by arguing that "on the border of North American culture, the binary trap of nature/representation could recur with still more force," and the image Fuller "conjures at the foot of the falls" draws "on the fact that women were often identified *with* the forces of nature" (101). The identification of women with nature that haunts Fuller at the falls exemplifies the way in which certain types of feminist critique/subversion (such as Fuller's assertion of the "genius of woman") can become, in Zwarg's words, "the site of political deformation or annihilation." To help solve the dilemma presented by the corporeal aspect of identity, Fuller makes a rhetorical leap:

> I realized the identity of that mood of nature in which these waters were poured down with such absorbing force, with that in which the Indian was shaped on the same soil. For continually upon my mind came, unsought and unwelcome, images, such as never haunted it before, of naked savages stealing behind me with uplifted tomahawks; again and again this illusion recurred, and even after I had thought it over, and tried to shake it off, I could not help starting and looking behind me. (*Summer*, 72)

If Fuller does not want to be aligned with "nature/representation," then she averts this "trap" by recognizing that the "mood of nature" that created the falls also created the Indian. By reflecting on the similar "identity" shaping the soil and the Indian (rather than reflecting on the similar "identity" that shaped the soil and herself) Fuller shifts readers' associations of herself with nature to the Native Americans, who come to embody the American landscape. She becomes the observer who, although seeking the sublime, is incapable of an unmediated affinity with nature. It is no coincidence, then, that Fuller repeatedly connects Native Americans to the sublime in the rest of *Summer*. As Lucy Maddox argues, "Fuller can do with her views of the Indians what she could not do with her views of the whites: she can look through the disappointing present and locate the buried sources of sublimity."[29] Rather than merge with the sublime, or have her body associated with it, she locates it in Native Americans.

Fuller cannot completely merge with nature, then, because like "the civilized man" she describes later who "is a larger mind, but a more imperfect nature than the savage," she carries the burden of intellect with her to the falls.[30] Presumably this gear does not hinder Native Americans because, as she describes them at a different point, "[t]he red man, when happy, was thoroughly happy; when good, was simply good" (*Summer*, 222). Encumbered by the weight of civilization, rather than by her body, Fuller assumes the role of mediator or interpreter of nature, both to herself and her readers. Zwarg's assertion that Fuller evokes Native Americans in the scene to question the "binary trap" of "nature/representation" is astute. However, her contention that Fuller questions this binary in terms of race and gender—to reveal the "manner in which women and Native Americans are both trapped by a tendency in Western thought to appropriate by opposition" (101)—clouds the means by which Fuller relegates Native Americans to an association with nature in order to break the binary for Euro-American women. She sets herself up in opposition to the Indians in order to authorize herself as a writer of the American landscape.

If Fuller evokes the noble savage in her alignment of the Indian with the landscape, her next sentences draw upon the idea of the Indian as just plain savage. The image of Indians sneaking up behind a white woman with uplifted tomahawks was common in the nineteenth century, particularly in the captivity narrative, a genre that was experiencing newfound popularity on the frontier. Kolodny links frontier women's identification with captive heroines to a shared sense of entrapment. Many women went west unwillingly and felt like captives in a land and culture that was not their own.[31] Yet Fuller's experience contradicts captivity, as she heads west deliberately and temporarily, regretting only that her adventures cannot be more extensive. The Native Americans she meets wield no tomahawks and serve as silent, submissive guides, or mark the landscape with their "picturesque" poverty (*Summer*, 175). She is a tourist, not an explorer. Why, then, does Fuller evoke the common cultural motif of the captive at this point in her narrative? In part, one could argue that her response harks back to her conflicting fear of, and desire for, the sublime. The "savages" are naked, and this could represent her fear of merging (because the Indians may want to rape her, thus forcing her to merge with the landscape they now symbolize) or her desire to merge despite the corporal vulnerability it exposes her to (encoded in her envisioning the "savages" as naked and therefore potentially desirable). All of these interpretations point to the vulnerability that Fuller may feel as an embodied woman at the falls, whether she is susceptible to her own corporeal desires, the threat of merging symbolically with Native Americans, or the threat of being too readily aligned by her body with the natural sphere. Those uplifted tomahawks are poised for something: is it capture or decapitation? In either case, Fuller represents herself as corporeally exposed. Even her mind seems easily penetrable, as "again and again this illusion recurred" though it came "unsought and unwelcome" (*Summer*, 72).

Why does Fuller envision herself in danger of being taken captive, especially if, as she claims, these images are not welcome? Zwarg suggests that Fuller is "determined to displace the image she summoned at the foot of the falls" in the rest of *Summer* and therefore pursues "a change in the attitude toward Native Americans and a change in the attitude toward women in general" (104). Although Fuller certainly wants to "displace the image" that she creates at the falls, she does not do so by arguing for a different attitude toward Native Americans. If anything, *Summer* is rather predictable in its lament for fated and vanishing Indians.[32] Rather, Fuller draws upon the captivity narrative to change attitudes about Euro-American women. As June Namias argues in *White Captives*, in the antebellum era a shift occurred in the way white women were portrayed in captivity narratives. Whereas earlier captives were often either adaptable or physically defiant, narratives from the 1830s and 1840s are based on "the poor, hapless woman who is taken unawares," the "frail flower," who "rarely emerges from her shock, distress, and misery." Significantly, these changes "correspond to the rise of True Womanhood and the mass marketing of sentimental fiction"; in short, they helped to reaffirm a woman's *naturally* weaker status and the need for men to protect her from the potentially dangerous public sphere.[33]

Certainly, Fuller would resent this image of corporeal vulnerability and weakness. But how does one escape the role of captive in one's society, especially as the belief that women were naturally weaker and destined to a separate sphere was becoming increasingly prevalent? One way is to enact a reversal. No longer will a white woman be held captive, either by "savages" or by the Euro-American men in the East. Instead, she will hold the "savages" captive in her text. If the genre of captivity does not serve her well, she will leave it at the falls and replace it with several discourses, including ethnology. No longer will Fuller be the Euro-American woman who is an object of pity, a frail flower held captive. No longer will she be associated primarily with the natural sphere. No longer will she be a woman who is scrutinized by scientists for evidence of physical laws that would define her status in society. All of these roles will be transferred onto the Native Americans in the rest of *Summer*. They will be taken "captive" in her text as specimens to be studied at her readers' leisure. In this sense, Rosowski is correct in suggesting that Fuller "made the West imaginatively accessible to other women." But part of the process of making the West accessible to women from the East entailed making the "savages" objects of Fuller's study.

Repeatedly Fuller calls for establishing Native American archives to collect both physical artifacts and samples of oral literary traditions. In effect, her text becomes the "monument" to Native American culture that she calls for in *Summer*. For example, after dismissing the feasibility of the Chippewa people's becoming citizens of Michigan because she has no hope that they could "be admitted, as brothers, to the heart of the white man," Fuller asserts that the demise of all Native Americans is inevitable. She adds: "Yet, ere they depart, I wish there might be some masterly attempt to reproduce, in art or literature, what is proper to them, a kind of beauty and grandeur, which few of the every-day crowd have hearts to feel, yet which ought to leave in the world its monuments, to inspire the thought of genius through all ages" (*Summer*, 189). Later Fuller expands her appeal for the collection of Native American relics by encouraging the establishment of a "national institute, containing all the remains of the Indians" (*Summer*, 211). After calling for the salvation and collection of these materials, Fuller proceeds to collect and comment upon various aspects of Native American culture in her text, drawing upon travel narratives, histories, and ethnological works. Her accumulation of Native American relics—like the Native American "mementoes" she later keeps in her room at Cambridge—can be read as her attempt to be a "master" ethnologist, cataloging texts and narratives instead of skulls.[34]

In this respect, Fuller was very timely. Just two years before Fuller wrote *Summer*, the American Ethnological Society was formed to provide the United States government with information about various tribes.[35] In a compelling assessment of Fuller's relationship to the Harvard Library and early American ethnology, Nicole Tonkovich argues that Fuller includes extensive summaries of recent ethnological work to "buttress" her own authority. Because Fuller was the first woman to be granted access to the Harvard Library (in order to research *Summer*), Tonkovich suggests that we read the work as a "synecdoche of the library itself." "Like the curators who would establish Harvard's Peabody Museum of American Archaeology and Ethnology twenty years later," Tonkovich contends, Fuller perceives Native Americans within a preexisting framework and reiterates these categories to affirm her status as a scholarly authority. As Fuller's choice of verbs demonstrates, she wants a Native American historian to "collect much that we could interpret" (*Summer*, 210). The power of interpretation rests with Euro-Americans, and typically with males. Fuller usurps this traditionally masculine task, assuming the role of a metaphysical self examining embodied others.[36] At the same time, she provides eastern women readers with access to abstracts from ethnological texts, implicitly inviting them to scrutinize the cultural "remains" of the Native Americans.

The parallels between Fuller and the early ethnologists are striking. Her claim, for example, that "it seems most probable, that a peculiar race was bestowed on each region, as the lion on one latitude and the white bear on another" (*Summer*, 203–204) anticipates Samuel Morton's assertion of polygenesis, the theory that humankind was created "in many pairs; and they were adapted, from the beginning, to those varied circumstances of climate and locality." Likewise, when Fuller rejects assimilation as a possible option for Native Americans, she does so by commenting on amalgamation, noting that those "of mixed blood fade early, and are not generally a fine race. They lose what is best in either type, rather than enhance the value of each, by mingling" (*Summer*, 188). Here her beliefs parallel those of Josiah C. Nott and George R. Gliddon, who, when addressing "hybridity" in relation to Negroes and Caucasians, claim that mulattoes are the shortest-lived of any class, are less capable of enduring fatigue and hardship than either of the "pure" races, and are prone to low fertility rates and abortions.[37] By rejecting racial mixing while arguing that it is the only means through which Native Americans can achieve "civilization," Fuller leaves no role for Native Americans in the body politic. Although she does not advocate or condone their violent removal, she does assume their demise is inevitable.

Interestingly, to build her argument against amalgamation, Fuller draws not only upon ethnology but also upon oral literary tradition, including a Native American story entitled "Muckwa, or the Bear." It is no coincidence that Fuller mentions that the story has "not before appeared in print" (*Summer*, 193). By discovering the tale and by neglecting to name its source, Fuller can serve as its sole translator. Certainly, as someone who comprehended several languages and had translated German texts, Fuller was sensitive to the complexity of translation.[38] However, in this case, she elides the cultural intricacies and says that the "little tale" shows the Indians' "human way of looking on [bears], even when engaged in their pursuit" (*Summer*, 193). Fuller's assumption that she can easily discover, translate, and interpret the tale is troublesome. As Cheyfitz argues, representations of seemingly seamless translations are inextricably associated with colonization. Often the process of translation "attempted to displace . . . Native Americans into the realm of the proper, into that place where the relation between *property* and *identity* is inviolable, not so these Americans could possess the proper but so that having been translated into it they could be dispossessed of it . . . and relegated to the territory of the figurative."[39] Through her inclusion of this tale (and the subsequent lesson she draws from it) Fuller justifies the removal of the Native Americans from their property, relegating them to the symbolic realm.

The story itself details the plight of a Native American bear hunter, Muckwa (the Chippewa word for bear), who relinquishes the chase to live among bears. His marriage to a bear produces one bear and one human. Despite several happy years, the hunter grows restless, returns to his hunting, and accidentally kills his bear sister-in-law. To complicate matters further, his human friends track him back to his new habitat, hoping to kill bears. Consequently his bear wife tells Muckwa to return to his people and concludes: "The Indian and the bear cannot live in the same lodge, for the Master of Life has appointed for them different habitations." Muckwa departs with his human child, leaving his bear wife and child behind. At the tale's close, Fuller concludes that it is "a poetical expression of the sorrows of unequal relations; those in which the Master of Life was not consulted" (*Summer*, 193–195).

Through its placement in Fuller's text, the story can be read as an allegory for the relationship between Euro-Americans and Native Americans, especially if they are proposed as different "species." Muckwa could be the Native American who will not give up hunting to adopt "bear" (or white) ways. He could also represent the Saxon man, whose desire to hunt or violent nature is far too ingrained to allow for a shared peaceable existence (as Fuller maintains about the Native Americans and settlers in Michigan).[40] Whomever Muckwa symbolizes, the overall implication of the story is that species cannot adapt. Therefore they must live in different habitations, or, as nineteenth-century governmental policy would demonstrate, some must be relegated to reservations. Also, the children produced from these two "species" are not a mixture of the best qualities of both and cannot remain together as siblings. Interestingly, Fuller has Native Americans voice this belief: the tale itself claims that the "Master of Life" has appointed for them different habitations. By then allegedly distancing herself from this viewpoint—by interpreting the tale as a "a poetical expression" of "unequal relations . . . in which the Master of Life was not consulted"—Fuller insinuates that disapproval of amalgamation is a Native American viewpoint. As the narrator, Fuller assumes a tone of regret regarding the "unequal relations," which apparently are not part of the Master of Life's plan, but her more explicit statements about amalgamation elsewhere in the text contradict the sincerity of this purported regret and align Fuller with a more typical gesture of lamenting the inevitably fated Indian.[41]

Fuller's role of cultural translator and mediator is connected to her use of the captivity narrative genre in her opening scene at the falls. If captivity narratives of the 1830s and 1840s were objectionable to Fuller, earlier versions of captivity— still popular in the antebellum era—may have provided a model by which she could authorize herself as a writer and cultural mediator. Namias argues that during the Colonial era the predominant image of the woman captive is that of the "survivor," a woman who is not a "passive victim" but rather knows how to "adapt." For example, in Mary Rowlandson's 1682 account of King Phillip's War (a narrative still popular in Fuller's time), Rowlandson asserts her authority as the creator and narrator of her own story, translates and mediates between Native American and Western cultures, and displays an extensive mastery of textual (biblical) material. Like Rowlandson, Fuller tells her story, mediates between cultures, and proves herself an authority on text. Indeed, the acts of mediation, adaption, and writing all become crucial ways in which Fuller distinguishes herself from the Native Americans. "Unlike the Indians," Tonkovich argues, "some white women are capable of resisting that marginality, representing themselves in writing and having these representations preserved in institution of cultural memory."[42] Even Fuller's insistence that the races cannot mix is based, in part, on the idea that the Indians are somehow outside the realm of adaptability, unlike the Euro-American women who can survive, even thrive, in the West.

If Fuller's assertions of the impossibility of cultural mixing seem contrary to her declaration of the unity of soul and her derision of the scientists who try "in vain" to form physiological rules, they can be explained, in part, by her hopes for Euro-American women. Within this framework, Fuller's extensive descriptions of Native Americans primarily foster her status as a woman who is able to observe and write on different cultures. Fuller's desire to elevate white women to the status of cultural observers becomes particularly evident in her discussion of the roles and status of Native American women. Although she says that women's "observations of women" are "always more valuable than those of men"—a claim that certainly elevates her status as author and affirms her belief that embodied experiences matter in terms of knowledge—she contends that the observations of Anne MacVicar Grant were "much nearer" to the truth than those of Jane Schoolcraft (a woman of Ojibwa and Irish heritage) because Grant's "observation did not bring her so close" and, therefore, she was able to look "more at both sides to find the truth" (Summer, 177). Fuller's dismissal of Jane Schoolcraft as somehow less objective than a Euro-American woman is troubling, especially when considered in relation to Fuller's reliance on the work of Schoolcraft's Euro-American husband: earlier in Summer, she describes Henry Rowe Schoolcraft's Algic Researches, a text on which Jane Schoolcraft collaborated with her husband, serving as interpreter and translator, as a "valuable book" (Summer, 88). Fuller gives more credit to Euro-American women and men than to a woman of mixed cultural and racial heritage who is fluent in the language and customs of the Ojibwa people, as well as educated in Euro-American traditions.[43] Although the embodied experiences of Euro-American women are claimed as an asset, the body of Jane Schoolcraft seems to hinder her objectivity.

This denigration of Jane Schoolcraft's ability to represent adequately Native Americans results, in part, from Fuller's need to elevate the white woman to the status of the literate observer of Native American bodies and cultures. By privileging objectivity over subjectivity and embodied experience, Fuller also marks herself, at least temporarily, as part of an Enlightenment-based privileging of the visual. Not only does this shift to the objective/visual move away from the romantic epistemology Fuller claims for herself and other Euro-American women in her feminist essays, but it also aligns Fuller with what Mary Louis Pratt aptly calls the narrative of "anti-conquest" common to much Euro-American travel writing. Narratives of "anti-conquest" contain strategies of representation "whereby European bourgeois subjects seek to secure their innocence in the same moment as they assert European hegemony." Pratt focuses on several separate, but related, strategies, including natural history and ethnography, and argues that all usually contain the protagonist of the "seeing man," the "male subject of European landscape discourse—he whose imperial eyes passively look out and possess." When Fuller privileges Euro-American visual and objective knowledge over that of Jane Schoolcraft, she in effect assumes a masculine role. Like Emerson, who Cheyfitz argues assumes that generally it is women "who exhibit the mean egotism of a soul unable to free itself from the body,"[44] Fuller here assumes that it is Native Americans, and Native American women in particular, who are unable to "free" themselves from their bodies, unable to obtain the Enlightenment status of the objective spectator.

Fuller's repudiation of Jane Schoolcraft not only helps her separate Euro-American women "subjects" from Native American women "objects," but also it allows her to dismiss any evidence that Native American women are less oppressed than Euro-American woman. Fuller spends several pages analyzing the status of Native American women and professes to present a balanced view of the relationship between the "Red man" and his wife. "Why will people look only on one side?" she asks; "they either exalt the Red man into a Demigod or degrade him into a beast" (Summer, 175). But even while recognizing that most people define Native Americans either as noble savages or as just plain savages, Fuller eventually determines that Native American women are different from their Euro-American counterparts. They may "suffer less than their white sisters, who have more aspiration and refinement, with little power of self-sustenance," she surmises, adding that "their place is certainly lower, and their share of the human inheritance less" (*Summer*, 178). Therefore, although it is true that provocative readings can be made by juxtaposing the various sections of *Summer* with one another and that Fuller does at times describe scenes, especially those with Native American women, with some sympathy, her concern should not be interpreted as deconstructing her overall premise of Euro-American superiority. Joan Burbick correctly suggests that ultimately Fuller creates a hierarchy of women's oppression: "Her insight is not that all women are alike, but that in their oppressed position they ironically mark an additional hierarchy of values. The native women's extreme oppression, in one sense, legitimates the inevitability of their demise."[45]

Moreover, when Fuller professes sympathy for Native Americans, she does so, in part, to demonstrate her superior cultural sensibility. She is more refined, she implies, than those women who loathe the "dirt" and "smell" of Native Americans (*Summer*, 180). Fuller's need to distance herself from these women may also be further evidence of her desire to rewrite captivity narratives of the 1830s and 1840s. Often, according to Namias, these narratives turned uncleanliness and "disgusting Indians" into "highly salable works." By stating her distance from the women who find Native Americans dirty, Fuller once again differentiates herself from the writers of antebellum captivity narratives. Later she distinguishes herself further from the rude "masses," putting the question of Native Americans' future into the past tense: "Had they been truly civilized or Christianized, the conflicts which sprang from the collision of the two races, might have been avoided; but this cannot be expected in movements made by masses of men. The mass has never yet been humanized, though the age may develop a human thought" (*Summer*, 212). In this passage Fuller assumes the role of the superior person, developing a "human thought" that the masses are as yet unable to comprehend. This intellectual maneuver allows her to wash her hands of any responsibility for the government's actions against Native Americans and to propose, instead, a feeble response to the question of colonizers' responsibility for the suffering of those whom they have colonized. The "white," she says, should "look on him in pity and brotherly goodwill, and do all he can to mitigate the doom of those who survive his past injuries" (*Summer*,

212). As she states earlier: "The whole sermon may be preached from the text, 'Needs be that offenses must come, yet wo them by whom they come'" (*Summer*, 189). For Fuller, the mark of the "superior" race is the way it interprets, collects, and cares for what remains of an "inferior" and "fated" race.[46]

Fuller's absorption of Native American "relics" into her text becomes more troublesome when considered in relation to national identity. Because she believes Native Americans are fated to extinction, she wants to assimilate their spirit into American identity. McKinsey argues that Fuller's vision at the falls strikes a "personal chord," reminding her that "[o]ne must accept the savage nature in oneself, just as whites must recognize the inhumanity of their treatment of the Indians." As McKinsey suggests, Fuller wishes to absorb part of the "savage" into the "civilized" man, and her highest praise goes to those settlers who adopt Native American values, which Fuller interprets as a sensibility that privileges the sanctity of nature over material gain.[47] She comments:

> Seeing the traces of the Indians, who chose the most beautiful sites for their dwellings, and whose habits do not break in on that aspect of nature under which they were born, we feel as if they were the rightful lords of a beauty they forbore to deform. But most of these settlers do not see it at all. . . . their mode of cultivation will, in the course of twenty, perhaps ten, years, obliterate the natural expression of the country.
>
>   This is inevitable, fatal; we must not complain, but look forward to a good result. (*Summer*, 96)

Fuller almost concedes that Native Americans are the "rightful lords" of the land due to their proper valuation of it, but retreats into what is "inevitable, fatal"—the domination of the United States. This domination, she believes, will eventually produce an outcome that will be positive, presumably because it includes the advancement of Euro-American women, paving the way for a ravishing harmony of spheres.

Fuller reiterates her esteem for Native American values throughout her text. At one point she says that critics "may blacken Indian life as they will, talk of its dirt, its brutality, I will ever believe that the men who chose that dwelling-place were able to feel emotions of noble happiness as they returned to it, and so were the women that received them" (*Summer*, 100). Here Fuller's praise of Native Americans is tied to their ability to recognize the beauty of the landscape in which they live, a sensibility she contrasts with the capitalistic, speculative vulgarity of the settlers. In this sense, Fuller moves from the scientific "anti-conquest" narrator described above to the stance of the "sentimental subject" and travel writer that Pratt also describes in *Imperial Eyes*. This narrator of travel, Pratt argues, "looks *through* the language of science and finds the alternative spiritual understanding of nature as image of the divine." Yet both the sentimental and scientific subject share the "crucial characteristics" of maleness, middle-classness, and a presumed innocence and passivity.[48]

Fuller continues joining Indian greatness with Indian ability to appreciate the landscape through eyes other than scientific or commercial by stating that she understands how an "Indian brave, accustomed to ramble in such paths, and be bathed by such sunbeams, might be mistaken for Apollo, as Apollo was for him by West" (*Summer*, 100). As McKinsey points out, Fuller alludes to the painter Benjamin West, who, upon first seeing the Apollo Belvedere in Rome, declared that it looked like a young Mohawk warrior. McKinsey maintains that just as West's remark "implied that American nature should be accorded equal consideration with classical culture, so Fuller's comparison elevates the Indian to the stature of classical heroism." Although this is a possibility, Fuller's comparison of Native Americans to Greeks is problematic. Emerson indicates in "History" that the Grecian state, which he believed every person passes through, "is the era of the bodily nature, the perfection of the senses." Not surprisingly, as the intellect becomes more prominent, one danger is that a man can entirely dismiss the "Greek" component of his identity. "The idiot, the Indian, the child, and unschooled farmer's boy, stand nearer to the light by which nature is to be read," Emerson cautions, than "the dissector of antiquary."[49] In the overall context of *Summer*, it is highly probable that Fuller intended her allusion to suggest that the American continent also produced a "Greek" stage of humankind, similar to the one that Europe claimed as its roots. The emerging race of Americans will incorporate this sensual, childlike race through the appropriation of their positive values. This process of viewing Native Americans as a "lost version of the self," according to Lora Romero, is typical of many nineteenth-century writers. Citing both Fuller and James Fenimore Cooper, Romero argues that "aboriginals represent a *phase* that the human race goes through but which it must inevitably *get over*."[50] The formulation of American identity, then, rests on the supposedly fatal extinction of Native Americans and the romantic appropriation of their cultural traditions.

Toward the end of her text Fuller states the importance of appropriating the symbolic value of Native Americans for a distinctly American identity. "I feel acquainted with the soul of this race," she claims; "I read its nobler thought in their defaced figures. There *was* a greatness, unique and precious, which he who does not feel will never duly appreciate the majesty of nature in this American continent" (*Summer*, 222). Once Native Americans no longer inhabit the frontier, Fuller implies, a writer like herself—one who is "acquainted with [their] soul"—can then translate their disembodied sensibility for an American readership. No longer a corporeal representative of the natural and the sublime, Fuller instead is the translator of these qualities, which she locates in Native American bodies and culture. Through Fuller's text, the Native American helps Euro-Americans distinguish their own heritage from that of their European counterparts. This is why Fuller longs, when looking upon "picturesque groups" of Chippewa and Ottowa tribes, for "Sir Walter Scott to have been there. . . . I was so taken up with the spirit of the scene" (*Summer*, 175). Scott, Fuller implies, would recognize that America, too, has the raw material necessary to produce great literature. It just takes the right kind of observer to turn it into art.

By the end of *Summer*, a reader is left with the impression that the Native Americans are victims of their own bodies. Incapable of change, amalgamation, or assimilation, they are fated by their corporeality to vanish; their bodies will soon be a part of the past; their presence will remain only in art. Unlike Native Americans, one has the impression that Euro-American women will excel in the West, primarily because they are able to adapt and to participate in their culture's literary and scientific projects. It is not too much of an imaginative leap to suggest that, consciously or not, Fuller reacts to fears of being defined solely by her body, of being relegated to the position of a feminine woman in the nineteenth century, by juxtaposing her own identity with that of Native Americans. She becomes the disembodied woman with an ethnological and ethnographical eye who can look across cultures to dismiss concerns about her corporeal inferiority.

Fuller returns from the West having bolstered her authority in at least two significant ways. First, as my analysis of the additions in *Woman in the Nineteenth Century* suggests, she was freer to elaborate upon the positive ramifications of the "genius of woman," having symbolically transferred the negative "fatal" implications of corporeality onto Native Americans in *Summer*. Second, although she flirts with the prospect of acquiring a "tan" in the West—of joining the frontier and Native American women, who were carving out a new definition of gender that was not as reliant on white womanhood—she ultimately leaves her role as tourist and returns to the East even "whiter" than when she departed. She headed west with gender on her mind and returned with a newfound sense of racial solidarity. Like Emerson after his second trip to England, Fuller returns home with an understanding of the power and benefits bestowed by whiteness. Proceeding to the Harvard Library to tackle the tasks of ethnologist and writer, Fuller authors her first book-length manuscript and in the process authorizes herself as a Euro-American woman capable of participating in a Euro-American man's world. As Rosowski notes, when *Summer* was published it "attracted the attention of one of the West's more enthusiastic boosters," Horace Greeley, who subsequently invited Fuller to become the *New York Tribune*'s chief reviewer and critic.[51] Rosowski is correct in arguing that in many ways Fuller becomes a "pioneer" in the "preserve of men" after her trip west, be that preserve the Harvard Library or the profession of journalism. Yet pioneering, as Fuller was well aware after her trip west, comes with cultural costs, costs from which she was not exempt.

When Fuller stood at the Niagara Falls, she was caught in a profound dilemma. Torn between her desire to become one with the sublime and to escape the societal trappings of her female body, she took a rhetorical and political leap. As such, Fuller's texts demonstrate the conflicting and unresolved relationships between her body, her politics, and her philosophical goals. Although she wants to trust her body, she also recognizes that a woman in the nineteenth century has cause to fear an association with the natural and corporeal. In this respect, she complicates the response to a question that Walt Whitman had not yet posed. In his 1855 edition of *Leaves of Grass*, he brazenly demands to know: "Who need be afraid of the merge?" For Whitman, Emerson's hierarchy, which ultimately privileges the soul over the body, is not acceptable. Like Fuller, he perceives a vital link between corporeality and philosophy, seeking a cosmic understanding that can only be reached through the integration of corporeality and spirituality. In doing so, he challenges not only scientific essentialism, but also the romantic premise of corporeal transcendence. Yet as Fuller stands on the threshold of the West in 1843, simultaneously resisting and longing for the sublime, she demonstrates that many people legitimately fear "the merge" of which Whitman sings.

6

"WHO NEED BE AFRAID OF THE MERGE?"

Whitman's Radical Promise and the Perils of Seduction

> A child said, What is the grass? fetching it to me with full hands,
> How could I answer the child? I do not know what it is any
> more than he. . . .
>
> Or I guess it is a uniform hieroglyphic,
> And it means, Sprouting alike in broad zones and narrow zones,
> Growing among black folks as well as among white,
> Kanuck, Tuckahoe, Congressman, Cuff, I give them the same, I
> receive them the same.
> —Walt Whitman, "Song of Myself"

"Who need be afraid of the merge?" Walt Whitman dares readers in the debut edition of "Song of Myself" (l. 136).[1] Indeed, the rest of *Leaves of Grass* (1855) seems to repeat, "Who?" For Whitman, the "merge" is an all-encompassing force, blending sexuality with politics, philosophy, and spirituality to produce unprecedented generative power. Politically Whitman's merge promises to fuse the disparate bodies that make up the body politic, to create a "race of races" in a teeming "nation of nations." Philosophically the merge has the potential to reverse what Whitman perceives as the devastating effects of the Cartesian split between mind and body, thereby reinvigorating an individual's capacity for knowledge. Spiritually the merge links sexuality to the process of cosmic revelation and quest. The first edition of *Leaves of Grass* delights in the seemingly inexhaustible potential of the merge, positioning the body and sexuality as forces of cosmic significance.

By the time Whitman first published *Leaves of Grass*, two scientific "truths" were becoming accepted by many Americans: the concept of a sexually fragile middle class and the belief that race and gender were innate categories of difference. Aspects of these beliefs offended Whitman's most cherished convictions—his faith in the inevitable realization of democracy on the continent and his idealization of Americans as a new, healthy, vital race. Consequently, it is against these related dogmas that Whitman launches some of his most masterful attacks. He turns sexuality and the body into "uniform hieroglyphic[s]" (l. 97) that consecrate democracy. He champions a polymorphic, nonprocreative sexual energy to challenge antebellum associations between productivity and sexuality. Most importantly, he creates an epistemology of the body that fundamentally challenges the modern structures of knowledge then coming to dominate his age. Unlike scientists who taught about the body, Whitman trusted his body as a teacher, welcoming it as an equal partner in the search for knowledge. The first part of this chapter explores the radical implications of Whitman's merge, demonstrating how his poetry can be read in opposition to the discourse of science, despite his personal fascination with the scientific innovations of his age.[2]

Yet Whitman's question, "Who need be afraid of the merge?," betrays the potential threat implicit in his work, indicating by its interrogative and bold tone that the poet expects some resistance to his call to merge. As Margaret Fuller's reluctance to merge with the sublime at Niagara Falls indicates (see chapter 5), for those who were often defined by their corporeality in politically precarious ways the merge represented peril as well as promise. Whitman's masterful absorption threatens to obliterate difference, to assume too much, to consume readers entirely as he fuses them into his ideal race of Americans. To learn Whitman's lesson, the reader must be absorbed into the poet, as Whitman aspires one day to be reabsorbed "affectionately" by America.[3] The jeopardy associated with a corporeal merge parallels the threat of a literary one. Professing to speak for those who are silenced, Whitman assures readers that he is a comrade to people of "every hue and trade and rank, of every caste and religion" (l. 343). Welcoming both sexes with remarkable enthusiasm for his time, he yearns to be the "poet of the woman the same as the man" (l. 426) and to speak for forbidden and silenced voices. Yet how can one "act as the tongue of" another (l. 1244) without risking the silencing of that other's voice?

The danger the merge posed to certain groups, particularly women, African Americans, and Native Americans, is evident in Whitman's texts; it is one of the contradictions his poetics attempts to contain, especially through parataxis and the catalog technique. Whitman's use of the poetic catalog seems to be, as

Lawrence Buell proposes, an "inherently 'democratic' technique," one that suggests "the vast, sprawling, loose-knit country which America is" and "adheres to a sort of prosodic equalitarianism: each line or image is of equal weight in the ensemble; each is a unit unto itself."[4] Despite what Betsy Erkkila likewise identifies as Whitman's attempt to create an "egalitarian poetics," the potential peril of Whitman's poetics appears subtly in the 1855 edition of *Leaves of Grass* and becomes more pronounced in subsequent editions. Although Whitman strives toward gender equality, he is, for example, ultimately unable to conceive of women's sexuality outside the realm of procreation. Similar to Ralph Waldo Emerson, Whitman often confines women to a corporeal identity, reserving the power of a spiritual/corporeal merge primarily for men. Along with the revolutionary homosexual potential of the "Calamus" series in the 1860 edition comes the simultaneous exclusion of women from his sexually charged political sphere. Additionally, although Whitman longs for a merge that would produce a "race of races," his method of reading the body, of discerning "the expression of a wellmade man," and his glorification of the Jacksonian myth of the frontier/working man often make Whitman sound like a member of a chorus of writers, scientists, and politicians who were busily defining and defending the Caucasian/American race. The second part of this chapter articulates the limitations of Whitman's merge and his call for an epistemology of the body, especially when considered in relation to the body politics of mid-nineteenth-century America.

Whitman's Epistemology of the Body

> Through me forbidden voices,
> Voices of sexes and lusts . . . . voices veiled, and I remove
>   the veil,
> Voices indecent by me clarified and transfigured.
> (ll. 518–520)

Whitman wanted to be the translator of the "many long dumb voices" of the oppressed and repressed, and his explicit celebration of sexuality and the body certainly struck a powerful chord in many readers. However, to read Whitman only in terms of the dynamic of expression in an age of repression is to award an exaggerated role to repression, as Michel Foucault suggests, "because power would be a fragile thing if its only function were to repress, if it worked only through the mode of censorship, exclusion, blockage and repression . . . exercising itself only in a negative way." Rather, power "produces effects at the level of desire—and also at the level of knowledge." In nineteenth-century America, scientific scrutiny of the body became one of the most powerful means of containing desire, and scientific knowledge was often understood as a potent tool for mastering corporeality. "The more perfectly scientific the young mind becomes in anatomy and physiology," a popular 1837 lecturer guaranteed, "the more strongly it is secured against the undue influence of lewd associations."[5] In this context, what makes Whitman so revolutionary is his attempt to alter radically the connections between sex, the body, and knowledge. In an age that sought to know sex, that regarded both the body and sexuality as sites to be objectively mastered, Whitman proposed to know *through* sex. Nonprocreative sexual acts, which many of his contemporaries considered antisocial, undemocratic, and criminal, were represented as generating spiritual and cosmic knowledge in Whitman's verse.

When arguing about Whitman's glorification of nonprocreative sexual acts, it is easy to open oneself to charges of reading his poetry in a manner that reflects our era's post-Freudian obsession with sexuality, rather than placing Whitman within his historical context. For example, scholars argue that passages we now interpret as homosexual received only "scattered gay readings" in the 1870s, and they rightly note that Whitman, in his own day, was mostly accused of being a womanizer rather than a proponent of male-male sexuality.[6] Similarly, as I discuss below, many modern readers of Whitman (including myself) are troubled by his appropriation of a physiological discourse that, despite its purported call for women's liberation, tended to reduce women's identity to their reproductive capabilities, yet women of his own era were often Whitman's greatest supporters. These shifting responses point to the historical context and construction of sexuality and gender roles and complicate any readings of sexuality ("coded" or otherwise) in his poems. My intent, then, is not to reduce Whitman's poetry to what it "says" about sex or gender, any more than my intent in chapter 4 is to reduce Emerson to what he "says" about race. Yet we must acknowledge that, in many respects, Whitman's poetry is among the most corporeally suggestive of his era. As Michael Moon argues, Whitman's texts exhibit the dual impulse toward "extreme literality and extreme indeterminacy."[7] We certainly want to acknowledge the dialectical relationship between "extreme literality" (the sexual acts that may be suggested in his verse) and "extreme indeterminancy" (the manner in which many of his passages move from the literal to a vague concept of kosmos). To do so, we must ponder the potential literal implications of his most explicit passages and explore lines of poetry that on one reading appear to be graphic, particularized representations of sexuality and, on another reading, seem to have very little to do with the body itself.

We can also presume that Whitman's investment in his age's discourses of the body and sexuality was personal, as well as political, leading us to ask how a man searching for the vocabulary with which to describe his erotic desire for, and possibly his sexual encounters with, men might represent sexuality in the last half of the nineteenth century. As David S. Reynolds argues, the question of Whitman's sexuality has been asked "either directly or indirectly ever since *Leaves of Grass* first appeared." Despite the understandable interest in the correlation between Whitman's physical experiences and the representations of corporeality in his poetry, Reynolds notes that "knowledge of his sexual activities has not gone much beyond" John Burroughs's, Whitman's first biographer's, "maddeningly vague statement" that between 1837 and 1848 Whitman had "'sounded all the experiences of life with all their passions, pleasures, and abandonments.'"[8] Some scholarship indicates that Whitman had probably engaged in what we would now identify as homoerotic and/or homosexual activity by the time he published his first edition of *Leaves of Grass*. For example, Charley Shively's collection of Whitman's letters, together with those of various male correspondents, indicates that Whitman actively pursued and maintained intense male-male relationships throughout his life. Byrne R. S. Fone has analyzed Whitman's early prose works and notebooks and likewise demonstrates that Whitman's desire for men began early in his life. As Jerome Loving argues, the "ongoing debate" about Whitman's sexual orientation "will probably continue in spite of whatever evidence emerges." Nonetheless, "[o]ne fact is clear: he required from his earliest adult years the company of young men, working men, and 'roughs.'"[9]

Although Reynolds argues that Whitman's relations with men can "be best understood as especially intense manifestations of the kind of same-sex passion that was seen everywhere in antebellum America,"[10] he also points to times when Whitman struggled with his desire for men, anguish that hints at Whitman's sense that his same-sex passion might not have been comparable to his era's typical male-male friendships. Whitman's most explicit statement regarding this desire is in his journal entry of 15 July 1870 on Peter Doyle. As is well known, Whitman coded Doyle in his journals with the numeral 16.4, for the letters in Doyle's name. The fact that Whitman adopted a code suggests that he might have sensed something unusual, perhaps culturally deviant, in his desire for, and relationship with, Doyle. In this passage, Whitman resolves, in what Reynolds identifies as the discourse of phrenological self-regulation, "[T]O GIVE UP ABSOLUTELY & for good, from the present hour, this FEVER-ISH, FLUCTUATING, useless, UNDIGNIFIED PURSUIT of 16.4—too long, (much too long) persevered in,—so humiliating—It must come at last & had better come now . . ."[11] Typically, Whitman's language neither demonstrates a sexual pursuit of Doyle nor explicitly disavows this possibility. It is also unclear what specifically is "undignified" and "humiliating," his desire for Doyle or the fact that Doyle may not reciprocate Whitman's passion.

The ambivalence Whitman displays in this 1870 passage toward his pursuit of Doyle can be compared with his ambiguous denial of the sexual implications of the "Calamus" series in his summer 1890 letter to John Addington Symonds. Symonds was a homosexual, who had written to Whitman on several occasions, and—in this instance—asked if Whitman contemplated in his conception of comradeship "the possible intrusion of those semi-sexual emotions and actions which no doubt do occur between men? I do not ask, whether you approve of them, or regard them as a necessary part of the relation? But I should much like to know whether you are prepared to leave them to the inclinations and the conscience of the individuals concerned?" To this, Whitman replies that the "morbid inferences" Symonds finds in the "Calamus" series were "quite at the time entirely undream'd & unreck'd" and are "disavow'd by me & seem damnable." Yet even in this angry letter of denial, Whitman proceeds to elaborate that the "one great difference" between himself and Symonds is "restraint," wording that certainly leaves open the possibility that Whitman sympathizes with Symonds's physical impulses toward other men, even if he portrays himself as someone who does not act on those impulses. Of course, it certainly makes sense if, in the repressive environment for homosexuals of the 1890s, Whitman was quick to deny any such interpretation of his poems. This letter, like his journal entry on Doyle, indicates a tension between Whitman's passionate desires for men and an equally strong desire to restrain, control, or deny them.[12]

If Whitman's poetry often masks his ambivalence toward male-male desire by portraying male adhesiveness as a powerful, creative force, one could speculate (and, admittedly, speculate is all we can do) that Whitman's evolving struggle with his sexuality led him to sympathize with others who might also be labeled deviant or criminal. Like Lydia Maria Child, who (as I argue in chapter 2) responds to the figurative vulnerability of her body in the public sphere by creating tactful strategies with which to represent the slave's body, Whitman may also have reacted to the vulnerability of his body—the possibility that his desires were deviant, or would be labeled as such—with compassion for others who experienced socially unacceptable desires, such as the women whose sexual passion, often categorized as deviant or monstrous in mid-nineteenth-century America, he celebrated. In this respect, Reynolds traces a suggestive incident regarding Whitman, sexuality, and criminality that is purported to have taken place during 1841 in the remote village of Southold, Long Island, where Whitman was a school teacher. According to Reynolds, Southold oral tradition and the oral tradition of the Whitman family indicate that Whitman may have been publicly denounced from the pulpit of Southold's First Presbyterian Church because of what was deemed his inappropriate relationship with some of the (younger) male students he taught, and with whom he most likely lodged, sharing a bed. As the legend went, members of the congregation formed a mob, seized Whitman, and tarred and feathered him, inflicting enough physical harm to force him into a month's recuperation.[13] Reynolds is careful to point out that this story cannot be proven, although he has located evidence that Whitman resided in Southold during this time period, a fact Whitman omits from all of his subsequent biographies and correspondence. Indeed, we should be cautious about an oral tradition that links a presumed homosexual with the sodomizing of young men, as it too conveniently fits into the criminalization of the homosexual identity that takes place during Whitman's lifetime. That said, we do not have to interpret this story as evidence of Whitman's criminality. Rather, we could interpret it as demonstrating the townspeople's hostility toward a person they suspected was criminal or deviant or both.

As chapter 1 details, anxiety over nonprocreative sexual acts intensified in the nineteenth century due to concern over the nation's productivity. Unlike the nation's seemingly inexhaustible natural resources, the energy of young (presumably bourgeois and white) couples was considered a rare and culturally important commodity. Harking back to earlier conceptions of semen as a condensed form of blood, physicians admonished young men about the dangers of spending their "seed" too often or carelessly. William Alcott, one of the century's most popular health and conduct-guide writers, warned against participating in a free economy of sexuality that separated sexuality from the responsibility of productivity: "They wish for full liberty to scatter their seed; it is a pleasure to them, a luxury to which they seem to think themselves entitled;

but they do not wish to have a crop. . . . Hence it is that ways, almost innumerable, are devised for evading nature's laws altogether. . . . They are all evasions. They are all criminal, even though they should be, as they seem to be, crimes without names."[14] In this context, sodomy and other nonprocreative sexual acts were considered "crimes without names," criminal evasions of one's social responsibility to produce for and within society. As the century progressed, men were arrested not only for nonconsensual acts of sodomy, but increasingly for consensual ones as well.[15] Within this context it is fair to suggest that the sympathy Whitman expresses in his poems toward those deemed criminal could result from his embodied experiences, from either the pain inflicted on him if he was, in fact, labeled a sodomite and tarred and feathered as a result, or from his fear of this type of retribution.[16] For example, in his 1860 poem that would eventually be titled "You Felons on Trial in Courts," Whitman assumes a criminal persona: "I feel I am of them—I belong to those convicts and prostitutes myself" (l. 14). Whitman's "Calamus" confession reveals that he was struggling to find a way to express male-male desire in a period that increasingly offered the negative motifs of criminality or disease. Part of this process entailed reassessing the meaning of sex and sexuality.

The 1860 "Calamus" series illustrates the magnificent use of the confessional form for the expression of homosexual desire; however, the 1855 version of "Song of Myself" is exceptional neither for its expression nor for its confession of sexuality. Both of these modes were common in Whitman's age. "The fact is that, far from being alone in his treatment of sex," Reynolds contends of Whitman, "he was adopting and transforming sexual imagery from popular sensational writings." Many writers, Reynolds notes, had already employed a metaphor similar to Whitman's, that of "lifting the veil" off social corruption by addressing issues of corporeality and sexuality.[17] Likewise, as Foucault argues, the confession had long served as Western civilization's means of expressing sexuality. By the nineteenth century, the confession metamorphosed into a scientific form, and speaking openly about sexuality became a scientifically sanctioned act. Foucault describes this process: "On the face of it at least, our civilization possesses no *ars erotica*. In return, it is undoubtedly the only civilization to practice a *scientia sexualis*; or rather, the only civilization to have developed over the centuries procedures for telling the truth of sex which are geared to a form of knowledge-power strictly opposed to the art of initiations and the masterful secret: I have in mind the confession."[18] In some instances Whitman participated in the mode that Foucault describes. As my analysis of "I Sing the Body Electric" indicates, Whitman repeatedly vindicates expression of sexuality by claiming that civic responsibility calls for a free discussion of procreative heterosexual sex.

Yet even if talking about sex was more common in the nineteenth century than ideas of repression may lead some to believe, not all utterances can be said to fall into a homogenous *"scientia sexualis."* Rather than discussing sexual activity in order to condemn or master it, Whitman describes sex—including nonprocreative sex—to celebrate it. For example, in the often cited section 5 of "Song of Myself" Whitman portrays a sexually charged encounter with another being, a "you" who could be, among others, the speaker's soul, the reader, or an unidentified lover. The specific identification and gender of the lover are not defined, but the act that follows evokes, among other possibilities, a nonprocreative sexual act being performed on the speaker:

> You settled your head athwart my hips and gently turned over upon me,
> And parted the shirt from my bosom-bone, and plunged your tongue to my
>   barestript heart,
> And reached till you felt my beard, and reached till you held my feet.
> (ll. 79–81)

Regardless of the partner's identity, to return to the physician Alcott's description, the act, if sexual, is criminal. As the rest of the passage shows, Whitman clearly rejoices in scattering his seed without producing the required crop of children. Yet Whitman links this act to creation and generation. With orgasm comes not the depletion and debilitation that the antionanism literature of the day threatened, but rather fruition. The speaker gains a knowledge of oneness with the universe:

> Swiftly arose and spread around me the peace and joy and knowledge that
>   pass all the art and argument of the earth;
> And I know that the hand of God is the elderhand of my own,
> And I know that the spirit of God is the eldest brother of my own,
> And that all the men ever born are also my brothers .... and the women my
>   sisters and lovers, ...
> (ll. 82–85)

Orgasm teaches the poet that he is a sibling in the human family. Sexuality is once again portrayed as a democratizing and social force, one that unites the human family. Although the passage may valorize nonprocreative sexual activity, it is often interpreted as symbolizing a merge between the poet's soul and the poet's body, or "the other I am," which "must not abase itself" to the soul.

By depicting the merge between the body and soul as generative, Whitman emphasizes that both components of identity (the transcendent and the corporeal) are critical in the search for knowledge, and he refuses to endorse a hierarchy that would situate one over the other. Whether the passage is interpreted as representing a sexual act between two people or as symbolically portraying the union of the body and soul, it nonetheless indicates that the body should not be subordinate to the soul.

Whitman repeats the pattern of creation through "nonprocreative" orgasm several times in "Song of Myself," but his most poignant depiction comes in the sequence that begins with section 28 and ends with section 30. In this section, the autoerotic imagery is quite suggestive. Loving argues that it is as if in his late twenties Whitman "had discovered masturbation."[19] Asking, "Is this then a touch?" Whitman proceeds to describe a battle with desire in rape- and warlike images. Overtaken by yearning, he is "given up by traitors" and, losing all senses, proceeds to touch himself:

> I talk wildly. . . . I have lost my wits. . . . I and nobody else am the
>   greatest traitor,
> I went myself first to the headland. . . . my own hands carried me there.
> (ll. 637–638)

Whitman portrays himself as a reluctant victim of his own sexual desire and mimics the language of antionanism by depicting the masturbator as insane. However, immediately following orgasm, Whitman insists that the masturbatory act has been creative. Indeed, as the earlier passage has taught us, the hand of God is the elderhand of the poet, and thus God can be said to figuratively enact the sexual act. He continues to describe the moments immediately following orgasm:

> Parting tracked by arriving . . . . perpetual payment of the perpetual
>   loan,
> Rich showering rain, and recompense richer afterward.
>
> Sprouts take and accumulate. . . . stand by the curb prolific and vital,
> Landscapes projected masculine full-sized and golden.
> (ll. 643–646)

Here nonprocreative sexuality is again shown as a productive action. Going beyond this, Whitman claims that his semen is a generative force: it becomes a "rich showering rain" capable of creating vegetation. He proceeds:

> All truths wait in all things,
> They neither hasten their own delivery nor resist it,
> They do not need the obstetric forceps of the surgeon, . . .
> (ll. 647–649)

By employing the language of childbirth, Whitman hints that his masturbatory act has given birth to knowledge. In effect, Whitman revises the language of sexual productivity to include types of productivity that cannot be measured in the marketplace. He argues that sex *produces* knowledge, spiritual awakening, and democracy.

Glorification of nonprocreative sexuality was in itself a radical act, however, Whitman goes beyond this and uses these passages to flesh out his epistemology of the body. For Whitman, sex was not to be known, but rather to be a way of knowing, a method for understanding one's relation to the universe. Whitman attempts to return the reader to earlier versions of sexuality that are closer to what Foucault describes in the passage I quote above as "*ars erotica*," as "the art of initiations and the masterful secret." If nineteenth-century American discourse tended to express sexuality through scientific language and/or the confession, *Leaves of Grass* attempts, instead, to initiate readers into a method of learning *through* sexuality, not *about* it. In forging what many call a modern view of sexuality because of its valorization of sex, Whitman was in fact drawing upon earlier conceptions of orgasm and cosmic relation. In prenineteenth-century Western thought, orgasm was placed on a spectrum with other forces that kindled "heat." According to Thomas Laqueur, in classical and Renaissance terms, "[o]rgasm's warmth, though more vehement and exciting, is in kind no different from other warmth and can be produced in some measure by food, wine, or the power of the imagination."[20] In this context, orgasm can be linked to a powerful force, paralleling the heat of imagination. It can, in effect, become a muse. The earlier definition, which may have been familiar to Whitman through classical readings, helps to justify sex in a decidedly nonmodern way.

Just as orgasm was linked directly to imaginative power, so too was it connected with a better understanding of the cosmos. Laqueur describes a fundamental shift in the understanding of the body's relationship to the cosmos that occurred with the rise of modern science in the nineteenth century. During the classical era and the Renaissance, images of the body reflected an intricate relationship between the micro- and the macrocosm. However, as modern science began to evolve, it explained the relationship between man and nature "in one neutral mathematical language" instead of emphasizing the "connectedness between and within the micro- and the macrocosm."[21] Whitman's work attempts to restore this lost connection. What many viewed as an either intensely personal or outright antisocial act—the orgasm—becomes a means of knowing unity not only with other people, but also with nature. Whitman's insistence that his orgasms lead beyond pleasure to cosmic comprehension may strike us either as romantic in its transcendence or as modern in its explicitness. It is both, and more. It is a backward glance to an ideology that allowed for something beyond confession or science to frame sex. It is, perhaps, the closest that nineteenth-century American poetry gets to an *ars erotica*. Pleasure, for Whitman, produces knowledge.

In this context, all of *Leaves of Grass* can be read as an attempt to create an enduring pedagogy of sex. Scholars have often noted the "presence" of Whitman's body in his text, an idea that Whitman also emphasized.[22] Figuratively, Whitman's desire for presence can be read as a yearning for a sexual encounter with his readers, one that would transmit knowledge, in Foucault's words, through an "initiation" into the "masterful secret." Whitman understood physical contact as a means of relaying knowledge, sexual and otherwise, as evidenced by the mentoring relationships between boys and men in his early prose works and by some of the complex relationships he had with young men throughout his life.[23] In formulating an epistemology of the body, Whitman echoes classical models of sexuality, particularly Greek. Foucault reminds us: "In Greece, truth and sex were linked, in the form of pedagogy, by the transmission of a precious knowledge from one body to another; sex served as a medium for initiations into learning. For us, it is in the confession that truth and sex are joined, through the obligatory and exhaustive expression of an individual secret."[24] Thus, if Whitman cannot literally be present for his reader to serve as the master teacher, he will replace sexual experience with a posthumous confession. The revelation he coyly hints at throughout his work substitutes for a pedagogy of sex. More than a solitary singer of expression in an age of repression, Whitman is a corporeal explorer. He pleasurably challenges the scientific structures that defined and confined knowledge in his day, while simultaneously arousing others to find truth in sex.

The "Uniform Hieroglyphic": Sexuality and the Body as Signs of a Potent Democracy

As argued above, Whitman's invention of an epistemology of the body is motivated by his desire to elevate corporeality to what he perceives as its rightful status in relation to poetry, politics, philosophy, and spirituality. The knowledge produced through corporeality, he implies in the 1855 edition of *Leaves of Grass*, is the equality and relatedness of humankind regardless of race or gender. In this edition, Whitman turns sexuality and corporeality into symbols as powerful as the grass itself, into "uniform hieroglyphic[s]" that evoke the potential for unity, vitality, and generation. In many ways, this edition is arguably Whitman's most radical experiment in a democratic poetics. As I discuss below, and as Reynolds also notes, Whitman became increasingly conservative and derogatory about African Americans in the postwar period, in part due to theories of ethnological science.[25] Also, his journalism before 1855 exhibits a hesitation regarding abolition and a tendency to privilege the native-born white working class over African Americans, Native Americans, and immigrants. Indeed, scholars of Whitman are often hard-pressed to account for editorials in the 1840s that seem to be written by Whitman, yet blatantly contradict the democratic promise he asserts in the 1855 *Leaves of Grass*.[26] As Loving demonstrates, throughout the 1840s Whitman wanted slavery abolished because it hindered the progress of free white labor. Like many mainstream editors and journalists, Whitman paid the antislavery movement "scant attention" until the Mexican-American War, which he then framed primarily as an issue of Free (white) Labor. Loving argues that Whitman had "mixed feelings" about African Americans and Native Americans throughout his lifetime and was "more concerned with the problems of whites in a growing democracy" than with questions of racial equality and justice.[27]

In many ways, then, we can read the 1855 *Leaves of Grass* as Whitman's imaginative space, a literary site onto which he projects a poetics of democracy that he could not translate into the America he inhabited. As Donald E. Pease suggests, to Whitman, "America is the place where things in the world take on the life they more normally would within the mind. As a poem, America is not a thought in the mind or a place on a map, but the medium through which everything passes on the way to becoming all it can be."[28] In this sense, the 1855 version of "Song of Myself" represents Whitman's most strident efforts to imagine what America could be. The presentation of the body as a "uniform hieroglyphic" of equality, relatedness, and democracy is most pronounced in the 1855 version of "I Sing the Body Electric," a poem that celebrates the "expression of the body" by cataloging descriptions of bodies in motion, celebrating the sexuality of the male and female form, and depicting male and female slaves at auction. Throughout the poem, Whitman not only glorifies the bodies of all people, but also claims their basic equality. According to Pease,

Whitman's doctrine of the "body electric" develops "a correspondence between an individual's inner impulses and the democratic masses." Indeed, "in the electric suddenness of movement in and among crowds persons encounter equality as an everyday experience."[29] Whitman begins the poem by seemingly echoing the reform language of his day, but in actuality he asks readers to reconsider the meaning of corporeal corruption:

> Was it dreamed whether those who corrupted their own live bodies could
>   conceal themselves?
> And whether those who defiled the living were as bad as they who defiled
>   the dead?
> (ll. 3–4)

Whitman had already prepared readers to reconsider sexual corruption through the glorification of nonprocreative sexuality in his "Song of Myself." Nonetheless, in "I Sing the Body Electric," he justifies his most explicit material by linking it to the more socially accepted idea of the production of healthy Americans. He describes a robust "common farmer" who at eighty is still the ideal of health and potency: "[H]e was the father of five sons . . . . and in them were the fathers of sons" (l. 29). Having supplied the patriarchal justification for the "procreant urge," Whitman is free to celebrate sexuality.

In the poem's explosive fifth section, Whitman begins with the presentation of a female and ends with what can be interpreted as an orgasmic description of heterosexual sex. Although he seems to evoke the ideology of the angelic Victorian woman by starting, "This is the female form, / A divine nimbus exhales from it from head to foot," he immediately collapses the binary of the passionless female/lusty male by continuing: "It attracts with fierce undeniable attraction" (ll. 46–48). In what follows, Whitman grants women as much sexual capacity as men, claiming that the female is "both passive and active" (l. 63) and the male is "action and power" (l. 67). The passage also implicitly blurs sexual difference, returning to eighteenth-century conceptions of sexuality. Until the eighteenth century, scientists perceived males and females as inverted versions of one another. Female orgasm was thought to be not only necessary to procreation, but also "masculine," with the clitoris described as becoming "erect" when aroused. As the sexual merge occurs, the bodies themselves become indistinguishable, even interchangeable. Lines such as "Ebb stung by the flow, and flow stung by the ebb" (l. 52) connote a fluid site where the boundaries of male/female bodies themselves lose significance. Who, for instance, is the source of the "ebb" and who is the "flow"? Likewise, descriptions such as "loveflesh swelling and deliciously aching," "quivering jelly of love," and "delirious juice" (ll. 52–54) can refer, especially in late-eighteenth-century terms, to either the male or female body during sex or to the physical results of the sexual act itself. If, as Laqueur suggests, these earlier interpretations of sexuality relied upon an "unimaginably—indeed terrifyingly—porous body," then Whitman may be harkening back to them to challenge his day's rigid corporeal categories. Moon argues that Whitman proposes fluidity "[i]n the face of his culture's massive anxiety about the loss of boundaries between mind and body, of erotic boundaries between males, of boundaries of gender between men and women, and of boundaries between races and social classes."[30] The sexual merge depicted in "I Sing the Body Electric," then, does more than celebrate sexuality in an age tending toward repression. It symbolically defies scientific assertions that members of the body politic could not merge—that racial, gendered, and sexual borders could not be crossed.

In the sections that follow, Whitman turns from his sexual argument to a racial one, pushing his corporeal philosophy to its fullest potential. Significantly, the poem was first titled "Slaves," an indication of how important the question of race and slavery was to Whitman's contemplation of corporeality at this time.[31] Immediately preceding Whitman's section on the slave auction, he reminds us of the grass, the most democratizing symbol in his volume. Whitman challenges those who would call the slave ignorant: "Do you think matter has cohered together from its diffused float, and the soil is on the surface and water runs and vegetation sprouts for you . . . and not for him and her?" (l. 82). With his reference to vegetation, Whitman evokes the most pervasive image of "Song of Myself," the "uniform hieroglyphic" of the grass. Here Whitman's symbol can be read literally. All matter is connected. Translated racially, this means that just as all vegetation sprouts from a common source, so too do all people contain the same original matter. Organically, difference is denied.

Whitman then becomes more explicit as to the common origins and innate equality of humankind, deriding his age's growing belief in polygenesis, the theory of human races as distinct species. Ironically assuming the position of the slave auctioneer, he challenges proslavery science by stripping the body, "red black or white" (l. 91). Once exposed, he shows those watching the slave auction and his readers that all bodies contain the same essence. Significantly, Whitman points to the brain and the blood to argue that slaves are physiologically equal to all Americans. This choice cannot be coincidental. Just a year before the first edition of *Leaves of Grass* was printed, Josiah C. Nott and George R. Gliddon published *Types of Mankind*, a scientifically hailed text that continued their predecessor's, Samuel George Morton's, *Crania Americana* *(1839)*. Both works catalog human skulls to argue that the races are distinct and that the Caucasian race is superior. Whitman responds by glorifying the slave's brain: "In that head the allbaffling brain, / In it and below it the making of the attributes of heroes" (ll. 89–90). By calling the slave's brain "allbaffling," Whitman not only suggests that the Negro brain is as complex as that of the Caucasian, but also implies that scientists cannot fully understand the brain. It will continue to mystify them despite their weighty surveys. But Whitman most forcefully drives his point home by enacting his striptease of the slave's body. By the time Whitman wrote "I Sing the Body Electric," almost all parts of the body were translated as indicating racial difference. Whitman unravels the layers of the slave's body—the eyes, the limbs, the breast muscle. Asking readers to join his examination, he finally arrives at "the same old blood . . . the same red running blood" (l. 96). Like scientists and slave owners, Whitman has inspected the publicly accessible slave's body. However, unlike them, Whitman ascertains evidence only of common humanity.

For the scientists of Whitman's day, physical characteristics indicated intellectual and moral capability. Following this lead, Whitman also couples physiological features with the attributes he considers crucial for the "race of races," the Americans. Like the farmer and the woman in previous passages, the slaves in "I Sing the Body Electric" also contain seeds of mighty generations, of potential heroes and "rich republics." Whitman focuses on the female slave as the "teeming mother of mothers" who deserves respect on a par with his readers' own mother or lover. By emphasizing the sexuality of the presumably Caucasian woman earlier in the poem and concentrating on the maternal instincts of the slave woman, Whitman challenges two of his age's most hypocritical and damaging "truths"; he contradicts the twin myths of the oversexed Negro woman, who is portrayed as a temptress to white men, and of the passionless Caucasian woman, who is labeled abnormal if she desires sex. Through his descriptions, Whitman proposes that all women have the same emotional and sexual capability.

Despite his emphasis on bodily equality, Whitman does not link identity solely to corporeality. Rather, he contends that both male and female slaves are capable of the same intelligence and emotions as are Caucasians, an idea hotly contested by the scientists of his day. Immediately following his discovery of the "same red running blood," Whitman continues:

There swells and jets his heart . . . . There all passions and desires . . .
   all reaching and aspirations:
Do you think they are not there because they are not expressed in parlors
   and lecture-rooms?
(ll. 97–98)

In this passage Whitman extends the meaning of "passion" to a more general drive: the slave, like all humans, has "aspirations." By indicating that these emotions exist even though they are not in "parlors," Whitman confronts readers' class assumptions. At the same time, by adding "lecture rooms" to the places where these "passions" and "aspirations" are not expressed, Whitman implies that the type of knowledge one finds through lectures (scientific ones included) is not adequate. Whitman also mocks the notion of fixed racial identity. Just as scientists were arguing that the "types" of humankind were permanent, Whitman asks readers a most unsettling question about the slave man: "How do you know who shall come from the offspring of his offspring through the centuries?" (l. 102). Not only might slaves produce "rich republics," but also, Whitman hints, the offspring of all races could combine to create an entirely new race. He continues with an even more haunting question for the majority of Americans: "Who might you find you have come from yourself if you could trace back through the centuries?" Although Caucasian Americans had to acknowledge the presence of racially mixed people in the body politic, they were reluctant to consider the possibility of any Negro blood in their own lineage. Whitman plays on this fear, hinting that there is no pure Caucasian type. By suggesting that these types are not permanent, Whitman repudiates the justification for racial slavery.

   In the last two stanzas, Whitman returns to the question of corruption that he introduced at the poem's beginning. By placing this idea immediately following his depiction of the slave woman at auction, he indicates that the person most guilty of corruption is the white man who would defile the maternal body by sexually exploiting a slave woman. Like Frances E. W. Harper, he draws upon and reverses the common stereotypes of his age that define which bodies are the most corrupt or uncontrollable. He intimates that the ultimate sin of slavery is that it desecrates the body, the symbol of equality in a potent democracy. By the poem's end, the "typical" nineteenth-century corrupter (the masturbator, the oversexed youth) has been replaced with a more vicious villain—the person who would hawk the glorious body in a common slave market. "I Sing the Body Electric" stands as the logical extension of Whitman's democratic yearning; it is his powerful testimony to the sexuality that vitalizes us and the common humanity that defines us.

Although "I Sing the Body Electric" may be Whitman's most sustained and radical declaration of bodily equality, several passages in "Song of Myself" also propose corporeal solutions to political dilemmas. For example, in lines 178–182, Whitman describes a marriage between a "trapper in the open air in the far-west" and his bride, "a red girl." The marriage crosses both culture and race, as the trapper has presumably shed his European fashions to be dressed "mostly in skins" and the ceremony seems to be Native American in character, with the girl's father and friends dressed in traditional clothes and smoking pipes in what probably symbolizes a show of peace. Through the marriage, Whitman represents racial and cultural hybridity that might allow both races to join in the formation of a new national identity. Typical of Whitman, the merge is sexually charged, because the girl is described as having "long eye-lashes" and "voluptuous limbs" (l. 182). It is through sexual blending, through the "mixed" children signified by the marriage, that a new "race of races" might be formed. Going against the science of his day, which saw Indians as a separate species that could not mix with Caucasians, Whitman proposes cultural mixing and assimilation as an alternative national identity.

Immediately following the marriage between the trapper and the Native American girl, Whitman describes an encounter with a runaway slave, whom he attempts to heal before sending him north. As Whitman brings a tub for "his sweated body and bruised feet" (l. 187) and puts "plasters on the galls of his neck and ankles" (l. 190), he assumes a subservient position, performing the labor that would have commonly been performed by a slave on a white person's body. By not only touching but also helping to mend the corporeal lacerations caused by slavery, Whitman implies symbolically that the body of the nation might also recuperate from slavery if the white man were willing to reverse roles and become a wound dresser rather than a master. Through these passages, Whitman wields corporeality as a fundamental indicator of equality. However, he goes beyond this radical symbolism to suggest that corporeality can be used as a methodology, as a means of achieving political solutions. Whether it be through racial hybridity, or through the physically based healing process between the enslaved and the free, Whitman grants the body the power to create political change.

A New Kind of "Radicalism": The 1860 Edition

The 1860 edition of *Leaves of Grass* marks a significant change in Whitman's portrayal of sexuality in particular and of the body in general. Whitman's daring new "Calamus" series boldly confesses and exonerates the male-male desire at which earlier editions had hinted, but never avowed as openly. It exposes love between men as a private bond and a public force. However, Whitman covers his homosexual confession by prefacing it with "Enfans d'Adam," his tribute to heterosexuality. He continues to justify heterosexual desire by linking it to procreation, thereby relegating women's sexuality, in particular, to reproductive biology. Thus, even while cultivating a central text of homosexual expression, the 1860 edition establishes those binaries of sexual identity that continue to dominate popular understanding of sexuality. In effect, he participates in the construction of what would later be called "homosexual" and "heterosexual" identities.

To explore the amorous attachments that would eventually be labeled homosexual and heterosexual, Whitman employs the language of phrenology, a quasi science with which he was well acquainted through two of its main proponents, the Fowler brothers of New York, who were the distributors and, according to Loving, the "de facto" publishers of the first edition of *Leaves* (1855). Indeed, rather than rejecting scientific scrutiny of the body (as his 1855 epistemology of the body seems to do), Whitman's 1860 edition turns to this quasi science to authorize his representations of sexuality. According to Reynolds, phrenology provided Whitman the means by which to refer to sex with "candor and tact." Indeed, phrenological terms "were a convenient means of deflecting criticism of potentially risqué passages," because their addition could "lend scientific purity to bold passages."[32] Phrenologists believed character was manifested physically and could be read through the bumps on a person's head. When Whitman first heard Orson S. Fowler's lecture on phrenology in March 1846, he dismissed the system as fraudulent. Yet in the summer of 1849, he had a phrenological exam and was pleased with the results. Indeed, he scored a six (the safest high score) in the categories of "amativeness" (sexual passion) and "adhesiveness" (friendship).[33] These were considered two of the most powerful phrenological attributes, and they are also the two categories that Whitman employs to organize "Enfans d'Adam" and "Calamus." Borrowing these two terms, Whitman juxtaposes male-female and male-male desire, as well as procreative and nonprocreative sexual acts. As a result of his adaptation of phrenological terms, Whitman turns from his earlier polymorphic, nonspecific sexual descriptions to the solidification of what would later be called homosexual and heterosexual identities. Fone succinctly argues that "Whitman stands at the beginning of this changing discourse and is an initial and powerful participant in it, clearly seeing what Foucault describes—namely, that language could translate a solitary or a shared act of physical release into a community, even a communion, of desire, changing sex into sexuality."[34] As Fone indicates, Whitman's search for a positive way to formulate and express "a community, even a communion, of desire" had the effect of changing "sex" into "sexuality," of aiding in the solidification of sexual acts into sexual categories of identity.

To represent heterosexuality, Whitman chose amativeness, the force that aids in generation. Phrenologically, the characteristic was considered stronger in men, which might help explain why the virile Adam dominates this grouping of poems. Although Whitman attempts to reclaim the innocence of sexuality by depicting Adam and Eve as "potent mates" in the New World, he nonetheless crafts Adam as more forceful than Eve. Adam, who is often identified with the poet, symbolizes the creative energy of the phallus, as in the poem that would eventually be titled "From Pent-up Aching Rivers":

> From my own voice resonant—singing the phallus,
> Singing the song of procreation,
> Singing the need of superb children, and therein superb grown people, . . .
> (ll. 4–6)[35]

This passage, which links the poet's voice to the fertile phallus and then to the production of future citizens, represents aptly what Jimmie M. Killingsworth calls Whitman's "*phallic* poetic/political complex": "Presence, in Whitman's formulation, is defined by sexual power, which in turn stands for creative power; the penis becomes the originary word, the logos, that creates and gives meaning to the world." For Whitman, the poet and the power of the phallus are inextricably linked. As David Leverenz argues, "despite his quasi-parental androgyny, Whitman's voice also proclaims a very phallic self-extension, which seems inseparable from his will to inseminate, embrace and dominate." To Leverenz, resistance to Whitman is not necessarily limited to the female reader. "If I resist his specifically homosexual desires," Leverenz argues about his reaction to Whitman, "I resist them not simply out of erotic anxiety but also because Whitman makes me feel feminized or non-existent, rather than either masculine or androgynous."[36]

No other poem in the series better demonstrates Whitman's phallic project than the poem eventually titled "A Woman Waits for Me," which was published in the 1856 edition and also included in "Enfans d'Adam." Here Whitman reveals his ideology of womanhood quite nakedly. As in "I Sing the Body Electric," he depicts active women, who know how to "swim, row, ride, wrestle, shoot, run, strike, retreat, advance, resist, defend themselves, / They are ultimate in their own right—they are calm, clear, well-possessed of themselves" (18–19). Whitman's repetition of active verbs seems to answer figuratively Fuller's call in *Summer on the Lakes* for a new kind of woman. There Fuller laments that women who have been educated in the eastern United States are not prepared for frontier life, pointing specifically to some of the activities that they have not accomplished with the same sense of urgency that marks Whitman's passage: "[W]hen they can leave the housework, they have not learnt to ride, to drive, to row, alone."[37] Although Whitman portrays the vigorous women Fuller beckons, he betrays their primary role in the poem's opening lines: "A woman waits for me—she contains all, nothing is lacking, / Yet all were lacking, if sex were lacking, or if the moisture of the right man were lacking." Returning to the classical conception of semen as the vital procreative force, Whitman depicts women as passive agents, waiting to receive the male's generative power. She may have "heroes and bards" enveloped in her, yet "[t]hey refuse to awake at the touch of any man" but the speaker (l. 24). Betsy Erkkila argues that their "union seems less the occasion for a dynamic pairing of equals and more the scene of a domestic rape."[38] If not quite rape, the encounter certainly is a rather unpleasant task. The powerful man works arduously to fill up the lacking woman. He has to "make" his "way," and "brace" himself, being careful to hurt the woman as little as possible. This is a difficult job, but one that is necessary to produce the "sons and daughters fit for These States" (ll. 25–29).

By the poem's end, the woman has become a mere vessel for the speaker and state, the depository into which the man puts "what has so long accumulated" within him. In keeping with phrenology, which asserted that normal women had more love of children than men, Whitman ultimately enveloped women in one role, the mothers of the Republic. The last stanza begins by emphasizing the passivity of the woman through a powerful repetition of prepositions:

Through you I drain the pent-up rivers of myself,
In you I wrap a thousand onward years,
On you I graft the grafts of the best-beloved of me and of America,
The drops I distill *upon you* shall grow fierce and athletic girls, new artists, musicians, and singers,
The babes I beget *upon you* are to beget babes in their turn [emphasis mine], . . .
(ll. 31–35)

Halfway through the stanza, the poem turns to underscore the all-important "I" of the poet, concluding, "I shall look for loving crops from the birth, life, death, immortality, I plant so lovingly now" (39). The speaker/poet has spent his seed, and like the advice books he implicitly criticizes in his earlier poetry and the yeoman farmer he idealizes, he wants a return on his investment.

Contrasting with the procreative qualities of amativeness, Lorenzo Fowler describes adhesiveness as extending to "attachments not founded upon the generative instinct."[39] Although Fowler stresses that adhesiveness was usually stronger in women, and although adhesiveness was not commonly associated in the nineteenth century with what we would now call homosexual desire or acts,[40] Whitman adapts the term to articulate male-male attachments. Because Whitman associated sex with cosmic knowledge, adhesiveness became a fitting way to express the complex relationship between male-male desire, the political sphere, and cosmic revelation. Fowler further describes the characteristic as "the bond of society, the mental chain which is infinitely more efficacious in uniting families and nations than the naked law of force or interest."[41] For Whitman, this quality of adhesiveness helped to express the political power he believed could come from male-male desire. In "States!" he predicts that America will not be held together by lawyers or contracts, but rather through "a new friendship" between men, which consecrates the political union:

> The most dauntless and rude shall touch face to face lightly,
> The dependence of Liberty shall be lovers,
> The continuance of Equality shall be comrades.
> (ll. 31–33)

As the Civil War approached, the rejuvenating force of male-male desire becomes one of Whitman's only prospects for saving the corporeal body of America from dismemberment. Robert K. Martin argues: "Whitman, like Melville, is suggesting that only when men accept their innate homosexuality can there be any hope for real change and a final victory over the aggression, acquisitiveness, and death-drive which, he believes, are rooted in heterosexuality. This is indeed a revolutionary idea; no wonder, then, that some critics have been so alarmed that they have been unable to address it."[42] Whitman, as Martin proposes, is revolutionary. However, by basing the continuance of the soul of American democracy primarily on male-male desire, Whitman seriously undercuts his radical potential. The 1860 edition reduces women to passive recipients of male vitality, rendering them sexually and symbolically irrelevant to democracy's primary bond.

Why, then, if Whitman's poetry renders women sexually and symbolically irrelevant to the primary bond of democracy, did so many women read, enjoy, and defend Whitman's *Leaves of Grass* in general and his 1860 edition in particular? Indeed, Sherry Ceniza challenges the "persistent strand in Whitman criticism that sees Whitman as a less than positive force for his female readers," arguing that such critiques have been launched without sufficient attention to historical context, particularly to Whitman's friendship with, and knowledge of, radical women in the 1850s. Although some passages in his poetry may be problematic, Ceniza contends that Whitman adopts rhetorical strategies similar to those of women representing sexuality, and she argues that we need to read Whitman's inconsistencies as we would those within nineteenth-century women's fiction, as contradictions that did not necessarily disempower female readers. Similarly, Reynolds suggests that although "Whitman did stress motherhood and female athleticism in his poetry," he "by no means limited women to these roles," and rightly points to the connections between Whitman's representation of female corporeality, especially in his early editions, and his deployment of the rhetoric of physiology. As noted, Reynolds demonstrates how Whitman appropriates the language of physiology to create a model for his poetic treatment of sexuality. By employing physiological rhetoric, Whitman was able to join with those who were trying to "cleanse popular culture" of its pornographic tendencies, while also being "frank" about sexuality. Whitman, like the physiologists, had a "deep-seated belief in the sacredness and purity of sex when rightly treated"; they both "hoped to reinstate sex as fully natural, the absolute center of existence."[43] Ceniza's and Reynolds's arguments contain merit. That said, we can now read Whitman's two models for expressing sexuality in the 1860 edition—the physiological model for women's sexuality and the phrenological model for male-male desire—as pointing to the paradoxes inherent in scientific discourses in the nineteenth century. Whitman's zeal for physiology, for example, caused him to review enthusiastically Edward Dixon's *Woman and Her Diseases*, in part because it was graphic and explicit about women's sexual nature. However, as I argue in chapter 1, with the advantage of historical hindsight we can also read this text as limiting women's identities and roles through their bodies. If we recall, for example, Dixon's claim that a woman without a uterus was not really womanly at all, that for those "females in whom there exists a complete absence of the ovaria . . . [t]he passion of love is unknown . . . and they present an aspect altogether at variance with the harmony of nature,"[44] we understand just how precarious the use of physiological rhetoric was in this era. One need not doubt Whitman's overt intent to represent women as sexual, active, and powerful in their procreative abilities to interrogate also the assumptions of the rhetoric he appropriated to make these claims. Likewise, one need not dismiss his creative deployment of phrenological "adhesiveness" to develop a language for male-male desire that moved beyond the motifs of criminality, disease, or both to suggest also that this rhetoric, consciously or not, contributed to the solidification of homo/hetero identities that some find prohibitive.

The finding of "radicalism" in the 1860 edition, then, depends very much on the perspective of the reader. "Calamus" will remain a celebration of male-male desire, but some, such as Killingsworth, lament Whitman's turning away from the polymorphic, nonspecific, and what some would now call "queer" sexuality of his earlier versions.[45] For women, the 1860 edition proves ominous. Swept away by the potent male, the female's corporeal integrity is very much in peril. The youthful Adam is an American male with a job to do; progress demands that he thrust "with slow rude muscle" onward. The body of the poet, which incarnates the body of the nation, is ever-swelling, moving westward, and absorbing all that remains in its path. As the next section demonstrates, Whitman so aligns the "body" of his poetry with the "body" of the nation that his poetics become inextricably tied to the politics of expansion. Like Fuller, Whitman believed in the inevitable fulfillment of democratic progress, a project that necessitated land. If other bodies stood in the way of the expansion of the nation or the integrity of the Union—be they Native Americans or slaves—they had to be either overlooked or removed.

Fear the Merge

Best exemplifying the dilemma posed by Whitman's merge is "By Blue Ontario's Shore," first published in 1856 as "Poem of Many in One." The 1867 edition clarifies the poem's narrative framework. As the poet sits by the side of Lake Ontario, a phantom beckons him to chant the poem *"that comes from the soul of America"*(l. 4). To fulfill this task, Whitman champions the role of the American poet, creating a female muse of democracy who empowers the male poet with the ability to sing the nation's spirit. As the speaker further demarcates his role, he repeatedly and parenthetically returns to the ideal of democracy, which he envisions as a woman to whom he must remain true. In a line added in the 1867 edition, the nature of the female muse of democracy becomes clear: "Ah, Mother! prolific and full in all besides—yet how long barren, barren?" (l. 136). Like the female in "A Woman Waits for Me," who is passive until activated by male power, democracy also awaits the masculine poet who will arbitrate, equalize, and supply what "wants supplying" (ll. 141–143).

While the poem erases the real bodies of women by relegating them to the realm of feminized muse, the poet, emphasized as both masculine and male, comes to incarnate the land itself. In a particularly poignant passage, the body of the poet merges with the land:

> Used to dispense with other lands, incarnating this land,
> Attracting it Body and Soul to himself, hanging on its neck with
>   incomparable love,
> Plunging his semitic muscle into its merits and demerits,
> Making its cities, beginnings, events, diversities, wars, vocal in him,
> Making its rivers, lakes, bays, embouchure in him,
> Mississippi with yearly freshets and changing chutes—Columbia,
>   Niagara, Hudson, spending themselves lovingly in him,
> If the Atlantic coast stretch, or the Pacific coast stretch, he stretching
>   with them north or south,
> Spanning between them east and west, and touching whatever is
>   between them.
> (ll. 71–78)

In language typical of Whitman, this merge is sexual. Masculine rivers "spend" themselves lovingly in the poet and he, in turn, plunges his "semitic muscle" into the land (he later changes the word to "seminal"). Although Whitman's depiction of a "seminal muscle" figuratively impregnating the barren countryside would traditionally evoke the common motif of a feminine/maternal landscape,[46] Whitman has already established a symbolic order in *Leaves of Grass* in which non-procreative acts can be generative, and this passage suggests a masculine landscape merging with a male poet. The poet, after all, hangs "on its neck with incomparable love," as do so many of the comrades in the "Calamus" series, and both the land and the poet are depicted as spending themselves in one another. While Whitman breaks with the passive/feminine landscape that is common in American literature (which, perhaps, added to the appeal of his poetry to female readers), women are nonetheless excluded from the primary bond. The work of the poet is seminal and male; landscapes are projected as masculine.[47]

Just as the poem figuratively erases women's bodies, so too does it overlook slavery's corporeally determined experiences, which are swallowed by the poem's overall declaration of national identity. Although slavery is not in the poem's forefront, it is an important subtext. Erkkila argues that Whitman's insistence on the preservation of the Union regardless of the status of slavery led him to rewrite history, often inventing "founding fathers and an American republic more committed to the cause of emancipation than was in fact the case."[48] In this poem, Whitman once again places the survival of the Union above the slave's cause. In the 1867 edition, celebrating Americans as "[a] breed whose proof is in time and deeds," he assures his readers:

> We are the most beautiful to ourselves, and in ourselves;
> We stand self-pois'd, in the middle, branching thence over the world;
> From Missouri, Nebraska, or Kansas, laughing attacks to scorn.
>
> Nothing is sinful to us outside of ourselves,
> Whatever appears, whatever does not appear, we are beautiful or sinful in
>   ourselves only.
> (ll. 17–21)

In this passage the poet attempts to contain contradiction and depicts America as a perfect manifestation of a self-contained plan. However, Whitman's inclusion of Missouri, Nebraska, and Kansas hints at how his poetic claims contradict political reality. These states were pivotal in the debate over slavery. The 1820 Missouri Compromise allowed slavery to exist in Missouri, but banished it from any new territory north of the 36°30′ parallel, an understanding that the 1854 Nebraska-Kansas Act effectively dismantled by allowing settlers to vote on the status of a new state. Kansas was particularly volatile, as pro- and antislavery proponents migrated to the territory to claim it as their own. Tensions exploded into violence by 1855, earning the state the epithet "bleeding Kansas."[49] By adding the line "From Missouri, Nebraska, or Kansas, laughing attacks to scorn" to the 1867 edition, Whitman erases the violence and specific struggles of history and portrays these states as part of a "most beautiful" nation. As Erkkila argues, Whitman's tendency to mythologize events was common to many romantics who then "read these struggles back into history as part of an inevitable and providentially ordained revolutionary process." Additionally, the impulse to omit painful accounts of injustice probably resulted from the intensely personal impact that the threat of war, and the war itself, had on Whitman. Erkkila describes how "Whitman internalized the war, experiencing the assault on the political Union as an assault on the body and the personality structure of the democratic self."[50] For Whitman, the postwar healing process necessitates his-torical re-presentation. Lost in his process is the specificity of corporeal experience, in this case that of slavery.

Whitman's rewriting of history may also indicate his reluctance to accept newly emancipated African Americans as potential citizens. The presence of African Americans in the nation's capital increased during Whitman's residence there, first as contrabands during the war and later as freed men and women. In a letter written to his mother in April 1867, Whitman comments that "Washington is filled with *darkies*—the men & children & wenches swarm in all directions" and adds, "I am not sure but the North is like the man that won the elephant in a raffle."[51] We must base an understanding of Whitman's racial beliefs on his private as well as his public and poetic statements; although I have already indicated that Whitman's 1855 *Leaves of Grass* creates a space for corporeal equality and democratic potential, this letter is distressing in the same manner as his 1871 "Ethiopia Saluting the Colors," which describes a newly freed slave woman as "so ancient hardly human." Whitman's crude humor and animal imagery reveal a duplicity in his attitude toward African Americans. He demonstrates that he feels a difference between his (white) self and the "darkies," perhaps because the war brought him into much greater contact with the "other" race. His comparison of freed slaves to an "elephant" won at a "raffle" seems to beg the question of what the North will do with such an exotic, but perhaps in Whitman's assessment worthless or inappropriate, prize. Whitman's primary postbellum concern was solidifying the myth of a newly unified and redeemed nation, one that ultimately he envisioned as predominately white.

Just as Whitman cannot merge the bodies of African Americans fully into the body politic of postwar America, so too is he reluctant to associate Native Americans with what he calls the nation's "white neighborhood." In the same section of "By Blue Ontario's Shore," the poet—now incarnating the land—thrusts forward to "surround" everything in both time and space:

> Surrounding the essences of real things, old times and present times,
> Surrounding just found shores, islands, tribes of red aborigines, . . .
> (ll. 85–86)

In this passage, the "red aborigines" belong to the "old times." They are a part of history and no longer a corporeal presence. This erasure becomes increasingly significant several lines further down, as the poet continues to list all that he embodies, moving westward to the "unsurvey'd interior, log-houses, clearings, wild animals, hunters, trappers; / Surrounding the multiform agriculture, mines, temperature, the gestation of new States" (ll. 91–92). Conspicuously missing from Whitman's westward gaze are specific depictions of Native Americans, many of whom had been forced to move to the "unsurvey'd interior" prior to the Civil War. Like so many nineteenth-century American writers, Whitman implicitly supports the idea of the Indians as vanishing Americans.[52] Whitman adds to his erasure of Native American bodies by ending the passage with two concepts that support Caucasian domination. He returns once again to the Jacksonian "noble character of mechanics and farmers, especially the young men," taking particular notice of the "freshness and candor of their physiognomy" and the "copiousness and decision of their phrenology" (ll. 94–96). Both physiognomy and phrenology were thought to prove Native Americans' inferiority and therefore supported their removal from "white" lands east of the Mississippi. Furthermore, Whitman glorifies the "railroad and steamboat lines, intersecting all points" (l. 102). To many Native Americans, the railroad was not only a sign of the white man's unwanted advance, but also a direct threat to their survival, plunging through their territories and further disrupting the grazing habits of their game animals.[53]

Maurice Kenny summarizes Whitman's attitude toward Indians as "indifference." Kenny points out that Whitman's indifference is made all the more troubling by his employment at the Indian Bureau for several months in 1865: the "worthless treaties were at his fingertips; the recorded injustices perpetrated upon Indians were under his naked eyes; documents and letters of unscrupulous officials prodding the extermination of the 'savages' most certainly would have been familiar to him." Yet, according to Loving, Whitman was not all that interested in the Bureau's politics or mission: it "appears [Whitman] did not take his new situation all that seriously. . . . The work was easy enough but apparently only as engaging as his passing interest in the Indian at this time."[54] Indeed, Whitman's personal notes support Kenny's distrust of Whitman's politics. In February 1863 Whitman heard a lecture detailing Sioux attacks in Minnesota and wrote in his journal: "The poetical Indian is all lollypop. The real reds of our northern frontiers, of the present day, have propensities, monstrous and treacherous, that make them unfit to be left in white neighborhood."[55] Clearly Whitman doubted the desirability of assimilating Native Americans into a "white neighborhood" or into the expanding white body of America. Whatever their "poetical" potential, real Indians were "monstrous and treacherous." Whitman's conception of America necessitated colonization, and he was willing to achieve it by force. As Erkkila notes, Whitman's faith in a Jeffersonian America linked his poetry to the politics of expansion, because "Jeffersonian ideology became tied to a national policy of violation. . . . the national government pursued a more aggressive policy of territorial expansion in the name of preserving American democracy."[56] For Whitman, who came to envision the Civil War as a triumphant test of the American democratic spirit, the postwar period was a time when America had symbolically chosen to recommit itself to its original mission of democracy, a duty that he, and many others, tied inextricably to possession of western land.

Some critics are hesitant to critique the expansionist and racist tendencies of Whitman's work. Martin, who edited the anthology that includes Kenny's essay, deprecates Kenny's criticism of Whitman's romanticized descriptions of the Native American body. He charges Kenny with assuming incorrectly that Whitman sees only American Indians "as pure body."[57] It is interesting that Martin comes to this conclusion. Certainly Whitman wants to reclaim corporeality as a fundamental component of everyone's identity, and he does not focus solely on the bodies of women, African Americans, or Native Americans. However, given the complicated body politics of nineteenth-century America, such a move was not without negative implications for those who were all too often defined by their corporeality. As this chapter suggests, for women, African Americans, and Native Americans, Whitman's merge threatened to erase them figuratively, to subsume their identity into the category "American," a category that was implicitly white and male. Similarly, to suggest that those who are often defined corporeally should claim knowledge through their bodies creates the dilemmas (described in chapter 5) that Fuller encounters when writing her feminist philosophy, dilemmas over how one can celebrate the "pure body" in politically precarious times.

Who need be afraid of the merge? Margaret Fuller needed to be cautious about it. Frances E. W. Harper also had much to dread about being associated with a body that could be perceived as "grotesque" and "carnivalesque" (see chapter 3). Similarly, chapter 7 will show that Harriet Jacobs's status as a mulatto woman necessarily complicated any claim to an epistemology of the body. Rather than receiving knowledge *through* sexuality, Jacobs quickly gained knowledge *of* sexuality and its relation to power. As a mulatto woman, Jacobs could afford neither Emerson's transcendent optimism nor Whitman's exaltation of the sexual body. Like Fuller, she had to find a way to write about the knowledge that came from her embodied experiences and simultaneously create space for her disembodied will. At the same time, she had to do so while not reconfirming notions of the mulatto woman as defined primarily by her corporeality. In *Incidents in the Life of a Slave Girl, Written by Herself*, she accomplishes these tasks with force.

7

"NEVER BEFORE HAD MY PUNY ARM

FELT HALF SO STRONG"

Corporeality and Transcendence in Jacobs's Incidents

When he told me that I was made for his use, made to obey his command in *every* thing; that I was nothing but a slave, whose will must and should surrender to his, never before had my puny arm felt half so strong.—Harriet Jacobs, *Incidents in the Life of a Slave Girl*

My master had power and law on his side; I had a determined will. There is might in each.—Harriet Jacobs, *Incidents in the Life of a Slave Girl*

On a "lovely spring morning" that mocks her sadness, the young, beautiful slave Linda Brent is accosted by her master, who scathes her ears with "stinging, scorching, words" designed to corrupt her mind and hasten her deliverance into his licentious grip. Like so many nineteenth-century heroines, she is indignant at his suggestions. Yet unlike them, she is denied the privilege of sexual modesty due to her status as a slave. Considered "naturally" immoral and lustful by most Americans, she could have been suspected as the perpetrator, rather than the victim, of the "seduction." But these weighty possibilities, backed as they were by science and law, do not convince Linda of her innate depravity. Nor does her master's authority persuade her of an inherent frailty. This young girl discovers not vulnerability, but muscle: "Never before had my puny arm felt half so strong" (18). Linda knows that her body must become a site of resistance because it signifies her oppression.

Harriet Jacobs, who crafts the persona Linda Brent in her 1861 autobiographical work *Incidents in the Life of a Slave Girl, Written by Herself,*[1] situates this confrontation in a chapter titled "The Slave Who Dared to Feel like a Man." Although this chapter purportedly highlights Linda's uncle Benjamin, who beats his master in a fight and then escapes north, it also refers to Linda. For it is when she is most marked by society for her gender and race—the moment when her master, a physician, could call upon scientific and legal precedent to substantiate his claim that she was "made for" his sexual use—that this young slave girl does the extraordinary: she "dares to feel like a man" (in nineteenth-century terms), envisioning her body as a source of strength and her arm as a potential weapon. Like her uncle, Linda decides that corporeal resistance is an acceptable, even heroic, response to slavery. "The war of my life had begun; and though one of God's most powerless creatures, I resolved never to be con-quered" (19). Jacobs shows us through *Incidents* that this is a war she has to fight on many related ideological fronts. Jacobs has to refute the racialized dis-courses of the men of science and law, symbolized in her text by her master, the physician Flint, and her sexual liaison, the lawmaker/congressman Sands; she has to learn how to manage the knowledge of sex in a corrupt and corrupting world; she has to break the racial dialectic of true womanhood; she has to carve a literary space for her claim of a disembodied, metaphysical will in a era that denied such a possibility to women of color and in a literary genre that also complicated this assertion; like Frances E. W. Harper, she has to reverse the gaze of spectatorship, literally and figuratively turning the power of surveil-lance onto the white slaveholders and away from her own body, a task made all the more difficult by the sexual history she feels compelled to confess.

Throughout *Incidents*, Jacobs constantly flings "punches" at her readers similar to those in the chapter "The Slave Who Dared to Feel like a Man," forc-ing them to reconsider fundamental conceptions of womanhood and race. She draws upon her embodied experiences to defy essentialist notions of racial infe-riority, especially those applied to mulatto and Negro women. From her limi-nal space as a slave woman, she offers her women readers, in particular, a new view of their bodies, their sexuality, and their potential roles. Yet even though Jacobs comprehends and depicts the carnal horror of slavery, she dismisses cor-poreality as the sole factor in a slave's and woman's identity. For literary, polit-ical, and philosophical reasons, Jacobs insists on a transcendent will that exists outside of the slave's body. Like Margaret Fuller, she invents a dual strategy that demonstrates the importance of corporeality to identity, but ultimately proposes that it can be transcended. Unlike Fuller, she does not do so at the expense of another race. Besides allowing her to evade the essentialism and voyeurism that haunted so many African American women during her era, Jacobs's crafting of a disembodied will enables her to carve literary and philo-sophical space in the debates that dominated her time. Like Ralph Waldo Emer-son, Jacobs asserts a "me" that is "not me."[2] Yet by doing so as an African

204 FLESHING OUT AMERICA

American woman and by questioning Emerson's transcendental optimism, Jacobs ruptures the nineteenth-century binary of metaphysical self/embodied other. She also breaks the "dialectical relationship" between white and black womanhood, suggesting (as does the text's editor, Lydia Maria Child, in her earlier antislavery writing) that Caucasian and African American women are capable of a full range of human emotions.

Jacobs's ordeal as a slave woman provides her with a unique perspective, and the study of her work significantly enhances our understanding of body politics in relation to both scientific essentialism and romanticism. However, interpretations of her text are complicated by the fact that Jacobs was writing in part to influence northern white Christian women's beliefs about slavery. According to Frances Smith Foster, unlike other African American women of her time, Jacobs "identifies white women as a significant portion of her readership" and "attempts to write across the color line, to mediate between the races and if not to resuscitate their former coalition then at least to establish that they did have mutual concerns." Having very few literary models to draw upon for this task, Jacobs revises several genres and forms, including the antislavery novel, the slave narrative, the religious confession, sentimental fiction, and the autobiography.[3] As is well documented, Jacobs's authenticity as an author was repeatedly questioned, and the prospect of doubt and censure most likely affected her as she wrote.[4] Her text contains solicitation and confrontation, revealing ambivalence about her white readers. For example, when the narrative closes, Linda is bought and freed by her current employer and friend, Mrs. Bruce. In her final chapter, Linda expresses uncertainty about her life in the North and her newly bought "freedom." In an often cited passage, Jacobs writes: "Reader, my story ends with freedom; not in the usual way, with marriage. I and my children are now free! We are as free from the power of slaveholders as are the white people of the north; and though that, according to my ideas, is not saying a great deal, it is a vast improvement in *my* condition. The dream of my life is not yet realized. I do not sit with my children in a home of my own" (201).

This excerpt typifies much of Jacobs's text. Linda begins by appealing to her "reader[s]"—whom she intends to be partially made up of white, northern Christian women—but immediately breaks with their expectations by saying, "[M]y story ends with freedom; not in the usual way, with marriage." As she does throughout her text, Jacobs implies that a common sympathy could be reached between women, but also accents how her embodied experiences lead to not only different, but perhaps new, endings to both fiction and life. As a mulatto woman born into slavery, she can teach readers not only about her life, but also about new possibilities for womanhood in the nineteenth century. In order to do so, she first has to deconstruct racist assumptions about female nature, and then reconstruct womanhood to include notions of strength, independence, and will. Indeed, as Hazel V. Carby argues, *Incidents* serves as the "most sophisticated, sustained narrative dissection of the conventions of true womanhood by a black author before emancipation."[5]

Women in the Nineteenth Century

Jacobs is often identified in contemporary criticism as an African American or black woman, but in the first paragraph of her text she introduces Linda as the daughter of mulatto parents. Her particular racial distinction is significant, because mulatto women were categorized differently from Negro women during Jacobs's lifetime. However, neither mulatto nor black women writers could assume, as many white authors did, a commonality between themselves and "all" women readers. The ideal of an angelic feminine nature was not only not extended to women of color, but, as Carby argues and as chapter 1 details, actually rested upon a "dialectical relationship with the alternative sexual code associated with the black woman."[6] Therefore it is not enough for Jacobs to attempt to extend true womanhood to Negro and mulatto women in order to argue against slavery. Rather, she has to break the racial binary that upholds the white woman's privileged status. Writing *Incidents*, Jacobs has to refute scientific notions about Negro, mulatto, and Caucasian women. Although Jacobs may not have accepted the category of mulatto, one strategy to discredit notions about women of mixed racial heritage was to speak from her own embodied experience as a mulatto and serve as corporeal evidence against false scientific theories.

One of the most powerful ways Jacobs serves as physical evidence for her readers is her depiction of Linda as a spirited mother who would sacrifice everything for her children. As such, she contradicts charges made by proslavery writers such as John H. Van Evrie, who contrasts the "lofty sentiment" of white motherhood with the maternal instincts of the Negro woman, which he claims resemble those of an "animal." Citing science, Van Evrie argues that although the Negro mother has a "boundless affection" for her infant, at age twelve to fifteen she "is relatively indifferent to it" and "at forty she does not recognize it."[7] These proslavery sentiments are expressed in *Incidents* by

Linda's mistress, Mrs. Flint, who declares that Linda "hasn't so much feeling for her children as a cow has for its calf. . . . The good-for-nothing hussy!" (102). Far more than just an appeal to an audience familiar with the cult of motherhood, Jacobs's portrayal of Linda as what Joanne Braxton has aptly characterized as the archetype of the "outraged mother" writes Linda into Jacobs's readers' conceptions of womanhood and therefore into humanity. As demonstrated by the titles of the chapters that depict the birth of her children—"The New Tie to Life" and "Another Link to Life"—motherhood not only empowers Linda's escape, but also gives her a reason to live. The most important decisions in Linda's life stem not from what she wants as an individual, but rather from what is best for her children. At one point she reminds readers that although she could have escaped alone, "it was more for my helpless children than for myself that I longed for freedom. Though the boon would have been precious to me, above all price, I would not have taken it at the expense of leaving them in slavery" (89). As Braxton argues, Jacobs's concerns are typical of female slave narrators: "Implied in all her actions and fueling her heroic ones is abuse of her people and her person."[8]

At all points in her journey, Linda's concern for her children prompts her most daring actions. After Flint jails Linda's brother William and her children as punishment for Linda's escape, her first impulse is to surrender, a move that could result in physical punishment, permanent separation from her family, or even death. However, her brother sends her a note imploring her to stay away, arguing that she will only endanger her family further if she capitulates. Encouraged, she remains a fugitive and schemes to free her children. Later, after Linda has been hiding in the crawl space, she becomes convinced that the father of her children, Mr. Sands, has forgotten his promise to free them. Despite her semiparalysis caused by her confinement, she places herself and the other members of her family in jeopardy by crawling down to plead with Sands for her children's freedom. This incident reveals that if Linda is forced to decide between other members of her family and her children, she opts for her children's welfare. Linda calls her grandmother, who substitutes for her mother, "a great treasure." However, her grandmother's intense love for her family and desire to keep them together makes her prefer that they patiently try to buy their freedom, rather than escape north. Discovering that Linda has resolved to run away, she asks: "Linda, do you want to kill your old grandmother?" Not content to call on Linda's duties as a granddaughter, she continues: "Nobody respects a mother who forsakes her children." Linda's response is telling: "My courage failed me, in view of the sorrow I should bring on that faithful, loving old heart" (91). As a mother, Linda understands how much pain her grandmother would experience at their separation. However, she is not willing to sacrifice her children's future for her grandmother or for herself. Once she is convinced that her children are in immediate danger, she acts and flees. As her readers are made to understand, it is not a lack, but rather a surplus, of motherly love that motivates her flight.

Repeatedly Linda portrays all slave mothers, regardless of racial classification, as caring deeply and permanently for the fate of their children. In the third chapter, "The Slaves' New Year's Day," Linda describes the annual sale and hiring of slaves on the first day of the year. To the slave mother, Linda argues, the day brings "peculiar sorrows. . . . She may be an ignorant creature, degraded by the system that has brutalized her from childhood; but she has a mother's instincts, and is capable of feeling a mother's agonies" (16). To move beyond generalizations, Linda describes a particular mother, whose seven children are sold on one day: "I met that mother in the street, and her wild, haggard face lives to-day in my mind. She wrung her hands in anguish, and exclaimed, 'Gone! All gone! Why *don't* God kill me?' I had no words wherewith to comfort her. Instances of this kind are of daily, yea, of hourly occurance" (16). Here Jacobs joins other women slave narrators and demonstrates the maternal sufferings and subsequent strength of slave women not only through her personal story, but also through dramatic stories such as this one.

In addition to representing slave women's maternal emotions, Jacobs also challenges misconceptions about the health and reproductive capability of mulatto women. As in the case of myths about African American women's sexuality, Jacobs's life experience appears to support scientific assumptions about childbirth that she wants to dismiss. Chapter 1 details the proposition set forth by antebellum scientists that racial "hybrids" were weak, less prolific, and prone to become sterile in about four generations when kept separate from their "parent stock." Josiah C. Nott classified mulatto women as "bad breeders, bad nurses," who were "liable to abortions" and whose "children generally die young."[9] Jacobs, apparently in congruence with these scientific charges, is ill during her first pregnancy and gives birth prematurely to a "sickly" four-pound baby. As Diane Price Herndl details, African American women writers found themselves in a "peculiar double-bind" when trying to represent illness in their texts. "If they followed the conventions of nineteenth-century white fiction and represented their heroines as invalids, the dominant culture could interpret this as evidence of their unfitness for freedom." Yet if "they did not represent their heroines as ill," they "risked the lack of sympathy such representations could evoke" and hazarded fueling "the ideology that black women's bodies were fundamentally different and indestructible."[10] To negotiate this representational quandary, Jacobs shows that it is not her natural condition that debilitates her, but rather the slave system. It is during Linda's pregnancy, interestingly enough, that Flint's status as a physician becomes important to the text. As a slave woman in a small town, Linda has few medical options. She is not allowed to see any other doctor besides Flint, and he abuses his status to insult and harm her. She describes one "medical" visit by Flint when she is at her grandmother's house. Flint tells Linda that he has neglected "his duty" and "that as a physician there were certain things that he ought to have explained" to her. "Then followed such talk such as would have made the most shameless blush" (59). Because Flint abuses his status as a physician to insult Linda, she cannot receive proper medical attention, for she "could not have any doctor but my master, and [she] would not have him sent for" (60). After giving birth to her second child, Linda says she "begged my friends to let me die, rather than send for the doctor. There was nothing I dreaded so much as his presence" (78). Through her detailed representation of Linda's struggle with Flint, Jacobs turns Flint into a representative of the abusive physicians in the antebellum South.

Jacobs's life serves as compelling physical evidence against damaging conceptions of mulatto women, but she also includes numerous examples to show that her experience, especially in relation to sexual and reproductive issues, typifies the treatment of slave women. In a poignant passage, Linda tells of her aunt Nancy's pregnancy:

> Mrs. Flint, at that time, had no children; but she was expecting to be a mother, and if she should want a drink of water in the night, what could she do without her slave to bring it? So my aunt was compelled to lie at her door, until one midnight she was forced to leave, to give premature birth to a child. In a fortnight she was required to resume her place on the entry floor, because Mrs. Flint's babe needed her attentions. She kept her station there through summer and winter, until she had given premature birth to six children; all the while she was employed as night-nurse to Mrs. Flint's children. Finally, toiling all day, and being deprived of rest at night, completely broke down her constitution, and Dr. Flint declared it was impossible she could ever become the mother of a living child. (143)

By juxtaposing Mrs. Flint's pregnancy with that of her aunt Nancy, Jacobs suggests that white, slaveholding women were relatively pampered, doing little work during and after their pregnancy and indulging their "illness" as a lady should and could. What was true for many white, middle-class women in the North—that they accepted "the medical definition of childbirth as an illness" and hired "doctors as testimony to their economic and social status"—also applies to slaveholding women like Mrs. Flint. She demonstrates her class status as a white woman conspicuously through the display of expendable time for medically required rest.[11] By contrast, Aunt Nancy is so worn down by her double shift that her health falters, until the doctor "objectively" determines that she is infertile. Rather than having a natural tendency toward sickness or premature birth, mixed-race women are shown to be the victims of abusive circumstances, circumstances brought about in part by the white woman's presumed frailty.

Adding to Aunt Nancy's compelling narrative, Jacobs also dares to address the issue of birth control and abortion in relation to slave women. Once Linda tells Flint that she is pregnant, he suggests that if she had chosen him instead of Sands, he could "as a physician" have saved her from "exposure" (58). Flint's meaning is ambiguous; he may be indicating that he could have provided birth control or an abortion. As White concludes, evidence about birth control and abortion in slave society is scarce. Yet certainly, some slave women "had reason not to want to bear and nurture children who could be sold from them at a slave master's whim"; "had ample cause to want to deny whites the satisfaction of realizing a profit on the birth of their children"; and "had as much reason as any antebellum woman, white or free black, to shun pregnancy and childbirth," including fear of exposure to the community.[12] Through her briefly reported exchange with Flint, Jacobs suggests that, rather than being naturally "liable to abortions" (as Nott charged), some mulatto women may be forced into them by their masters to avoid exposure either to the master's wife or the community.

The implications of these incidents are striking, especially because they involve the person or household of Flint, who represents not only the master, but also the man who masters through medicine and science. During Jacobs's lifetime, scientists were busily examining slave populations to prove their inferior status. In the antebellum South, physicians and scientists had access to the bodies of living slaves for experimentation and to slave corpses for dissection. Often they would use African American women for public medical exhibitions in a manner that would not have been tolerated for white women.[13] Jacobs shows that these "objective" men abuse their authority and sicken those whom they allegedly cure. Moreover, their supposed proof of their "specimens'" inferiority is manufactured by the slave system itself. Thus they reify their own power by creating the "evidence" they purport to discover.

Clearly Jacobs was aware of the scientific debates surrounding the nature of the Negro. In chapter 8, titled "What Slaves Are Taught to Think of the North," Linda provides anecdotes showing how misinformed some slaves are about the North. However, she parallels these anecdotes, implicitly, with others that reveal how ignorant northerners are about slavery. Tellingly, she ends her discussion of misinformation by attacking science and directly confronting scientific essentialism: "I admit that the black man *is* inferior. But what is it that makes him so? It is the ignorance in which white men compel him to live," she insists. She goes on to dismiss the theory of polygenesis as "a libel upon the heavenly Father, who 'made of one blood all nations of men!' And then who *are* Africans? Who can measure the amount of Anglo-Saxon blood coursing in the veins of American slaves?" (44). These passages, coupled with the depiction of Flint's medical practices, unmask the men of science who categorized Jacobs as a member of an inferior species and insisted that the "races" in America could never mix because mulattoes were destined for extinction.

Jacobs offers a powerful critique of scientific assumptions about reproduction and motherhood and provides an equally compelling reassessment of sexuality. In arguing against the belief that Negro and mulatto women were sexually depraved, Jacobs had to tackle her most difficult task as a writer. Linda was, after all, a "fallen" woman in nineteenth-century cultural terms. Not only did she "allow" herself to be seduced into a sexual liaison before she was married, but she also remained in it for several years, producing two children. How, then, could her readers see her as anything but a Jezebel, a woman whose lust prevailed over her will? Would she not confirm what writers such as Nott and Gliddon proposed, that there was a "want of chastity among mulatto women, which is so notorious as to be proverbial?"[14] After all, her own mistress calls her a "hussy" (102). Jacobs confronts these accusations of sexual depravity in several ways. First, she shows that rather than being indiscriminate in her choice of partners, Linda opts to love only one man, a free man of color, who lives in the community and wants to marry her. When a family friend asks Flint to allow the marriage, he refuses, outraged that Linda prefers a "nigger" over him as her "master." "If you *must* have a husband, you may take up with one of my slaves," he offers, drawing upon the myth that slave women do not distinguish between partners. Linda replies, "Don't you suppose, sir, that a slave can have some preference about marrying? Do you suppose that all men are alike to her?" After Flint refuses permission, he threatens to shoot her lover "as soon as [he] would a dog" if he discovers them together. Recognizing danger, Linda tells her suitor not to come back from his upcoming visit to Savannah, because she does not want "to link his fate with my own unhappy destiny" (39–42).

Second, Linda's honorable first love demonstrates that she is pure and has been properly raised by her grandmother but prematurely and unnaturally corrupted by her master and, by extension, the slave system. Chapter 5, "The Trials of Girlhood," illustrates how young slave girls are defiled. "The light heart which nature had given me became heavy with sad forebodings," Linda reflects after having been cornered by Flint and forced to listen to "unclean images, such as only a vile monster could think of" (27–28). She describes the fate of the slave girl, who learns early why the mistress hates particular slave women, perhaps even the girl's own mother: "She will become prematurely knowing in evil things. Soon she will learn to tremble when she hears her master's footfall. She will be compelled to realize that she is no longer a child. If God has bestowed beauty upon her, it will prove her greatest curse. That which commands admiration in the white woman only hastens the degradation of the female slave. . . . I cannot tell how much I suffered in the presence of these wrongs, nor how I am still pained by the retrospect" (28). Linda reminds readers that a slave's beauty "hastens" her degradation, wording that suggests her "fall" is often inevitable. Like Eve, these women know too much about the nature of good and evil to symbolize innocence.

Despite the bleakness of these passages they also suggest that the slave girl gains at least one tool—she becomes *knowing*, and this knowledge can translate into power. She comprehends the potency sexuality has in antebellum society. Not only can it destroy the serenity of the master's home, but it can also determine a slave woman's treatment and destiny. Although a slave woman had scarce support for demonstrating her sexual autonomy in a society that ruled that her body was not her own, she may nonetheless have been able to negotiate the complex sexual landscape to achieve a state "akin to freedom" (55). In other words, Jacobs's most powerful argument against the innate depravity of Negro and mulatto women is her ploy to show sexuality not as an uncontrollable emotion, but as a tool, used, in her own words, with "deliberate calculation." The young Linda learns early that to survive in a corrupt world, she must manage the knowledge of sex. For example, in chapter 2, Linda witnesses an incident that occurs just several months after she arrives in Flint's household. Flint sells one of his slave women, severing her forever from her husband, family, and friends. Linda reports their final exchange: "[S]he said, 'You *promised* to treat me well.' To which he replied, 'You have let your tongue run too far; damn you!'" The young Linda concludes, "She had forgotten that it was a crime for a slave to tell who was the father of her child" (13). This exchange teaches Linda valuable lessons about the management of sexuality. First, she realizes that she cannot trust Flint's promises and must not assume that she will receive better treatment by entering into a liaison with him. To have any leverage, a slave girl must choose her partner based upon whatever indication of his character she can glean. Second, even if she cannot remain a virgin, she must try to deploy the knowledge of sex with caution. The woman has erred, presumably, in letting Mrs. Flint know her children's identity. Linda will ultimately choose an unmarried man for her partner but will also hide his identity from white society.

By the time Linda enters into her liaison with Sands, then, she is no longer pure, in that she understands that sex holds power in slave society. Although her deed is the most corporeal act imaginable to her readers, Jacobs does not represent it as physical, but rather as intellectual, in content: "I would do any thing, every thing, for the sake of defeating him. What *could* I do? I thought and thought, till I became desperate, and made a plunge into the abyss." Linda's sexual choices, for which she feels shame throughout her life, are confessedly designed to seek revenge on Flint while possibly gaining her freedom: "I knew what I did, and I did it with deliberate calculation" (53–54). William Andrews notes that Jacobs "drains her affair with Sands of all its pornographic potential" by disclosing only the psychological factors that made her go into it and not the facts of how it was carried out.[15] In short, Linda asks readers to reconstruct her experience and understand how her liaison with Sands was a reasonable response to a desperate situation.

Why does she choose Sands? Given her options in a small antebellum town, Sands is not a bad alternative. Although she does not love him—that emotion she reserves for the man she could not marry—Linda does not despise Sands (59) and has a "tender feeling" toward him (54). She assesses him as a man of "more generosity and feeling" than Flint and surmises that she might be able to obtain her freedom from him. Indeed, what we learn of Sands shows that he treats Linda with some consideration. He arranges to buy his children from Flint, sends his daughter north at Linda's request, and, when he marries, confesses his paternity to his new wife, who treats his children comparatively well. He does not turn Linda in when he learns that she is a fugitive and seems mildly concerned about her welfare even several years after their affair has ended. Sands's status as a single white man of property also helps Linda. Because he is a bachelor, Linda does not have to contend with complications brought on by a jealous wife, and she does not commit adultery. "[T]he wrong does not seem so great with an unmarried man," she reflects, "as with one who has a wife to be made unhappy" (55). Also, as a wealthy white man, Sands is exempt from any retribution by Flint and may serve Linda either as a buffer against him or as a possible means toward liberation. Once Flint recognizes that Sands is the father of Linda's child, he cannot do anything about it because Sands (a federal congressman) is a gentleman of property and prestige in the community and immune from Flint's control. When we recall the slave mother whom Flint sold south, we see that, given her options, Linda chose effectively. Not only do the ramifications of this decision endorse the idea that Linda has chosen *rationally* to engage in a sexual encounter, but they also help Jacobs move beyond the tragic-mulatto plot. As noted in chapter 2, the tragic-mulatto plot often results in the death of the mulatto woman. Additionally, as in the case of Child's "Slavery's Pleasant Homes," the mulatto mistress usually causes devastation to the white family upon the discovery of her liaison with the master. Linda shows readers that she is not an accomplice in the destruction of a southern home; in this sense, Jacobs reveals an astute awareness of her readers' uneasy relationship with the supposedly sexually depraved mulatto woman.

Linda's decision demonstrates her perceptive sense not only of Jacobs's readers' and Flint's psychology, but also of the delicate dynamic upon which a man or a race base their presumed authority. Linda understands that Flint's identity is intertwined with her submission and that to refuse him is to deny the pretense upon which he bases his claims. In the slave system, Angela Davis argues, "[r]ape was a weapon of determination, a weapon of repression, whose covert goal was to extinguish slave women's will to resist."[16] However, Flint will not "rape" Linda by force; he prefers to coerce her into submission, to extinguish any sense of herself outside of his power. Flint, Linda reminds us, "loved money, but he loved power more" (80). He needs Linda to submit to his force willingly, to approve of both the physical brutality of slavery and the

racist, sexist suppositions that attempted to justify it. He wants her to accept
cheerfully her preordained role as a sexual being whose duty is to fulfill the
white man's needs. Dana D. Nelson presents this argument in her analysis of
Linda's assertion, early in the narrative, that Flint has a (legal) right to kill her,
but that Flint has "no right to do as [he] like[s] with [Linda]" (39). As Nelson
argues, this scene demonstrates how, in fact, Flint cannot kill Linda before "she
has confirmed his mastery of her (her symbolic death). His own identity
depends on her recognition of it. He apparently cannot feel his mastery until
she reflects it to him."[17] Therefore, Linda's decision to give her body to Sands,
however riddled with the painful contradictions of her oppression, is also a
mark of her declaration of personhood, her control of the politics of body. She
will not let Flint see a reflection of his identity in her body; instead, she maintains the ability to give herself at will.

Linda's rebellion is not unaccompanied by guilt, and the "painful and humiliating memory" continues to haunt her, as she shows by asking readers to
"pity" and "pardon" her. Yet she also repeatedly insists that they do not understand her situation: "You never knew what it is to be a slave; to be entirely
unprotected by law or custom; to have the laws reduce you to the condition of
a chattel, entirely subject to the will of another." Given her circumstances, she
suggests, she should be subject to different moral criteria: "[L]ooking back,
calmly, on the events of my life, I feel that the slave woman ought not to be
judged by the same standard as others" (55–56). Indeed, Linda searches for abso-
lution from within the female slave community. Immediately after Linda tells
Flint of her pregnancy, she seeks her grandmother's pardon and eventually
receives her love, if not her verbal forgiveness. In one of the text's final chapters, "The Confession," Linda begins to reveal her sexual past to her daughter,
but her daughter interrupts her, telling her that she already knows everything
and loves her anyway. Situated, as it is, so close to the end of the book, this confession shows that Linda seeks acceptance and love from within her own community, and not from readers.[18]

By telling readers that they cannot judge her life, Linda is doing more than
providing a justification for her sexual actions to a genteel population. She is
questioning assumptions not only about Negro and mulatto women's sexuality, but also about sexuality in general. She indicates that a woman's sexual
choices are contingent on her environment, on cultural and political factors.
Additionally, by showing that slave women are not innately promiscuous,
Jacobs breaks the binary that constructs white women's sexual identity as pas-

sionless. Neither "naturally" lustful nor "innately" pure, she hints, women may in practice respond to the sexual standards society deems proper for them. As such, she offers her readers a means of reassessing the value and validity of their own sexual codes, opening space for cultural relativism.[19] Jacobs's status as a fallen woman is a powerful example of this challenge to readers' sexual standards. After her "fall," Jacobs has the strength and audacity not only to live, but also to escape north and write an autobiography. She solicits and receives the love and assistance of members of her community, both men and women, whites and blacks, in her efforts. Might her readers not question, then, the stories about sexuality they tell themselves? Like the heroine in a sentimental novel, Jacobs is confronted with sexual choices, none of which are entirely unfamiliar to her readers. Although she chooses rationally to "fall," she manages to rewrite the ending and thus to reconfigure the dynamic of choice and consequence.[20]

In a similar move, Jacobs destabilizes the essentialist justification for true womanhood by exposing the actions and attitudes of various southern "ladies," who exhibit anything but an innate spiritual superiority or nurturing sympathy. We receive the most information about Mrs. Flint, who like a proper lady is "totally deficient in energy" and has "not the strength to superintend her household affairs." Nonetheless, she has nerves so strong "that she could sit in her easy chair and see a woman whipped, till the blood trickled from every stroke of the lash"(12). She comes home from church services to spit in the pots that hold Sunday dinner, just to ensure that her half-starved slaves do not eat any food. In addition to Mrs. Flint, we learn about numerous slaveholding women, such as one who chastises a dying young slave girl for giving birth to her master's child: "Her mistress stood by, and mocked at her like an incarnate fiend. 'You suffer, do you?' she exclaimed. 'I am glad of it. You deserve it all, and more too'" (13). True, these incidents can be read as suggesting that slavery corrupts the innate purity of all women. They could function in a similar manner as those Frederick Douglass relates about his mistress, Mrs. Auld, who at first is kind toward Douglass but later is corrupted by slavery; they could, in effect, serve as allegories for the loss of natural feminine innocence through wicked institutions. In the overall context of *Incidents*, however, it is just as reasonable to conclude that they contest essential conceptions of womanhood linking white women with purity. As Carby describes Mrs. Flint, "[t]he qualities of delicacy of constitution and heightened sensitivity . . . appear as a corrupt and superficial veneer that covers an underlying strength and power in cruelty and brutality."[21] These women are twisted versions of the young Linda, who "dares to feel like a man." They have the "masculine" characteristics of aggression and revenge. After all, in Linda and in numerous other southern slave women, we see the same characteristics—aggression and revenge—resulting in positive acts of defiance and survival. Does not a sense of revenge empower Linda to defy Flint? Does not her aggression enable her to plot courageously to free her children? Her grandmother, we are told, once tried to shoot a white man who offended her daughter. These southern women may not be ladies, but they offer northern readers entrenched in the cult of domesticity's angelic view of women a range of emotions and responses outside the "feminine" realm. Full members of humanity, they are just as capable of evil as they are of good.

Certainly Jacobs crafted her work for a northern audience, and one of the primary ways to reach it was to appeal to its notions of virtue, motherhood, and Christianity. However, to argue, as Elizabeth Fox-Genovese does, that Jacobs portrays "slave women as essentially like their northern white sisters in their goals and sensibilities" instead of presenting an argument for individual women's rights, is to overlook the text's power.[22] The radical nature of Jacobs's text resides in her comparison of women cross-culturally and cross-racially to expose the bourgeois conceptions of women's sexuality and femininity as constructed and historical, not natural and universal. In doing so, Jacobs concurs with Fuller, who analyzes slave and Native American women in *Woman in the Nineteenth Century* to interrogate the attributes ascribed to Caucasian women, and with Child, who offers readers a cross-cultural view of women in her *History of the Condition of Women*. Jacobs's embodied experiences as a mulatto woman led her to reassess the meaning and applicability of "womanhood" itself. To read her text as merely a humble appeal to the pity of white women— as written solely on their terms—is to miss the most radical implications of her work in relation to women in the nineteenth century.

Averting the Eye of the Spectator through the Force of Will

Jacobs destabilizes readers' assumptions about racial and gendered identity at the price of exposing her life to her audience's gaze, by revealing her most private secrets in a public form. Like Harper and Child, Jacobs took considerable risk by going public with stories of slavery. But unlike Child's, Jacobs's body aligned her with harmful racial concepts, and unlike Harper's, Jacobs's slave story was personal, her past sexual. The public revelation of these incidents, even under an assumed name, disturbed her. She writes in a letter to Amy Post: "I have My dear friend—Striven faithfully to give a true and just account of my own life in Slavery—God knows I have tried to do it in a Christian spirit—there are somethings that I might have made plainer I know—Woman can whisper—her cruel wrongs into the ear of a very dear friend—much easier than she can record them for the world to read."[23] This passage suggests that Jacobs aspired to write a "true and just" account of her life that, as she says in her preface, would "arouse the women of the North to a realizing sense of the condition of two millions of women at the South." Yet to do so, she had to bare the wounds of slavery, which she preferred be left dressed. Linda expresses concern over exposure at two key points in her narrative. When she arrives in Philadelphia after her escape, a prominent African American minister hears her tale and assures her that he requested details not from "idle curiosity" but rather from a wish to help. He warns her that she should not tell everyone her life story, because it might "give some heartless people a pretext for treating you with contempt." Linda remarks that the "word *contempt* burned me like coals of fire" (160–161). In this context, how could Jacobs ensure that her readers would hear her with the aspiration to help or learn, rather than with a desire for entertainment, titillation, or judgment?

This dilemma is also evident when the second Mrs. Bruce buys Linda's freedom. Linda comments: "The bill of sale is on record, and future generations will learn from it that women were articles of traffic in New York, late in the nineteenth century of the Christian religion. It may hereafter prove a useful document to antiquaries, who are seeking to measure the progress of civilization in the United States" (200). The word *traffic* that Jacobs uses to describe her sale can also refer to prostitution. One reason for the bourgeois campaign against prostitution in northern cities in the nineteenth century was that prostitution took what was supposed to be a private practice and made it, quite unpolitely, public. Like those of the prostitute, Jacobs intimates, her body and her life are also inappropriately public. In a society that privileged the privacy of the female body and wanted to confine sexuality to the interior space of the bourgeois home, the slave woman was forced onto a platform and inspected for her childbearing potential and sexual appeal.[24] Her body was publicly accessible, open to the gaze of anyone who would look upon her with lust, contempt, or pity. While the institution of slavery and proslavery writing commonly reduced African Americans to a corporeally based identity, some antislavery rhetoric likewise emphasized the physical aspects of slavery in a way that risked associating slave identity too readily with corporeality. As William Andrews suggests, when describing a female slave, male slave narrators often emphasized the "futility of her continual resistance unless she chooses suicide as her ultimate recourse, and her eventual humiliation and betrayal after she finally yields or is worn down by force." Jean Fagan Yellin analyzes a central symbol of the women's antislavery movement as a female figure who, "black, half nude, chained, kneeling in supplication," emphasizes the presumed helplessness and sexual vulnerability of slave women.[25] How, then, could Jacobs confess her life in a public mode to her readers without reinforcing the idea of herself as a spectacle, readily accepting anyone's impertinent stare? Like Child and Harper, she had to invent a strategy of representation that did not reinforce a structure resting upon the binary of an "embodied" slave woman and a "disembodied" observer. Unlike them, she had to do so as a slave woman with a history that included corporeal actions readers might deem shocking and questionable, but that were nonetheless central to crafting her argument against slavery. As Lauren Berlant argues, "sexual knowledge stands for a kind of political counter-intelligence, a challenge to the norms of credibility, rationality, and expertise that generally organize political culture; and yet, as an archive of injury and private sensation, sexual knowledge can have the paradoxical effect of *delegitimating* the very experts who can represent it as a form of experience."[26]

To devise a solution to this predicament and to dismiss herself as a potential spectacle, Jacobs becomes the spectator, a role she assumes in chapter 21, "The Loophole of Retreat." Having found refuge from the gaze of fugitive-slave hunters in the garret above her grandmother's house, Linda is, for the first time in her life, no longer looked upon by slave society. She is liberated, paradoxically, by the darkness that surrounds her, although the cost of this liberation is being forced to sit "in a cramped position day after day, without one gleam of light" (114). Yet it is in this horrific prison that Linda discovers the power associated with surveillance, a method often deployed against slaves: "One day I hit my head against something and found it was a gimlet. . . . I said to myself, 'Now I will have some light. Now I will see my children.' . . . I stuck the gimlet in and waited for evening. I bored three rows of holes, one above another; then I bored out the interstices between" (115). Even though Linda drills the holes to see her children, the first person she sees is Flint. At first she deems this a bad omen, but she quickly ascertains the power her position as spectator provides. Indeed, she becomes quite the "peeper," assuming the role of voyeur that Flint had so mercilessly played on her: "I peeped at him as he passed on his way to the steamboat," she reveals (116). Taking this newfound resource even further, she reports: "Southerners have the habit of stopping and talking in the streets, and I heard many conversations not intended to meet my ears" (117).

By refusing to depict herself as an object to be looked upon and by becoming the subject rather than the object of the gaze, Jacobs reverses one of the most damaging conceptions of African American women. She also shows that surveillance is a two-way process in slave society and that slaves are scrutinizing their masters every bit as much as the masters are leering at them. Linda comments dryly: "If the secret memoirs of many members of Congress should be published, curious details would be unfolded" (142). Jacobs's courageous revelation of private secrets in a public form demonstrates the collective strength that slave women in particular, and slaves in general, could gain by crossing the border between public and private spheres. This power is underscored by Sands's status as a legislator and Flint's role as a physician. By revealing their secrets in a public autobiography, Jacobs unmasks the physician and law maker, symbolically challenging the discourses of law and medicine that sought to define her as chattel. She also challenges her audience to consider their complicity in these discourses and, therefore, in her exploitation. Berlant asks what it would "mean to write a genealogy of sexual harassment in which not an individual but a nation was considered the agent of unjust sexual power" and suggests that Jacobs does so, "making America accountable for the private sexual transgressions of its privileged men and radically transforming the history of the 'public' and the 'private' in America."[27]

Jacobs's reversal is forceful. However, her most radical strategy for maintaining a sense of self beyond one that is marked corporeally and gazed upon by society is her revision of romantic rhetoric to assert her natural "will." She forges a sense of self that is not corporeal, that cannot be enslaved or sexually abused. Jacobs's depiction of a transcendent will is as powerful a tendency in her narrative as is her corporeal resistance. Affirming her individual will, Jacobs repeatedly suggests that both oppression and liberation must be viewed as more than bodily states. When analyzing both the embodied and disembodied representations in Jacobs's text, I do not want to imply that these divisions are necessarily feasible or that Jacobs endorsed them. Jacobs wants to create a literary space where her experience as an African American woman matters and to demonstrate how a person's embodied status leads to different societal treatment and expectations. Also, she illustrates how physical conditions affect a person's will. For romantic authors such as Henry David Thoreau, who believed in a metaphysical self, the body could be severed from the will. In his essay "Resistance to Civil Government" (1849) Thoreau argues that the state "never intentionally confronts a man's sense, intellectual or moral, but *only his body*" (emphasis mine).[28] Jacobs demonstrates that such divisions are difficult to maintain when the body is subjected to torture or continuous deprivation. When sent to her master's plantation, Linda observes the slaves who have been physically broken: "The spirit of the mothers was so crushed by the lash, that they stood by, without courage to remonstrate. How much more must I suffer, before I should be 'broke in' to that degree?" she wonders (87). Jacobs comprehends that bodily pain—if severe and prolonged—can create political paralysis.

Jacobs's insistence on both corporeal identity and disembodied will may be partly attributed to conflicting conceptions of identity in Jacobs's time. The nineteenth century was certainly invested in defining people corporeally according to race, gender, and sexuality, and science was generally used to fix identity as innate. However, as my analysis of Emerson and Fuller indicates, there was also a philosophical understanding of identity as transcendent and disembodied, a concept that coincided with romanticism. Sidonie Smith traces the rise of the metaphysical self in the eighteenth and nineteenth centuries (see chapter 4). This self, which was disembodied and dissociated from social and communal roles, privileged the "eye" and the "I" of the observer. It relied on the construction of women and non-Caucasian races not only as embodied, but also as often encumbered and defined by biology. Many romantic writers took this I/eye for granted, a privilege that was ironically obtained through their embodied status in society. However, as a mulatto woman, Jacobs could not assume that readers would allow her the status of a disembodied observer. To complicate matters further for Jacobs, the metaphysical self, Smith argues, was intimately connected with the growth of autobiography in nineteenth-century America, because "[a]utobiography itself functioned as guarantor of 'metaphysical selfhood.'"[29] The genre of autobiography relied heavily upon the belief in an extralinguistic and extracorporeal basis of identity. Therefore, when Jacobs picked up her pen, she was marked by science, philosophy, and genre as "other," as a corporeal phenomenon rather than transcendent being or equal citizen. By insisting so firmly on the disembodied will, Jacobs asserts an Emersonian "me" that is "not me," and breaks the binary of metaphysical self/embodied other. She also draws upon the ideal of the American citizen as a race- and gender-neutral political subject. In doing so, she carves a space for African American women in literary, philosophical, and political spheres.

From the first chapter of her narrative, Linda portrays herself as having an identity not defined by slave society, and freedom as not only a corporeal state. "I was born a slave; but I never knew it till six years of happy childhood had passed away." Linda's sense of an independent self comes from her family. Her father, a carpenter, "had more of the feelings of a freeman than is common among slaves" (9), and her grandmother gains status in the white community and secures her freedom through her baking skills. Both the young Linda and her uncle Benjamin reason, as did the Revolutionary forefathers, that God wills people to be free (17). At the end of the chapter "The Slave Who Dared to Feel Like a Man," in which Linda confronts her master, Linda's grandmother has bought one of her sons, and the other has finally escaped north. The family members conclude: "He that is *willing* to be a slave, let him be a slave" (26).[30] The members of her family can liberate themselves, she indicates, because their minds are able to envision freedom. Both slavery and freedom are therefore philosophical as well as corporeal, and the will must triumph over corporeal incarceration. Or, as Fuller puts it in a different but applicable context, if "principles could be established, particulars would adjust themselves aright."[31]

The lessons Linda learns from her family are critical to her sense of self and at times can be read as allegorical, as can be the grandmother's life story. Born to a slave woman and her owner, Linda's grandmother is freed when her master/father dies during the Revolutionary War, only to be captured and sold back into slavery. Given the promise of the Revolution to liberate all persons subject to tyranny, Linda's grandmother should have been emancipated during the Revolution. However, as the radical potential of the Revolution gave way to the expansion of slavery on American soil, so too did the concept of the theoretically disembodied citizen give way to racial slavery based on a person's embodied status. Throughout her journey, Linda seeks the promise of the Revolution and the New Republic. She represents revolutionary ideals, ironically embodied in the physique of a slave. In chapter 4 she declares war on Flint, resolving "never to be conquered" (19), and, when her relatives want her to turn herself in after she flees, she reminds herself that there would be "no turning back. 'Give me liberty, or give me death,' was my motto" (99), echoing Patrick Henry's Revolutionary vow. While her body is fettered, her mind yearns—naturally and rightfully—to be free.

Repeatedly, Linda insists that she has an identity outside the one that Flint—and slavery—forces upon her. To return to a passage I analyze above, when Flint refuses to let Linda marry the man of her choice, Linda tells him that she despises him. Flint, infuriated, responds: "Do you know that I have a right to do

as I like with you,—that I can kill you, if I please?" Linda answers: "You have
tried to kill me, and I wish you had; but you have no right to do as you like with
me" (39). By saying that Flint may kill her, Linda condescends to the southern
practice that gives a master control over his slave woman's body. However, by
adding that "you have no right to do as you like with me," she suggests that
there is a noncorporeal part of her that he cannot touch, be it spirit, soul, or
will. At the end of her story Linda once again reiterates the dialectical relationship between mind and body, but hints that the mind must take precedence for
her whole self to be free. She comments on her ambivalence about having her
freedom bought by Mrs. Bruce: "The more my mind had become enlightened,
the more difficult it was for me to consider myself an article of property; and to
pay money to those who had so grievously oppressed me seemed like taking
from my sufferings the glory of triumph" (199). In this passage Linda's "mind"
governs her understanding of her body, as she begins to realize even more fully
how her body cannot be an "article of property."

These examples indicate that Jacobs depicts a dialectical relationship
between the mind and the body throughout her narrative, keeping transcendent optimism in check through her embodied experience. However, beginning
with chapter 15, one can detect a narrative shift, as the representation of the
corporeal wrongs of slavery gives way to a depiction of disembodied will. Chapter 15 centers around Flint's proposal that Linda become his concubine. Linda
determines that she will "fight" her "battle alone," and once again poses a
sense of will against the objective facts of her existence: "My master had power
and law on his side; I had a determined will. There is might in each" (185).
From that moment Linda begins what she calls in chapter 25 a "competition in
cunning." Pitting herself against Flint—wit against wit, pen against pen, and
will against will—she masters him and therefore becomes her own master.
Ironically, she first asserts her will forcefully when she is imprisoned in her garret space. From her garret she not only surveys southern society, but also draws
upon the power of literacy (the same power she deploys to avoid recapture
when she is in the North) to secure her freedom. The spoken and written word
are represented as noncorporeal and therefore as spaces where Linda can compete on more equal terms with Flint. Certainly, emphasizing the power of literacy was not unique to Jacobs. The slave narrative genre often links literacy
with freedom, because slaves had to write their way into humanity and citizenship by demonstrating their ability to master the written word.[32] Because
Linda is taught relatively early to read and write, her narrative does not incor-

porate the story of becoming literate as a primary motif. Yet she certainly shows the power that language provides to help her defend herself and escape. Thus Jacobs connects the conventions of the slave narrative to the genre of sentimental fiction, whose readers might approve of nonviolent resistance even if they did not dare to meet Jacobs's challenge to feel like "men" by accepting aggression and physical resistance. If they cannot use the strength of their bodies, Linda implies, her readers certainly can wield their voices and their pens to free themselves and their country from oppression.

Jacobs's early acts of defiance come through the oral, rather than the written, word. Braxton defines Jacobs's "sass," which she identifies as a word of "West African derivation that is associated with the female aspect of the trickster." She continues, "Whenever Linda is under sexual attack, she uses sass as a weapon of self-defense."[33] Braxton's reading is suggestive, as one of Flint's most powerful tools is his use of language. He is described in serpentlike images, whispering obscene language into Linda's ear to harass and dominate her. In contrast to Eve, Linda defeats the serpent by talking back to it. At one of their most intense moments of confrontation, instead of hitting Flint, Linda reacts with words: "You have struck me for answering you honestly. How I despise you!" (39). After becoming pregnant with Sands's child, Linda most cherishes the "thought of telling" Flint (56). Flint often holds a razor to Linda's throat, symbolically underscoring both his hatred of her voice and her determination to use it despite the violence of slavery.

Once Linda escapes from Flint, her primary weapon becomes the letter. Repeatedly she pretends to send letters from the North when in fact she is across the street from Flint. Part of the deadly game Linda plays rests on who has the knowledge to read the truth in her letters. The members of Linda's family must recognize that Flint tampers with Linda's letters. They often communicate through code, "knowing" that part of a letter to one of the family members indirectly applies to Linda. When she goes north, this contest continues, and Linda regularly searches the newspapers for word of visitors from the South and corresponds with the Flints, trying to negotiate her freedom. Throughout all of these scenes, Linda proves to be an astute reader of letters and people. She detects fraudulent promises and mocks Flint's conspicuous attempts to lure her back under false pretenses. "Verily," Linda says of Flint when reading one of his letters to her after her escape north, "he relied too much on 'the stupidity of the African race'" (172). This emphasis on literacy can be interpreted as Jacobs's means of creating a space in which she is not identified solely by her body. She suggests that the "Republic of Letters," although certainly not colorblind, offers a "competition in cunning" that is at least on fairer ground. As more African Americans and women published in the nineteenth century, the territory of the written word was fertile soil to set her sights on. However, she is hardly naive. As a writer who is also a former slave, she knows full well the power that more influential figures could attempt to exert over her text, and though she does everything she can to project her own voice, she understands that her life and work will continue to be a struggle.[34]

Clearly Jacobs is proud of her heritage and perceives the importance of the body to both identity and resistance. Yet she also moves away from the body as the sole source of character or knowledge. When she visits England as a fugitive slave, Linda displays what could be read as Jacobs's ideal. She says that for the "first time in my life I was in a place where I was treated according to my deport-ment, without reference to my complexion. I felt as if a great millstone had been lifted from my breast. . . . I laid my head on my pillow, for the first time, with the delightful consciousness of pure, unadulterated freedom" (183). Linda pictures her model society as one in which a person's embodied status is not more impor-tant than her individual character. By ironically situating that ideal in the domain of England, Jacobs reminds readers that the Revolutionary potential of America has been hindered through the understanding of identity not only as essential, but also as determined by race and gender. Her "unadulterated free-dom" comes from not having to define herself solely as society has categorized her. America's freedom will come, she intimates, when it ceases to mark people with arbitrary and false categories to deny them rights of citizenship.

Jacobs professes noncorporeal identity to participate fully in the literary, political, and philosophical debates that dominate her times. Like Fuller, Jacobs has reason to fear Whitman's "merge" with corporeality because it risks reaf-firming notions of a physiologically inferior self. Yet Jacobs knows that the body is a source of knowledge, and she refuses to dismiss the often harsh lessons that it teaches her about American society. Therefore, in a fashion similar to Fuller's, Jacobs establishes a dual strategy that demonstrates the importance of corpore-ality to identity, but ultimately proposes that it can be transcended. However, unlike Fuller—who dissociates herself from negative corporeal implications by transferring them to an "other" race—Jacobs breaks the binary of the embodied/passionate African American woman and the disembodied/passionless white woman that supported the cult of true womanhood without reestablishing a comparison between herself and an "other" race that affirmed her as superior.

A survivor, Jacobs could leave us her tale, "written by herself." Nonetheless, as she informs us in that story, there are some slaves who are broken beyond rebellion, beyond the ability to articulate their pain or imagine liberation. Therefore, she finds a way to write about their pain, to speak about the corporeal nature of oppression, without leaving them, symbolically, victims or spectacles. In this sense, Jacobs manages to speak the knowledge of the body and to transcend racially harmful discourses of corporeality. In doing so, she dismisses, rather than appropriates, the discourses of science that were attempting to define and confine her. By comparison, Martin R. Delany also attempts a dual strategy with respect to racialized concepts of corporeality. Like Jacobs, he points to his own body—to his status as the "blackest of the black" men[35]—as testimony against claims of natural racial inferiority. Yet, unlike Jacobs, he does not assert a simultaneous claim to a disembodied, transcendent will and dismiss the men of science and their racialized discourses. Rather, he dares to do "what white men have ever dared and done,"[36] to become a man of science himself and appropriate the discourse to substantiate his globalized vision of the future of people of color.

Martin R. Delany and the Politics of Ethnology

I desire to dare do, what white men have ever dared and done.—Martin R. Delany

In chapter 7 I suggest that Harriet Jacobs's dual strategy for negotiating the precarious body politics that dominated her age was to carve a literary space for her transcendent, disembodied will and to reverse the gaze of spectatorship, to become a "peeper" who unmasks the men of science and law and their oppressive discourses. Frances E. W. Harper similarly reverses the politics of the gaze, but perhaps goes a step further, directing her readers to spectate upon the intemperate, unruly bodies of Caucasian characters. As I argue in chapter 3, this rhetorical strategy enabled her to question the physiological basis for citizenship, a power explicitly reserved prior to Reconstruction for those whose bodies were white and male and, many would argue, implicitly reserved for them thereafter. I also proposed that Harper was able to forge figuratively a reversal of power through her representations of corporeality. Yet one might ask how far removed Harper's strategy is from that of Margaret Fuller, whose tendency to transfer unwanted corporeal associations onto the bodies of Native Americans, as I suggest in chapter 5, could be considered a regrettable rhetorical and political gesture. Don't both strategies, in effect, flirt dangerously with reconfirming the polarization that the authors presumably want to transcend? Or does the question of which race they draw attention to (or deflect it from) influence our assessment of their textual body politics? Can we call Harper's strategy, for example, a move toward deconstruction, a reversal of body politics that splinters the corporeal narratives of her day? Can we then juxtapose this with Fuller's strategy, which seems to replicate in a conventional manner the trope of the "fated" Indian? Does it matter that one author was embodied white and one black? Or do both strategies—and those of the other authors in this study—suggest that scientists and medical experts of the era dominate the discourse of the body in a way that, if not totalizing, nonetheless defines the terms of the debate?

These questions lead us back to the queries I pose in my introduction. There I ask: Can the new politics of the body be liberating or useful? How can authors engage in a critique of nineteenth-century sciences if those very discourses define them as incapable of participating in the debate? When and why do authors decide to deploy "strategic essentialism" and speak the knowledge that comes from their body or from their embodied experiences? How do authors negotiate the dynamics of spectatorship either in relation to their own bodies or the bodies of those they represent? The previous chapters explore these concerns in relation to particular texts and specific authors. Yet I also suggest in my introduction that these inquires lead to the one that dominates this book: Can we combat the disturbingly divisive nature of the politics of the body through the imaginary space that literature provides? As I indicate above in relation to Fuller and Harper, such a question may lead us to the uncomfortable conclusion that an author's corporeality matters in terms of the politics of the work. It may lead us, for example, to consider a claim to an "essential" feminine nature—such as the "genius of woman"—liberational when voiced by Fuller but oppressive when suggested by Emerson, or to suggest that proposing specific traits of the English/American/Saxon smacks of racial superiority when voiced by Emerson, Fuller, or Whitman (or any number of nineteenth-century writers) but somehow sounds different when proposed by African American authors. To consider this dilemma further, it seems natural to turn to the work of Martin R. Delany, a man who, perhaps more than any other African American in the nineteenth century, confronted and interrogated the science of race, forging a theoretical/scientific basis for what he believed to be the destiny of colored people throughout the world.

By briefly considering three pivotal texts by Delany—*The Condition, Elevation, Emigration and Destiny of the Colored People of the United States* (1852), "The Political Destiny of the Colored Race" (1854), and *Principia of Ethnology* (1879)—in relation to the issues this study has explored, we can understand better how theories of the body, bolstered by science, cannot be conceived solely as a discourse defining women and people of color in a strictly hierarchal manner. Rather, as the previous chapters suggest, despite the disadvantage at which scientific discourses of the body placed those it labeled inferior, many participated in the definitions of identity that were forming in the mid- to late nineteenth century. Perhaps more than any other individual,

Delany, a man of science himself, employed scientific discourse to revolution-ize his world view and challenge Caucasian claims of superiority. If Delany risked, as Frederick Douglass suggested in 1862, going "about the same length in favor of black, as the whites have in favor of the doctrine of white superior-ity,"[1] if he hazarded, in other words, solidifying theories of difference that could and would be employed against him and those he wished to assist, his theories also can be argued to provide a crucial stage in the deconstruction of racial difference, because they enact a reversal that challenges the hierarchy and superiority established by the white men of science analyzed in chapter 1.

To assess Delany's deployment of the science of race, we can begin by con-sidering Delany's work during the same year that opens chapter 1, 1854. This year loomed large for those involved in the antislavery movement and the struggle for African American rights. This was the year that the monumental *Types of Mankind* was published, a work that in many ways epitomized the "phalanx of learned men—speaking in the name of *science*" who, Douglass argues, were forbidding "the magnificent reunion of mankind in one brother-hood" by establishing supposed proof of permanent difference and hierarchy among the races of humankind. As Robert S. Levine argues, in Douglass's speech to the Literary Societies of Western Reserve College, Douglass was cer-tainly invested in proving the ethnological equality of Africans, displaying his "pride in 'the African' by moving beyond egalitarian arguments to assertions of the greatness, indeed the superiority, of ancient black civilizations." Nonethe-less, Levine demonstrates that Douglass was primarily concerned with estab-lishing "not the oneness of the 'African race' but the 'oneness of the human family.'" In this same speech, Douglass challenges ethnologists to study those who will give the correct idea of the "mental endowments of the negro" and proposes Delany as a subject worthy of their scrutiny.[2] Douglass's pointing to Delany as representative of Negro endowments was not atypical. Levine argues throughout his study of Delany and Douglass that Delany often capitalizes on his status as an African American of unmixed (and, he claimed, royal) ancestry to achieve his political objectives. By 1854 Delany had already earned a reputa-tion as a medical doctor, editor, and political leader. By the end of the Civil War, he could add becoming the first African American major in the United States Army and the first African American to lead an exploratory expedition into Africa to his list of accomplishments. His 1868 biography, a work that was written by Frances Rollins but heavily influenced by Delany himself, repre-sents Delany as embodying a challenge to ethnology. Early in the biography

Rollins points to Delany as physical proof against scientific theories of Negro inferiority, noting in particular Delany's pure blackness:

> The isolated and degraded position assigned the colored people precluding the possibility of gaining distinction, whenever one of their number lifts himself by the strength of his own character beyond the prescribed limits, ethnologists apologize for this violation of their established rules, charging it to some few drops of Saxon blood commingling with the African. But in the case of the individual of whom we write, he stands proudly before the country the blackest of the black . . . evidencing in his splendid career the fallacy of the old partisan theory of negro inferiority and degradation.[3]

As this quote shows, Delany was often satisfied with, and indeed encouraged, portrayals of himself as the "blackest of the black" men of success and leadership in the nation. Unlike Douglass, who, ethnologists could claim, demonstrated intelligence due to his mixed racial heritage, Delany's accomplishments merged with his physical status to refute ethnological assertions of African inferiority.[4]

Delany's deployment of his body as a repudiation of ethnologists' claims of Negro inferiority is indicative of his tendency to deploy a strategic essentialism that supported theoretically the concept of innate differences between the races. Unlike Douglass, whose politics consistently led him to argue for the basic unity of humankind, Delany dared to do "what white men have ever dared and done,"[5] to invent and build upon theories of racial essentialism that not only served his personal politics, but also provided the theoretical background for his globalized vision of the future of people of color, a vision that he came to believe necessitated a racialized national identity. The same year that Douglass argued for the basic unity of humankind in the address discussed above (an argument that coincided with Douglass's lifelong resistance to colonization and emigration), Delany presided over the National Emigration Convention in Cleveland, Ohio. This group agreed before attending the convention that emigration was desirable, thus separating themselves from those in Douglass's leadership circles. In his 1854 "Political Destiny of the Colored Race," the address Delany gave at the convention, he responds both to ethnologists and to Douglass. To Delany, the strategy of remaining in America and working for equality was faulty because the achievement of equality for African Americans in the United States would only come "as in Europe, by an entire destruction" of the identity of those seeking equality. Delany envisioned assimilation as enacting a type of racial suicide. Noting that "friends" in the United States have been urging free people of color to "lose our identity as a distinct race, declaring that we were the same as other people; while at the very same time their own representative was traversing the world, and propagating the doctrine in favor of a *universal Anglo-Saxon predominance*," Delany declares his belief in innate differences between the races, a conviction that concurs with his calls for emigration and the formation of a new nation in Central America (later he would return to his earlier proposal that Africa was the most appropriate destination for emigrants). "The truth is," he argues, "we are not identical with the Anglo-Saxon, or any other race of the Caucasian or pure white type of the human family, and the sooner we know and acknowledge this truth the better for ourselves and our posterity." After all, he asks, "[t]he English, French, Irish, German, Italian, Turk, Persian, Greek, Jew, and all other races, have their native or inherent peculiarities, and why not our race?"[6] This type of racial thinking was not new to Delany, nor would it end in the 1850s. His faith in a radical Reconstruction led him to move away from pondering racial difference and emigration immediately after the Civil War, but he returned to these theories more earnestly after the collapse of Reconstruction in the late 1870s, publishing *Principia of Ethnology* in 1879.

Although Delany emphasizes his theories of racial difference in "The Political Destiny of the Colored Race" (1854) and expands upon them in some detail in *Principia of Ethnology* (1879), his *Condition* (1852) struggles with competing ideologies of race, fluctuating from declarations of unity to assertions of difference. In part, we can understand the conflicted nature of the work by placing it in the context of his relationship with the scientific community in general and the medical community in particular. Trained as a doctor by the white physician Andrew McDowell of Pittsburgh, Delany often supported himself and his family by practicing medicine.[7] In 1851 he hoped to expand upon his apprenticeship background by attending formal medical school. After being rejected by several institutions due to his race, he was admitted to Harvard Medical School and attended classes, but was soon asked to leave due to white students' protests. One letter by a medical student in the Boston *Journal* clarified that white students resented being "classed with blacks, whom they themselves, their professors, and the community generally, considered to be of inferior mental ability."[8] The irony of this rejection could not have escaped Delany. Here, once again, was the familiar tautology: science (in this case the medical profession) declared African Americans to be inferior and then barred them from participating in formalized scientific discourse because of their allegedly inferior nature. Yet Delany's dismissal from Harvard did not stop him from participating in scientific debates as a man of science. Immediately after leaving Harvard, he undertook a western tour of abolition circuits, lecturing on the comparative anatomy and physiology of the races. According to Victor Ullman, Delany's lectures drew upon both anatomical and ethnological knowledge and "were planned to reassure his black audiences as to their equality with Caucasians, at least in volume of brain matter, and in their equal capacity for the acquisition of knowledge and skills." Indeed, in his biography Delany (via Rollins) downplays the pain of expulsion, skipping immediately from his admission to Harvard to informing readers that after "leaving Harvard, he traveled westward and lectured on physiological subjects—the comparative anatomical and physical conformation of the cranium of the Caucasian and negro races."[9] Delany wanted readers to deduce that he left Harvard not as a rejected and inferior African American man, but rather as a person well equipped to participate in scientific debates. Nonetheless, Delany's removal from medical school served to heighten his disillusionment with white abolitionists in particular and with white America in general. Levine argues that the passing of the Fugitive Slave Law in the fall of 1850 also added to Delany's disgust and probably contributed to his exploration of emigration. As Delany laments in Condition, "We love our country, dearly love her, but she don't love us—she despises us, and bids us begone, driving us from her embraces; but we shall not go where she desires us." For Delany, in 1852, the answer was to emigrate not to Africa but to Central America, a plan that determined the design of Condition, a book Delany regretted and apologized for in his biography.[10]

Unlike "The Political Destiny of the Colored Race" and Principia of Ethnology, Condition overtly represents race not as indicative of innate differences but rather as a convenient, and tragic, constructed sign of difference that served the ruling classes of the original colonies and of the United States. Like Lydia Maria Child in her Appeal in Favor of that Class of Americans Called Africans (1833), Delany repeatedly represents race as class, emphasizing this categorization by comparing African Americans with Europe's oppressed classes in the book's first chapter.[11] Indeed, he downplays the idea that Africans were enslaved as a result of hatred toward them or their color, arguing instead that they were enslaved solely because they made the best laborers. The man who had just been expelled from Harvard because of his race very much wanted to establish an equality of racial capability. His statement in chapter 9 clarifies this position, as Delany argues that once he has established the "equality" of the "pure descendants of Africa" with the "European race," "the equality of every person intermediate between the two races" will be confirmed, and this "establishes, beyond contradiction, the general equality of men."[12]

Yet Delany often contradicts his representation of race as a socially constructed marker of difference, turning to language that conflates racial essentialism and social difference and pointing to the radical shift in racial theory that his 1854 "Political Destiny" reveals. Delany's move toward assertions of racial difference is evident as early as chapter 4, which begins by affirming his belief in the "universal equality of man" and the "declaration of God's word, in which it is there positively said that, 'God has made of one blood all the nations that dwell on the face of the earth.'" However, in the very next paragraph, Delany repeats racialized romantic tropes that could just as easily be found in Emerson's antislavery lectures or *English Traits*, claiming that the "colored races are highly susceptible of religion; it is a constituent principle of their nature, and an excellent trait in their character. But unfortunately for them, they carry it too far." Although he begins by conflating race with class, by chapter 7 he has already slipped into categories of race that are not aligned with a concept of class, declaring that the "African race" has from "the earliest periods of the history of nations . . . been known as an industrious people" and that they "had proven themselves physically superior either to the European or American races—in fact, superior physically to any living race of men."[13]

Clearly one cause of the conflict that marks *Condition* is Delany's struggle to define exactly what constitutes race, a question he automatically associates with its political ramifications.[14] Although Delany spends a large portion of *Condition* establishing the right of African Americans to remain in the United States, noting their contributions to the Colonial era and the Revolutionary War and other wars, and their attainment of a high degree of literary and business success despite the oppression they face, he nonetheless concludes that "[w]e must abandon all vague theory, and look at *facts* as they really are; viewing ourselves in our true political position in the body politic. . . . We are politically, not of them, but aliens to the laws and political privileges of this country." Working toward the association between national identity, racial identity, and citizenship that "Political Destiny" makes explicit, Delany begins to formulate a theory of race based on the notion of inherited traits influenced by environmental conditions. For example, Delany tries to account for what he believes is a tendency toward submissiveness on the part of African Americans, proposing that slave parents pass on their degradation to their children, thereby repeating "a system of regular submission and servitude, menialism and dependence, until it has become almost a physiological function of our system, an actual condition of our nature." By the end of *Condition*, Delany turns his assertion of inheritable traits into a defense of emigration. Comparing his people's lot to that of the Irish and Germans in America, Delany argues that when in their native countries, "their spirits were depressed and downcast; but the instant they set their foot upon unrestricted soil; free to act and untrammeled to move; their physical condition undergoes a change, which in time becomes physiological, which is transmitted to the offspring, who when born under such circumstances, is a decidedly different being to what it would have been, had it been born under different circumstances." Likewise, he suggests, African American children born into oppression in the United States will be very different beings from those born to the same parents in a new nation.[15] Delany's assertion that racial traits are both innate and changeable anticipates Emerson's 1856 *English Traits* by two years. As chapter 4 demonstrates, in *English Traits* Emerson considered race something of "appalling" importance in particular eras, yet also a condition that could be altered, based on environment. Indeed, Emerson's 1863 "Fortune of the Republic" suggests a process similar to what Delany imagines in 1852, the making of a new man in a new nation. However, unlike Emerson, who forecasts the transformation of the Englishman "John" into a new English American "Jonathan," Delany predicts an era when people of color, led by Africans who once resided in America, will properly rule over the portions of the world designed for them.[16]

As I have suggested, Delany's strategy to label some characteristics racial and some environmental coincides with the theory of national identity and power he develops later in his life. In his address "The Political Destiny" Delany elaborates on his developing belief that national identity, citizenship, and racial identity are permanently intertwined. Early in the address he asserts that it must be "understood, as a great principle of political economy, that no people can be free who themselves do not constitute an essential part of the *ruling element* of the country in which they live." Indeed, as Gregg D. Crane argues, by the time he published his novel *Blake* (1859) Delany had accepted, for pragmatic purposes, the definition of citizenship that Justice Roger B. Taney provided in the devastating 1857 Dred Scott Decision. In that decision, Crane argues, Taney "overtly equates power, rights and community in commenting that black Americans 'had no rights but such as those who held the power and the Government might choose to grant them.'" Crane suggests that Delany's acceptance in *Blake* "of majority status as the sine qua non of citizenship rights threatens to swallow his appeal to the moral restraints that a liberal natural rights theory of American law would impose on the legal exercise of the will of the majority."[17] Because he conflates majority status and citizenship rights, Delany argues that to liberate themselves, African Americans must turn their attention toward "those places where the black and colored man comprise, by population, and constitute by necessity of numbers, the *ruling element* of the body politic . . . where our political enclosure and national edifice can be reared, established, walled, and proudly defended on this great elementary principle of original identity." Here Delany conflates majority rule, citizenship, and race. Delany elaborates on this point extensively, arguing that "every substantial political structure" in the world shares an original identity and "cannot exist without it." Using a scientific analogy to underscore the naturalness of this societal law, Delany argues that if a people lose their "nucleus" and "centre of attraction," "a dissolution must as naturally ensue as the result of the neutrality of the basis of adhesion among the particles of matter." Indeed, Delany goes so far as to suggest that an original identity, which he defines as racial, is the "great secret of the present strength of Great Britain, Russia, the United States, and Turkey" as well as the "endurance of the French nation."[18] Delany sounds far more similar to Emerson in *English Traits*, defining a nation's success based on its racial origins, and to Whitman, whose journal notes calling America a "white neighborhood" indicate that national identity is the most seamless when it is also a racial identity, than he does to Jacobs, who reports feeling free in the predominantly white England (and thus defines freedom based on a country's laws and customs, not race). To Delany, then, the political solution to the dilemma of racial oppression is for African Americans to emigrate, in this case to Central America, because he believes that it is God's will that the African race remain on the continent it helped to found and is best suited to labor upon.[19]

Thirty-five years passed between Delany's "Political Destiny" address and the publication of *Principia of Ethnology: The Origin of Races and Color*. During these years, Delany published *Blake*, led an expedition to Africa, visited England, settled for a while in Canada, served as a major in the United States Army from the late Civil War to the early Reconstruction years, and worked in several other capacities for the recently emancipated slaves in the South. His hopes for a truly radical Reconstruction led him temporarily to abandon his emigration schemes, but by the mid-1870s Delany's disillusionment with Reconstruction was leading him to some odd political decisions, such as his March 1875 speech in New York

City that castigated carpetbaggers for misguiding African Americans in the South, his strangely restrained judgement of Andrew Johnson (even when he was among African Americans), and his support of the Democratic Party (in which he served both as a promoter of former slave owners for office and as a candidate himself). Yet when the violence of 1876 in his then home state of South Carolina all but disenfranchised African Americans and it became clear that the Democrats had no intention of surrendering white power, Delany's disillusionment became intense and he turned, once again, to emigration as a possibility.[20]

It is in this mood of despondency that Delany wrote and published *Principia of Ethnology*, his last major statement on race. Levine calls the work a "compelling and disturbing statement of Delany's late 1870s thinking on the origin and characteristics of the races," one which, if read out of context, "presents absolutist notions of racial difference that can seem quite noxious," but he also notes that when it is read in the context of the failure of Reconstruction, *Principia* becomes "one of Delany's most moving efforts to argue for black pride and to make sense of the failure of his efforts to achieve black elevation in the United States."[21] Levine's comments point to the central dilemma posed by the work: Should we read it as a radical work, one in which Delany speaks as a man of science to men of science about racial difference, reversing devastating notions of black inferiority? Or should we understand the work as trapped in the paradigms of racial identity created primarily by white men and fortified by years of racial science, as a work that fails to challenge the body politics of the age because it endorses a notion of innate difference playing too easily into racial explanations for the political failure of Reconstruction?

Certainly Delany's work sets out to address directly the theories of race that were so harmful to the politics of his time. Despite the importance of Charles Darwin's work *On the Origin of Species* (1859), Delany basically ignores the theory of evolution, dismissing it with the circular argument that the theory of biblical Creation will be used as his starting point because this "narration is acceptable to us."[22] Therefore, just like the ethnologists of the 1850s with whom he argues, Delany bases his work on a mixture of religious, ethnological, and physiological arguments. He sets out to establish several claims: the original unity of the races as per biblical Creation; the permanent separation of these races after the biblical Flood into three "grand divisions" of yellow, black, and white; the physiological sameness of the cause of color in humans despite permanent racial difference; the connections between the biblical Ham and the early rulers of Egypt and Ethiopia; and the preeminence of Africa in the history of world civilization. Unlike *Condition* and "Political Destiny," this work has no overt political aim and comes attached with no call for action. Instead, Delany offers it to the "scientific and serious enquirer" who desires to know the "facts" that would help answer "the all-important question in social science," the origin of the races of man.[23]

Of course, Delany's claims to a disinterested investigation are no more valid than those of the ethnologists he argues against. The implicit connection between his theory of racial origin and his politics is hinted at as early as chapter 4. In this chapter Delany builds upon his theory of the original unity of the races, a unity he claims was ended permanently after the biblical Flood. In doing so, he harkens back implicitly to Samuel Morton's argument in *Crania Americana* (1839), which also proposed that the races were permanently separated after the Flood. In chapter 3 Delany asserts that Adam most resembled "the lightest of the pure-blood North American Indians" and that "the peoples from Adam to Noah, including his wife and sons' wives, were all of one and the same color." Yet Delany argues that God desired the progress of civilization, an event he believes comes about by three means: revolution, conquest, and emigration. Of these three, Delany proposes, emigration is the "most effective" because it is "voluntary." Therefore, in addition to separation by language, God used the "basis of race distinction" to establish the "grand divisions" that composed the world's settlement. Once the permanent difference of color was established, the divine command also "fixed in the people a desire to be separated by reason of race affinity" and created a "new progress in life, as three distinct peoples, of entirely different interests, aims and ends."[24] In this passage the connections between Delany's theories of race and his political goals in the late 1870s seem clear: emigration from the United States is not only necessary, but natural. Although some may consider Delany's theory of permanent racial difference curious, given how such theories were deployed against people of color, to him it offered a scientific and religious justification for emigration schemes and, perhaps, a way to comprehend the seemingly incomprehensible alliance of whites that allowed the violence against African Americans to thwart Reconstruction.

Delany's commitment in *Principia* to the permanent division of races is unflinching. Among the three "sterling" races, Delany claims, the European and African races are the most distinct, but he asserts that both "are of equal vitality and equally enduring; absorbing and reproducing themselves as races, with all of their native external physical properties of complexion and hair."

Therefore, the races are "indestructible" and "*miscegenation* as popularly understood—the running out of two races, or several, into a *new race*—cannot take place." Delany's assertion that both races are "equally enduring; absorbing and reproducing themselves" offers a powerful rebuttal to the common assumption that the European/Saxon race was powerful enough to absorb all other races into its fold; it typically positions Delany as the most representative of a "pure" race as well. However, it also leads him to disparage those of mixed racial origin in a manner that aligns him uneasily with the ethnologists he wishes to refute. At one point he goes so far as to call any mixed race "abnormal" and predicts the eventual extinction of Malays and other "abnormal" races, who will be absorbed into one of the original, sterling races. How far, then, is Delany from Nott and Gliddon, who in *Types of Mankind* conclude that "[n]o two distinctively-marked races can dwell together on equal terms"?[25]

Despite Delany's passionate insistence that the sterling races are indestructible, he argues that the physiological cause of color is in fact the same in all humans. In what is perhaps his most interesting chapter, "How Color Originates," Delany draws upon the religious argument in his preceding chapter that suggests that the sons of Noah, although born to the same parents, had different complexions that became the impetus for the three primary races. Investigating the layers of the human skin, Delany quickly turns to a discussion of the *rete mucosum*, the layer in which he says coloring matter, or *rouge*, is located. Delany argues that all races contain the same essential *rouge* and the appearance of each race is determined solely by the amount of concentration of *rouge* in the *rete mucosum*. In the African race, he argues, the coloring matter "*is the same* as that in the other two races, being *rouge* concentrated, which makes a pigment—the *pigmentum* nigrum of physiology—or a black matter." Thus, he argues, the "color of the blackest African is produced by *identically the same* essential coloring matter that gives the 'rosy cheeks and ruby lips,' to the fairest and most delicately beautiful white lady."[26]

Why would a man so confident when asserting racial difference claim the same cause of color? Part of the answer lies in his sarcastic description of the "rosy cheeks" and "ruby lips" of the "white lady." Certainly, Delany—who had heard for so long that the Caucasian race was superior in beauty—asserts a basic sameness of color to unsettle notions of Caucasian superiority. Another reason for this claim may be that Delany is challenging the scientific/Enlightenment belief in vision that backed racial ideology. As Robyn Wiegman notes, "the visible has a long, contested, and highly contradictory role as the primary vehicle

for making race 'real' in the United States."[27] To prove his theory of racial commonality, Delany strips away the layers of skin, seeing beyond the mere surface. In effect, he argues that vision betrays the observer when one observes
color as a mark of difference, and he uses new technologies that render the previously invisible visible as the basis of his classification. Unlike other scientists, who tended to interpret the invisible as evidencing racial distinction,
Delany "sees" human unity. Much like Whitman's slave auctioneer in "I Sing
the Body Electric," Delany strips the body in an act of revisioning and reveals
commonality. Thus, he appropriates the dominant means by which difference
was defined—the observation of the "invisible" with new technologies—and
declares unity in the face of his otherwise racially separatist theories.

Delany's unmasking of the supposed truth of objective scientific vision shows
the extent of his interrogation, appropriation, and reversal of the corporeal theories that were so devastating to his race. Yet the case of Delany raises as many
questions as it answers. Did he, as Douglass suggests, stand up so straight as to
lean backwards? Did he, in other words, become so entrenched in racial ideology that he lost sight of the precarious political implications of his assertions?
After all, his "Political Destiny" speech represents a clear case of Delany's theories being employed against his political plans. When Abraham Lincoln was
considering recolonization of African Americans during the Civil War, the
House of Representatives (on behalf of Lincoln) attached "Political Destiny" to
its "Report of the Select Committee on Emancipation and Colonization," using
it for its political aims, which were contrary to Delany's goals at the time.[28] In
his biography, Delany (clearly uncomfortable with how easily his racial beliefs
could be used against him) calls the inclusion of "Political Destiny" the "most
successful *coup d'état* of the president," because it "set the opinion at rest forever that the colored people could be induced to emigrate from *their home, and
this their country, en masse.*"[29] Delany's rewriting of Lincoln's motives indicates just how precarious Delany's racial strategies were. All too often his con-
firmation of innate difference and incompatibility could be used to confirm
political plans grossly at odds with his vision. In this respect, he was not radically altering scientific discourse for political gain, but rather reconfirming its
significance by defining the races as permanently incapable of composing the
same body politic. Levine, too, notes that Delany's vision in *Principia*, particularly his denunciation of miscegenation, "is a vision that both counters and contributes to the contemporaneous white efforts to impose a color line."[30]

Yet Delany considered his scientific writing a radical appropriation and
reversal of white men's science. Sending the manuscript of *Principia* to one of

his mentors, Dr. William Elder, Delany asks for his opinion, noting that "[o]ne friend, a professor of a college, writes me, 'I am glad to see the time when a colored person can capture the sciences, and appropriate them to the endowment of his own will.'" Delany adds, "And this I know to be your feelings. I desire to dare do, what white men have ever dared and done."[31] Indeed, Delany becomes a scientist (a role underscored by his invitation to, and introduction at, the International Statistical Congress in England in 1860),[32] thus breaking the tautology that defined him as incapable of participating in the very discourses that labeled him inferior. The fact that he bases his racial theories, which so radically contradict the claims of white male scientists regarding the nature of the Negro and Caucasian, on science puts into play the question of what can be objectively known about race, about the body, about—in effect—what is true.

Delany's case underscores the complexity of creating a strategy to negotiate the precarious, pervasive, and consequential body politics of the nineteenth century. One critical dilemma is how to disrupt harmful narratives of corporeality that seek to define one without transferring them onto another type of body or reinforcing racial, gendered, or sexual polarization in a politically detrimental way. Can authors create representations of the body that do not rely on oppositional strategies, that do not pose a binary between oneself and another? Certainly none of the authors in this study create flawless methods of corporeal representation. Nonetheless, their struggle is evolutionary and ongoing. Corporeal strategies, their work suggests, are historically specific, contingent on the theories and texts they embrace or refute. At times, all of these authors are able to challenge their age's destructive binaries and classifications. Yet their works also reveal how central the science of the body was to the literary imagination during this era. If writers like Fuller, Emerson, Whitman, and Delany, for example, begin with a theory of corporeal transcendence or basic racial unity, they finish their careers farther entrenched in ideas of difference that dominated racial science. This suggests how difficult it was (and is) to flesh out a new America, to imagine a multiracial democracy, one that contains what Fuller calls "a ravishing harmony" between genders, one that does not criminalize or even categorize so-called deviant sexualities. Their work points to the struggle to build, in other words, Whitman's "nation of nations." Despite the challenges they faced, when these authors were at their best, they were able to use literature to rupture oppressive corporeal narratives by the continual invention of counternarratives, by the continual deployment of counterstrategies. Within coercive systems of corporeal control are sites from which an author can devise strategies of resistance, however shifting those sites may be.

NOTES

Introduction

I use "Negro," "Caucasian," "Anglo-Saxon," "Aboriginal," and "mulatto" throughout this study in order to evoke their specific connotations, which are not the same as "African American," "Native American," or "white." Although I recognize that nineteenth-century terminology may be offensive, I employ it because these words signify the specific categories the authors in this study were struggling within and against. At times, when I believe it is more appropriate to do so, I use current classifications.

1 Sánchez-Eppler, *Touching Liberty*, 3, 1.
2 Gates, "Writing 'Race,'" 5.
3 Lauter, *Canons and Contexts*, 97–101.
4 Horsman, *Race and Manifest Destiny*; Nelson, *Word in Black and White* and *National Manhood*; Roediger, *Wages of Whiteness*.
5 Fetterley, "Commentary," 602.
6 Ibid., 604–605.
7 See, for example, Bizzell, "Opinion," 163–169, and Pratt, *Imperial Eyes*.
8 Modleski, *Feminism without Women*, 15.
9 Ibid.
10 Christian, "Race for Theory," 55.
11 Peterson, *"Doers of the Word,"* 21.
12 Fuller, *Woman in the Nineteenth Century*, 310.
13 Laqueur, *Making Sex*, 42.
14 Nelson, *Word in Black and White*, x.

1. The Body in the Body Politic

1 Blassingame, introduction to "Claims of the Negro Ethnologically Considered," 498.
2 Douglass, "Claims of the Negro," 498–503. Douglass refers to Josiah C. Nott, George R. Gliddon, Jean Louis Rodolphe Agassiz, and Samuel Morton. Morton, *Brief Remarks*, 6, 15–16; Morton, *Letter to the Reverend John Backman*, 14.
3 Foucault, *Order of Things*, 144.
4 Linné, *from System of Nature*, 13.
5 Pratt, *Imperial Eyes*, 32.
6 Gates, "Writing 'Race,'" 1–20.

7 Jefferson, *Notes on the State of Virginia*, 140, 142.

8 The eighteenth-century racial and gendered hierarchal concept drew upon the earlier concept of the "Great Chain of Being," a hierarchal ordering of the cosmos. See Lovejoy, *Great Chain of Being*.

9 Horsman, *Race and Manifest Destiny*, 46.

10 For an extensive analysis of conceptions of race prior to the nineteenth century, see Winthrop, *White over Black*.

11 Equiano, *Narrative of the Life of Olaudah Equiano*, 45.

12 Foucault, *Order of Things*, 138.

13 Wiegman, *American Anatomies*, 31.

14 Mary Louis Pratt analyzes the link between the supposedly anticonquest natural historian and the colonial project in the first part of *Imperial Eyes*.

15 Fredrickson, *Black Image in the White Mind*, 12–13. Horsman also argues that the "contrast in expansionist rhetoric between 1800 and 1850 is striking" because the debates and speeches of the early nineteenth century "do not have the jarring note of rampant racialism that permeates the debates of mid-century." See Horsman, *Race and Manifest Destiny*, 1.

16 Sánchez-Eppler, *Touching Liberty*, 3.

17 Robyn Wiegman also suggests that we need to take caution when applying Foucault's overarching claim to an "epistemic leap" from the classical age to the modern age and to the United States in the antebellum era. Wiegman, *American Anatomies*, 33–34.

18 Fisher, *Laws of Race*, 11–12.

19 Nott and Gliddon, *Types of Mankind*, 79.

20 Nott and Gliddon, *Types of Mankind*, 402; Van Evrie, *Negroes and Negro "Slavery,"* 111–112; Fredrickson, *Black Image in the White Mind*, 70; Pulte, *Woman's Medical Guide*, 24; Stepan, "Race and Gender," 360–361; Pulte, *Woman's Medical Guide*, 44; Young, *Colonial Desire*, 9.

21 Gould, *Mismeasure of Man*, 63; Van Evrie, *Negroes and Negro "Slavery,"* 196–197; Nott and Gliddon, *Types of Mankind*, 79.

22 Horsman, *Race and Manifest Destiny*, 56, 142–143; Morton, *Brief Remarks*, 15–16; Bieder, *Science Encounters the Indian*, 55, 68–69; Gould, *Mismeasure of Man*, 85.

23 Horsman, *Race and Manifest Destiny*, 57–58; Combe, appendix to *Crania Americana*, 274–275; Bieder, *Science Encounters the Indian*, 73–101.

24 Nott and Gliddon, *Types of Mankind*, 189, 462; Van Evrie, *Negroes and Negro "Slavery,"* 124–125; Colfax, *Evidence against the Views of the Abolitionists*, 25–26.

25 Caldwell, *Thoughts on the Original Unity of the Human Race*, 56–58. Horsman notes that Caldwell was an "opinionated and argumentative physician" who "consistently and loudly defended the cause of innate racial difference." A native North Carolinian who went to the University of Pennsylvania for his medical training, he became a prominent member of the medical profession. See Horsman, *Race and Manifest Destiny*, 117.

26 Van Evrie, *Negroes and Negro "Slavery,"* 93–95; Fredrickson, *Black Image in the White Mind*, 49; Van Evrie, *Negroes and Negro "Slavery,"* 217–218, 72; Douglass, "Claims of the Negro," 510.

27 Nott and Gliddon, *Types of Mankind*, 53, 68; Van Evrie, *Negroes and Negro "Slavery,"* 52; Nott and Gliddon, *Types of Mankind*, 260; Van Evrie, *Negroes and Negro "Slavery,"* 156.

28 *Oxford English Dictionary*, 747; Nott and Gliddon, *Types of Mankind*, 397, 373.

29 Nott and Gliddon, *Types of Mankind*, 407. Fears over amalgamation intensified throughout the century. By the 1870s scientific theories of hybridity were used to uphold various states' antimiscegenation laws. According to Michael Grossberg, thirty-eight states prohibited interracial marriage during the nineteenth century. These bans, which were without English precedent, contradicted the overall tendency to view marriage as a contract that the state should not interfere with. See Grossberg, *Governing the Hearth*, 126–127.

30 Fisher, *Laws of Race*, 18; Horsman, *Race and Manifest Destiny*, 208.

31 Abolitionists were concerned about the manipulation of class tensions. In an inaugural edition of the *National Anti-Slavery Standard*, a column "To the Abolitionists" included a discussion of class: "We shall have to endeavor to convince the hard-handed workingman at the North that whatever may be the condition of others, his fate is indissolubly linked to that of the Southern slave. He must be made to feel that his brother, dark-skinned though he be, must find his way up to his level, or he must sink to the level of chattelship" (11 June 1840, p. 3).

32 Van Evrie, *Free Negroism*, 29, 292; Van Evrie, *Negroes and Negro "Slavery,"* 336–337; Horsman, *Race and Manifest Destiny*, 249.

33 See Roediger, *Wages of Whiteness*, and Ignatiev, *How the Irish Became White*.

34 Todd Savitt concludes that in southern antebellum medical practice African Americans "comprised a substantial proportion" of living subjects and almost all of the corpses. In extreme cases, the body was amputated unnecessarily to let students observe an operation. See Savitt, *Medicine and Slavery*, 281–288.

35 Fredrickson, *Black Image in the White Mind*, 114. The comparison of women to children was so firmly embedded in medical thought that the two were added as joint topics of study to medical curricula in the early nineteenth century. See Rothstein, *American Physicians in the Nineteenth Century*, 33. Pulte, a physician of women and children, argues that "the female has retained more or less the character of the child . . . a fact, which will have great influence in the better understanding and appreciation of the female character and destiny." See Pulte, *Woman's Medical Guide*, 21–22.

36 According to Stepan, phrenology was one of the first discourses to compare women with the "lower" races in relation to functions other than reproduction. See Stepan, "Race and Gender," (366). In addition to phrenological observation, women's facial angle, prognathism, cranial capacity, and brain weight were also assumed to correlate with intelligence. See Haller and Haller, *Physician and Sexuality*, 48–49.

37 Fowler, *Principles of Phrenology*, 132–133. Cynthia Eagle Russett argues that phrenology could support reform, because both men and women were encouraged to know their strengths and weaknesses in order to improve them. See Russett, *Sexual Science*, 21–22.

38 Russett, *Sexual Science*, 24–36; Pulte, *Woman's Medical Guide*, 43.

39 Schiebinger, "Skeletons in the Closet," 65; Russett, *Sexual Science*, 38.

40 Pulte, *Woman's Medical Guide*, 26–27. Just as women exploited the Doctrine of Separate Spheres to achieve a public voice, so too did many manipulate the idea of their natural, feminine "susceptibility" to gain power. This was particularly evident in the spiritualist movement. Ann Braude summarizes how women employed the concept of feminine passivity and bodily susceptibility to become trance speakers and mediums, gaining access for the first time in large numbers to the public platform. See Braude, *Radical Spirits*, 85.

41 Jordanova, *Sexual Visions*, 23; Pulte, *Woman's Medical Guide*, 53.

42 Smith-Rosenberg analyzes the relationship between mid-century medical literature and later cases of hysteria and concludes that the hysterical female "emerges from the essentially male medical literature of the nineteenth century as a 'child-woman'" (212).

43 Schiebinger, "Skeletons in the Closet," 42–63.

44 For informative analysis of the Doctrine of Separate Spheres, see Kerber, *Toward an Intellectual History of Women*, 155–199. See also the edition of *American Literature* dedicated to an investigation of the concept of separate spheres, *American Literature* 70.3 (September 1998), ed. Cathy N. Davidson.

45 The fertility rates cited are from D'Emilio and Freedman, *Intimate Matters*, 58. Horsman, *Race and Manifest Destiny*, 295, 286.

46 Hoffert, *Private Matters*, 15–16; Dixon, *Woman and Her Diseases*, 245.

47 Grossberg, *Governing the Hearth*, 159; Smith-Rosenberg, *Disorderly Conduct*, 221. Grossberg points to a fundamental conflict between private practice and public policy in the nineteenth century. Although public prohibitions on birth control and abortion increased throughout the century, private practice indicates a desire to limit families. The discrepancy resulted in laws that made the public distribution of information illegal, but its use a private (and thus relatively unregulated) matter. See Grossberg, *Governing the Hearth*, 156–159. Similarly, Barbara Meil Hobson argues that with increased urbanity, sexual regulation shifted from overseeing indoor sex offenses ("private" offenses such as fornication, adultery, and sodomy) to outdoor offenses (considered "public" such as prostitution). See Hobson, *Uneasy Virtue*, 31.

48 Hoffert suggests that the cult of motherhood intensified in relation to the availability of birth control techniques and urbanization. As the birth rate dropped and families fragmented, numerous writers placed an increased ideological value on children. Popular advice books and medical doctors presented pictures in which "[d]omestic bliss . . . was a condition made possible only by the presence of a child, whose birth was guaranteed to enhance the affection that husband and wife felt for each other." See Hoffert, *Private Matters*, 2.

49 Smith-Rosenberg, *Disorderly Conduct*, 184; Laqueur, *Making Sex*, 213. Laqueur contends that sexual difference was created despite new scientific advances in developmental anatomy that pointed to the common origins of both sexes in an androgynous embryo. See Laqueur, "Orgasm, Generation, and the Politics of Reproductive Biology," 3.

50 Dixon, *Woman and Her Diseases*, 71–72.

51 Smith-Rosenberg, *Disorderly Conduct*, 187.

52 Pulte, *Woman's Medical Guide*, 121; Dixon, *Woman and Her Diseases*, 32; Pulte, *Woman's Medical Guide*, 87.

53 Pulte, *Woman's Medical Guide*, 157.

54 Hobson summarizes the Victorian sexual code in relation to prostitution, noting it "assumed that women and men had distinct biological and moral natures and that sexual passion was a sign of pathology in the female sex." See Hobson, *Uneasy Virtue*, 111.

55 Smith-Rosenberg's *Disorderly Conduct* provides an excellent analysis of puberty and menopause as biological "facts" in Victorian America. Both stages, she argues, were viewed as "peculiarly sensitive physiological turning points in a woman's life—stages at which new physical and emotional equilibria had to be established." See Smith-Rosenberg, *Disorderly Conduct*, 184.

56 Dixon, *Woman and Her Diseases*, 5.

57 Hoffert, *Private Matters*, 15, 20–21; Pulte, *Woman's Medical Guide*, 206.

58 Hoffert offers an astute analysis of the class implications of midwifery, physician assistance, and childbirth in *Private Matters*. She concludes, with respect to many middle-class white woman in the urban North, "Fear as well as concern for establishing or maintaining their reputations as genteel and respectable . . . encouraged women to accept the medical definition of childbirth as an illness and to hire doctors as testimony to their economic and social status" (63). Also, by the 1850s, too rapid recovery from childbirth was interpreted as vulgar, because working-class women were believed to give birth with relative ease. Middle-class women, as a result, were expected to convalesce at least a month after birth (116–117).

59 Haller and Haller, *Physician and Sexuality*, 47–48.

60 White, *Ar'n't I a Woman?*, 32.

61 Carby, *Reconstructing Womanhood*, 30.

62 Van Evrie, *Negroes and Negro "Slavery,"* 89.

63 Nott and Gliddon, *Types of Mankind*, 398.

64 White, *Ar'n't I a Woman?*, 28–29, 68–70.

65 Van Evrie, *Negroes and Negro "Slavery,"* 223–229.

66 For example, Smith-Rosenberg juxtaposes the bourgeois myth of "cleanliness, order, and sexual repression" with the David Crockett tales, which, "dirty, drunken, and sexual," glorified the independent male. See Smith-Rosenberg, *Disorderly Conduct*, 103.

67 Alcott, *Young Husband*, 38; Haller and Haller, *Physician and Sexuality*, 192–194.

68 Foucault, *History of Sexuality*, 40–41.

69 Ibid., 69.

70 Russett, *Sexual Science*, 109–113.

71 By the end of the century the relationship between the brain and the nervous system was emphasized to a point that could be considered frantic. "Neurasthenia," a nervous exhaustion caused by excessive "brain work," was discovered in 1869 and considered almost epidemic among the urban middle class by the century's end. Haller and Haller interpret the disease as "in a very real sense, a rationalization of America's new social order." Through the disease, middle-class Americans embodied their difference by elevating their labor above that of the working-class. See Haller and Haller, *Physician and Sexuality*, 42.

72 Graham, *Lecture to Young Men*, 36.

73 Alcott, *Physiology of Marriage*, 66–72.

74 Alcott, *Young Wife*, 101–107.

75 Haller and Haller, *Physician and Sexuality*, 195–196.

76 *Works of Aristotle*, 9; Alcott, *Physiology of Marriage*, 86.

77 Although men were the targeted audience for the majority of anti-onanism literature, women were not exempt from threats. Dixon warned readers that masturbation could prevent menstruation and that women masturbators would suffer as much as men. See Dixon, *Woman and Her Diseases*, 52–59.

78 Graham, *Lecture to Young Men*, 107–108, 23–24. Smith-Rosenberg aptly analyzes the symbolic importance of the American male in the Jacksonian era. As the apprenticeship system gave way to a more mobile economy and urbanization increased with great rapidity, young males were uprooted from their homes. At the same time "frightened and frightening" figures (81), they "became the symbol of both the vitality and the problems inherent in these massive social changes" (88).

79 D'Emilio and Freedman, *Intimate Matters*, 57.

80 *Works of Aristotle*, 18.

81 Laqueur, *Making Sex*, 51; *Works of Aristotle*, 34.

82 *Works of Aristotle*, 15.

83 Laqueur, *Making Sex*, 8; *Works of Aristotle*, 16, 10.

84 Laqueur, *Making Sex*, 42.

85 Alcott, *Young Husband*, 249.

86 Alcott, *Physiology of Marriage*, 167. D'Emilio and Freedman point to regional differences in the interpretation of female sexual nature. Whereas the bourgeois northern population tended to understand woman as passionless, southern families emphasized moral weakness rather than natural purity. Determined to protect family lines from racial mixture, southern men enforced stronger controls on married women's mobility and personal freedom. See D'Emilio and Freedman, *Intimate Matters*, 94–95.

87 As Kevin Mumford notes, "[b]y the 1830s, it was widely believed that lost womanhood—unlike lost manhood—could not be redeemed." See Mumford, "'Lost Manhood' Found," 81.

88 D'Emilio and Freedman, *Intimate Matters*, 121. In "Female World of Love and Ritual," Smith-Rosenberg argues that same-sex relationships between women in the first half of the nineteenth century were generally perceived as innocent, even when they were extremely close and would be considered erotic today. See Smith-Rosenberg, *Disorderly Conduct*, 53–76. Although the formation of the category "lesbian" occurred slightly later, the "diseased and corrupting lesbian" became a familiar figure in the early twentieth century. See Smith-Rosenberg, *Disorderly Conduct*, 245–296.

89 D'Emilio and Freedman, *Intimate Matters*, 121–129. Jonathan Ned Katz provides a selection of primary sources from 1884 to 1974 that chronicle the "treatment" of "diseased" homosexuals and lesbians in *Gay American History*, 129–207.

90 Foucault, *History of Sexuality*, 43.

91 Wiegman, *American Anatomies*, 1.

92 Fredrickson, *Black Image in the White Mind*, 41.

93 Horsman, *Race and Manifest Destiny*, 225; Fredrickson, *Black Image in the White Mind*, 43.

94 Foucault, *History of Sexuality*, 123.

95 D'Emilio and Freedman, *Intimate Matters*, 108.

96 Gould, *Mismeasure of Man*, 66, 101; Nelson, *National Manhood*, 113.

97 Nelson, *National Manhood*, 127; Gould, *Mismeasure of Man*, 74. Robert J. Young likewise points to the connections between the American Confederacy of Southern States and the deployment of "the new racial science" in London. See Young, *Colonial Desire*, 133–141. Horsman also notes that the "American intellectual community" not only absorbed European ideas, but also "fed European racial appetites with scientific theories stemming from the supposed knowledge and observation of blacks and Indians" (3).

98 Nelson, *National Manhood*, 133.

99 Rothstein's work traces the growth of medicine as a profession. See in particular *American Physicians in the Nineteenth Century*, chapters 3, 4, and 6.

100 Colfax, preface to *Evidence Against the Views of the Abolitionists*; Combe, appendix to *Crania Americana*, 268; Nott and Gliddon, *Types of Mankind*, 54.

101 Nott and Gliddon, *Types of Mankind*, 49. Russett likewise argues that anthropology was not tied to the eighteenth-century concept of monogenesis and emerged, instead, from a combination of anatomy, zoology, and medicine. From its inception, it displayed a bias for medical analysis and an emphasis on classification of race by physical structure. See Russett, *Sexual Science*, 25.

102 Caldwell, *Thoughts on the Original Unity of the Human Race*, 76–77.

103 Schiebinger points to the specific problems scientific definitions of difference created for women. Science became legitimized through the investigation of woman's nature, but, based on its "objective" findings, women (portrayed as less rational) were excluded from participating in the profession. Thus, "discoveries" served both to define the profession and to exclude many women from equal participation in it. See Schiebinger, "Skeletons in the Closet," 43.

104 Nott laments that racial categories are "hopelessly vague" and admits that, "based on the present state of knowledge," he must "testify how arbitrary all classifications inevitably must be." Scientists could not agree as to the number or exact origins of races of humankind, and even the word "Caucasian," although in general use, carried with it ambiguities about origin and characteristics. See Nott and Gliddon, *Types of Mankind*, 97, 67.

105 Douglass, "Claims of the Negro," 503–504.

2. The Spectacle of the Body

1 Child, preface to *An Appeal in Favor of That Class of Americans Called Africans*. All further citations will be given in parenthesis in the text.

2 Karcher concludes that Child frames her decision to join the antislavery movement with language evoking a religious conversion. See Karcher, *First Woman*, 175.

3 Karcher's title of *First Woman* comes from William Lloyd Garrison, who called Child "the first woman in the republic" in the November 20, 1820, issue of *Genius of Universal Emancipation*. See Karcher, *First Woman*, 173. Karcher notes the irony of Child's contemporary reputation as primarily the editor of Jacobs's autobiography in her preface to *First Woman*, xii.

4 For information on Child's wartime and postbellum promotion of Jacobs's text, see Karcher, *First Woman*, 437.

5 Deborah M. Garfield, coeditor of *Harriet Jacobs and "Incidents in the Life of a Slave Girl,"* focuses her conclusion on what she calls the "vexed alliances" between white and African American women, citing Child as an example. See Garfield, "Conclusion: Vexed Alliances," 275–291. Sidonie Smith groups Child with other editors of slave narratives, referring to their editing practices as "editorial colonization." See Sidonie Smith, "Resisting the Gaze of Embodiment," 98. Sandra Gunning says that Child "bypasses Jacobs's authorship—and therefore the notion of Jacobs as a self-conscious critic of an American political and social system." See Gunning, "Reading and Redemption," 136.

6 Garfield also argues that "the dynamic between African American and white academics continues to haunt the present scholarly revisiting of *Incidents*." See Garfield, "Conclusion: Vexed Alliances," 287. Rafia Zafar, the coeditor of *Harriet Jacobs and "Incidents in the Life of a Slave Girl,"* likewise contends that the "alliance" between Jacobs and Child "could only sign at the fissures in the purported transracial sisterhood of American abolitionism." See Zafar, "Introduction: Over-Exposed, Under-Exposed," 2.

7 Numerous scholars have expressed concern about or criticism of Child's wording in her introduction to *Incidents* as well as her overall role as editor. For example, Valerie Smith analyzes the same section of Child's introduction that I place at the beginning of this chapter and concludes that Child "rather awkwardly imposes the reader in the precise grammatical location where the slave woman ought to be," thus paralleling "the potential for narcissism of which Child suggests her reader is guilty." See Valerie Smith, "'Loopholes of Retreat,'" 222. Gabrielle P. Foreman elaborates on Smith's concern, suggesting that readers believe Child's claim of presenting the "veil withdrawn" and, therefore, "continue to accept Jacobs as a narrator who has internalized, or at least deferred to, unmediated tenets of true womanhood." See Foreman, "Manifest in Signs," 78. Deborah M. Garfield claims that, while Child is "militating against polite deafness," she "actually enacts her audience's skittishness," presiding "like a blushing impresaria over Jacobs's textual performance" and then leaving it to the black voice to reveal the particularities of the subject. See Garfield, "Earwitness," 108. Frances Smith Foster acknowledges that Child's introduction to *Incidents* conveys Child's support of Jacobs and confirms her right to claim selfhood, but also aligns Child with Jacobs's "foes"; she indicates that Jacobs had to "confront" Child "[o]n more than one occasion . . . in order to retain control over the form, the emphasis, and even the proofreading of her text." See Foster, *Written by Herself*, 106. Bruce Mills argues that Child's changes "significantly affected the narrative's final shape," appealing to "eternal values" rather than "to passions engendered by contemporary events." See Mills, "Endings," 256.

8 Carby, *Reconstructing Womanhood*, 30.

9 Halttunen, *Confidence Men and Painted Women*, 57.

10 Pulte, *Woman's Medical Guide*, 24. Although the first edition of this text was published in 1853, the concepts it expresses were developing throughout the antebellum era.

11 Phillip Lapsansky analyzes these and other graphic images in "Graphic Discord," 201–230.

12 Sánchez-Eppler, *Touching Liberty*, 1; Yellin, *Women and Sisters*, 5.

13 Karcher discusses Child's role at this antislavery convention and the reproach she received. See Karcher, *First Woman*, 244–248.

14 Grimké, *Appeal to the Women of the Nominally Free States*, 21–22. See Yellin, *Women and Sisters*, 34–38, for a discussion of Angelina Grimké's authorship.

15 Grimké, *Appeal to the Women of the Nominally Free States*, 23; Halttunen, *Confidence Men and Painted Woman*, 105.

16 For example, Yellin investigates the relationship between the public and private spheres, concluding that antislavery white women often "asserted their own right . . . to act in the public sphere" while condemning "slavery because it excluded women from patriarchal definitions of true womanhood and from the domestic sphere." See Yellin, *Women and Sisters*, 25. Smith-Rosenberg's *Disorderly Conduct* also analyzes how nineteenth-century women manipulated the domestic ideal to perform public and political activities.

17 Karcher, *First Woman*, 33.

18 Karcher traces Child's editorship of the periodical *The Juvenile Miscellany* in *First Woman*, 57–79, and also provides information on the success of Child's books *The Frugal Housewife* and *The Mother's Book*, 126–146.

19 Karcher, *First Woman*, 191–192.

20 Child, *Selected Letters*, 31.

21 Karcher, *First Woman*, 3, 16–17.

22 Fowler's reading of Child's head is quoted in Karcher, *First Woman*, 295.

23 Karcher, *First Woman*, 40–42. The quote regarding her portrait appears in Karcher, *First Woman*, 51. According to Karcher, both Edgar Allan Poe and James Russell Lowell testified to the "transfiguration" Child underwent when her intellect and passions were aroused. See Karcher, *First Woman*, 310.

24 Quoted in Karcher, *First Woman*, 297.

25 Karcher analyzes Child's decision not to speak at public gatherings and proposes several motives, one of which is that Child might not have wanted to be associated with the radicalism of women such as Frances Wright, whom she criticized in 1829 articles. Child also might have been reluctant to compete with her husband in yet another arena, particularly because she was already a more successful editor than he and also provided the couple's income. Karcher, *First Woman*, 216.

26 Child, *Selected Letters*, 64.

27 In *First Woman* Karcher contends that Child "envisaged women's emancipation as a byproduct of their unselfish labors, rather than as a goal in its own right" (247). For further analysis of Child's views on women's liberation in the early part of her career,

see also chapters 10 and 14 of *First Woman*. Additionally, Yellin indicates that in the *History of the Condition of Women* Child "restricts herself to presenting a geographically organized chronology of woman's wrongs" rather than "asserting woman's rights." See Yellin, *Women and Sisters*, 55.

28 Child is quoted in Karcher, *First Woman*, 247.

29 Although Sánchez-Eppler's and Noble's critiques are most relevant to my argument in this chapter, other scholars voice similar concerns about sentimentalism in particular or reform literature in general. Richard H. Brodhead, for example, links the act of mastering through the body to the act of mastering through text in *Cultures of Letters*. David S. Reynolds also charges that "slavery was—horribly enough—exploited for its sensationalism by some reformers and editors who wished to provide arousing, masochistic fantasies to an American public accustomed to having its reform well spiced with violence and sex." See Reynolds, *Beneath the American Renaissance*, 73.

30 Halttunen, "Humanitarianism and the Pornography of Pain," 304, 318, 330; Sánchez-Eppler, *Touching Liberty*, 20. In *Women and Sisters*, 24, Yellin investigates the female antislavery emblem to analyze the complex relationship between white women abolitionists and the female slaves they wanted to help, arguing that the emblem made it "poss.ole to ignore the crucial differences" and "conflate the condition of free women and slaves." At times white antislavery feminists identified with female slaves on the basis of gender, but articulated "a feminist consciousness that was race-specific."

31 Sánchez-Eppler, *Touching Liberty*, 25.

32 Noble, *Masochistic Pleasures of Sentimental Literature*, 127–138.

33 Ibid., 145.

34 Nudelman, "Harriet Jacobs," 946.

35 Ibid., 964; Scarry, *Body in Pain*, 4. Further citations will appear in parenthesis in the text.

36 Douglass states that it was not until his body was at least tolerably comfortable that he was able to begin to analyze his oppression and plan escape. See Douglass, "Narrative of the Life of Frederick Douglass," 91. Likewise, Harriet Jacobs portrays mothers who have been so abused that they no longer protest when their own children are beaten and recognizes that she could be reduced to such a state. See Jacobs, *Incidents in the Life of a Slave Girl*, 87.

37 Mills, *Cultural Reformations*, 33–46. Karcher also points out that one of the primary arguments Child needed to refute was that it was in the "masters' interests to treat their slaves kindly" and that "simple expediency" would "result in making cruelty the exception rather than the rule." See Karcher, *First Woman*, 175.

38 Foucault, *Discipline and Punish*, 8. Further citations will appear in parenthesis in the text.

39 Brodhead, "Sparing the Rod," 67.

40 Child, *Letters from New York*, 3d ed., 223–224. In letter 29 Child calls for prison reform, indicating further her awareness of debates over the nature of criminality. See Child, *Lydia Maria Child Reader*, 319–327.

41 I consider a "sustained" narrative to be at least the major portion of a paragraph and to focus on an individual slave. In chapter 1 of *Appeal in Favor of That Class of Amer-*

icans called Africans, as I interpret it, Child includes four shorter sustained narratives of torture: the flogging and torture of a child on a slave ship (17); the hunting and shooting of a fugitive slave (26); the beating of a slave woman by her female slave owner (28); and the beating and murder of a pregnant slave woman (28). The two longest narratives of torture are placed together, with the story of Kate preceding the narrative of the Kentuckian slave (23–26).

42 My argument draws upon the work of Carla L. Peterson, who, as discussed in chapter 3, analyzes Frances E. W. Harper's poetry in relation to "an aesthetics of restraint." See Peterson, *"Doers of the Word,"* 119–137.

43 Although the genre of the slave narrative was not fully developed in the 1830s, Child had access to the stories of fugitive slaves. Karcher concludes that William Lloyd Garrison's antislavery newspaper, the *Liberator,* was an "invaluable mine of information" for Child. See Karcher, *First Woman,* 176.

44 Theodore Dwight Weld, along with his wife, Angelina Grimké Weld, and her sister, Sarah Grimké, repeated Child's strategy of using southern testimony six years later in *American Slavery as It Is* by collecting evidence from more than twenty thousand copies of southern newspapers to dismiss southern claims of benevolence. Their work provides an interesting contrast to Child's, because it does not trace a similar shift from corporeal to noncorporeal representation but, instead, provides unrelenting accounts of torture and abuse. See Weld and Grimké, *American Slavery as It Is.*

45 Child influenced not only numerous women, but also many prominent men, who credited Child's text with being a major inspiration in their lives. Leaders such as William Ellery Channing (a Unitarian minister), Wendell Phillips (a lawyer), Thomas Wentworth Higginson (the first man to lead a black regiment in the Civil War), and the fiery Radical Republican senator Charles Summer, all attested to the influence that Child's *Appeal* had on their thoughts and actions. See Karcher, *First Woman,* 193–194.

46 Karcher, *First Woman,* 185–186; Sánchez-Eppler, *Touching Liberty,* 38.

47 Karcher, *First Woman,* 183, 185.

48 Karcher also argues that *Appeal* "violates the prevailing norms of feminine discourse by its very engagement in political controversy, as well as by its authoritative display of erudition and its preoccupation with such matters as law, economics, and congressional apportionment." See Karcher, *First Woman,* 185.

49 Although this chapter does not analyze "The Black Saxons," it is a suggestive story in relation to the changing conceptions of race in antebellum America. As its title suggests, Child conflates the heroic cause of the "Saxons," the race from which, as chapter 1 details, many nineteenth-century Caucasians were believed to be descended, with the revolutionary impulses of slaves. See Child, *Lydia Maria Child Reader,* 182–191.

50 Quoted in Karcher, *First Woman,* 320.

51 Karcher, *First Woman,* 333.

52 Child, "The Quadroons," 88–98. All further citations will appear in parenthesis in the text. Yellin credits Child with inventing the "tragic mulatto" archetype, which she defines as "a slave woman of mixed race who wants to conform to patriarchal definitions of true womanhood but is prevented from doing so by the white patriarchy"

(53). As Yellin indicates, one problem with the "tragic mulatto" is that it permits "white female readers to identify with the victim by gender while distancing themselves by race and thus to avoid confronting a racial ideology that denies the full humanity of nonwhite women." See Yellin, *Women and Sisters*, 71–74. Karcher also notes that "stories like 'The Quadroons' could move such readers, but only at the cost of dangerous concessions to the very prejudices and misconceptions abolitionists sought to overcome." See Karcher, *First Woman*, 343.

53 Child, "Slavery's Pleasant Homes: A Faithful Sketch," in *Lydia Maria Child Reader*, 238–242. All further citations will be given in parenthesis in the text.

54 Karcher, "Rape, Murder, and Revenge in 'Slavery's Pleasant Homes,'" 71.

55 Karcher notes that Child might have been influenced by a *Portsmouth Journal* article comparing southern women to harem slaves. See Karcher, *First Woman*, 338.

56 Jennifer Fleischner also analyzes this scene in "Slavery's Pleasant Homes" and concludes that Child is working against sentimentalism. She maintains that Child is able to resist sentimentalizing the relationship between female slave owners and slave women because she "gives literary life to fantasies of a real sisterhood, fraught with tensions of rivalry, competition, hatred, and revenge" (51). In this sense, she "opens up the possibilities of a secret alliance based not on passivity and recognition of mutual suffering, but rather on the capacity for aggression against one another and, finally, against men." See Fleischner, *Mastering Slavery*, 45–46.

57 The narrator's reference to newspaper accounts is fictional. Child combined several sources for her story, including newspaper accounts and personal narratives she heard from fugitive slaves. See Karcher, "Rape, Murder, and Revenge in 'Slavery's Pleasant Homes,'" 64–65.

58 Child, "Stars and Stripes: A Melo-Drama." Further citations will be given in parenthesis in the text. Karcher indicates that Child based at least part of this piece on the story of William and Ellen Craft's escape from slavery. See Karcher, *First Woman*, 413.

59 Child is quoted in Karcher, *First Woman*, 436.

60 Jacobs wrote in a letter to Amy Post that Child was "a whole souled Woman—we soon found the way to each others heart." See Jacobs's *Incidents*, edited by Yellin, 247. Nonetheless, I do not mean to imply that Jacobs did not have to overcome significant obstacles in publishing *Incidents* or that Child had no influence over the final version of the text. As Yellin documents, Jacobs at first wanted to produce a dictated narrative with the help of Harriet Beecher Stowe. However, Stowe inappropriately forwarded Jacobs's story to her employer for verification without Jacobs's permission and wanted to include it in her *Key to Uncle Tom's Cabin* rather than publish it in its own right. This exchange outraged Jacobs, and she decided to write her story herself. After Jacobs tried for several years to get her manuscript accepted, Boston's Thayer and Eldridge said they would publish it if Jacobs could get an introduction from Child. Although Jacobs was grateful to have Child's support, she was upset about having to miss a final meeting to review proofs before publication because of her work as a domestic. For more information on Jacobs's attempts to publish *Incidents*, see Yellin, Introduction to *Incidents in the Life of a Slave Girl*, xviii–xxiii. See also the letters at the end of Yellin's edition of Jacobs's *Incidents*, 244–249. Karcher also examines

Child's role as editor and concludes that Child "displayed the same hardheaded editorial judgment" in adapting her own works for a larger audience. See Karcher, *First Woman*, 436. Despite legitimate concerns about "vexed alliances" between African American and white women, I agree with Peterson, who concludes that Jacobs, having "established close relationships with Amy Post and Child" and having been able to express her distress over Stowe's inappropriate behavior, "could accept collaboration as historically inevitable and seek to turn it to her advantage." See Peterson, *"Doers of the Word,"* 153.

61 Peterson, *"Doers of the Word,"* 20–21.

3. Deflecting the Public's Gaze and Disciplining Desire

1 Harper is quoted in Still, *Underground Rail Road*, 786.
2 Harper, "Oh, How I Miss New England," in *Brighter Coming Day*, 46.
3 Van Evrie, *Negroes and Negro "Slavery,"* 89.
4 White, *Ar'n't I a Woman?*, 29.
5 Foster, Introduction to *Brighter Coming Day*, 3; Peterson, *"Doers of the Word,"* 8, 16–17.
6 Peterson, *"Doers of the Word,"* 21.
7 Ibid., 18–19.
8 Quoted in Still, *Underground Rail Road*, 806–807.
9 Harper, "Almost Constantly Either Traveling or Speaking," in *Brighter Coming Day*, 126–127.
10 Foucault, *Discipline and Punish*, 187.
11 Rosenthal, "Deracialized Discourse," 162, 156.
12 As my analysis reveals, Peterson also argues for the importance of placing Harper's Reconstruction fiction in relation to temperance rhetoric and for the examination of the political implications of self-discipline. See Peterson, "Frances Harper, Charlotte Forten, and African American Literary Reconstruction," 39–61.
13 Tate, "Allegories of Black Female Desire," 98–126; duCille, *Coupling Convention*, 3–12.
14 Peterson, *"Doers of the Word,"* 124.
15 The review is by Grace Greenwood and appeared in the *Independent*. It is quoted in Still, *Underground Rail Road*, 812.
16 Graham, Introduction to *The Complete Poems of Frances E. W. Harper*, lii. Graham notes that "the vast majority" of Harper's poems from this time period "used conventional metrical patterns, ranging from the rhymed couplet to the four-line ballad stanza." Therefore, "for the modern reader these poems seem imitative and forced, wedded to a metrical system and style that too often sacrificed depth of thought, subtlety of imagery, and precision of language for melodrama and didacticism." Yet Harper's poems should be analyzed in relation to the setting in which they were performed as well as her poetical and political goals. See Graham, Introduction to *The Complete Poems of Frances E. W. Harper*, xliii–xliv. Paul Lauter also asserts that the "aesthetic counter-tradition which emerged in the work of writers like Henry James has continued to dominate our own training," making it difficult for us to interpret

writers like Harper. This tradition can be blamed, in part, for the exclusion of Harper from the modern literary canon despite her popularity during her lifetime. See Lauter, "Is Frances Ellen Watkins Harper Good Enough to Teach?," 29. By 1858, for example, her *Poems on Miscellaneous Subjects* had reached twelve thousand copies in print, and by 1872 fifty thousand copies of Harper's first four books were published. See Boyd, *Discarded Legacy*, 77.

17 Boyd argues that Harper's use of the ballad links her abolition poems to folk poetry, contending that Harper's poems "are folk poems, poetic slave narratives adapted from Underground Railroad stories about runaways, from reports she heard from escaped slaves, or from scenes she witnessed with her own eyes." See Boyd, *Discarded Legacy*, 59–60. Even though Harper employs the ballad to suggest an alignment with the folk, she neither writes folk literature nor allows slaves direct testimony. As Susan Stewart argues about the ballad in general, it is imperative not to confuse the evocation of a folk tradition with the "folk" itself. See Stewart, *Crimes of Writing*, 103.

18 Stewart, *Crimes of Writing*, 124–125; Peterson, "*Doers of the Word*," 128. Peterson builds upon Buell's discussion of the aesthetics of restraint in his introduction to the *Selected Poems of Henry Wadsworth Longfellow* (New York: Penguin, 1988), xii, xi.

19 In *Hard Facts*, Philip Fisher argues that "separation and mental anguish" are the "primary forms of suffering" in sentimentalism, and often this anguish is best exemplified by the parting of "the essence of the family, mother and child" (106).

20 All quotations of Harper's poems are taken from Harper, *Complete Poems of Frances E. W. Harper*.

21 Peterson, "*Doers of the Word*," 125.

22 Foster compares "The Slave Mother" to John Greenleaf Whittier's "At Washington" and "The Slave Auction" to Whittier's "Panorama," arguing that Harper concentrates to a greater extent on the "feelings and sensibilities" of the victimized women. Foster, Introduction to *Brighter Coming Day*, 31–33.

23 Stowe, *Uncle Tom's Cabin*, 149; Noble, *Masochistic Pleasures*, 130; Ernest, "Motherhood beyond the Gate," 180.

24 Scarry, *Body in Pain*, 29.

25 Foucault, *Discipline and Punish*, 60–66.

26 Scarry, *Body in Pain*, 35–36.

27 John 20.25, *Harper Collins Study Bible*, 2053.

28 For example, James Baldwin charges Stowe with robbing Tom of "his humanity" and divesting him of his sex. See Baldwin, *Notes of a Native Son*, 17.

29 Harper's 1854 edition of *Poems on Miscellaneous Subjects* includes two poems based, in part, on *Uncle Tom's Cabin*: "Little Eva's Farewell" and "Eliza Harris." Also, in 1854 she published a tribute to Stowe titled "To Mrs. Harriet Beecher Stowe" in *Frederick Douglass's Paper*. See Harper, *Brighter Coming Day*, 57.

30 Peterson, "*Doers of the Word*," 125.

31 Harper, "The Two Offers," in *Brighter Coming Day*, 114.

32 Foster, *Written by Herself*, 141.

33 Rosenthal, "Deracialized Discourse," 155.

34 Foster, Introduction to *"Minnie's Sacrifice," "Sowing and Reaping," and "Trial and Triumph,"* xxiii–xxv.

35 Quoted in Frances Smith Foster, *Brighter Coming Day*, 105. For a brief discussion of the *Anglo-African*, see Burks, "First Black Literary Magazine," 318–321.

36 Tate, "Allegories of Black Female Desire," 124.

37 Harper, *"Minnie's Sacrifice," "Sowing and Reaping," and "Trial and Triumph,"* 46. In all further citations the collection of the three novels will be referred to as MST in parenthesis in the text.

38 See Crowley, "Slaves to the Bottle," 117. Peterson links Harper's Joe Gough with the historical John Gough. See Peterson, "Frances Harper, Charlotte Forten, and African American Literary Reconstruction," 48.

39 Crowley, "Slaves to the Bottle," 122–123.

40 Yacovone, "Transformation of the Black Temperance Movement," 290.

41 Van Evrie, *Negroes and Negro "Slavery,"* 196–197; Levine, *Martin Delany, Frederick Douglass, and the Politics of Representative Identity*, 103.

42 Carby, *Reconstructing Womanhood*, 85.

43 Gough, *Autobiography*, 35, 52, 89.

44 Rosenthal argues that Harper's readers, encountering the novels in the Afro-Protestant press, "probably did not find the deracialized discourse curious, but instead assumed Harper's characters to be black." See Rosenthal, "Deracialized Discourse," 155.

45 Foucault, *Discipline and Punish*, 8, 137.

46 Clearly punishment did not disappear in the postbellum South. However, there was a time period, especially when Harper would have been writing *Sowing and Reaping*, when African American authors were generally optimistic about the nation's future in general and about the disappearance of violence in particular. See, for example, Andrews, "Reunion in the Postbellum Slave Narrative," 5–16.

47 Peterson, "Frances Harper, Charlotte Forten, and African American Literary Reconstruction," 43.

48 Tate, "Allegories of Black Female Desire," 119–120.

49 Romero, "Vanishing Americans," 102; Foucault, *History of Sexuality*, 122.

50 Romero, "Vanishing Americans," 101. One work that exhibits this tendency is Brodhead's "Sparing the Rod," 67–96.

51 See Smith-Rosenberg, *Disorderly Conduct*, for an analysis of the rhetoric of nineteenth-century reform movements.

52 Peterson, "Francis Harper, Charlotte Forten, and African American Literary Reconstruction," 43.

4. Saxons and Slavery

1 My reading of Emerson's desire to look at the bodies of "his" dead is indebted to Richardson's biography, which begins with the story of Emerson staring at Ellen and works toward its conclusion by focusing on Emerson's decision to peer at Waldo's remains. See Richardson, *Emerson: The Mind on Fire*, 3, 540.

2 In contrast to my interpretation, Ralph L. Rusk interprets Emerson's decision to view Ellen's body as atypical, suggesting that an "obscure unreasonable and uncontrollable impulse caused him" to have her coffin opened. See Rusk, *Ralph Waldo Emerson*, 150.

3 Leverenz, *Manhood and the American Renaissance*, 39–40. Rusk also notes a connection between Emerson's physical illnesses and his state of mind, commenting that Emerson's trouble with rheumatic pain and sight are related to his "unrealized ambition" early in his life. See Rusk, *Ralph Waldo Emerson*, 115.

4 Richardson, *Emerson: The Mind on Fire*, 224. Emerson's task of coming to terms with Charles's legacy was complicated by Emerson's discovery that Charles had no "notable literary talent," which led Emerson to redefine Charles as an outstanding orator. See Rusk, *Ralph Waldo Emerson*, 231.

5 Barbara Packer argues that the final chapters of *Nature* must be considered in relation to the "sudden catastrophe" of Charles's death, an incident that forced Emerson to reconsider his writings on "spirit." See Packer, *Emerson's Fall*, 29–30; see also 48–63. Julie Ellison notes that Emerson splits identity between the body and the spirit and that, for Emerson, the body was the "less prestigious pole." As a result, Ellison argues, Emerson often associated Henry David Thoreau with the body, as the "concrete embodiment" that Emerson often set in opposition to the "abstract spirit." See Ellison, "Aggressive Allegory," 159.

6 Richardson concludes that Emerson and Ellen's relationship was full of sensuality and warmth. See in particular *Emerson: The Mind on Fire*, 84–86.

7 Reynolds, *Beneath the American Renaissance*, 85–94; Gougeon, *Virtue's Hero*, 66.

8 Gougeon, *Virtue's Hero*, 178–179. Eduardo Cadava also suggests that there can be "little doubt" that by the early 1840s Emerson is not persuaded by the arguments for racial determinism. See Cadava, *Climates of History*, 58.

9 Robinson, *Conduct of Life*, 3.

10 Cayton, *Emerson's Emergence*, 33–42; Cadava, *Climates of History*, 14.

11 Rowe, *At Emerson's Tomb*, 21. See Nicoloff, *Emerson on Race and History*, 29. Robinson also notes that Emerson's trip to England served as a "catalyst" in his thought, accelerating his movement toward incorporating social and political concerns into his conception of moral action. See Robinson, *Conduct of Life*, 113.

12 The view that Emerson shifted toward a reluctant and ambivalent acceptance of fate later in life is expressed by Stephen E. Whicher in *Freedom and Fate*. Although I agree that Emerson's philosophy shifted throughout his lifetime, this chapter clearly disagrees with Whicher's claim that Emerson's second trip to England in 1847–48 can "be conveniently taken to mark the conclusion of the real development of his thought" (154). Sacvan Bercovitch, linking a movement from the "radical" early essays to the more "conservative 'later Emerson'" with the "theory and practice of socialism," also notes a shift in Emerson's thinking. See Bercovitch, "Emerson, Individualism, and the Ambiguities of Dissent," 110. Nicoloff likewise argues that the 1840s were a time of transformation for Emerson as he moved from "a radical faith in man's illimitable possibilities to an emphasis upon a constitutional determinism." See Nicoloff, *Emerson on Race and History*, 106. In her work, which traces Emerson's thought in rela-

tion to three unique responses to the "fallen" state of humanity, Packer argues that Emerson's third and final account of the fall—one that equates self-consciousness with the fall—is a myth that is more pessimistic than his earlier solutions of the same dilemma. See Packer, *Emerson's Fall*, 148–149.

13 Cadava, *Climates of History*, 9; Buell, *Literary Transcendentalism*, 16.

14 For an analysis of Emerson's "transcendental style," see Buell, *New England Literary Culture*, 62.

15 Whicher, *Freedom and Fate*, 58. Clearly Whicher writes before deconstruction influenced American literary criticism. However, more recent work by Robinson notes that "criticism has taught us the ironic and dramatic complexity" of Emerson's essays, "complicating any reading of them as a straight declarative philosophy or a simple narrative of the self. Instead, we must approach the essays as *the sties at which Emerson hoped to work through his conflicting impulses*" (emphasis mine). Although Robinson notes that Emerson's rhetoric is complex and even contradictory, he also indicates that Emerson wanted to "work through" his conflicting impulses. See Robinson, *Conduct of Life*, 9.

16 Jefferson, *Notes on the State of Virginia*, 143.

17 Whicher, *Freedom and Fate*, 112–113.

18 West, *American Evasion of Philosophy*, 31.

19 Buell, *Literary Transcendentalism*, 149; Swedenborg is quoted in Packer, *Emerson's Fall*, 38.

20 Emerson, *Nature*, in *Collected Works*, 1:19–21.

21 Packer, *Emerson's Fall*, 39.

22 Emerson, "The Transcendentalist," in *Collected Works*, 1:206–207.

23 Emerson, "The Method of Nature," in *Collected Works*, 1:123.

24 Rusk describes how Emerson came relatively early to distinguish "reason" from "understanding," a distinction with which he credited Milton, Coleridge, and various German philosophers. "Reason," Emerson wrote to his brother Edward, "is the highest faculty of the soul—what we mean often by the soul itself; it never *reasons*, never proves, it simply perceives; it is vision. The Understanding toils all the time, compares, contrives, adds, argues, near-sighted but strong-sighted. . . . Beasts have some understanding but no Reason." Quoted in Rusk, *Ralph Waldo Emerson*, 203–204. By associating understanding with the "beasts" and reason with the soul, Emerson suggests, even in this letter, that understanding is associated with one's animal nature, that is, corporeality, whereas reason is disembodied.

25 Emerson, "Compensation," in *Collected Works*, 2:61; Emerson, "Over-Soul," in *Collected Works*, 2:162. Emerson, "Poet," in *Collected Works*, 3:16–17; Emerson, "The Transcendentalist," in *Collected Works*, 1:212.

26 Emerson, "Experience," in *Collected Works*, 3:31.

27 Combe, Appendix to *Crania Americana*, 269.

28 Emerson, "Address on Emancipation," in *Emerson's Antislavery Writings*, 29.

29 Emerson, "Poet," in *Collected Works*, 3:3–4.

30 Emerson, "Over-Soul," in *Collected Works*, 2:173.

31 Buell, *Literary Transcendentalism*, 168–169.
32 Emerson, "American Scholar," in *Collected Works*, 1:53.
33 Emerson, "Address on Emancipation," in Emerson, *Emerson's Antislavery Writings*, 32; "Lecture on Slavery," in Emerson, *Emerson's Antislavery Writings*, 92; "To the Citizens of Concord," in Emerson, *Emerson's Antislavery Writings*, 64.
34 Child, "Letter from New York," no. 34, in Child, *Lydia Maria Child Reader*, 361–362.
35 For a discussion of Emerson's published and unpublished essays on women's rights, see Gougeon, "Emerson and the Woman Question."
36 Deese, "'A Liberal Education,'" 248.
37 Gougeon, "Emerson and the Woman Question," 572.
38 Emerson, *Nature*, 8. Robert E. Spiller discusses Emerson's connections with German idealism in his introduction to Emerson's *Collected Works*, 1:xxii–xxiii.
39 Ann Braude provides an analysis of American spiritualism, as well as details about the relationship between mediumship and gender and race in *Radical Spirits*, 29, 83.
40 Emerson, *Nature*, 38.
41 Emerson, *Nature*, 10.
42 Ellison, *Delicate Subjects*, 11, 268; Cheyfitz, *Trans-Parent*, 59; Leverenz, *Manhood and the American Renaissance*, 47.
43 Sidonie Smith, "Resisting the Gaze of Embodiment," 76.
44 Ibid., 77.
45 Emerson, *Nature*, 44.
46 For an analysis of the trope of women and the domestic sphere as entrapping men in nineteenth-century fiction, see Baym, "Melodramas of Beset Manhood." Emerson's representation of the feminine sphere as a trap calls to mind his feelings about teaching in a young ladies' school after finishing his studies at Harvard. According to Rusk, Emerson viewed his teaching of young women an obstacle "circumscribing his freedom of thought and action." See Rusk, *Ralph Waldo Emerson*, 101.
47 Emerson, "Divinity School Address," in *Collected Works*, 1:91.
48 Emerson, "Love," in *Collected Works*, 2:106.
49 Emerson, "Character," in *Collected Works*, 3:64–65.
50 Emerson, "Manners," in *Collected Works*, 3:88–89.
51 Emerson, "Man the Reformer," in *Collected Works*, 1:147.
52 Ibid., 1:148–153.
53 Emerson, "Self-Reliance," in *Collected Works*, 2:32.
54 Alcott, *Young Husband*, 38; Emerson, "Self-Reliance," in *Collected Works*, 2:41.
55 Emerson evokes biblical language in this passage, particularly Matthew 10.37, which instructs readers that "Whoever loves father or mother more than me is not worthy of me; and whoever loves son or daughter more than me is not worthy of me," in *Harper Collins Study Bible*, 1876.
56 Emerson, "Self-Reliance," in *Collected Works*, 2:43.
57 Ibid., 2:29; Leverenz, "Emerson's Man-Making Words," 138.
58 Emerson, "Self-Reliance," in *Collected Works*, 2:41.

59 Horsman, *Race and Manifest Destiny*, 14.

60 Emerson, "Self-Reliance," in *Collected Works*, 2:48.

61 Emerson, *English Traits*, 23.

62 Horsman, *Race and Manifest Destiny*, 158–159.

63 Buell argues that early Emerson scholars concentrated too much on Emerson's connections with the Puritans and American Enlightenment debate, sources that Emerson mentions only sporadically. Instead, Buell suggests Emerson should be viewed as "a nineteenth-century Bostonian with a very limited, indeed quasi-amnesiac memory of American history . . . yet with an intellectual range positively global in scope." See Buell, "Emerson in His Cultural Context," 49.

64 Bercovitch, "Emerson, Individualism, and the Ambiguities of Dissent," 122.

65 Emerson, "Address on Emancipation," in *Emerson's Antislavery Writings*, 29.

66 Gougeon, *Virtue's Hero*, 85.

67 Emerson, "Address on Emancipation," in *Emerson's Antislavery Writings*, 29–31.

68 Ibid., 31.

69 Ibid., 8–10.

70 Ibid., 26, 30.

71 Ibid., 20, 30.

72 George Fredrickson describes the preponderance of romantic racialism in the antebellum era in *The Black Image in the White Mind*. Fredrickson argues that whereas biological schools could construct the Negro as a "pathetically inept creature who was a slave to his emotions," evangelical religion and romanticism saw these "traits" as redeeming virtues or evidence of black superiority (101).

73 See Combe, Appendix to *Crania Americana*, 272.

74 See Horsman, *Race and Manifest Destiny*, 177. For a discussion of Emerson's belief in the "doomed" Indian, especially in relation to the question of the Cherokees' removal from Georgia, see Alexander, "Emerson and Cherokee Removal."

75 Emerson, "Address on Emancipation," in *Emerson's Antislavery Writings*, 15, 33.

76 Emerson, "To the Citizens of Concord," in *Emerson's Antislavery Writings*, 67.

77 Emerson, "Kansas Relief Meeting," in *Emerson's Antislavery Writings*, 115.

78 Emerson, *English Traits*, 18–19.

79 Ibid., 35–36.

80 Emerson, *English Traits*, 172, 19–20.

81 Buell, *New England Literary Culture*, 203.

82 Nicoloff's discussion of Emerson's view of history demonstrates how Emerson's chapters "Race" and "Literature" can be understood as attempts to synthesize two opposing concepts, the scientific view of ascent and the religious view of the Fall. See Nicoloff, *Emerson on Race and History*, 234.

83 Emerson, *English Traits*, 155.

84 Nicoloff, *Emerson on Race and History*, 112.

85 Emerson, "Young American," in *Collected Works*, 1:230–231.

86 Morton, *Brief Remarks*, 6.

87 According to Rusk, Agassiz was a founding member of the "Saturday Club" that

Emerson helped to form and also the schoolmaster of Emerson's daughter, Ellen. See Rusk, *Ralph Waldo Emerson*, 392. As Gougeon notes, Agassiz was Emerson's "greatest friend in the scientific community" and "Emerson could not help but be affected in some way" by Agassiz's opinions and theories on race. See Gougeon, *Virtue's Hero*, 181–182.

88 Nicoloff, *Emerson on Race and History*, 123. Horsman calls Knox's work "a passionate espousal of racial doctrines" with "a wild irrational streak." Chief among Knox's beliefs is that, although Saxons love liberty, they only want to grant democratic rights to other Saxons. See Horsman, *Race and Manifest Destiny*, 71–73.

89 Robinson, *Conduct of Life*, 116.

90 Emerson, *English Traits*, 24; Nott and Gliddon, *Types of Mankind*, 53.

91 Nicoloff, *Emerson on Race and History*, 146.

92 Emerson, *English Traits*, 28.

93 Emerson, *Journals*, 8:86.

94 Emerson, *English Traits*, 26.

95 Ibid., 24–28.

96 Horsman, *Race and Manifest Destiny*, 225.

97 Emerson, *Journals*, 8:226.

98 Emerson, *English Traits*, 36.

99 Emerson, *English Traits*, 25–26, 51, 55.

100 Robinson, *Conduct of Life*, 115. Although my argument differs with the conclusion Robinson reaches regarding racial determinism and *English Traits*, we share the belief that Emerson's antislavery lectures are critical when assessing *English Traits* and Emerson's later philosophy and that his 1850s lectures can be understood as a "tense dialectic over American possibilities" (131).

101 Gougeon, *Virtue's Hero*, 184; Cadava, *Climates of History*, 58.

102 Nicoloff, *Emerson on Race and History*, 96.

103 Emerson, *English Traits*, 45.

104 When discussing Emerson's "President's Proclamation," I do not want to imply that this brief essay should be taken as his definitive statement on emancipation. Certainly, "Boston Hymn," which was delivered in celebration of emancipation, and "Voluntaries," among other texts, should also be considered. See Emerson, *Poems* (1867; Boston: Houghton Mifflin, 1918), 201–209. For a reading that differs with my understanding of Emerson's view of race during the Civil War years, see Cadava's provocative assessment of these poems in the final chapter of *Climates of History*, 149–201.

105 Emerson, "President's Proclamation," in *Emerson's Antislavery Writings*, 131–132.

106 See Gougeon and Myerson, *Emerson's Antislavery Writings*, 223.

107 Emerson, "Fortune of the Republic," in *Antislavery Writings*, 140–144.

108 Ibid., 139.

109 Ibid., 146–147, 151.

110 Nicoloff, *Emerson on Race and History*, 112–114.

111 See Gougeon, *Virtue's Hero*, 314.

112 Whicher, *Freedom and Fate*, 103, 131.

113 See Cayton, *Emerson's Emergence*, 57–79.

5. The New Face of Empire

1 *Benét's Readers Encyclopedia*, 842, 855.
2 Fuller, *Woman in the Nineteenth Century*, 260. Further citations will be given in parenthesis in the text. Steele connects Fuller's aversion to "wolfish" energy with the founding of Rome in the footnotes to his edition of her text. See Fuller, *Summer on the Lakes*, 453 n. 12.
3 Rosowski, "Margaret Fuller, an Engendered West, and *Summer on the Lakes*," 138.
4 Ibid., 141.
5 In May 1843, before leaving for the Great Lakes and Wisconsin territory, Fuller completed "The Great Lawsuit," which was published in the *Dial* while she was on her trip. In May 1844 she published *Summer on the Lakes, in 1843*, and in November 1844 she completed her revision of "The Great Lawsuit," titling it *Woman in the Nineteenth Century*. Several scholars have commented upon the chronological proximity of the texts and their relation to one another. For example, Annette Kolodny argues that *Summer* is "everywhere informed . . . by the concerns for women that Fuller had so recently explored in 'The Great Lawsuit,'" and, in turn, *Woman* is "informed by the new insights (and frustrated fantasies) awakened on the prairies but only imperfectly analyzed" in *Summer*. See Kolodny, *Land before Her*, 128–129. Lucy Maddox also points to the correlation between *Summer on the Lakes* and *Woman in the Nineteenth Century*, noting that "many of the anecdotes she first records" in *Summer* "are repeated—having become examples used to support Fuller's argument for female equality" in *Woman*. See Maddox, *Removals*, 132. Although it is not the focus of her article, Rosowski likewise indicates that by "turning toward the future with hope for other, younger women" in *Summer*, Fuller "anticipates the serious argument" of *Woman*. See Rosowski, "Margaret Fuller, an Engendered West, and *Summer on the Lakes*," 131.
6 Zwarg, *Feminist Conversations*, 104. Further citations will be given in parenthesis in the text.
7 Ellison, *Delicate Subjects*, 270–271.
8 Quoted in Karcher, *First Woman*, 226.
9 Pulte, *Woman's Medical Guide*, 157.
10 Fuller, "Autobiographical Romance," in *Essential Margaret Fuller*, 25; Blanchard, *Margaret Fuller*, 76.
11 Capper, *Margaret Fuller*, 160, 70–71, 65.
12 Emerson, Channing, and Clarke, eds., *Memoirs of Margaret Fuller Ossoli*, 229. Although this quote may reflect Fuller's conception of herself during her adolescence, I do not want to overemphasize its significance. Some scholars contend that *Memoirs* reveals more about the anxieties of its editors than it does about Fuller's personality or appearance. For example, Dorothy Berkson argues that the "extreme emphasis" on Fuller's appearance in *Memoirs* is a "constant reminder that Fuller is a woman, an unwomanly woman who has stepped out of her role." See Berkson, "'Born and Bred in Different Nations,'" in *Patrons and Protégées*, 25. In an insightful essay, Lindsey Traub investigates Emerson's representation of Fuller in the *Memoirs* in relation to

his private statements about Fuller, arguing that his representation of Fuller depends, in part, on his need to situate her as a private audience to his public work. See Traub, "Woman Thinking."

13 Emerson also experienced disease and bodily pain, although it was not as severe as Fuller's sufferings. Eric Cheyfitz argues that Emerson's disturbance in his lungs during 1826–27 was not the only time when doubts about "a particular professional identity" coincided with physical symptoms such as eye disease and recurrent diarrhoea. See Cheyfitz, *Trans-Parent*, 48–49; Fuller, *Letters*, 2:99.

14 Fuller, *Letters*, 3:55.

15 Ellison argues that physiological or "nervous" weakness functions as an indication of mental dominance in romantic literature. See Ellison, *Delicate Subjects*, 269. Her assertion is supported by Higginson's recollections of Fuller, which establish Fuller's pain as a type of muse. He says her pain "acted like a girdle, to give tension to her powers." Emerson, Channing, and Clarke, *Memoirs of Margaret Fuller Ossoli*, 229.

16 Fuller, *Woman in the Nineteenth Century*, 302.

17 Despite her challenges to scientists, Fuller was intrigued with phrenology, had her head read on at least two occasions, and had a professional relationship with the Fowler brothers of New York. For a summary of the relationship between Fuller, phrenology, and the Fowler brothers, see Stern, "Margaret Fuller and the Phrenologist-Publishers," 229–237.

18 In *Disorderly Conduct*, Smith-Rosenberg demonstrates how many women reformists enacted political change within the ideology of domesticity. Likewise, Jane Tompkins shows how much nineteenth-century sentimental literature exploited the reformist potential of domesticity. See Tompkins, "Sentimental Power."

19 Ellison, *Delicate Subjects*, 270–271. Mary Wood also argues that Fuller "returns repeatedly to conventional nineteenth-century notions that masculine and feminine characteristics are essential and distinct, even if those characteristics may inhabit either men or women." See Wood, "'With Ready Eye,'" 9.

20 Cheyfitz, *Trans-Parent*, 59; Foucault, *Order Of Things*, 144.

21 Fuller justifies the inclusion of this story by saying that German lore will soon be mingled with that of the Indians in the West. See *Summer on the Lakes*, 170.

22 Jean Fagan Yellin and Karen Sánchez-Eppler analyze feminist-abolitionist rhetoric and the rhetorical linking of free women of the North with slaves. See Yellin, *Women and Sisters*, and Sánchez-Eppler, *Touching Liberty*.

23 Rosowski, "Margaret Fuller, an Engendered West, and *Summer on the Lakes*," 133.

24 Richard Slotkin analyzes the frontier as a symbolic site of renewal in *Regeneration through Violence*. Although Fuller challenges the idea that violence creates renewal, she nonetheless endorses the concept of the frontier as edenic in its possibility.

25 Rosowski, "Margaret Fuller, an Engendered West, and *Summer on the Lakes*," 125; Kolodny, *Land before Her*, 113.

26 Rosowski shows how the West was crucial to Fuller's imagination at least a decade before embarking on her trip. See Rosowski, "Margaret Fuller, an Engendered West, and *Summer on the Lakes*," 125–128. For the Puritans, social experimentation was, of

course, rooted in their religious faith rather than democratic experimentation. However, Fuller draws upon Puritan conceptions of the "New World" as a sacred testing
ground. For example, John Winthrop calls his new community a "city upon a hill"
that the world will be watching. If the Puritans "deal falsely with our God in this
work," they "shall be made a story and a by-word through the world." See Winthrop,
"A Model of Christian Charity," 91.

27 McKinsey, *Niagara Falls*, 219, 3.

28 For a discussion of Emerson's "transparent eyeball" as it relates to nineteenth-
century conceptions of the self, see chapter 4.

29 Maddox, *Removals*, 143. Similar to my interpretation, Maddox argues that Fuller
viewed Native Americans as fated, suggesting that Fuller "confronted the question of
Indians' participation in the society to come in *Summer on the Lakes*" and "concluded that their political destiny was not to be equality within a free society but
inevitable removal from it." See Maddox, *Removals*, 140.

30 Fuller's phrasing echoes Emerson's statement in "Self-Reliance" that "[t]he civilized
man has built a coach, but has lost the use of his feet." See Emerson, "Self-Reliance,"
in *Collected Works*, 2:48.

31 See Kolodny, *Land before Her*, 17–34.

32 Reginald Horsman demonstrates that "after 1830 neither the mass of the American people nor the political leaders of the country believed that the Indians could be melded into
American society," a belief based on nineteenth-century conceptions of race. See Horsman, *Race and Manifest Destiny*, 190. See also Dippie, *Vanishing American*, 45–78.

33 Namias, *White Captives*, 36–37.

34 Rosowski, "Margaret Fuller, an Engendered West, and *Summer on the Lakes*," 133.
Fuller writes to Maria Rotch in 1844 that her room in Cambridge has "some Indian
things mementoes of my Western experiences and Indian cradle &c." See Fuller, *Letters*, 3:170–173.

35 Bieder, *Science Encounters the Indian*, 43.

36 Tonkovich, "Traveling in the West," 80–83.

37 Morton, *Letter to the Reverend John Backman*, 14; Nott and Gliddon, *Types of
Mankind*, 373.

38 Zwarg provides a detailed analysis of Fuller's role as translator in *Feminist Conversations*.

39 Cheyfitz, *Poetics of Imperialism*, 59.

40 Horsman demonstrates how some mid-nineteenth century scientists attributed not
only positive, but also negative traits such as aggression and a desire for conquest to
the "superior" Anglo-Saxons. See Horsman, *Race and Manifest Destiny*, 72.

41 Tonkovich also interprets the "Muckwa" story as establishing "Fuller's position as
an opponent to 'amalgamation.'" See Tonkovich, "Traveling in the West," 87.

42 Namias, *White Captives*, 25; Tonkovich, "Traveling in the West," 90.

43 Jane Schoolcraft was educated both in her mother's and in her father's traditions. For
brief information on Jane Johnston Schoolcraft's life and work, see Lavonne Brown
Ruoff's entry in *Handbook of Native American Literature*.

44 Pratt, *Imperial Eyes*, 7; Cheyfitz, *Trans-Parent*, 59.

45 Burbick, "Under the Sign of Gender," 76.

46 Namias, *White Captives*, 36–37. This is the type of benevolence that Horsman describes as common to New Englanders' particular brand of cultural racism and that resembles Emerson's views on Native Americans, as well. See Horsman, *Race and Manifest Destiny*, 176–177.

47 McKinsey, *Niagara Falls*, 222. For Fuller's comments on aesthetic sensibility, the new immigrants, and Native Americans, see *Summer on the Lakes*, 96–100.

48 Pratt, *Imperial Eyes*, 78.

49 McKinsey, *Niagara Falls*, 220; Emerson, "History," in *Collected Works*, 2:14, 23.

50 Romero, "Vanishing Americans," 93.

51 Rosowski, "Margaret Fuller, an Engendered West, and *Summer on the Lakes*," 137.

6. "Who Need Be Afraid of the Merge?"

1 All references to Whitman's poems are to the first edition of Whitman, *Leaves of Grass* (1855), unless otherwise noted.

2 David S. Reynolds documents Whitman's fascination with scientific theories of the body, arguing that Whitman was so influenced by mid-nineteenth-century thought that he attributed the source of two of the most important words and concepts of *Leaves of Grass*—"leaves" and "kosmos"—to scientific works. See Reynolds, *Walt Whitman's America*, 241–245. For additional analysis of Whitman and science, see pages 194–278 and 471–474.

3 Whitman ends the preface to his 1855 edition of *Leaves of Grass* by proposing that "the proof of a poet is that his country absorbs him as affectionately as he has absorbed it" (24).

4 Buell, *Literary Transcendentalism*, 167; Erkkila, *Whitman the Political Poet*, 88. Reynolds also notes that Whitman's fear over disunion caused him to "begin testing out statements that balanced opposite views, as though simple rhetorical juxtaposition would dissolve social tensions," and thus began "what would become a long-term strategy of his: resolving thorny political issues by linguistic fiat." See Reynolds, *Walt Whitman's America*, 119.

5 Foucault, *Power/Knowledge*, 59; Graham, *Lecture to Young Men*, 9.

6 Reynolds, *Walt Whitman's America*, 197–198.

7 Moon, *Disseminating Whitman*, 38. Indeed, many scholars are rightfully concerned about the tendency to interpret Whitman's poems as primarily sexual. Reynolds notes that current commentary on Whitman is influenced by interest in "the erotic and the psychological in our post-Freudian age," making many scholars overlook his spiritual themes. See Reynolds, *Walt Whitman's America*, 252. Loving argues against interpretations of Whitman's poems that seem to contradict their reception in the nineteenth century. Noting that *Leaves of Grass* was "hardly ever, if at all, assailed in the nineteenth century for its suggestions of homosexuality" (202), he also dismisses the implications of oral sex in "Song of Myself." Analyzing the "Twenty-Eight Bathers"

section of that poem (which has often been interpreted as representing an oral sex act), Loving argues that the passage has been made "racier" by modern readers as the suggestion of oral sex "was probably out of the question in the nineteenth century—at least with such middle-class women as the 'twenty-ninth bather'" (195). See Loving, *Song of Himself*.

8 Quoted in Reynolds, *Walt Whitman's America*, 197.

9 Shively, *Calamus Lovers*. Fone interprets Whitman's "Child's Champion" (1841) as exhibiting an erotic and redemptive friendship between a young man and one who is slightly older. See Fone, *Masculine Landscapes*, 53; Loving, *Song of Himself*, 19.

10 Reynolds, *Walt Whitman's America*, 198.

11 Quoted in Reynolds, *Walt Whitman's America*, 250.

12 For the correspondence between Whitman and Symonds, see Katz, *Gay American History*, 340–358. Whitman's disavowal, of course, does not end the debate. As Kaplan documents, Whitman made many attempts late in his life to destroy or alter documents, especially by switching the gender descriptions of various men to women. See Kaplan, *Walt Whitman*, 19.

13 Reynolds, *Walt Whitman's America*, 70–74.

14 Alcott, *Physiology of Marriage*, 179.

15 See D'Emilio and Freedman, *Intimate Matters*, 121–123.

16 By suggesting that Whitman's compassion for criminals may stem from anxiety over his "deviancy," I am not dismissing the more overtly political reasons for his concern. Reynolds comments on Whitman's "passionate" sympathy for the unjust treatment of criminals in the mid-1840s, tracing this sympathy, in part, to the stereotype of the justified criminal in the sensational press. See Reynolds, *Beneath the American Renaissance*, 312.

17 Ibid., 322.

18 Foucault, *History of Sexuality*, 58.

19 Loving, *Song of Himself*, 177.

20 Laqueur, "Orgasm, Generation, and the Politics of Reproductive Biology," 7.

21 Laqueur, *Making Sex*, 115.

22 Whitman often repeated his desire to embody himself in his book. For example, in a *St. Louis Post-Dispatch* interview in 1879, Whitman said, "[M]ore than all I determined from the beginning to put a whole living man in the expression of the poem, without wincing. . . . Curious as it may appear, it had never yet been done. An entire human being physically, emotionally, and in his moral and spiritual nature." See Myerson, *Whitman in His Own Time*, 17.

23 Shively's collection of the letters the older Whitman wrote to younger men demonstrates how Whitman cultivated mentoring relationships with young, relatively uneducated boys. See Shively, *Calamus Lovers*.

24 Foucault, *History of Sexuality*, 61.

25 See Reynolds, *Walt Whitman's America*, 464–474. In *Beneath the American Renaissance*, Reynolds proposes that Whitman's move toward conservatism later in life can be attributed, in part, to the fact that "reform rhetoric had carried him to rather

frightening extremes" (111). Moon, in *Disseminating Whitman*, also notes a postbellum change in Whitman's work, suggesting that Whitman completed his radical project in his first four editions and felt that "newly emergent political realities demanded quite different strategies and practices" than exhibited in his earlier editions (221).

26 See, for example, Loving's discussion of the *Aurora*'s "Native American" campaign in *Song of Himself*. Loving finds it incomprehensible that the "same person" who wrote *Leaves of Grass* could be involved in such editorials and eventually absolves Whitman of writing them (62–66). Reynolds suggests in *Beneath the American Renaissance* that we should "not be shocked at apparent inconsistencies in Whitman's attitudes toward current social issues," because he explored the "*imaginative*" rather than the "*political*" possibilities of reform rhetoric (107).

27 Loving, *Song of Himself*, 108–110, 90.

28 Pease, *Visionary Compacts*, 129–130.

29 Ibid., 110.

30 Laqueur, *Making Sex*, 42; Moon, *Disseminating Whitman*, 59.

31 Loving, *Song of Himself*, 212.

32 Loving, *Song of Himself*, 213. See also Kaplan, *Walt Whitman*, 146–156; and Reynolds, *Beneath the American Renaissance*, 326–327.

33 Loving, *Song of Himself*, 150.

34 Fone, *Masculine Landscapes*, 30.

35 All quotations from "Calamus" and "Enfans d'Adam" have been edited to reflect their 1860 version, as per Bradley's variorum.

36 Killingsworth, *Poetry of the Body*, 73, 81; Leverenz, *Manhood and the American Renaissance*, 31–32.

37 Fuller, *Summer on the Lakes*, 106.

38 Erkkila, *Whitman the Political Poet*, 138.

39 Fowler, *Principles of Phrenology and Physiology*, 132, 29.

40 Reynolds, *Beneath the American Renaissance*, 328. Martin interprets Whitman's use of adhesiveness as a way of constructing a homosexual identity not defined solely by sex. Martin, *Homosexual Tradition in American Poetry*, 45.

41 Fowler, *Principles of Phrenology and Physiology*, 29.

42 Martin, *Homosexual Tradition in American Poetry*, 59.

43 Ceniza, "'Being a Woman,'" 111; Reynolds, *Walt Whitman's America*, 208–214.

44 Dixon, *Woman and Her Diseases*, 71–72.

45 Killingsworth reads Whitman as growing progressively conservative. As Whitman depicted sexuality as either heterosexual or homosexual and made his eugenic program more specific, he lost some of the "broad human appeal that is the goal of the liberal romantic." See Killingsworth, *Poetry of the Body*, 45.

46 Kolodny summarizes the motif of the American landscape as a feminine presence, beckoning the male son/lover. See Kolodny, *The Land before Her*, 3.

47 Fone's analysis of Whitman's early notebooks supports the idea that Whitman viewed masculinity as the active force. See Fone, *Masculine Landscapes*, 97.

48 Erkkila, *Whitman the Political Poet*, 46.

49 McPherson, *Battle Cry of Freedom*, 145–150.

50 Erkkila, *Whitman the Political Poet*, 58, 197.

51 Whitman, *The Correspondence: 1842–1867*, vol. 1, ed. Edwin Haviland Miller (New York: New York University Press, 1984), 323.

52 See Dippie, *Vanishing American*, 12–78.

53 Pioneer wagon trains and the railroad had a devastating effect on the grazing habits of buffalo and other animals, significantly reducing various tribes' ability to support themselves and adding to tension between colonists and Native Americans. See Lazarus, *Black Hills/White Justice*, 14.

54 Kenny, "Whitman's Indifference to Indians," 30; Loving, *Song of Himself*, 284.

55 Whitman, *Notebooks and Unpublished Prose Manuscripts*, 3:565. The revolt was launched by the Sioux after repeated treaty infringements by the government and violence by the military. The Sioux killed an estimated 750 settlers on the frontier. See Lazarus, *Black Hills/White Justice*, 27.

56 Erkkila, *Whitman the Political Poet*, 40.

57 Martin, Introduction to *The Continuing Presence of Walt Whitman*, xv–xvi. Erkkila critiques Whitman's expansionist tendencies in "Whitman and American Empire." She argues that Whitman's catalog technique allowed him "to keep the actual blood and violence and struggle that accompanied American western expansion at bay by avoiding the potential danger of historical narration" (63).

7. "Never Before Had My Puny Arm Felt Half So Strong"

1 Because of her text's highly sensitive subject material, Jacobs created a persona, Linda Brent, and changed the names of those she wrote about. I refer to Linda Brent when remarking upon the central character of the text and use Jacobs's name when highlighting choices that were made by the author or referring to aspects of Jacobs's life that are not represented in the text. When referring to other people in the text, I use the name Jacobs ascribes to them. Their real identities are documented in Yellin's 1987 edition of Jacobs, *Incidents*. Citations for *Incidents* are given in parenthesis in the text.

2 In his 1836 *Nature*, Emerson establishes nature, art, other men, and his own body as "Not Me." See Emerson, *Nature*, 8–45. See also my analysis of Emerson in chapter 4.

3 Foster, *Written By Herself*, 96. Jean Fagan Yellin argues that Jacobs was "bolstered" by a fully developed ideology of antislavery and antiracism, but had "no comparable articulation of an antisexist ideology" to support her views about women. See Yellin, *Women and Sisters*, 95.

4 Jacobs's persona and doubts about the authenticity of works written by African American authors in the nineteenth century led many to conclude that *Incidents* was fiction rather than autobiography. Many also assumed erroneously that the book was either written or drastically altered by its editor, Lydia Maria Child. Yellin discusses the doubt surrounding Jacobs's authenticity in her introduction to Jacobs's *Incidents*,

xxii–xxiii. Both Yellin and Lydia Maria Child's biographer, Carolyn L. Karcher, agree that Child's role as an editor did not unduly influence Jacobs's text and that their relationship was cordial. See Karcher, *First Woman*, 435–437. Nonetheless, skepticism about Jacobs's veracity continues to linger. For example, Elizabeth Fox-Genovese disputes Jacobs's claims that she was never raped by Flint and that she spent seven years confined to an attic space. See Fox-Genovese, *Within the Plantation Household*, 374–392. See my second chapter for more information about contemporary critical debate over Child's and Jacobs's relationship.

5 Carby, *Reconstructing Womanhood*, 47. My language about "reconstructing womanhood" draws upon Carby's work and is indebted to her argument.

6 Ibid., 30.

7 Van Evrie, *Negroes and Negro "Slavery,"* 223–229.

8 Braxton, *Black Women Writing Autobiography*, 21.

9 Nott and Gliddon, *Types of Mankind*, 397, 373.

10 Herndl, "Invisible (Invalid) Woman," 558.

11 Hoffert, *Private Matters*, 63.

12 White, *Ar'n't I a Woman?*, 86.

13 See Savitt, *Medicine and Slavery*, 289–305.

14 Nott and Gliddon, *Types of Mankind*, 398. As noted in chapter 1, White proposes that the sexually tempting Jezebel was one of the most pervasive images of the black woman in the antebellum South. See White, *Ar'n't I a Woman?*, 28–29.

15 Andrews, *To Tell a Free Story*, 252.

16 Davis, *Women, Race, and Class*, 23–24.

17 Nelson, *Word in Black and White*, 136.

18 Carby makes a similar point, arguing that by seeking her daughter's forgiveness, Jacobs "bound the meaning and interpretation of her womanhood and motherhood to the internal structure of the text, making external validation unnecessary and unwarranted." See Carby, *Reconstructing Womanhood*, 61.

19 Yellin also suggests that Jacobs "makes possible a discussion of alternative sexual standards for women." See Yellin, *Women and Sisters*, 94.

20 Rachel Blau DuPlessis argues that the primary mode of resolution in nineteenth-century fictive plots dealing with women is an ending in which "quest or *Bildung* . . . is set aside or repressed, whether by marriage or by death." The novelist's task was to write beyond the romance plot that "muffles the main female character, represses quest, valorizes heterosexual as opposed to homosexual ties," and "incorporates individuals within couples as a sign of their personal and narrative success." By ending her story with "freedom," not "marriage," Jacobs breaks the romance plot and begins to forge a new cultural ending to women's stories. See DuPlessis, *Writing beyond the Ending*, 3–5.

21 Carby, *Reconstructing Womanhood*, 53–54.

22 Fox-Genovese, *Within the Plantation Household*, 375–376.

23 Jacobs, *Incidents in the Life of a Slave Girl*, 242.

24 White, *Ar'n't I a Woman?*, 32. For an analysis of the anxiety surrounding prostitution

in relation to the rise of the city in the nineteenth century, see Hobson, *Uneasy Virtue*, 27–33.

25 Andrews, *To Tell a Free Story*, 241; Yellin, *Women and Sisters*, 3, 9. Foster also confirms Jacobs's desire to shift away from the "prevalent literary construct of slave women as completely helpless victims." See Foster, *Written By Herself*, 95.

26 Berlant, "Queen of America," 457–458.

27 Ibid., 459.

28 Thoreau, *Walden and Other Writings*, 97.

29 Smith, "Resisting the Gaze of Embodiment," 79.

30 Although this statement appears harsh, it should be considered in relation to Jacobs's more sensitive realization at the plantation that people can be physically broken to a point where they can no longer envision liberation. For further discussion of the relationship between pain and freedom, see chapter 2.

31 Fuller, *Woman in the Nineteenth Century*, 258.

32 Henry Louis Gates Jr. establishes the relationship between literacy and liberation. See Gates, Introduction to *Slave's Narrative*, xxiii–xxviii.

33 Braxton, *Black Women Writing Autobiography*, 31.

34 Yellin documents Jacobs's effort to maintain her autonomy as an author. See her introduction to Jacobs's *Incidents*, xviii–xix. Jacobs's relationship with Harriet Beecher Stowe demonstrates the mistreatment Jacobs could receive from authors. See Hedrick, *Harriet Beecher Stowe*, 248–249.

35 Rollin, *Life and Public Services of Martin R. Delany*, 11. As I argue in the epilogue, we can read Rollin's biography of Delany, in part, as an autobiography because Delany had much control in its production.

36 Quoted in Ullman, *Martin R. Delany*, 511.

Epilogue

1 Frederick Douglass writes this comment about Martin R. Delany in the August 1862 issue of *Douglass' Monthly* after witnessing three of Delany's lectures detailing his exploratory trip to Africa. Quoted in Ullman, *Beginnings of Black Nationalism*, 249.

2 Douglass, "Claims of the Negro," 503–504; Levine, *Martin Delany, Frederick Douglass, and the Politics of Representative Identity*, 10–12.

3 Rollin, *Life and Public Services of Martin R. Delany*, 11. Rollin's biography is not representative of Delany's philosophy. Written during Reconstruction, a period when Delany had temporarily abandoned his commitment to emigration and was entrenched in his work as the first African American major after the Civil War, it downplays his desire to leave the country and represents him as a model Reconstruction citizen. Typical of many biographies and narratives by former slaves or people of color during the years immediately after the Civil War, Delany seems willing to minimize the prejudice against him in the spirit of reconciliation. For an analysis of Reconstruction slave narratives, see Andrews, "Reunion in the Postbellum Slave Narrative."

4 Levine's *Martin Delany, Frederick Douglass, and the Politics of Representative Identity* presents a convincing argument about the complex relationship between Douglass and Delany, a relationship that negotiated—among other things—the politics of their claims to representative status, because Douglass often emphasized his former status as a slave and Delany pointed to his unmixed racial heritage.

5 Quoted in Ullman, *Beginnings of Black Nationalism*, 511.

6 Delany, "Political Destiny of the Colored Race," 199–203.

7 See Sterling, *Making of an Afro-American*, 48–55, for information on Delany's medical apprenticeship.

8 Quoted in Sterling, *Making of an Afro-American*, 132. For more information on Delany and medical school, see pages 132–137. See also Ullman, *Beginnings of Black Nationalism*, 123–125.

9 Ullman, *Beginnings of Black Nationalism*, 123–125; Rollin, *Life and Public Services of Martin R. Delany*, 69.

10 Levine, *Martin Delany, Frederick Douglass, and the Politics of Representative Identity*, 61; Delany, *Condition, Elevation, Emigration, and Destiny of the Colored People of the United States*, 203. In Rollin's biography, Delany downplays *Condition*, suggesting it was "published without proper revision," and although it was "nearly dashed to pieces in the storm it encountered" of criticism, "[n]one criticized it so severely as himself." He also calls it "an episode illegitimate in his role" in American politics (80–81). See Rollin, *Life and Public Services of Martin R. Delany*. Although these comments may result from the criticism the work received, it was also understandable for Delany to downplay his emigratory scheme once Reconstruction held forth the promise of radical change.

11 Delany, *Condition, Elevation, Emigration, and Destiny of the Colored People of the United States*, 11–13.

12 Ibid., 21, 87.

13 Ibid., 36–37, 53–56.

14 Levine also suggests that *Condition* reveals Delany's conflict, arguing that the prospect of emigration remains "strictly utopian" to Delany at this point in his career, with Central and South America serving primarily as symbolic sites. See Levine, *Martin Delany, Frederick Douglass, and the Politics of Representative Identity*, 63–66.

15 Delany, *Condition, Elevation, Emigration, and Destiny of the Colored People of the United States*, 157–158, 48, 207–208.

16 Although Delany resists much in American ideology, his politics are clearly influenced by American concepts such as self-reliance and colonization. His 1861 "Report of the Niger Valley Exploring Party," for example, calls upon readers to move beyond mere missionary work and undertake the "establishment of all those social relations and organizations, without which enlightened communities cannot exist." See Delany, "Report of the Niger Valley Exploring Party," 110. For more information on the elitist and colonialist presumptions of Delany's political theory, see Painter, "Martin R. Delany," 149–171.

17 Delany, "Political Destiny of the Colored Race," 197; Crane, "Lexicon of Rights," 529–530.

18 Delany, "Political Destiny of the Colored Race," 200–201.

19 Ibid., 211–216, 221.

20 See Ullman, *Beginnings of Black Nationalism*, 428–500.

21 Levine, *Martin Delany, Frederick Douglass, and the Politics of Representative Identity*, 234.

22 Delany, *Principia of Ethnology*, 10.

23 Delany, Preface to *Principia of Ethnology*.

24 Delany, *Principia of Ethnology*, 11, 14–15, 27, 37.

25 Delany, *Principia of Ethnology*, 91–94; Nott and Gliddon, *Types of Mankind*, 79.

26 Delany, *Principia of Ethnology*, 23.

27 Wiegman, *American Anatomies*, 21.

28 Ullman, *Beginnings of Black Nationalism*, 271–272.

29 Rollin, *Life and Public Services of Martin R. Delany*, 137.

30 Levine, *Martin Delany, Frederick Douglass, and the Politics of Representative Identity*, 235.

31 Quoted in Sterling, *Making of an Afro-American*, 324.

32 Rollin, *Life and Public Services of Martin R. Delany*, 99–133.

WORKS CITED

Alcott, William A. *The Young Husband; or, Duties of Man in the Marriage Relation.* 3d ed. Boston, 1839.

———. *The Young Wife; or, Duties of Woman in the Marriage Relation.* 3d ed. Boston, 1839.

———. *The Physiology of Marriage, by an Old Physician.* Boston, 1856.

Alexander, Floyce. "Emerson and Cherokee Removal." ESQ: *A Journal of the American Renaissance* 29.3 (1983): 127–137.

Andrews, William L. *To Tell a Free Story: The First Century of Afro-American Autobiography, 1760–1865.* Urbana: University of Illinois Press, 1986.

———. "Reunion in the Postbellum Slave Narrative: Frederick Douglass and Elizabeth Keckley." *Black American Literature Forum* 23.1 (spring 1989): 5–16.

Baldwin, James. *Notes of a Native Son.* New York: Dial Press, 1963.

Baym, Nina. "Melodramas of Beset Manhood: How Theories of American Fiction Exclude Women Authors." In *The New Feminist Criticism: Essays on Women, Literature, and Theory,* ed. Elaine Showalter, 63–80. New York: Pantheon Books, 1985.

Benét's Reader's Encyclopedia. 3d ed. New York: Harper and Row, 1987.

Bercovitch, Sacvan. "Emerson, Individualism, and the Ambiguities of Dissent." In *Ralph Waldo Emerson: A Collection of Critical Essays,* ed. Lawrence Buell, 101–127. Englewood Cliffs, N.J.: Prentice Hall, 1993.

Berkson, Dorothy. "'Born and Bred in Different Nations': Margaret Fuller and Ralph Waldo Emerson." In *Patrons and Protégées: Gender, Friendship, and Writing in Nineteenth-Century America,* ed. Shirley Marchalonis, 3–30. New Brunswick, N.J.: Rutgers University Press, 1988.

Berlant, Lauren. "The Queen of America Goes to Washington City: Harriet Jacobs, Frances Harper, Anita Hill." In *Subjects and Citizens: Nation, Race, and Gender from Oroonoko to Anita Hill,* ed. Michael Moon and Cathy N. Davidson, 455–480. Durham, N.C.: Duke University Press, 1995.

Bieder, Robert E. *Science Encounters the Indian, 1820–1880: The Early Years of American Ethnology.* Norman: University of Oklahoma Press, 1986.

Bizzell, Patricia. "Opinion: 'Contact Zones' and English Studies." *College English* 56.2 (February 1994): 163–169.

Blanchard, Paula. *Margaret Fuller: From Transcendentalism to Revolution.* Reading, Mass.: Addison-Wesley Publishing, 1987.

Blassingame, John W. Introduction to "The Claims of the Negro Ethnologically Considered." In *The Frederick Douglass Papers*, ed. John W. Blassingame. 2 vols. New Haven, Conn.: Yale University Press, 1982.

Boyd, Melba Joyce. *Discarded Legacy: Politics and Poetics in the Life of Frances E. W. Harper, 1825–1911*. Detroit, Mich.: Wayne State University Press, 1994.

Braude, Ann. *Radical Spirits: Spiritualism and Women's Rights in Nineteenth-Century America*. Boston, Mass.: Beacon Press, 1989.

Braxton, Joanne. *Black Women Writing Autobiography: A Tradition within a Tradition*. Philadelphia, Pa.: Temple University Press, 1989.

Brodhead, Richard H. "Sparing the Rod: Discipline and Fiction in Antebellum America." *Representations* 21 (1988): 67–96.

———. *Cultures of Letters: Scenes of Reading and Writing in Nineteenth-Century America*. Chicago: University of Chicago Press, 1993.

Buell, Lawrence. *Literary Transcendentalism: Style and Vision in the American Renaissance*. Ithaca, N.Y.: Cornell University Press, 1973.

———. *New England Literary Culture: From Revolution through Renaissance*. New York: Cambridge University Press, 1986.

———. "Emerson in his Cultural Context." In *Ralph Waldo Emerson: A Collection of Critical Essays*, ed. Lawrence Buell, 48–60. Englewood Cliffs, N.J.: Prentice Hall, 1993.

Burbick, Joan. "Under the Sign of Gender: Margaret Fuller's *Summer on the Lakes*." In *Women and the Journey: The Female Travel Experience*, ed. Bonnie Frederick and Susan H. McLeod, 67–83. Pullman: Washington State University Press, 1993.

Burks, Mary Fair. "The First Black Literary Magazine in American Letters." CLA *Journal* (March 1976): 318–321.

Cadava, Eduardo. *Emerson and the Climates of History*. Stanford, Cal.: Stanford University Press, 1997.

Caldwell, Charles. *Thoughts on the Original Unity of the Human Race*. 2d ed. Cincinnati, Ohio, 1852.

Capper, Charles. *Margaret Fuller: An American Romantic Life: The Private Years*. New York: Oxford University Press, 1992.

Carby, Hazel V. *Reconstructing Womanhood: The Emergence of the Afro-American Woman Novelist*. New York: Oxford University Press, 1987.

Cayton, Mary Kupiec. *Emerson's Emergence: Self and Society in the Transformation of New England, 1800–1845*. Chapel Hill: University of North Carolina Press, 1989.

Ceniza, Sherry. "'Being a Woman . . . I Wish to Give My Own View': Some Nineteenth-Century Women's Responses to the 1860 *Leaves of Grass*." In *The Cambridge Companion to Walt Whitman*, ed. Ezra Greenspan, 110–208. Cambridge: Cambridge University Press, 1995.

Chevigny, Bell Gale. *The Woman and the Myth: Margaret Fuller's Life and Writings*. Rev. ed. Ann Arbor, Mich.: Northeastern University Press, 1994.

Cheyfitz, Eric. *The Trans-Parent: Sexual Politics in the Language of Emerson*. Baltimore, Md.: Johns Hopkins University Press, 1981.

————. *The Poetics of Imperialism: Translation and Colonization from "The Tempest" to Tarzan*. Enl. ed. Philadelphia: University of Pennsylvania Press, 1991.

Child, Lydia Maria. *Letters from New York*. 3d ed. 1845. New York: Books for Libraries Press, 1970.

————. "The Stars and Stripes: A Melo-Drama." *Liberty Bell*. Boston, Mass., 1858.

————. *Selected Letters, 1817–1880*. Ed. Milton Meltzer and Patricia G. Holland. Amherst: University of Massachusetts Press, 1982.

————. "The Quadroons." In *Rediscoveries: American Short Stories by Women, 1832–1916*, ed. Barbara H. Solomon, 88–98. New York: Penguin, 1994.

————. *An Appeal in Favor of That Class of Americans Called Africans*. 1833. Ed. Carolyn Karcher. Amherst: University of Massachusetts Press, 1996.

————. *A Lydia Maria Child Reader*. Ed. Carolyn Karcher. Durham, N.C.: Duke University Press, 1997.

Christian, Barbara. "The Race for Theory." *Feminist Studies* 14.1 (1988): 51–63.

Colfax, Richard. *Evidence against the Views of the Abolitionists, Consisting of Physical and Moral Proofs, of the Natural Inferiority of the Negroes*. New York, 1833.

Combe, George. Appendix to *Crania Americana*, by Samuel Morton. Philadelphia, Pa., 1839.

Crane, Gregg D. "The Lexicon of Rights, Power, and Community in *Blake*: Martin R. Delany's Dissent from Dred Scott." *American Literature* 68.3 (September 1996): 527–553.

Crowley, John W. "Slaves to the Bottle: Gough's *Autobiography* and Douglass's *Narrative*." In *The Serpent in the Cup: Temperance in American Literature*, ed. David S. Reynolds and Debra J. Rosenthal, 115–135. Amherst: University of Massachusetts Press, 1997.

Davidson, Cathy N. *Revolution and the Word: The Rise of the Novel in America*. New York: Oxford University Press, 1986.

————, ed. *No More Separate Spheres!* Special issue of *American Literature* 70.3 (September 1998).

Davis, Angela. *Women, Race, and Class*. New York: Random House, 1981.

Deese, Helen R. "'A Liberal Education': Caroline Healey Dall and Emerson." In *Emersonian Circles: Essays in Honor of Joel Myerson*, ed. Wesley T. Mott and Robert E. Burkholder, 237–260. Rochester, N.Y.: University of Rochester Press, 1997.

Delany, Martin R. "Report of the Niger Valley Exploring Party." In *Search for a Place: Black Separatism and Africa, 1860*. Ann Arbor: University of Michigan Press, 1969.

————. "The Political Destiny of the Colored Race." 1854. In *The Ideological Origins of Black Nationalism*, ed. Sterling Stuckey, 195–236. Boston, Mass.: Beacon Press, 1972.

————. *Principia of Ethnology: The Origin of Races and Color*. 1879. Baltimore, Md.: Black Classics Press, 1978.

————. *The Condition, Elevation, Emigration, and Destiny of the Colored People of the United States*. 1852. Baltimore, Md.: Black Classics Press, 1993.

D'Emilio, John, and Estelle B. Freedman. *Intimate Matters: A History of Sexuality in America*. New York: Harper and Row, 1988.

Dippie, Brian. *The Vanishing American: White Attitudes and U.S. Indian Policy*. 1982. Lawrence: University Press of Kansas, 1991.

Dixon, Edward H. *Woman and Her Diseases, from the Cradle to the Grave*. 10th ed. Philadelphia, Pa., 1859.

Douglass, Frederick. "The Claims of the Negro Ethnologically Considered: An Address, before the Literary Societies of Western Reserve College." 1854. In *The Frederick Douglass Papers*, ed. John W. Blassingame, 497–525. 2 vols. New Haven, Conn.: Yale University Press, 1982.

———. *Narrative of the Life of Frederick Douglass, an American Slave*. 1845. In *Early African-American Classics*, ed. Anthony Appiah. New York: Bantam, 1991.

duCille, Ann. *The Coupling Convention: Sex, Text, and Tradition in Black Women's Fiction*. New York: Oxford University Press, 1993.

DuPlessis, Rachel Blau. *Writing Beyond the Ending: Narrative Strategies of Twentieth-Century Women Writers*. Bloomington: Indiana University Press, 1985.

Ellison, Julie. *Delicate Subjects: Romanticism, Gender, and the Ethics of Understanding*. Ithaca, N.Y.: Cornell University Press, 1990.

———. "Aggressive Allegory." In *Ralph Waldo Emerson: A Collection of Critical Essays*, ed. Lawrence Buell, 159–170. Englewood Cliffs, N.J.: Prentice Hall, 1993.

Emerson, Ralph Waldo. *Journals of Ralph Waldo Emerson*. Vol. 8. Ed. Edward Waldo Emerson and Waldo Emerson Forbes. Boston, Mass.: Houghton Mifflin, 1912.

———. *The Collected Works of Ralph Waldo Emerson*. Vol. 1. Ed. Alfred R. Ferguson. Cambridge, Mass.: Harvard University Press, 1971.

———. *Nature*. In *The Collected Works of Ralph Waldo Emerson*. Vol. 1. Ed. Alfred R. Ferguson. Cambridge, Mass.: Harvard University Press, 1971.

———. *The Collected Works of Ralph Waldo Emerson*. Vol. 2. Ed. Joseph Slater. Cambridge, Mass.: Harvard University Press, 1979.

———. *The Collected Works of Ralph Waldo Emerson*. Vol. 3. Ed. Joseph Slater. Cambridge, Mass.: Harvard University Press, 1983.

———. *The Collected Works of Ralph Waldo Emerson*. Vol. 5. Ed. Robert E. Spiller, Alfred R. Ferguson, et al. Cambridge, Mass.: Harvard University Press, 1994.

———. *English Traits*. In *The Collected Works of Ralph Waldo Emerson*. Vol. 5. Ed. Robert E. Spiller, Alfred R. Ferguson, et al. Cambridge, Mass.: Harvard University Press, 1994.

———. *Emerson's Antislavery Writings*. Ed. Len Gougeon and Joel Myerson. New Haven, Conn.: Yale University Press, 1995.

Emerson, Ralph Waldo, W. H. Channing, and J. F. Clarke, eds. *Memoirs of Margaret Fuller Ossoli*. New York: Lenox Hill Publishers, 1972.

Equiano, Olaudah. *The Interesting Narrative of the Life of Olaudah Equiano, Written by Himself*. 1789. Ed. Robert J. Allison. New York: Beford Books, 1995.

Erkkila, Betsy. *Whitman the Political Poet*. New York: Oxford University Press, 1989.

———. "Whitman and American Empire." In *Walt Whitman of Mickle Street: A Centennial Collection*, ed. Geoffrey M. Still, 54–69. Knoxville: University of Tennessee Press, 1994.

Ernest, John. "Motherhood Beyond the Gate: Jacobs's Epistemic Challenge in *Incidents in the Life of a Slave Girl."* In *Harriet Jacobs and "Incidents in the Life of a Slave Girl": New Critical Essays*, ed. Deborah M. Garfield and Rafia Zafar, 179–198. New York: Cambridge University Press, 1996.

Fetterley, Judith. "Commentary: Nineteenth-Century American Women Writers and the Politics of Recovery." *American Literary History* 6.3 (fall 1994): 600–611.

Fisher, Philip. *Hard Facts: Setting and Form in the American Novel.* New York: Oxford University Press, 1985.

Fisher, Sidney George. *The Laws of Race, as Connected with Slavery.* Philadelphia, Pa., 1860.

Fleischner, Jennifer. *Mastering Slavery: Memory, Family, and Identity in Women's Slave Narratives.* New York: New York University Press, 1996.

Fone, Byrne R. S. *Masculine Landscapes: Walt Whitman and the Homoerotic Text.* Carbondale: Southern Illinois University Press, 1992.

Foreman, Gabrielle P. "Manifest in Signs: The Politics of Sex and Representation in *Incidents in the Life of a Slave Girl."* In *Harriet Jacobs and "Incidents in the Life of a Slave Girl": New Critical Essays*, ed. Deborah M. Garfield and Rafia Zafar, 76–99. New York: Cambridge University Press, 1996.

Foster, Frances Smith. Introduction to *A Brighter Coming Day: A Frances Ellen Watkins Harper Reader*, ed. Frances Smith Foster, 3–40. New York: Feminist Press, 1990.

———. *Written by Herself: Literary Production by African American Women, 1746–1892.* Bloomington: Indiana University Press, 1993.

———. Introduction to *"Minnie's Sacrifice," "Sowing and Reaping," and "Trial and Triumph": Three Rediscovered Novels by Frances E. W. Harper*, ed. Frances Smith Foster, xi–xxxvii. Boston: Beacon Press, 1994.

Foucault, Michel. *The Order of Things: An Archaeology of the Human Sciences.* New York: Vintage, 1971.

———. *The History of Sexuality: An Introduction.* Trans. Robert Hurley. Vol. 1. New York: Pantheon Books, 1978.

———. *Discipline and Punish: The Birth of the Prison.* Trans. Alan Sheridan. New York: Random House, 1979.

———. *Power/Knowledge: Selected Interviews and Other Writings, 1972–1977.* Ed. Colin Gordon. New York: Pantheon Books, 1980.

Fowler, Lorenzo N. *The Principles of Phrenology and Physiology Applied to Man's Social Relations; Together with an Analysis of Domestic Feelings.* Boston, Mass., 1842.

Fox-Genovese, Elizabeth. *Within the Plantation Household: Black and White Women of the Old South.* Chapel Hill: University of North Carolina Press, 1988.

Fredrickson, George. *The Black Image in the White Mind: The Debate on Afro-American Character and Destiny, 1817–1914.* New York: Harper and Row, 1971.

Fuller, Margaret. "The Great Lawsuit." *Dial* 4.1 (July 1843). Reissued: New York: Russell and Russell, 1961.

———. *The Letters of Margaret Fuller.* Ed. Robert N. Hudspeth. 5 vols. Ithaca, N.Y.: Cornell University Press, 1983–.

———. *The Essential Margaret Fuller.* Ed. Jeffrey Steele. New Brunswick, N.J.: Rutgers University Press, 1995.

————. *Summer on the Lakes, in 1843*. In *The Esssential Margaret Fuller*. Ed. Jeffrey Steele. New Brunswick, N.J.: Rutgers University Press, 1995.

————. *Woman in the Nineteenth Century*. In *The Essential Margaret Fuller*. Ed. Jeffrey Steele. New Brunswick, N.J.: Rutgers University Press, 1995.

Garfield, Deborah M. "Earwitness: Female Abolitionism, Sexuality and *Incidents in the Life of a Slave Girl*." In *Harriet Jacobs and "Incidents in the Life of a Slave Girl": New Critical Essays*, ed. Deborah M. Garfield and Rafia Zafar, 100–130. New York: Cambridge University Press, 1996.

————. "Conclusion: Vexed Alliances: Race and Female Collaboration in the Life of Harriet Jacobs." In *Harriet Jacobs and "Incidents in the Life of a Slave Girl": New Critical Essays*, ed. Deborah M. Garfield and Rafia Zafar, 275–291. New York: Cambridge University Press, 1996.

Gates, Henry Louis, Jr. "Writing 'Race' and the Difference It Makes." In *"Race," Writing and Difference*, ed. Henry Louis Gates Jr., 1–20. Chicago: University of Chicago Press, 1985.

————. Introduction to *The Slave's Narrative*, ed. Charles T. Davis and Henry Louis Gates Jr., xi–xxiv. New York: Oxford University Press, 1985.

Gougeon, Len. "Emerson and Abolition: The Silent Years, 1837–1844." *American Literature* 54.4 (1982): 560–575.

————. *Virtue's Hero: Emerson, Antislavery, and Reform*. Athens: University of Georgia Press, 1990.

————. "Historical Background." In *Emerson's Antislavery Writings*, ed. Len Gougeon and Joel Myerson, xi–lvi. New Haven, Conn.: Yale University Press, 1995.

————. "Emerson and the Woman Question: The Evolution of His Thought." *New England Quarterly* 71.4 (December 1998): 570–592.

Gough, John B. *Autobiography*. Boston, Mass., 1850.

Gould, Stephen Jay. *The Mismeasure of Man*. Rev. ed. New York: Norton, 1996.

Graham, Maryemma. Introduction to *The Complete Poems of Frances E. W. Harper*, ed. Maryemma Graham, xxxiii–lvii. New York: Oxford University Press, 1988.

Graham, Sylvester. *A Lecture to Young Men, on Chastity, Intended Also for the Serious Consideration of Parents and Guardians*. 2d ed. Boston, Mass., 1837.

Grimké, Angelina. *An Appeal to the Women of the Nominally Free States, Issued by an Anti-slavery Convention of American Women*. 2d ed. Boston, Mass., 1838.

Grossberg, Michael. *Governing the Hearth: Law and Family in Nineteenth-Century America*. Chapel Hill: University of North Carolina Press, 1985.

Gunning, Sandra. "Reading and Redemption in *Incidents in the Life of a Slave Girl*." In *Harriet Jacobs and "Incidents in the Life of a Slave Girl": New Critical Essays*, ed. Deborah M. Garfield and Rafia Zafar, 131–155. New York: Cambridge University Press, 1996.

Haller, John S., and Robin M. Haller, *The Physician and Sexuality in Victorian America*. Urbana: University of Illinois Press, 1974.

Halttunen, Karen. *Confidence Men and Painted Women: A Study of Middle-Class Culture in America, 1830–1870*. New Haven, Conn.: Yale University Press, 1982.

————. "Humanitarianism and the Pornography of Pain in Anglo-American Culture." *American Historical Review* 100.2 (April 1995): 303–334.

Handbook of Native American Literature. Ed. Andrew Wiget. New York: Garland, 1996.

The Harper Collins Study Bible. Ed. Wayne A. Meeks. New York: Harper Collins Publishers, 1993.

Harper, Frances E. W. *The Complete Poems of Frances E. W. Harper.* Ed. Maryemma Graham. New York: Oxford University Press, 1988.

———. *A Brighter Coming Day: A Frances Ellen Watkins Harper Reader.* Ed. Frances Smith Foster. New York: Feminist Press, 1990.

———. *"Minnie's Sacrifice," "Sowing and Reaping," and "Trial and Triumph": Three Rediscovered Novels by Frances E. W. Harper.* Ed. Frances Smith Foster. Boston, Mass.: Beacon Press, 1994.

Hedrick, Joan. *Harriet Beecher Stowe: A Life.* New York: Oxford University Press, 1994.

Herndl, Diane Price. "The Invisible (Invalid) Woman: African-American Women, Illness, and Nineteenth-Century Narrative." *Women's Studies* 24 (1995): 553–572.

Hobson, Barbara Meil. *Uneasy Virtue: The Politics of Prostitution and the American Reform Tradition.* New York: Basic Books, 1987.

Hoffert, Sylvia D. *Private Matters: American Attitudes toward Childbearing and Infant Nurture in the Urban North, 1800–1865.* Urbana: University of Illinois Press, 1989.

Horsman, Reginald. *Race and Manifest Destiny: The Origins of American Racial Anglo-Saxonism.* Cambridge, Mass.: Harvard University Press, 1981.

Ignatiev, Noel. *How the Irish Became White.* New York: Routledge, 1995.

Jacobs, Harriet. *Incidents in the Life of Slave Girl, Written by Herself.* 1861. Ed. Jean Fagan Yellin. Cambridge, Mass.: Harvard University Press, 1987.

Jefferson, Thomas. *Notes on the State of Virginia.* 1787. Ed. William Peden. New York: Norton, 1972.

Jordan, Winthrop. *White over Black: American Attitudes toward the Negro, 1550–1812.* New York: Norton, 1968.

Jordanova, Ludmilla. *Sexual Visions: Image of Gender in Science and Medicine between the Eighteenth and Twentieth Centuries.* New York: Harvester Wheatsheaf, 1989.

Kaplan, Justin. *Walt Whitman: A Life.* New York: Simon and Schuster, 1980.

Karcher, Carolyn L. "Rape, Murder, and Revenge in 'Slavery's Pleasant Homes.'" In *The Culture of Sentiment: Race, Gender, and Sentimentality in Nineteenth-Century America,* ed. Shirley Samuels. New York: Oxford University Press, 1992.

———. *The First Woman in the Republic: A Cultural Biography of Lydia Maria Child.* Durham, N.C.: Duke University Press, 1994.

Katz, Jonathan Ned. *Gay American History: Lesbians and Gay Men in the U.S.A.* Rev. ed. New York: Meridian, 1992.

Kenny, Maurice. "Whitman's Indifference to Indians." In *The Continuing Presence of Walt Whitman,* ed. Robert K. Martin, 28–38. Iowa City: University of Iowa Press, 1992.

Kerber, Linda K. *Toward an Intellectual History of Women.* Chapel Hill: University of North Carolina Press, 1997.

Killingsworth, Jimmie M. *Whitman's Poetry of the Body: Sexuality, Politics, and the Text.* Chapel Hill: University of North Carolina Press, 1989.

Kolodny, Annette. *The Land before Her: Fantasy and Experience of the American Frontier, 1630–1860*. Chapel Hill: University of North Carolina Press, 1984.

Lapsansky, Phillip. "Graphic Discord: Abolitionists and Antiabolitionist Images." In *The Abolitionist Sisterhood: Women's Political Culture in Antebellum America*, ed. Jean Fagan Yellin and John C. Van Horne, 201–230. Ithaca, N.Y.: Cornell University Press, 1994.

Laqueur, Thomas. "Orgasm, Generation, and the Politics of Reproductive Biology." In *The Making of the Modern Body: Sexuality and Society in the Nineteenth Century*, ed. Catherine Gallagher and Thomas Laqueur, 1–41. Berkeley: University of California Press, 1987.

———. *Making Sex: Body and Gender from the Greeks to Freud*. Cambridge, Mass.: Harvard University Press, 1990.

Lauter, Paul. "Is Frances Ellen Watkins Harper Good Enough to Teach?" *Legacy* 5.1 (1988): 27–32.

———. *Canons and Contexts*. New York: Oxford University Press, 1991.

Lazarus, Edward. *Black Hills / White Justice: The Sioux Nation versus the United States, 1775 to Present*. New York: Harper Collins, 1991.

Leverenz, David. *Manhood and the American Renaissance*. Ithaca, N.Y.: Cornell University Press, 1989.

———. "The Politics of Emerson's Man-Making Words." In *Speaking of Gender*, ed. Elaine Showalter, 134–162. New York: Routledge, 1989.

Levine, Robert. *Martin Delany, Frederick Douglass, and the Politics of Representative Identity*. Chapel Hill: University of North Carolina Press, 1997.

Linné, Carl von. From *The System of Nature*. 1735. In *Race and the Enlightenment: A Reader*, ed. Emmanuel Chuckwudi Eze, 10–14. Cambridge, Mass.: Blackwell Publishers, 1977.

Lovejoy, Arthur. *The Great Chain of Being: The History of an Idea*. Cambridge, Mass.: Harvard University Press, 1961.

Loving, Jerome. *Walt Whitman: The Song of Himself*. Berkeley: University of California Press, 1999.

Maddox, Lucy. *Removals: Nineteenth-Century American Literature and the Politics of Indian Affairs*. New York: Oxford University Press, 1991.

Martin, Robert K. *The Homosexual Tradition in American Poetry*. Austin: University of Texas Press, 1979.

———. Introduction to *The Continuing Presence of Walt Whitman*, ed. Robert K. Martin, xi–xxiii. Iowa City: University of Iowa Press, 1992.

McAleer, John. *Ralph Waldo Emerson: Days of Encounter*. Boston, Mass.: Little, Brown, 1984.

McKinsey, Elizabeth. *Niagara Falls: Icon of the American Sublime*. Cambridge: Cambridge University Press, 1985.

McPhearson, James M. *Battle Cry of Freedom: The Civil War Era*. New York: Ballantine Books, 1988.

Mills, Bruce. "Lydia Maria Child and the Endings to Jacob's *Incidents in the Life of a Slave Girl*." *American Literature* 64.2 (June 1992): 255–272.

———. *Cultural Reformations: Lydia Maria Child and the Literature of Reform*. Athens: University of Georgia Press, 1994.

Modleski, Tania. *Feminism without Women: Culture and Criticism in a "Postfeminist" Age*. New York: Routledge, 1991.

Moon, Michael. *Disseminating Whitman: Revision and Corporeality in Leaves of Grass*. Cambridge, Mass.: Harvard University Press, 1991.

Morton, Samuel G. *Crania Americana; or, A Comparative View of the Skulls of Various Aboriginal Nations of North and South America*. Philadelphia, Pa., 1839.

———. *Brief Remarks on the Diversity of the Human Species and on Some Kindred Subjects, Being an Introductory Lecture Delivered before the Class of Pennsylvania Medical College*. Philadelphia, Pa., 1842.

———. *Letter to the Reverend John Backman, D.D., on the Question of Hybridity in Animals, Considered in Reference to the Unity of the Human Species*. Charleston, S.C., 1850.

Mott, Lucretia. *A Sermon to the Medical Students*. Philadelphia, Pa., 1849.

Mumford, Kevin. "'Lost Manhood' Found: Male Sexual Impotence and Victorian Culture in the United States." In *American Sexual Politics: Sex, Gender, and Race since the Civil War*, ed. John C. Fout and Maura Shaw Tantillo, 75–99. Chicago: University of Chicago Press, 1993.

Myerson, Joel, ed. *Whitman in His Own Time*. Detroit, Mich.: Omnigraphics, 1991.

Namias, June. *White Captives: Gender and Ethnicity on the American Frontier*. Chapel Hill: University of North Carolina Press, 1993.

Nelson, Dana D. *The Word in Black and White: Reading "Race" in American Literature 1638–1867*. New York: Oxford University Press, 1993.

———. *National Manhood: Capitalist Citizenship and the Imagined Fraternity of White Men*. Durham, N.C.: Duke University Press, 1998.

Nicoloff, Philip L. *Emerson on Race and History: An Examination of "English Traits."* New York: Columbia University Press, 1961.

Noble, Marianne. *The Masochistic Pleasures of Sentimental Literature*. Princeton, N.J.: Princeton University Press, 2000.

Nott, Josiah C., and George R. Gliddon. *Types of Mankind; or, Ethnological Researches, Based upon the Ancient Monuments, Paintings, Sculptures, and Crania of Races, and upon Their Natural, Geographical, Philological, and Biblical History*. Philadelphia, Pa., 1854.

Nudelman, Franny. "Harriet Jacobs and the Sentimental Politics of Female Suffering." *ELH* 59 (1992): 939–964.

Oxford English Dictionary. Vol 6. Oxford: Oxford University Press, 1933.

Packer, B. L. *Emerson's Fall: A New Interpretation of the Major Essays*. New York: Continuum, 1982.

Painter, Nell Irvin. "Martin R. Delany: Elitism and Black Nationalism." In *Black Leaders of the Nineteenth Century*, ed. Leon Litwack and August Meier, 149–171. Chicago: University of Illinois Press, 1988.

Pease, Donald E. *Visionary Compacts: American Renaissance Writings in Cultural Context*. Madison: University of Wisconsin Press, 1987.

Peterson, Carla L. *"Doers of the Word": African-American Women Speakers and Writers in the North (1830–1880)*. New York: Oxford University Press, 1995.

————. "Frances Harper, Charlotte Forten, and African American Literary Reconstruction." In *Challenging Boundaries: Gender and Periodization*, ed. Joyce Warren and Margaret Dickie, 39–61. Athens: University of Georgia Press, 1999.

Pratt, Mary Louis. *Imperial Eyes: Travel Writing and Transculturation*. New York: Routledge, 1992.

Pulte, J. H. *Woman's Medical Guide: Containing Essays on the Physical, Moral, and Educational Development of Females, and the Homeopathic Treatment of Their Diseases in All Periods of Life*. Philadelphia, Pa., 1854.

Reynolds, David S. *Beneath the American Renaissance: The Subversive Imagination in the Age of Emerson and Melville*. Cambridge, Mass.: Harvard University Press, 1988.

————. *Walt Whitman's America: A Cultural Biography*. New York: Vintage, 1995.

Richardson, Robert D. *Emerson: The Mind on Fire*. Berkeley: University of California Press, 1995.

Robinson, David M. *Emerson and the Conduct of Life: Pragmatism and Ethical Purpose in the Later Works*. New York: Cambridge University Press, 1993.

Roediger, David R. *The Wages of Whiteness: Race and the Making of the American Working Class*. New York: Verson, 1991.

Rollin, Frank [Frances]. *Life and Public Services of Martin R. Delany*. Boston, Mass., 1868.

Romero, Lora. "Vanishing Americans: Gender, Empire, and New Historicism." In *Subjects and Citizens: Nation, Race, and Gender from Oroonoko to Anita Hill*, ed. Michael Moon and Cathy N. Davidson. Durham, N.C.: Duke University Press, 1995.

Rosenthal, Debra J. "Deracialized Discourse: Temperance and Racial Ambiguity in Harper's 'The Two Offers' and *Sowing and Reaping*." In *The Serpent in the Cup: Temperance in American Literature*, ed. David S. Reynolds and Debra J. Rosenthal, 153–164. Amherst: University of Massachusetts Press, 1997.

Rosowski, Susan J. "Margaret Fuller, an Engendered West, and *Summer on the Lakes*." *Western American Literature* 25:2 (August 1990): 125–144.

Rothstein, William. *American Physicians in the Nineteenth Century: From Sects to Science*. Baltimore, Md.: Johns Hopkins University Press, 1972.

Rowe, John Carlos. *At Emerson's Tomb: The Politics of Classic American Literature*. New York: Columbia University Press, 1997.

Ruoff, Lavonne Brown. "Jane Johnston Schoolcraft." In *Handbook of Native American Literature*. Ed. Andrew Wiget. New York: Garland, 1996.

Rusk, Ralph L. *The Life of Ralph Waldo Emerson*. New York: Columbia University Press, 1949.

Russett, Cynthia Eagle. *Sexual Science: The Victorian Construction of Womanhood*. Cambridge, Mass.: Harvard University Press, 1989.

Sale, Maggie. "Critiques from Within: Antebellum Projects of Resistance." In *Subjects and Citizens: Nation, Race, and Gender from Oroonoko to Anita Hill*, ed. Michael Moon and Cathy N. Davidson, 145–168. Durham, N.C.: Duke University Press, 1995.

Samuels, Shirley. "The Identity of Slavery." In *The Culture of Sentiment: Race, Gender, and Sentimentality in Nineteenth-Century America*, ed. Shirley Samuels, 157–171. New York: Oxford University Press, 1992.

Sánchez-Eppler, Karen. *Touching Liberty: Abolition, Feminism, and the Politics of the Body*. Berkeley: University of California Press, 1993.

Savitt, Todd. *Medicine and Slavery: The Disease and Health Care of Blacks in Antebellum Virginia*. Urbana: University of Illinois Press, 1978.

Scarry, Elaine. *The Body in Pain: The Making and Unmaking of the World*. New York: Oxford University Press, 1985.

Schiebinger, Londa. "Skeletons in the Closet: Illustrations of the Female Skeleton in Eighteenth-Century America." In *The Making of the Modern Body: Sexuality and Society in the Nineteenth Century*, ed. Catherine Gallagher and Thomas Laqueur, 42–82. Berkeley: University of California Press, 1987.

Shively, Charley, ed. *Calamus Lovers: Walt Whitman's Working Class Camerados*. San Francisco: Gay Sunshine Press, 1987.

Slotkin, Richard. *Regeneration through Violence: The Mythology of the American Frontier, 1600–1860*. Middletown, Conn.: Wesleyan University Press, 1973.

Smith, Sidonie. "Resisting the Gaze of Embodiment: Women's Autobiography in the Nineteenth Century." In *American Women's Autobiography*, ed. Margo Culley, 75–110. Madison: University of Wisconsin Press, 1992.

Smith, Valerie. "'Loopholes of Retreat': Architecture and Ideology in Harriet Jacobs's *Incidents in the Life of a Slave Girl*." In *Reading Black, Reading Feminist: A Critical Anthology*, ed. Henry Louis Gates Jr., 212–226. New York: Penguin, 1990.

Smith-Rosenberg, Caroll. *Disorderly Conduct: Visions of Gender in Victorian America*. New York: Oxford University Press, 1985.

Stepan, Nancy Leys. "Race and Gender: The Role of Analogy in Science." In *The "Racial" Economy of Science*, ed. Sandra Harding, 359–376. Bloomington: Indiana University Press, 1993.

Sterling, Dorothy. *The Making of an Afro-American: Martin Robinson Delany, 1812–1885*. New York: De Capo Press, 1996.

Stern, Madeline B. "Margaret Fuller and the Phrenologist-Publishers." In *Studies in the American Renaissance*, ed. Joel Myerson, 229–237. Boston, Mass.: Twayne Publishers, 1980.

Stewart, Susan. *Crimes of Writing: Problems in the Containment of Representation*. New York: Oxford University Press, 1992.

Still, William. *The Underground Rail Road: A Record of Facts, Authentic Narratives, Letters & C.* 1871. Chicago: Johnson Publishing, 1970.

Stowe, Harriet Beecher. *Uncle Tom's Cabin; or, Life among the Lowly*. 1852. New York: Penguin, 1981.

Tate, Claudia. "Allegories of Black Female Desire; or, Rereading Nineteenth-Century Sentimental Narratives of Black Female Authority." In *Changing Our Own Words: Essays on Criticism, Theory, and Writing by Black Women*, ed. Cheryl A. Wall, 98–126. New Brunswick, N.J.: Rutgers University Press, 1989.

Thoreau, Henry David. *Walden and Other Writings by Henry David Thoreau*, ed. Joseph Wood Krutch. New York: Bantam Books, 1962.

Tompkins, Jane P. "Sentimental Power: *Uncle Tom's Cabin* and the Politics of Literary History." In *The New Feminist Criticism: Essays on Women, Literature, and History*, ed. Elaine Showalter, 81–104. New York: Pantheon Books, 1985.

Tonkovich, Nicole. "Traveling in the West, Writing in the Library: Margaret Fuller's *Summer on the Lakes*." *Legacy*: 10.2 (1993): 79–102.

Traub, Lindsey. "Woman Thinking: Margaret Fuller, Ralph Waldo Emerson, and the American Scholar." In *Soft Canons: American Women Writers and the Masculine Tradition*, ed. Karen L. Kilcup, 281–305. Iowa City: University of Iowa Press, 1999.

Ullman, Victor. *Martin R. Delany: The Beginnings of Black Nationalism*. Boston, Mass.: Beacon Press, 1971.

Van Evrie, John H. *Negroes and Negro "Slavery": The First an Inferior Race: The Latter Its Normal Condition*. New York, 1861.

———. *Free Negroism; or, Results of Emancipation in the North and West India Islands*. New York, 1862.

Weld, Theodore Dwight, and Angelina Grimké. *American Slavery as It Is: Testimony of a Thousand Witnesses*. 1839. Ed. William Loren Katz. New York: Arno, 1968.

West, Cornell. *The American Evasion of Philosophy: A Genealogy of American Pragmatism*. Madison: University of Wisconsin Press, 1989.

Whicher, Stephen E. *Freedom and Fate: An Inner Life of Ralph Waldo Emerson*. Philadelphia: University of Pennsylvania Press, 1953.

White, Deborah Gray. *Ar'n't I a Woman?: Female Slaves in the Plantation South*. New York: Norton, 1985.

Whitman, Walt. *Leaves of Grass*. 1855. Ed. Malcolm Cowley. New York: Penguin Books, 1959.

———. *Leaves of Grass: A Textual Variorum of the Printed Poems*. Ed. Sculley Bradley. New York: New York University Press, 1980.

———. *Notebooks and Unpublished Prose Manuscripts*. Vol. 3. Ed. Edward F. Grier. New York: New York University Press, 1984.

Wiegman, Robyn. *American Anatomies: Theorizing Race and Gender*. Durham, N.C.: Duke University Press, 1995.

Winthrop, John. *White over Black: American attitudes toward the Negro, 1550–1812*. Baltimore, Md.: Penguin Books, 1969.

———. "A Model of Christian Charity." In *The Puritans in American: A Narrative Anthology*, ed. Alan Heimert and Andrew Delbanco, 82–92. Cambridge, Mass.: Harvard University Press, 1994.

Wood, Mary E. "'With Ready Eye': Margaret Fuller and Lesbianism in Nineteenth-Century America." *American Literature* 65.1 (1993): 1–18.

The Works of Aristotle, the Famous Philosopher, in Four Parts. New England, 1821.

Yacovone, Donald. "The Transformation of the Black Temperance Movement, 1827–1854: An Interpretation." *Journal of the Early Republic* 8 (fall 1988): 281–297.

Yellin, Jean Fagan. Introduction to *Incidents in the Life of a Slave Girl, Written by Herself*, ed. Jean Fagan Yellin, xiii–xxxiv. Cambridge, Mass.: Harvard University Press, 1987.

———. *Women and Sisters: The Antislavery Feminists in American Culture.* New Haven, Conn.: Yale University Press, 1989.

Young, Robert J. C. *Colonial Desire: Hybridity in Theory, Culture, and Race.* New York: Routledge, 1995.

Zafar, Rafia. "Introduction: Over-Exposed, Under-Exposed: Harriet Jacobs and *Incidents in the Life of a Slave Girl*." In *Harriet Jacobs and "Incidents in the Life of a Slave Girl": New Critical Essays,* ed. Deborah M. Garfield and Rafia Zafar, 1–10. New York: Cambridge University Press, 1996.

Zwarg, Christina. *Feminist Conversations: Fuller, Emerson, and the Play of Reading.* Ithaca, N.Y.: Cornell University Press, 1995.

INDEX